CANADENSIS

The Garden of Canada • CANADENSIS • Le Jardin du Canada •

OFFICIAL PLANT EMBLEMS OF CANADA
A BIODIVERSITY TREASURE

ERNEST SMALL, PAUL M. CATLING AND BRENDA BROOKES

Catalogue Number: A22-539/2012E
ISBN: 978-0-660-20057-6

Également disponible en français.

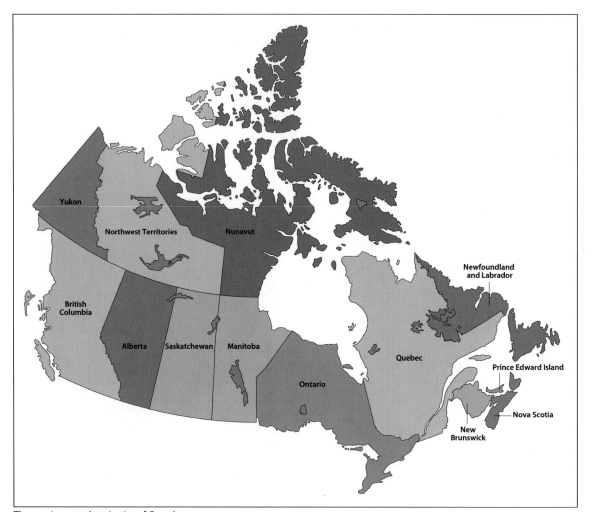

The provinces and territories of Canada.

PREFACE

In his well-known 1993 book *The Ecology of Commerce*, Paul Hawken stated that the average North American can name 1,000 commercial brands but perhaps only 10 plants. This is shocking, because plants are the indispensable basis of the necessities of life for humans—almost all food and fiber, and most medicine, energy, building materials, and commercial goods. Plants are the most significant of the abundant natural resources of Canada. They have sustained the inhabitants of this country for the last 10,000 years, and continue to generate the majority of employment and productivity. The indigenous flora of Canada is also a priceless cultural heritage, many species associated with fascinating and charming stories. We think that an improved knowledge of Canadian plants by the Canadian public will serve not only to promote wiser sustainable use, but also pride in the natural resources of our country.

Today, "biodiversity" ("biological diversity", particularly referring to all of the species in a region) has become a critical issue. Thousands of the world's species are rapidly undergoing extinction, due to the destruction of their supporting habitats and ecosystems. This is not merely a sentimental issue: the continuing elimination of species means that plants with undiscovered medicinal and agricultural potential will never contribute to the welfare of human beings. Addressing the growing threats to biodiversity has been a great international concern in recent decades, and the year 2010 was declared by the United Nations to be "The International Year of Biodiversity". All nations were requested to carefully examine their own biodiversity with a view to studying, cataloguing, and preserving the species that are present. Towards this goal, this book was initiated to review a highly select group of native plants that have extraordinary significance for Canada: those that have so greatly captured the public's interest that they have become "official" emblems of the provinces, territories, or the entire country. The 29 plant species featured in this book represent much fewer than 1% of Canada's plant species, but they are wonderful ambassadors for increasing awareness of the importance of the entire Canadian flora. We hope that the information collected in this book will serve as a vehicle for public education about Canadian plants, and the need to ensure their future welfare.

An impressive depiction of the wide range of biodiversity in Paradise at the moment of the Fall. Source: Ogilby, J. 1660. The Holy Bible Illustrated with chorographical sculps. 2 vols. Cambridge University, Cambridge, U.K.

ACKNOWLEDGMENTS

This book arose from our series of articles entitled "Native Plant Emblems of Canada", published in the Canadian Botanical Association Bulletin, beginning in 2006. We thank Christine Maxwell for her conscientious and helpful editing of this series.

Jacques Cayouette reviewed and considerably improved the manuscript.

Valuable reviews of one or more chapters were made by Anna Leighton and William Cody.

We also thank the staff of Public Works and Government Services Canada for their exceptional support of this project, particularly Paulette Thanase and Scott Butcher, who provided key publishing management, and Mary Boland, who skillfully laid out the text and illustrations.

Numerous individuals and organizations contributed photographs and drawings, and we are most grateful for their help. In some cases, Agriculture and Agri-Food Canada illustrators prepared drawings. All contributors are acknowledged in the captions to their illustrations. The photo of fireweed on the front cover was provided by the Government of Yukon. The frontispiece bouquet is reproduced by permission of Heritage Canada.

We also thank the following for information and advice: Susan Aiken, George Argus, and Laurie Consaul.

A Nova Scotia forest in the autumn. Source: Thinkstock.

TABLE OF CONTENTS

TABLE OF CONTENTS (CONT'D)

An Ontario forest in the autumn. Source: Thinkstock.

OVERVIEW OF CANADIAN PLANT SYMBOLS

A lowbush blueberry (*Vaccinium angustifolium*) field in New Brunswick. Lowbush blueberry, the provincial berry of Nova Scotia, grows naturally in open bogs, and in this photo, taken in the autumn, appears as a sea of red foliage. Source: Thinkstock.

A colourful autumn view of the plants of the Yukon. Source: Thinkstock.

INTRODUCTION

Although we humans think of ourselves as predominant in importance, in fact plants are the indispensable component of life on Earth, for without them virtually all life on the planet would cease. We depend on plants for food, shelter, medicines, and other essentials. Many important plants are native to foreign nations, but many others come from local places. "Indigenous" or "native" plants are ones that have grown naturally in a region for a long period (generally for thousands of years). The indigenous "flora" (the plants collectively) of an area is a priceless heritage that contributes to local wealth, life styles, traditions, and charm. More generally, the "biodiversity", meaning "biological diversity", particularly referring to all of the species in a region, has become a leading issue. The "biodiversity crisis" is the current rapid extinction of thousands of species, due to the destruction of their supporting habitats and ecosystems. This is not merely a sentimental issue: the continuing elimination of species means that plants with undiscovered medical and agricultural potential will never contribute to the welfare of human beings. Addressing the growing threats to biodiversity has been a great international concern in recent decades, and the year 2010 was declared by the United Nations to be "The International Year of Biodiversity". All nations were requested to carefully examine their own biodiversity with a view to studying, cataloguing, and preserving the species that are present. Towards this goal, this book addresses a highly select group of native plants that have extraordinary significance for Canada: those that have so greatly captured the public's interest that they have become "official" emblems of the provinces, territories, or the entire country.

There are hundreds of thousands of plant species in the world. Most of these are "higher plants", and these are the kinds discussed in this book ("Lower plants" include algae, mosses, liverworts, and other groups). Reminiscent of most animals, the higher plants have vascular tissues that transport water and chemicals from one part of the organism to other parts where they are needed. Accordingly, higher plants are sometimes called "vascular plants" (although some lower plants also have vascular tissues). Most vascular plants have flowers, although often the flowers are very small, and some, like ferns, lack flowers, and reproduce by spores rather than seeds. There are about 4,000 vascular plant species that are native to Canada (possibly 1,500 or so additional species have been naturalized, i.e., they have been introduced from outside the country, and have managed to become established in the wild). The 29 higher, vascular plant species featured in this book are flowering plants.

This introductory chapter provides general information on the symbolic use of plants with particular reference to prominent Canadian examples, and presents an overview of Canada's 29 official native plant emblems. Subsequent chapters are devoted to the official plant symbols of each of the ten provinces and three territories, and finally to the maples, representing Canada as a whole.

Part of Canada's heritage of biodiversity: an autumn scene along the Matapedia River, Quebec. Source: Thinkstock.

A BIODIVERSITY TREASURE

SOME FAMILIAR PLANT SYMBOLS

Plants are so critical to people that it is not surprising that they are among the most prominent and important of symbols. The olive branch signifies peace; the violet symbolized the anti-monarchist movement of France led by Napoleon; marijuana leaves on shirts conveyed a strong anti-establishment attitude in the 1960s; each spring, millions of tulips demonstrate the gratitude of the Dutch for Canada's help in sheltering their Princesses during the Second World War and for liberating their country; poppies were adopted by the Great War Veterans' Association in 1921 and represent the enormous sacrifice of Canadian soldiers; and daffodils are the Canadian Cancer Society's symbol of hope. There are many more plant symbols, but the favourites of most people are frequently their own regional symbols.

Tulips in front of the Parliament Buildings in Ottawa.
Source: Thinkstock.

PLANTS AS REGIONAL SYMBOLS

A very large proportion of the emblems of political regions originate in the natural world, including plants, animals, and minerals, but plants predominate. As noted above, plants sustain human life. People have a natural love and respect for plants that is mirrored in their choice of plant emblems. However, less than 1% of the flora of countries achieves the status of official emblems, and of course such plants need to be very special. What is required for a plant to become a regional symbol? These plants are extremely important economically or exceptionally impressive visually, and often have particular adaptation to the region they represent. Today virtually every country of the world is represented by a native plant emblem, as are numerous geographical subdivisions of countries.

WAR AND TULIPS

Over 3 million tulips are displayed in the spectacular Canadian Tulip Festival in Canada's capital each year. It all began in 1945, following World War II, when Canada planted a few thousand Dutch tulips on Parliament Hill in Ottawa. They were a gift that acknowledged the role of Canadian soldiers in liberating the Netherlands from Nazi control, and to thank Canada for providing a safe home for the Dutch Royal Family during the war. The gift of tulips became a tradition, and in 1953 the world's largest annual tulip festival became established in Ottawa. The tulip is one of the most prominent flowers of spring and as such it is a natural symbol of renewal. A "50 cent" ($24.95 issue price) selectively gold-plated coin was issued in 2002 to commemorate the fiftieth anniversary of the Canadian Tulip Festival (coin image© courtesy of the Royal Canadian Mint.). Similarly in 2005 a $1.05 stamp© was issued (image courtesy of Canada Post Corporation).

INDIGENOUS OR INTRODUCED?

Many plants are not native to a region but have become so well established that few realize that they originally came from other countries. One-fifth of the plant species that grow wild on the Canadian landscape have been introduced from other countries. The botanical emblems featured in this series are genuinely native (indigenous) species, but it is worth noting that sometimes well-established immigrants deserve consideration.

All of Canada's major crops are of foreign origin. Not surprisingly then, wheat (*Triticum* species), the leading crop of the Canadian Prairies, is encountered as a symbol there. Sheaves of wheat are found on the coat of arms, shield of arms, and flag of both Saskatchewan and Alberta (shields of arms are shown in the Centennial Canadian stamps, shown below), as well as the Coat of Arms of Manitoba, and in 1977 Manitoba adopted a stylized wheat sheaf as a general symbol for the province.

MARQUIS WHEAT: BORN IN CANADA

Wheat is not native to Canada, but one of the most famous varieties was born in Canada. Bred at Ottawa's Central Experimental Farm by Sir Charles E. Saunders, it became a major contribution to the Canadian economy. 'Marquis' matured early, avoiding frost damage and making possible a vast increase in wheat production on the Canadian prairies. One of the world's greatest feats in crop breeding, by 1911 it had produced the first 200 million bushel crop in the West's history. In 1915, during the First World War, it made up 90% of the wheat shipped by Canada to France, an essential source of food at that time since U-boats had cut off supplies from Australia and Argentina. A 46 cent stamp entitled "Sir Charles Saunders: The Marquis of Wheat" was printed in 2000 (image© Canada Post Corporation). A $100 coin was issued in 2003 to mark the 100th anniversary of the selection of 'Marquis' wheat (coin image© courtesy of the Royal Canadian Mint.)

DAFFODILS: DEFEATING CANCER

There is no more cheerful harbinger of spring than the golden sunshine of daffodils. They are said to say, "The sun is always shining when I'm with you". There is no better symbol of the inspired hope of the human spirit. An exceptional gala, the "Daffodil Ball", is one of the most successful cancer-related fundraisers in Canada. A black-tie dinner dance in Montreal's historic Windsor Station, it has often netted $9 million annually. For the event, the marbled interior of the station has been decorated with 65,000 daffodils. Daffodils (*Narcissus*, especially *N. pseudonarcissus*) are probably native to a small part of Europe but were introduced elsewhere, initially by the Romans. They are now cultivated around the world and hundreds of daffodil societies host shows and share information on how to grow them. A "50 cent" ($34.95 issue price) selectively gold-plated "golden daffodil" coin was issued in 2003 to honour the Canadian Cancer Society's symbol of hope, the daffodil (Coin image© courtesy of the Royal Canadian Mint). Similarly, two 50 cent daffodil stamps were issued in 2005 (one of these is shown here, the image© courtesy of Canada Post Corporation).

INFLUENCE OF POLITICS AND BUSINESS

In the United States, numerous plant species have been adopted as state symbols because politicians were pressured by organizations, schoolchildren (often persuaded by a teacher to take on a cause), and commercial interests. For example, the Bear Road Elementary School children in North Syracuse, New York, convinced the governor to sign a bill in 1987 making the apple muffin the official New York State muffin. Also, a fifth-grade class adopted the cause of making the cranberry (*Vaccinium macrocarpon*) the official berry of the state. Their 2 years of lobbying, petitions, and hearings were finally rewarded in 1994. In 2000, the huckleberry (*Vaccinium* species) was declared to be the "official fruit" of Idaho, a measure that was initiated by a group of fourth graders. Manitoba's official floral emblem was substantially determined by a poll of schoolchildren. British Columbia's choice of floral emblem was heavily influenced by the Women's Institute, an organization that in post Second World War times was quite influential.

The business world has sometimes adopted plants as corporate symbols. Examples representing the products sold include Mr. Peanut (Planters Nuts), Chiquita Banana (Chiquita Banana Company), and the California Dancing Raisins (State of California Department of Food and Agriculture). Of all corporate logos, the apple is perhaps most relevant to Canada. An apple with a bite out of the right side is the symbol of Apple Computer Inc. Jef Raskin (1943–2005), the man most often credited with the creation of the Macintosh computer (released in 1984), named it after his favourite fruit, the McIntosh apple, Canada's most famous contribution to the world of fruits. Raskin noted that he changed the spelling to "Macintosh" to avoid potential copyright conflicts with McIntosh, the audio equipment manufacturer.

CANADA'S APPLE: THE MCINTOSH

Over 3 million McIntosh apple trees flourish in North America and produce one of the world's most popular apples, but where did they come from? John McIntosh (1777–1846) moved to Canada from New York's Mohawk Valley and settled in Dundela, Ontario. In 1811 he found several apple seedlings in the woods around his new home. He transplanted these to his garden, and the one seedling that survived was the original McIntosh tree, and a mother of millions. A fire swept through the McIntosh farm in 1895, but the badly singed tree continued to bear fruit until 1906 and died shortly after. The original dead tree, shown here (amid some of its offspring) was left standing for some time, and a commemorative headstone was placed on the site. An uncirculated, collector silver dollar coin was issued in 1996 to mark the 200th anniversary of John McIntosh's arrival in 1796. (Coin image ©courtesy of the Royal Canadian Mint.)

SYMBOLS CAN CHANGE

The choice of given species as botanical symbols is sometimes not permanent, and in fact is sometimes subject to the strong influence of special interest groups. For example, the passion flower (*Passiflora incarnata*) was adopted as Tennessee's state flower in 1919. However, Nashville's Iris Association succeeded in having the iris adopted as the Tennessee state flower in 1933 (the passion flower wasn't forgotten; it was declared to be the "state wildflower" in 1973, while the iris is Tennessee's official "cultivated flower").

Changes of emblem are sometimes dictated by change in circumstances or gradual realization that a better choice is available. Some changes of official emblem in Canada provide examples. The white (Madonna) lily (*Lilium candidum*), a native of Greece, was officially designated as the floral emblem of Quebec in 1963, but there was confusion and debate as to whether it was the appropriate floral emblem. In 1999 the blue flag (*Iris versicolor*) was officially adopted as Quebec's new floral emblem. The change was considered by most to be desirable because the blue flag is native rather than introduced and is a characteristic element of the flora of the most inhabited part of the province. (The white fleur-de-lys that is used on Quebec's provincial flag and coat of arms is widely considered to be a floral symbol, but its identity is problematical, and there is even some doubt that it actually represents a plant.)

The Northwest Territories named the jack pine (*Pinus banksiana*) as its official tree in 1989. At that time, residents (mostly students) were polled. Trembling aspen (*Populus tremuloides*) received 369 votes, tamarack (*Larix laricina*) 593 votes, and jack pine 679 votes, resulting in the jack pine being proclaimed as the official tree of the Northwest Territories. However, in 1999, the new territory of Nunavut was carved away from the Northwest Territories, and that year, based on the recommendation of a Special Committee established in 1998,

The native North American passionflower (also known as Maypop, *Passiflora incarnata*). Source: the "Gottorfer Codex", a collection of gouache paintings on vellum depicting flowers of the garden of Schloss Gottorf, created between 1649 and 1659.

the newly delineated Northwest Territories replaced the jack pine with the tamarack.

Prince Edward Island chose the "lady's slipper" as its floral emblem in 1947, but did not stipulate the species. Of the three found in the province, the showy lady's slipper (*Cypripedium reginae*) was generally accepted as the floral emblem. However, in the early 1960s not enough plants of this very rare species could be found on the island to prepare a display for the Fathers of Confederation Building in Charlottetown. With concern that the showy lady's slipper was too rare in the province to represent it, the stemless lady's slipper (*C. acaule*) was chosen, and recognized in legislation in 1965. This latter species is a well known and widespread element of the island's flora.

COLLECTIBLES

During Canada's Centennial in 1968, the provincial and territorial official floral symbols (along with the maple leaf representing all of Canada) were placed on sets of commemorative coins and stamps (some of these are shown in this book). A similar set of medallions was distributed by Shell gas stations in Canada in the 1960s. The Canadian plant emblems also decorated plates and other objects. The coins, stamps, medallions, and similar items are still available as collector's memorabilia, as a search on the Web will reveal. See Coucill (1966), cited below, for reference to an outstanding set of paintings of the floral emblems, many of which are reproduced in this book. The floral symbols of the Centennial period differ from the present symbols in that Quebec changed its floral emblem as noted above, and Nunavut had not yet been recognized as a territory.

Uncirculated, collector $100 coin (92% gold, 8% silver) issued in 1977 to mark the 50th ("silver Jubilee") commemoration of Queen Elizabeth II. The coin shows a bouquet of the official flowers of the provinces and territories. Coin image © courtesy of the Royal Canadian Mint.

Pink Lady's Slipper
Prince Edward Island
Issued 1999

Pacific Dogwood
British Columbia
Issued 2000

Mayflower
Nova Scotia
Issued 2001

Wild Rose
Alberta
Issued 2002

White Trillium
Ontario
Issued 2003

Fireweed
Yukon
Issued 2004

Western Red Lily
Saskatchewan
Issued 2005

Blue Flag
Quebec
Issued 2006

Purple Violet
New Brunswick
Issued 2007

Purple Saxifrage
Nunavut
Issued 2008

Pitcher Plant
Newfoundland & Labrador
Issued 2009

Prairie Crocus
Manitoba
Issued 2010

Mountain Avens
Northwest Territories
Issued 2011

Canadian gold $350 coin series (0.99999% gold; 1999–2011) based on provincial and territorial symbols. Coin images © courtesy of the Royal Canadian Mint.

Alberta

British Columbia

Manitoba

New Brunswick

Newfoundland & Labrador

Northwest Territories

Nova Scotia

Ontario

Prince Edward Island

Quebec

Saskatchewan

Yukon

1967 Centennial floral emblem stamps (© Canada Post Corporation). Shields of arms are shown on the left of the stamps. As noted in the text, Quebec's emblem has changed, and Nunavut became a territory after 1967.

HOW MANY SYMBOLS ARE ENOUGH?

Canada is far behind many of the American states in providing official recognition of plants as symbols. The 50 U.S. states have spawned a seemingly endless variety of official symbols, including people, foods, beverages, tartans, etc. Tomato juice (from *Lycopersicon esculentum*) was made the official beverage of the state of Ohio in 1965. In 1986, Massachusetts declared the corn muffin (corn is *Zea mays*) to be its official state muffin. The blueberry muffin (based on *Vaccinium angustifolium*) was made Minnesota's "State Muffin" in 1988. In 1995, South Carolina declared tea (*Camellia sinensis*) to be its official state "Hospitality Beverage". The chocolate chip cookie (chocolate comes from *Theobroma cacao*) was declared to be the official state cookie of Massachusetts in 1997. Texas declared cotton (*Gossypium* species) to be its official State Fiber/Fabric in 1997. In 2001, Texas chose the pecan (*Carya illinoinensis*) to be its official state "Health Nut". While it seems unlikely that Canada will develop such enthusiasm for symbols, nevertheless the future will likely result in recognition of more plant species as Canadian emblems.

UNANTICIPATED PROBLEMS

Choosing a new botanical emblem requires careful consideration to avoid problems, as exemplified by the downy hawthorn (*Crataegus mollis*). Its blossom was declared to be the state floral emblem of Missouri in 1923. The legislature further asserted that the state department of agriculture should encourage hawthorn cultivation because of the beauty of the flower, fruit, and foliage. There are many in the state of Missouri, however, who think that hawthorn was a bad choice as an emblem. This is because in the British Isles hawthorns have an extraordinary reputation for being inhabited by fairies, which cause disasters should the trees be damaged. As late as 1968 an Irish road had to be realigned to pass a hawthorn that was on a new road being built from Ballintra to Rossnowlagh. In 1982, workers in the De Lorean car plant in Northern Ireland protested that the site was cursed because a hawthorn had been destroyed during construction of the plant. To calm everyone, management ceremoniously planted another "fairy tree" on the property. On the grounds of Belfast University people refused to trim a hawthorn for fear of offending the fairies, and it is said that when new buildings were planned, they had to be placed so that they would not disturb the tree.

How symbols are interpreted can change dramatically over time. Australia's national flower is the golden wattle (*Acacia pycnantha*), which was once popular. During the First World War, Australians wore sprigs to demonstrate patriotism and raise funds for the war effort. In more recent times, the golden wattle has often been mocked, and has become embroiled in the movement to change the country from a constitutional monarchy to a republic (the flower has become associated with the republican movement).

A zoological example of the conservation implications of conferring official status on species was provided by the state fishes of Alaska (the king salmon) and Nebraska (channel catfish). People for the Ethical Treatment of Animals, a well known animal rights group, recently petitioned the governors of the two states to ban fishing of the state fishes.

This book points out examples of choices that were made without either the guidance of botanists or adequate consideration of the potential problems, resulting in confusion about the identity of the species concerned.

Crataegus mollis, the floral emblem of Missouri. Source: Wikipedia, photo by Nadiatalent, released into the public domain.

THE SPECIAL SIGNIFICANCE OF BOTANICAL SYMBOLS

There is a subtle but very important significance to native plant emblems: they bridge the interests of professional botanists and society at large. Everyone is exposed to these indigenous plant emblem species on flags, signs, stamps, coins, and letterheads, and so these species are extremely memorable. Plant emblem species, therefore, are like ambassadors from the regions of the nation, calling attention to the importance of preserving the country's natural biological heritage—for practical sustainable harvesting in many cases—or simply in order to prevent the beauty of these species from disappearing from nature. Professional botanists now recognize their obligation to educate the public about the importance of plants to society and the natural world.

PLANT EMBLEM SPECIES ARE AMBASSADORS FROM THE REGIONS OF THE NATION, CALLING ATTENTION TO THE IMPORTANCE OF PRESERVING THE COUNTRY'S NATURAL BIOLOGICAL HERITAGE.

OFFICIAL PLANT EMBLEMS OF CANADA

SUMMARY OF CANADA'S INDIGENOUS PLANT SYMBOLS

Canada has 29 "official" indigenous plant symbols (i.e., recognized as such in legislation) at the federal, provincial, and territorial levels. The ten provinces and three territories each have a floral emblem, and all but Nunavut have an official tree. Also, Saskatchewan and Alberta have official grasses, and Nova Scotia has an official berry. In 1977, Alberta recognized "petrified wood" as its "official stone" (numerous fossil taxa could constitute petrified wood found in the province). Despite the botanical nature of this emblem, we are not interpreting it as a plant symbol. One genus of plants (*Acer* or maple in a generic sense) represents Canada collectively. An illustrated synopsis follows.

Canada

The "maple leaf" has been recognized as a Canadian emblem dating back to the early 1800s. The generalized leaf used as the Canadian symbol does not represent a particular species..

Official Tree: Sugar maple (*Acer saccharum* Marsh.; Adopted: 1996)

Alberta

Floral Emblem: Wild rose (Prickly rose, *Rosa acicularis* Lindl.; Adopted: 1930)

Official Tree: Lodgepole pine (*Pinus contorta* Dougl.; Adopted: 1984)

Provincial Grass: Rough fescue (*Festuca altaica* Trin., *F. campestris* Rydb., *F. hallii* (Vasey) Piper; Adopted: 2003)

A BIODIVERSITY TREASURE

SUMMARY OF CANADA'S INDIGENOUS PLANT SYMBOLS (CONT'D)

British Columbia

Floral Emblem: Pacific dogwood (Western Flowering Dogwood, *Cornus nuttallii* Audub.; Adopted: 1956)

Official Tree: Western red cedar (Western Arborvitae, *Thuja plicata* Donn; Adopted: 1987)

Manitoba

Floral Emblem: Prairie crocus (Pasque Flower, *Pulsatilla patens* (L.) Mill.; Adopted: 1906)

Official Tree: White spruce (*Picea glauca* (Moench) Voss; Adopted: 1991)

New Brunswick

Floral Emblem: Purple violet (assumed to be Bog Violet, also called Marsh Blue Violet), *Viola cucullata* Ait.; Adopted:1936)

Official Tree: Balsam fir (*Abies balsamea* (L.) Mill.; Adopted: 1987)

SUMMARY OF CANADA'S INDIGENOUS PLANT SYMBOLS (CONT'D)

Newfoundland & Labrador

Floral Emblem: Pitcher plant (Purple Pitcher Plant, *Sarracenia purpurea* L.; Adopted: 1954)

Official Tree: Black spruce (*Picea mariana* (P. Mill.) BSP.; Adopted: 1993)

Northwest Territories

Floral Emblem: Mountain avens (White Dryad, *Dryas integrifolia* M. Vahl; Adopted: 1957)

Official Tree: Tamarack (American larch, *Larix laricina* (DuRoi) K. Koch; Adopted: 1999)

Nova Scotia

Floral Emblem: Mayflower (Trailing Arbutus, *Epigaea repens* L.; Adopted: 1901)

Official Tree: Red spruce (*Picea rubens* Sarg.; Adopted: 1987)

Provincial Berry: Wild Blueberry (Lowbush blueberry, *Vaccinium angustifolium* Ait.; Adopted: 1996)

A BIODIVERSITY TREASURE

SUMMARY OF CANADA'S INDIGENOUS PLANT SYMBOLS (CONT'D)

Nunavut

Floral Emblem: Purple saxifrage (Purple mountain saxifrage, *Saxifraga oppositifolia* L.; Adopted: 2000)

Ontario

Floral Emblem: White trillium (Eastern White Trillium, Large-flower Wakerobin, *Trillium grandiflorum* (Michx.) Salisb.; Adopted: 1937)

Official Tree: Eastern white pine (*Pinus strobus* L.; Adopted: 1984)

Prince Edward Island

Floral Emblem: Lady's slipper (Pink lady's slipper, Stemless lady's slipper, *Cypripedium acaule* Ait.; Adopted:1947)

Official Tree: Red oak (Northern red oak, *Quercus rubra* L.; Adopted: 1987)

SUMMARY OF CANADA'S INDIGENOUS PLANT SYMBOLS (CONT'D)

Quebec

Floral Emblem: Blue flag (Harlequin blue flag, *Iris versicolor* L.; Adopted: 1999)

Official Tree: Yellow birch (*Betula alleghaniensis* Britton; Adopted: 1993)

Saskatchewan

Floral Emblem: Western red lily (Wood lily, *Lilium philadelphicum* L. var. *andinum* (Nutt.) Ker.; Adopted: 1941)

Official Tree: White birch (Paper birch, *Betula papyrifera* Marsh.; Adopted: 1988)

Provincial Grass: Needle-and-thread grass (*Hesperostipa comata* (Trin. & Rupr.) Barkw. subsp. *comata*; Adopted: 2001)

Yukon

Floral Emblem: Fireweed (*Chamerion angustifolium* (L.) Holub.; Adopted: 1967)

Official Tree: Subalpine fir (*Abies lasiocarpa* (Hook.) Nutt.; Adopted: 2002)

PROVINCIAL AND TERRITORIAL FLOWERS OF CANADA

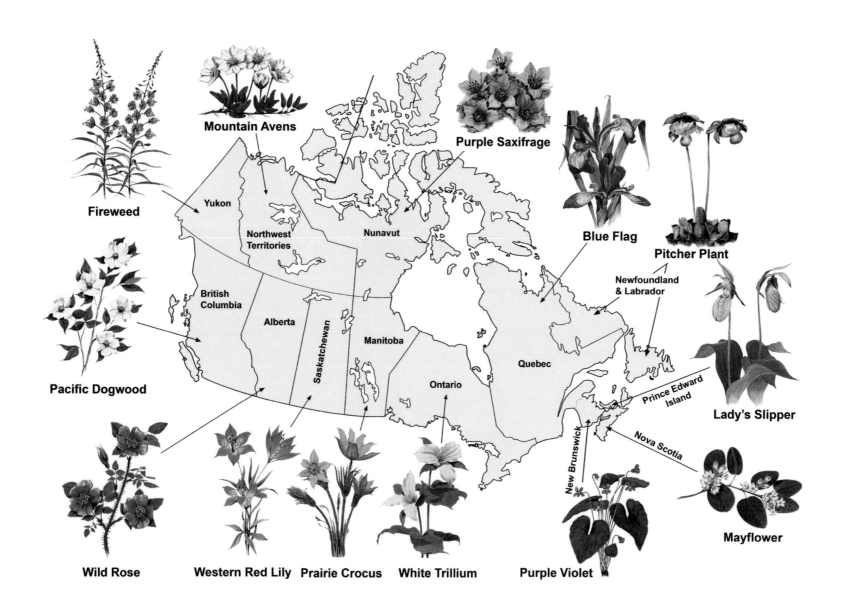

Mountain Avens

Purple Saxifrage

Fireweed

Blue Flag

Pitcher Plant

Pacific Dogwood

Yukon

Northwest Territories

Nunavut

British Columbia

Alberta

Saskatchewan

Manitoba

Ontario

Quebec

Newfoundland & Labrador

Prince Edward Island

Nova Scotia

New Brunswick

Lady's Slipper

Wild Rose   Western Red Lily   Prairie Crocus   White Trillium   Purple Violet

Mayflower

PROVINCIAL AND TERRITORIAL TREES OF CANADA

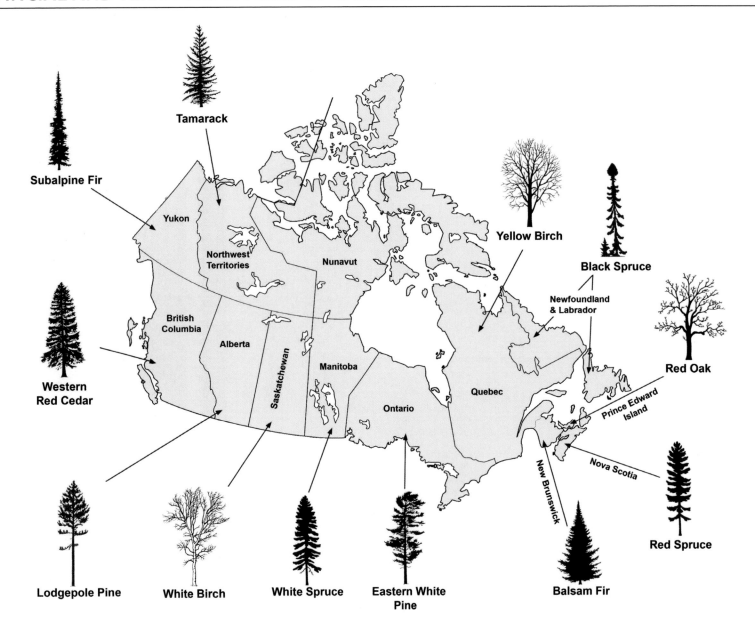

Subalpine Fir

Tamarack

Yellow Birch

Black Spruce

Yukon

Northwest Territories

Nunavut

Newfoundland & Labrador

Red Oak

British Columbia

Alberta

Saskatchewan

Manitoba

Quebec

Western Red Cedar

Ontario

Prince Edward Island

Nova Scotia

New Brunswick

Red Spruce

Lodgepole Pine

White Birch

White Spruce

Eastern White Pine

Balsam Fir

ACREAGE OF CANADA OCCUPIED BY THE COUNTRY'S ARBOREAL EMBLEMS

Province/Territory	Common Name	Scientific Name	Area in Canada	
			Square Miles	Square Kilometres
Newfoundland and Labrador	Black spruce	*Picea mariana*	2,208,078	5,718,922
Prince Edward Island	Red oak	*Quercus rubra*	149,905	388,254
Nova Scotia	Red spruce	*Picea rubens*	92,405	239,329
New Brunswick	Balsam fir	*Abies balsamea*	1,173,643	3,039,735
Quebec	Yellow birch	*Betula alleghaniensis*	231,656	599,989
Ontario	Eastern white pine	*Pinus strobus*	319,114	826,505
Manitoba	White spruce	*Picea glauca*	2,258,026	5,848,287
Saskatchewan	White birch	*Betula papyrifera*	2,222,603	5,756,542
Alberta	Lodgepole pine	*Pinus contorta*	416,690	1,079,227
British Columbia	Western red cedar	*Thuja plicata*	140,464	363,802
Yukon	Subalpine fir	*Abies lasiocarpa*	362,815	939,691
Northwest Territories	Tamarack	*Larix laricina*	1,918,585	4,969,135

The above table has been corrected from a version in evergreenmagazine.com/app/portal/mm/Canada.pdf.

Double stamp (note perforation across horizontal centre) honouring Canada's forests, issued by Canada Post (© Canada Post Corporation) to commemorate the 2011 International Year of Forests. The top stamp shows the West Coast rainforest, the bottom stamp shows biodiversity on the forest floor. Forests cover 41% of Canada's land mass.

KEY REFERENCES ON PLANT SYMBOLS OF CANADA

Note: the older references listed below do not report more recent changes in official emblems.

Breitung, A.J. 1954. Canadian floral emblems. Canadian Nature 16(2): 42–47. [Written for a general audience. Canadian Nature was published by the Audubon Society of Canada. It should not be confused with the Canadian Field-Naturalist.]

Canadian Heritage. 2002 (revised edition). Symbols of Canada. Canadian Heritage, Ottawa, ON. 57 pp. [Presentation is often elementary. Accompanied by a large poster. Very attractive colour drawings. Issued in French as: Les symboles du Canada.]

Coucill, W. 1966. Untitled [Official flowers of Canada's ten provinces and two territories]. National Trust, Ottawa, ON. [Bilingual format. "To commemorate Canada's Centenary, National Trust Company commissioned Canadian artist Walter Coucill to paint in their natural settings, the official flowers of Canada's ten provinces and two territories." This publication is a set of twelve superb coloured plates, based on the original paintings. The Bank of Nova Scotia acquired National Trust Company in 1997. The Coucill family deposited the paintings, while retaining copyright, with Library and Archives Canada.]

Department of the Secretary of State of Canada. 1967. The arms, flags and floral emblems of Canada. Department of the Secretary of State of Canada, Ottawa, ON. 80 pp. [Bilingual format, alternatively titled: Les armoiries, drapeaux et emblèmes floraux du Canada. The 1967 edition was issued with attractive drawings of plants in colour. Modified and co-published as a 3rd edition with Deneau Publishers, in unilingual formats, as The arms, flags, and emblems

of Canada, in 1984, with 112 pp. and (less attractive) colour photographs. The Department of the Secretary of State of Canada ceased to exist in 1996.]

Fletcher, M. 1998. Our fabulous flora. Legion Magazine May/June. [An article on Canada's floral emblems, written for a general audience, and available at various websites.]

International Wood Collectors Society. 2000. Canada's arboreal emblems. An overview of Canada's official trees and their wood. Canadian region of the International Wood Collectors Society. 32 pp.

Sherk, L.C. 1967. Growing Canada's floral emblems. Canada Department of Agriculture, (Publication 1288E) Ottawa, ON. 28 pp. [Issued in French as: Sherk, L.C. 1968 ("1967"). La culture des plantes emblèmes du Canada. Ministère de l'Agriculture du Canada (Publication 1288F), Ottawa, ON. 28 pp.] Photographs in colour.

Wayland, B. 2005. Symbolic blooms: a look at Canada's floral emblems. Wildlife (Canadian Wildlife Federation, Kanata, ON) 11(4): 38–41. [Has colour paintings of the flowers.]

Websites (current December 2011; these URLs have been available for several years)

Canadian symbols at Parliament. http://www.parl. gc.ca/information/about/education/CanSymbols/ about-e.asp [To celebrate Canada's 1967 Centennial, huge stained glass windows (each about 9 m high and containing around 2,000 pieces of cut glass) were installed in the House of Commons Chamber of the Parliament Buildings, with completion in

1973. This website provides detailed illustrations and background and (for the younger set) a floral emblem colouring book.]

Canadian Museum of Civilization. The Canada Garden: a tribute to Canada's indigenous flora. http://www.civilisations.ca/cmc/exhibitions/cmc/ plaza/plaza01eng.shtml#Menu [presents copies of a set of drawings of Canada's floral emblems by Lavonia R. Stockelbach (née Bonnie Hunter, 1874–1966). The original paintings are the property of Agriculture & Agri-Food Canada and are in the Saunders Building, Central Experimental Farm, Ottawa. Ms. Stockelbach, best known for illustrating birds, produced more than one copy of her set of paintings of the Canadian flora emblems, and had Chinaware engraved with the same paintings (the disposition of these is uncertain). The paintings were exhibited at the International Botanical Congress, Montreal in 1959.]

GeoSymbols/Plants. http://www.geosymbols.org/ [The largest website dealing with the symbolic use of plants of the world. Has a common sense explanation of the vernacular vs. technical use of terms like fruit, vegetable, tree, shrub, nut, berry, etc., which is important to the designation of representatives of these categories as official emblems.]

General Information on Plant Symbols

Rosenow, J. 2001. What role for national trees in promoting biodiversity conservation? Oryx 35(1): 1–2.

Vu, P. Can states ever have too many symbols? http:// www.infozine.com/news/stories/op/storiesView/ sid/6555/ [Discusses some absurd proposals.]

FIGURE SOURCES

Illustrated synopsis. The maple tree is from: Harter, J. (*Editor*). 1988. The plant kingdom compendium. A definitive volume of more than 2,400 copyright-free engravings. Bonanza Books, New York, NY. The remaining illustrations of trees are from Canada's arboreal emblems (cited above), reproduced with permission of C. Holder (author) and J. Monty (president) of the Canada Tree Foundation. The maple leaf is from: Sargent, C.S. 1891. The silva of North America. Houghton, Mifflin and Company, Boston, MA. vol. 2. Western flowering dogwood is from: Sargent, C.S. 1893. The silva of North America. Houghton, Mifflin and Company, Boston, MA. vol. 5. Lowbush blueberry is from: Vander Kloet, S.P. 1988. The genus *Vaccinium* in North America. Agriculture Canada Research Branch Publication 1828. Needle-and-thread grass is by A. Haynes (prepared for Agriculture and Agri-Food Canada). Rough fescue is from: Best, K.F., Looman, J., and Campbell, J.B. 1971 (prepared for Agriculture and Agri-Food Canada). Prairie grasses identified and described by vegetative characters. Canada Department of Agriculture, Ottawa, Publication 1413. The remaining floral emblems are from Canadian Heritage 2002 (cited above), with permission of Canadian Heritage, as well as Public Works and Government Services Canada.

Coins. All coin images are reproduced with the permission of the Royal Canadian Mint.

Stamps. All stamps are reproduced with the permission of Canada Post Corporation.

Map with provincial and territorial flowers. The illustrations are from Canadian Heritage 2002 (cited above), with permission of Canadian Heritage, as well as Public Works and Government Services Canada.

Map with provincial and territorial trees. The tree silhouettes are reproduced with permission from Trees in Canada by J.L. Farrar, published by the Canadian Forest Service and Fitzhenry and Whiteside (Markham, ON, Canada), 1995.

ALBERTA

Provincial flag of Alberta.

AN ALBERTA LANDSCAPE: autumn view from the prairies to the Rocky Mountains.

FLORAL EMBLEM: WILD ROSE

Wild prickly rose (*Rosa acicularis*) in flower. Courtesy of L. Hachey, Government of Alberta.

SYMBOLISM

The Alberta wild prickly rose has been applauded as an excellent choice for the floral emblem of Alberta because it is extraordinarily beautiful, widespread in the province, and exhibits hardiness in the northern climate of the province that reflects the spirit of the people. The thorniness of the plant has not generally been viewed as a virtue, but some have suggested that the prickliness is consistent with the tough nature of many Albertans.

The Coat of Arms of Alberta. Wild roses are at the base, above the provincial motto, Fortis et Libre, "strong and free".

NAMES

Latin Names
Rosa acicularis Lindl.

The genus name *Rosa* is based on the ancient Latin name for roses, *rosa,* which in turn originated from Akkadian (the ancient language of Mesopotamia) word *russu,* "red". The epithet *acicularis* is Latin for needle-like, a reference to the prickles.

English Names
Wild rose. Also: Alberta wild rose, Alberta wild prickly rose, arctic rose, bristly rose, circumpolar rose, northern prickly rose, prickly wild rose, wild prickly rose. The name "wild rose" is rather ambiguous; "prickly rose" is much more often used to refer to the species, and in the following we use "wild prickly rose".

French Names
Rosier aciculaire; also: églantier, églantine, rosier arctique.

Sunset viewed through wild prickly roses (*Rosa acicularis*). Source: Wikimedia (photographer: ufoncz; Creative Common Attribution 2.0 license).

HISTORY

Canada
The designation of a floral emblem for Alberta appears to have been initiated by a suggestion of the editor of an Edmonton newspaper. Alberta women's institutes took up the suggestion and passed it on to the province's Department of Education. School children made the final choice of the wild rose as the province's floral emblem. The provincial government adopted the wild rose officially in the Floral Emblem Act of 1930.

Foreign
Roses have been very popular choices as floral symbols of political regions, although often a particular species is not identified. Like Alberta, Iowa chose a "wild rose" as its emblem. The rose is the New York state flower. Georgia adopted the white Cherokee rose. The District of Columbia is associated with the American beauty rose. North Dakota chose the prairie rose. Roses have national significance in Bulgaria, England, Iran, Luxembourg, and the Maldive Islands in the Indian Ocean. The rose served as the national flower of Honduras from 1946 to 1969, but an orchid was adopted as the national flower in 1946. In 1986, the rose became the "national floral emblem" of the United States, when President Reagan signed the proclamation in the White House Rose Garden; according to one newspaper report, the president "rose to the occasion".

Wild prickly rose (*Rosa acicularis*) in flower (left) and in fruit (right). Source: Plates 344 and 345 (respectively) from Walcott, M.V. 1925. North American wild flowers. Smithsonian Institution, Washington, D.C. 5 vols.

APPEARANCE

Wild prickly rose is a deciduous, bushy shrub usually 0.5–1.5 m (20 inches–5 feet) tall, sometimes up to 2.5 m (8 feet) in height. The stems are usually densely covered with slender, straight thorns. The leaves are borne alternately; they have five to nine leaflets that are 3–5 cm (1.2–2 inches) long and coarsely toothed. The leaf stalks and the margins of the leaflets bear tiny glands and there are conspicuous stipules (small leaf-like bracts) at the base of the leaf stalk. The flowers are fragrant, 5–7 cm (2–2.8 inches) across, and are borne singly (occasionally in groups of a few) at the ends of lateral branches; the petals are pink or rose (rarely white) on the outside but often white and hairy on the inside; numerous stamens are present.

Wild prickly rose "fruits" (frequently called hips) are globose or pear-shaped, 1.5–2.5 cm (0.6–1 inch) long, fleshy, red or orange-red, and ripen in late summer and fall. They contain 10 to 30 small, hairy "seeds". Technically, rose hips are accessory or false fruits, not true fruits. The fleshy, outer portion that surrounds the "seeds" is a "hypanthium", developed from the top of the flower stalk; in contrast, the flesh of true fleshy fruits is developed from one or more ovary walls. The "seeds" of a rose are in fact the true fruits; these are categorized as "achenes", defined as single seeded, dry, indehiscent fruits in which the seed coat is separate from the fruit wall (sunflower "seeds" are another example of achenes).

CLASSIFICATION

Family: rose family (Rosaceae).

The genus *Rosa* consists of about 190 species of shrubs, distributed throughout the temperate and subtropical areas of the northern hemisphere. There are 14 native and 11 introduced species of the genus growing wild in Canada. Four species occur in the Prairie Provinces, three of these in Alberta: wild prickly rose (*R. acicularis*), prairie rose (*R. arkansana*) and common wild rose (*R. woodsii*). Unlike the wild prickly rose, the common wild rose has infrastipular prickles (paired prickles located below the stipules), and its fruit lacks a neck. Unlike the wild prickly rose, the prairie rose mostly dies back to ground level at the end of the season, and its leaves have 9–11 leaflets (compared to 3–7 in wild prickly rose). Hybridization between *R. acicularis* and other species of *Rosa* sometimes makes identification problematic.

Two subspecies of *R. acicularis* are widely recognized: subsp. *acicularis* occurs in Eurasia, extending into Alaska, and subsp. *sayi* (Schw.) Lewis is present in North America. The following key is from Lewis (1959; percentage frequencies of occurrence are in parentheses):

1. Pedicels glandular (89%); leaflets commonly 5 per leaf (91%), rarely glandular (22%), singly serrated (86%), the serrations rarely gland-tipped (22%), usually 17 or fewer per half leaflet (88%); sepals at their bases occasionally 3 mm or more wide (41%); one auricle often 5 mm or more wide (62%) . . . . subsp. *acicularis*

1. Pedicels rarely glandular (8%); leaflets 5 (47%) or 7 (53%) per leaf, commonly glandular (85%), usually biserrated (69%), the serrations usually glandular (67%), usually 18 or more per half leaflet (57%); sepals at their bases usually 3 mm or more wide (78%); one auricle occasionally 5 mm or more wide (42%) . . . . subsp. *sayi*

A white flowered form of *Rosa acicularis,* forma *alba,* occurs rarely throughout much of the range.

Wild prickly rose (*Rosa acicularis*) in fruit. Source: Wikimedia (photographer: Midori; Creative Commons Attribution-Share Alike 3.0 Unported license).

GEOGRAPHY

The circumpolar *R. acicularis* has the most extensive range of all species in the genus *Rosa*. In Eurasia, it occurs from Sweden across northern Eurasia to the Bering Strait, including Mongolia, northern China, Korea, and Japan. In North America, it extends in the north across Alaska, Yukon and Northwest Territories, from British Columbia to New Brunswick, and south to New Mexico and West Virginia.

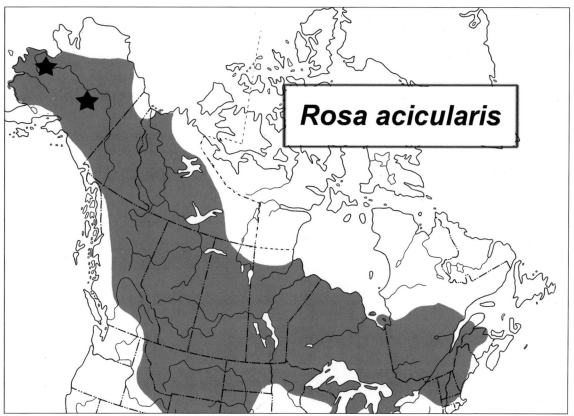

Rosa acicularis

Canadian and adjacent United States distribution of *Rosa acicularis.* subsp. *sayi* (shaded) and subsp. *acicularis* (stars in Alaska).

Wild prickly rose (*Rosa acicularis*). Source: Wikimedia (photographer: Ravedave; GNU Free Documentation license).

ECOLOGY

The wild prickly rose grows well in a considerable range of ecological conditions. The species is found in both fine-and coarse-textured soils, although it does not do well in peat. It can grow on soils low in nutrients, but is generally not present on the poorest soils. It occurs in both quite dry and quite moist locations, although it is not adapted to constantly wet substrates. *Rosa acicularis* is moderately shade tolerant, but fruits and seeds are produced more abundantly in sunnier locations. The species regenerates from its rhizomes following fires, and is often a colonizer of recently cleared sites. It is quite competitive in shrub associations and in young or open forests, but as forests mature it decreases markedly as shade increases.

Habitat

Rosa acicularis is a resident of habitats in the boreal forest, mixed forest, northern prairie, and western montane regions. The species typically occurs in the partial shade of open coniferous and hardwood associations. It is also found in more open circumstances, beside roads, in meadows, along streams and shores, on slopes, on rocky bluffs and ledges, and in swamps and floodplains.

Inter-species Relationships

Wild prickly rose is a significant food plant for wild vertebrate animals. Despite the presence of thorns that provide some protection for the plants, the twigs and leaves are browsed by deer, elk, moose, mountain sheep, grouse, hares, and rodents. Black and grizzly bears are fond of the fruits (bears are said to relish rose hips as a pre-hibernation food), which are also consumed by a variety of small mammals and birds. Insects of course also consume roses. Wild prickly rose thickets provide good nesting sites and cover for birds, and shelter for small mammals, as well as nectar and pollen for numerous insects. Because of numerous ecological interactions, *R. acicularis* is a "keystone species" (one upon which numerous other species depend).

Pollination and Dispersal

Rosa acicularis is an insect-pollinated species. In northern areas, it is a good source of nectar for bees maintained by beekeepers. The seeds are dispersed by birds and mammals. In addition to reproducing by seeds, *R. acicularis* propagates vigorously by rhizomes. Clones produced by rhizomes can live for hundreds of years.

Wild prickly rose (*Rosa acicularis*). Source: Wikimedia (photographer: Timholland; GNU Free Documentation license).

USES

Mostly in past times, wild prickly rose was among the roses used by Indigenous Peoples for medicinal purposes, both in the Old and New Worlds. In North America, roots, stems, bark, and hips of wild prickly rose were employed in medicinal preparations to treat a wide variety of problems, including cough, colds, fever, sore eyes, blindness, difficult birth, stomach difficulties, and diarrhea.

Roses are famous as ornamentals; more than 13,000 cultivars have been recorded, of which at least 5,000 are commercially available. Wild prickly rose is considered to be an attractive ornamental especially suited for cold areas. Its appearance is considerably enhanced by careful pruning. There are only a few North American cultivars of *R. acicularis,* including 'Aurora', a red-flowered selection; and 'Arctic Flame' and 'Nearly Wild', which are pink-flowered forms. There are also Old World cultivars, including 'Dornröschen' (German) and 'Tove' (Norwegian).

The use of rose "hips" (fruits) is minor, but nevertheless has a long history. A Neolithic archaeological site dated at 5000 BP shows evidence of humans intentionally collecting rose fruits for food, and they were also used as food by the Indians of North America. Rose hips are often covered with hooked, hairy outgrowths which should be removed before the fruits are cooked. In most species, the hairs on the outside are less troublesome than the fuzz on the inside. De-seeding the hips and removing the fuzz and hairs are tedious tasks. Rose hips should be picked when they are plump and red, but not softly over-ripe. They can be left on the bush until the first light frost, and picked when slightly soft to the touch. They should be processed quickly after harvest to prevent loss of vitamin C (in relation to its small amount of edible matter, the rose fruit is extraordinarily rich in this vitamin). The stem and blossom ends should be trimmed, the hips cut in half lengthwise, the seeds and fibres scooped out with a small spoon, and the halves dried on a screen in an airy, shaded room indoors. Alternatively, they can be dried by hot air from an electric heater, care being taken to prevent overheating and loss of natural colour. The hips can be screened in a rough wire container to remove their hair (unless the hairs are strained away, they can be irritating in foods prepared with the hips). Storage should be in a cool place, and as vitamin C decreases gradually, the hips and their products should not be kept longer than a year.

Rose flowers have limited, but interesting culinary uses. Drinks have been perfumed with roses, and rose petal wines have been made since classical times. During the Elizabethan era (sixteenth century), rose petals were extensively used to scent food and even washing water. Rose water for flavouring sweet dishes, rose petal jam, rose petal-flavoured honey, rose-flavoured candy and rose-flavoured vinegar are still marketed, albeit on a very limited scale.

Wild prickly rose has been recommended for revegetation and erosion control on moist to wet areas. It has moderate tolerance of oil-contaminated soil, a significant advantage in Alberta, one of the world's major oil producers.

Wild prickly rose (*Rosa acicularis*) by Lavonia R. Stockelbach (1874–1966). A collection of her paintings of Canadian provincial and territorial official flowers is associated with the herbarium of Agriculture and Agri-Food Canada in Ottawa.

A BIODIVERSITY TREASURE

CULTIVATION

Detailed instructions on how to grow wild prickly rose, from former Central Experimental Farm horticulturalist and co-worker Larry Sherk, are reproduced below from his popular but out-of-print (1967) guide to growing Canada's floral emblems (cited in the first chapter of this book).

"This shrub grows well in sandy, well-drained soil in full sun or part shade. You may either move a whole plant or take a sucker, preferably in the spring. The shrub spreads by underground suckers to form dense thickets, so plant it where it will not encroach on other plants.

"You may take semihard cuttings in July and root them in moist sand and peat moss in a closed frame. Powdery mildew is often a problem in a closed frame but it can be controlled with applications of dinocap or cycloheximide [due to health risks, use of cycloheximide as a fungicide is now discouraged].

"To start plants from seeds, take the seeds from the hips as soon as they are ripe and sow them at once in flats of soil, sand, and peat moss or in raised beds in the garden. If, on the other hand, you want to delay sowing until winter or spring, simply store the seeds in a cool dry place and sow them later. Before you sow stored seeds, you must stratify them in sand and peat at 40 °F (5 °C) for three months."

CONSERVATION STATUS

In much of its native area, *Rosa acicularis* is common and not in need of special conservation measures. However, it is mainly a western North American species, less common in the east, and is endangered in the states of Illinois, Iowa, Massachusetts, New Hampshire, New York, and Vermont. As noted below, it is also rapidly declining in a part of Saskatchewan due to recent range expansion of the rose stem girdler, with widespread declines anticipated.

THE ROSE STEM GIRDLER
Entomologist Doug Larson from Saskatchewan was the first to report an introduced beetle called the rose stem girdler (*Agrilus aurchalceus*) in the southern prairie provinces. In 2003 he found patches of wild roses in the Maple Creek area that were being devastated by the alien insect which tunnels under the bark of older canes. Larson suggested that the beetle has the potential of greatly modifying the vegetational landscape of parts of the prairies. This is because the dense, prickly stems deter livestock from grazing in the area, and thereby protect other plants that are susceptible to grazing. The bushes also provide numerous animals with protection from predators Because the beetle will likely cause wild roses to decrease, prairie shrub patches (which serve as protective oases for biodiversity) will become more open and accessible to grazing animals and predators. Since the roses may resprout from roots and root crowns, they are likely to persist as short roses with young short canes that are not attacked by the beetle. Nevertheless, a substantial decline seems likely.

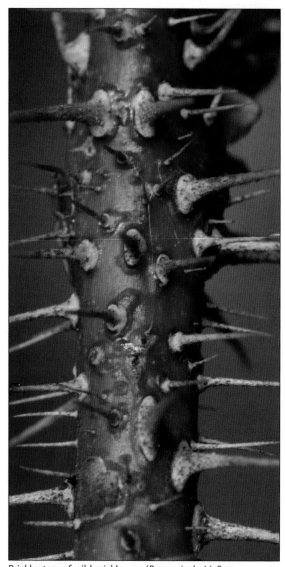

Prickly stem of wild prickly rose (*Rosa acicularis*). Source: Wikipedia (photographer: W. Siegmund; GNU Free Documentation license).

Painting of the official flower of Alberta, wild prickly rose (*Rosa acicularis*), from the Walter Coucill Canadian Centennial official flowers of Canada series (see Coucill 1966 cited in the first chapter of this book). Reproduced with the permission of the copyright holders, the Coucill family.

MYTHS, LEGENDS, TALES, FOLKLORE AND INTERESTING FACTS

🍁 Rose is translated as rose in Danish, French, German, and Norwegian; and as rosa in Italian, Portuguese, Russian, and Spanish.

🍁 The Roman Emperor Nero (37–68) reputedly used up the equivalent in modern currency of $100,000 in cut roses to decorate a single night's feast. He is also believed to have had pipes installed under banquet plates to allow his guests to be spritzed with rose scent between dinner courses.

🍁 Some privileged Romans slept on beds of rose petals, giving rise to the saying "It's not a bed of roses".

🍁 Since the time of the ancient Egyptians, roses have been associated with secrecy. According to Greek myth, Cupid, shocked by the conduct of his mother Venus, took her flower, the rose, to Harpocrates, god of silence, to keep her scandal confidential. This story is said to have brought about the expression "sub rosa", referring to activities conducted confidentially. Roses were customarily suspended over the dinner-table as a sign that confidences revealed under the influence of wine were to be kept secret. For many years the ceilings of European dining rooms featured formed plaster roses, with the same symbolism. The plaster ornament in the centre of a ceiling is still known as "the rose" or "rosette", even if it is no longer in the form of a rose. Beginning in the Middle Ages, a wood carving of a rose was placed in the space over confessional doors in Catholic churches, once again symbolizing confidentiality.

🍁 Rosaries are used to count prayers to Our Lady (the Virgin Mary). The first "rosaries" were made out of pounded rose petals, moulded into beads and threaded (the word rosary is derived from the Latin *rosarium*, rose garden). Rosaries were later made out of rose hips, and eventually out of various materials.

The scent of the beads was supposed to remind one of the roses in Mary's garden.

🍁 Roses have been a heraldic emblem on the shields of soldiers since the time of the Romans. The War of the Roses was a series of battles (1455–1487)

Wild prickly rose (*Rosa acicularis*) in flower. Courtesy of L. Hachey, Government of Alberta.

MYTHS, LEGENDS, TALES, FOLKLORE AND INTERESTING FACTS (CONT'D)

between two branches of the Royal Family Plantagenet in England. The House of Lancaster, represented by the red rose, defeated the House of York, represented by the white rose. The white rose is reputed to have been a form of *R. canina* (also said to be *R. ×alba* L., a hybrid involving *R. canina*). The two houses combined with the marriage of Henry VII of Lancaster to Elizabeth of York, Henry becoming the first Tudor king. He adopted a red and white Tudor rose as his symbol, and this is now the national flower of England. A rose cultivar called 'York and Lancaster' which develops both red and white flowers is currently marketed. This has been identified as a cultivar of the briar rose, *R. rubiginosa*.

* Roses were important medicinal plants during the Middle Ages, used to reduce fever, inflammation, pain, and to stop any kind of excessive flow, be it tears, diarrhea, or hemorrhage. The popularity of the rose eventually resulted in its elevation to the status of a wonder drug, used even for epilepsy, tuberculosis, goitre, and gout; during plagues, rose fragrance was used to purify the air in public places. Apothecaries even used rose galls, employing them to induce urination.

* Roses are the most popular of gravestone-inscribed flowers. In Victorian cemeteries, where a husband and wife were buried next to each other, the gravestone of the wife often showed a hand holding a lily (symbolic of innocence and purity) while that of the husband showed a hand with a rose. Children's gravestones often showed rose buds as symbols of innocence, and sometimes the stem of the rosebud was carved as broken, suggesting their short lives.

* During World War II, rose hips were eaten for their content of vitamin C while supplies of foreign fruit were limited. The British Ministry of Health distributed "National Hip Syrup". Similarly, German submarines and ships were supplied with rosehip syrup.

* In England, it was found that the vitamin C content of rose hips increases towards the north, with four times as much in plants grown in Scotland compared to those in southern England.

* In 1939 Frances Meilland, a rose specialist in France, found a rose with magnificent pale gold blossoms growing from one seed he had nurtured. He sent cuttings to a Pennsylvania rose grower, which were transported on the last American plane that got out of France in November 1940, a step ahead of the invading Nazis. The cuttings were used to propagate this rose which many experts consider the best ever developed, the Peace rose, which blooms on more than 30 million bushes throughout the world.

* The perforated nozzle on the end of the spout of a watering can, that produces a shower of water in order to minimize soil disturbance while watering potted plants, is called a "rose". The word originated from the French *aroser,* to irrigate, and so has no connection with roses.

* "Rosarians" are devoted rose hobbyists.

* The naming of roses has become a commercial venture. Some companies offer clients the possibility of having new rose varieties named for them, for a price, sometimes ranging up to $75,000. New rose varieties are being named for corporations ('Barbie' for the doll; 'Weight Watcher's Success' rose), causes ('Arthritis' rose, 'Veterans' Honour' rose), and of course famous personalities ('Billie Graham', 'Céline Dion', 'Chris Evert', 'Vidal Sassoon', 'Rosie O'Donnell', 'Barbra Streisand', 'George Burns').

SOURCES OF ADDITIONAL INFORMATION

Bruneau, A., Starr, J.R., and Joly, S. 2007. Phylogenetic relationship in the genus *Rosa*: new evidence from chloroplast DNA sequences and an appraisal of current knowledge. Syst. Bot. 32: 366–378.

Larson, D.J. 2003. The rose stem girdler (*Agrilus aurchalceus* Redtenbacher) (Insecta: Coleoptera: Buprestidae), a new threat to prairie roses. Blue Jay 61: 176–178.

Lewis, W.H. 1959. A monograph of the genus *Rosa* in North America. 1. *R. acicularis*. Brittonia 1: 1–24.

Mazza, G. 1979. Development and consumer evaluation of a native fruit product: Saskatoon, chokecherry and rose hip. J. Can. Inst. Food Sci. Technol. 12(4): 166–169.

Richardson, J.E. 1996. *Rosa acicularis:* the Arctic or circumpolar rose. New Plantsman 3: 147–149.

Alberta license plate. Source: Wikimedia (photographer: ziki88; Creative Common Attribution 3.0 Unported license).

ROSE PHILOSOPHY

"The rose has thorns only for those who would gather it."
—*Chinese Proverb*

"Gather ye rose-buds while ye may,
Old Time is still a-flying:
And this same flower that smiles to-day,
To-morrow will be dying."
—*Robert Herrick (1591–1674, English poet and clergyman)*

"One may live without bread, not without roses."
—*Jean Richepin (1849–1926, French writer)*

"The question of common sense is 'what is it good for?' A question which would abolish the rose and be answered triumphantly by the cabbage."
—*James Russell Lowell (1819–1891, American poet, critic, and editor)*

"I'd rather have roses on my table than diamonds on my neck."
—*Emma Goldman (1869–1940, Russian-born American philosopher, anarchist, and social activist)*

"An idealist is one who, on noticing that a rose smells better than a cabbage, concludes that it will also make better soup."
—*H.L. (Henry Lewis) Mencken (1880–1956, American journalist and critic)*

"Treaties are like roses and young girls. They last while they last."
—*Charles De Gaulle (1890–1970, President of France, in an interview in the July 12, 1963 issue of Time magazine)*

"The rose represents love, magic, hope, and the mystery of life itself. Its name, ordinary enough, refers to its colour . . . . But that is like saying the heart is a muscle situated on the left side of the rib cage."
—*Diana Wells, 100 flowers and how they get their names (1997), p. 187.*

"Time is money but it's also for smelling the roses and the rain."
—*Unattributed*

Wild prickly rose (*Rosa acicularis*) in flower. Courtesy of L. Hachey, Government of Alberta.

TREE: LODGEPOLE PINE

Shore pine (*Pinus contorta* var. *contorta*). Photo taken on Fidalgo Island, Washington State. Reproduced by permission of the photographer, Walter Siegmund.

SYMBOLISM

The lodgepole pine is a suitable choice as the official tree of Alberta because (1) it is very prevalent in the province (it is the most common tree species at lower and middle altitudes of the eastern slopes of the Rocky Mountains of Alberta); and (2) it has been important in the economic development of the region, and continues to play a major role in Alberta's forest industry. The tree's impressive stature, exceptional hardiness, and ability to thrive in an extraordinary range of habitats are characteristics that make the species an admirable emblem.

Extensive information on the symbolism of pines is given in the section on white pine, the official tree of Ontario, in the chapter on Ontario emblems.

Lodgepole pine (*Pinus contorta* var. *latifolia*) in Wyoming, U.S.A. Source: Wikimedia (photographer: stereogab; Creative Commons Attribution-Share Alike 2.0 Generic license).

NAMES

Latin Names
Pinus contorta Dougl. ex Loud.
West coast variety: var. *contorta*
Inland variety: var. *latifolia* Engelm.

The genus name *Pinus* is based on *pinus*, the Latin (ancient Roman) name for pine, derived from the Greek *pitus* or *pitys*, and the Sanskrit *pitu*. *Contorta* is from the Latin *con* (together) and *torquere* (to twist), a reference to the crooked appearance of the trunk of the west coast var. *contorta*. *Latifolia* is from the Latin *latus* (wide) and *folium* (leaf), referring to the needles, that are usually wider than those of the coastal variety.

English Names
Lodgepole pine (the name is based on the use of the tree for poles to support the lodges or tepees of indigenous people). Also: Rocky Mountain lodgepole pine, interior lodgepole pine, tall lodgepole pine, black pine, jack pine, western jack pine (the preceding three local names are undesirable as they are usually used for other pines; the name jack pine reflects a historical confusion of migrants from the east who were familiar with jack pine and mistakenly applied the name to lodgepole pine).

Variety *latifolia*: lodgepole pine; also: cypress. (Cypress (also known by the French cyprès) is a local name in Alberta and Saskatchewan, likely to lead to confusion with true cypress, *Cupressus* species of the western United States. Lodgepole pine east of the Rockies is confined to the Cypress Hills of southern Alberta and Saskatchewan. The Cypress Hills were named for the trees, not vice-versa.)

Variety *contorta*: shore pine; also beach pine, coast pine, scrub pine.

Variety *murrayana* (not native to Canada): Murray pine.

French Names
Pin lodgepole. Also: for var. *latifolia*: cypress, pin tordu latifolié; for var. *contorta*: pin tordu, pin á feuilles tordues; for var. *murrayana*: pin de Murray.

Silhouettes of the Canadian varieties of lodgepole pine (*Pinus contorta*). Left, var. *contorta*; right, var *latifolia*. Source: Farrar, J.L. 1995. Trees in Canada. Canadian Forest Service and Fitzhenry and Whiteside, Markham, ON, Canada. Reproduced with permission.

HISTORY

Canada

The Alberta Legislative Assembly designated the lodgepole pine as the provincial tree of the province in 1984, the result of efforts of the Junior Forest Warden Association of Alberta.

The eastern white pine (*Pinus strobus*) became the provincial tree of Ontario in 1984. The Northwest Territories named the jack pine (*Pinus banksiana*) as its official tree in 1989, but in 1999, after the new territory of Nunavut was carved away from the Northwest Territories, the jack pine was replaced with the tamarack.

Foreign

As detailed in the chapter on the emblems of Ontario, pine species are official trees of 12 U.S. states and two countries.

Male flowers of lodgepole pine (*Pinus contorta*). Source: U.S.D.A. Forest Service.

A stand of lodgepole pine (*Pinus contorta* var. *latifolia*) in Idaho. Photo courtesy of Chris Schnepf, University of Idaho and Bugwood.org.

Second year seed cones of lodgepole pine (*Pinus contorta*). Source: U.S.D.A. Forest Service.

A BIODIVERSITY TREASURE

APPEARANCE

Variety *latifolia* is typically found in dense stands, in which case it develops tall, straight, clean trunks up to 46 m (151 feet) tall and 80 cm (32 inches) in diameter. Trees in open stands form broad crowns. The branches generally curve upward. Variety *contorta* develops into a short, scrubby tree, 6–15 m (20–50 feet) tall with the trunks up to 50 cm (20 inches) in diameter. The latter often has a twisted trunk and an irregular crown shape.

The leaves (needles) of lodgepole pine are evergreen, 2.5–8 cm (1–3 inches) long, stiff and sharply pointed, in bundles of two (rarely in fascicles of three), often spirally twisted and spread apart. The flowers occur in male and female clusters (known as cones or catkins). The male catkins are 8–14 mm (0.3–0.6 inch) long, with pale yellow to yellowish orange flowers, the catkins occurring in clusters. The female catkins have 2–5 reddish purple flowers, and are 10–12 mm (0.3–0.5 inch) long. The mature female seed cones are 3–6 cm (1.2–2.4 inches) long, often asymmetrical, the tips of the cone scales with prickles at their tips. Lodgepole pines often live to 200 years of age, occasionally as long as 400 years. Variety *latifolia* is comparatively long-lived compared to var. *contorta;* one tree in British Columbia was determined to be 497 years of age.

CLASSIFICATION

Family: Pinaceae (pine family).

The Pinaceae is the largest family of conifers. There are about 100 species of *Pinus,* which includes trees or shrubs distributed in north temperate and mountainous, north tropical regions of the world. Thirty-eight species are native to North America north of Mexico, nine of these occurring in Canada, and three additional species are naturalized, including the mugo pine (*P. mugo*), which is a shrub. Almost all pines are in two major groups, subgenus *Pinus* (the hard pines) and subgenus *Strobus* (the soft pines). Lodgepole pine is a member of the hard pines, which have persistent (instead of deciduous) leaf sheaths and two, instead of a single vascular bundle, observable in a needle cross-section. Other hard pine trees found in Canada include black pine (*P. nigra*), red pine (*P. resinosa*), Scots pine (*P. sylvestris*), jack pine (*P. banksiana*), pitch pine (*P. rigida*), and ponderosa pine (*P. ponderosa*). There are only two other Canadian pines with two leaves in a cluster and needles of similar length. Introduced (and escaped) Scots pine always has cones that open and the cone scales are flat at the tip. Mature trees of lodgepole and jack pine (*P. banksiana*), on the other hand, often have cones that do not open. The cone scales of lodgepole pine have a short, curved spine at the tip that may or may not be present in jack pine. Jack pines also differ in having curved cones borne along the branches whereas lodgepole pines have straight cones borne at the branch tips. Lodgepole pine hybridizes extensively with the rather similar jack pine where the ranges of two species overlap, and the hybrids and their progeny may be difficult to identify.

In addition to *Pinus contorta* varieties *contorta* and *latifolia,* there is another variety, var. *murrayana* (Sierra lodgepole pine or tamarack pine), which occurs in the Sierra Nevada of California. Still another variety is sometimes recognized: var. *bolanderi* (Bolander pine) of Mendocino County, California.

Key differences between varieties *contorta* and *latifolia*

Character	Variety *contorta*	Variety *latifolia*
Height	Up to 15 m (49 feet); usually less than 10 m (33 feet)	Up to 46 m (151 feet)
Trunk shape	Typically crooked or deformed; with major trunk branches; tapering relatively abruptly upwards	Typically straight; with a single major trunk; tapering very gradually upwards
Crown	Often asymmetrical	Usually symmetrical
Bark of mature trunks	Evidently furrowed	Not evidently furrowed
Leaf (needle) colour	Dark green	Yellow-green

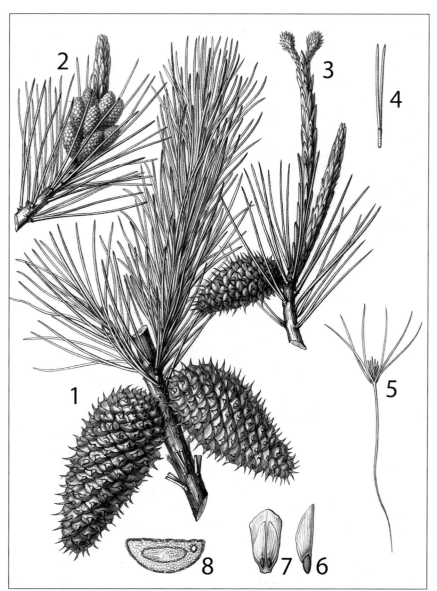

Lodgepole pine (*Pinus contorta*). 1, branch with mature cones; 2, branch with male flowers; 3, branch with female flowers; 4, cluster of young leaves; 5, seedling; 6, a mature seed with attached wing; 7, a young cone scale with two developing seeds; 8, cross section of leaf. Source: Sargent, C.S. 1897. The silva of North America. Houghton, Mifflin and Company, Boston, MA. Vol. 11, plate 567.

A lodgepole pine (*Pinus contorta*) forest in Alberta. Source: Thinkstock.

GEOGRAPHY

Pinus contorta is a widespread species native to North America. Forests dominated by lodgepole pine occur over 6 million ha (16 million acres) in the western U.S. and on 20 million ha (50 million acres) in Canada. The species also occurs locally in the mountains of Mexico (*Pinus contorta* is the only pine species that occurs both in Alaska and Mexico).

Variety *contorta* is native to a relatively narrow strip of the Pacific coast of North America, including southern Alaska, British Columbia, and the states of Washington, Oregon, and California.

In its northernmost locations, variety *latifolia* is native to southeastern Alaska, Yukon, and the Northwest Territories. It extends south through the western provinces, including interior British Columbia, much of western Alberta, part of southeastern Alberta and adjacent southwestern Saskatchewan. In its southernmost locations, it occurs in the states of Washington, Idaho, Montana, Oregon, Colorado, Wyoming, Utah, and South Dakota.

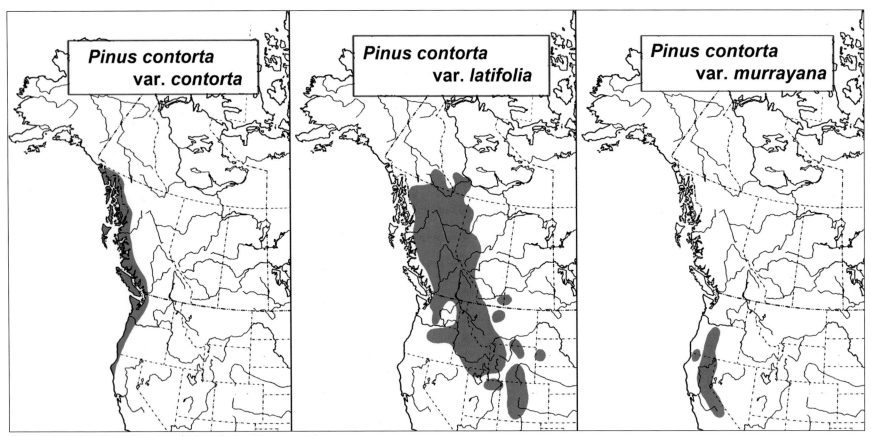

Geographical distributions of varieties of lodgepole pine (*Pinus contorta*).

ECOLOGY

As described below, fire is extremely important in the ecology of *Pinus contorta* (much more so for var. *latifolia* than for var. *contorta*). Several factors make the trees quite susceptible to fire: they contain considerable pitch; the bark is often thin, providing limited protection; and the dead lower branches often remain on the trunk, providing "fire ladders" facilitating burning. However, the species is adapted to very rapid recolonization of areas cleared by fires or other catastrophic events. Lodgepole pine is a fire or "pioneer" species, adapted to full sunlight and almost any forest soil, and to rapid early growth so that it can colonize and establish quickly. The species has relatively low shade tolerance, and so does not establish well in regions where forests are already well developed.

Variety *latifolia* often forms large, sometimes quite dense, pure stands, but also grows in associations with other species. It is an aggressive colonizer, rapidly populating an area after it has been cleared by fire or logging. As a result, even-aged stands are common. By contrast, variety *contorta* grows in a maritime climate in most of its range. It is a dominant species in the northern part of its distribution, but is less prominent farther south, where it typically occurs in scrubby thickets and as a component of sparse vegetation. Shore pine is adapted to habitats that are relatively inhospitable to most other plants, giving it a competitive advantage.

Habitat

Variety *latifolia* occurs at altitudes from 490–3,660 m (1,600–12,000 feet). It is found on a wide variety of soils, including gravelly and stony ridges, and grows in an extensive range of moisture, including both dry areas and swamps. It is intolerant of saline soils, and grows best on well-drained loam soil.

Variety *contorta* occurs from sea level up to 610 m (2,000 feet) in altitude, on coastal sand dunes, seaside bluffs, dry foothills, exposed rocky ridges and highlands, serpentine soils, muskeg, and in maritime fog forests and peat bogs. It is most common in poorly drained areas. The prevailing coastal winds often result in the crown of the tree becoming deformed and asymmetrical, developing best in the direction away from the wind. In very exposed areas, the plants may be reduced to shrubs by wind shear and salt spray.

Fire in a lodgepole pine forest, courtesy of the USDA Forest Service, Rocky Mountain Region, J.J. Witcosky, and Bugwood.org.

ECOLOGY (CONT'D)

Inter-species Relationships

Lodgepole pine furnishes food for a range of wildlife. Mule deer, moose, and elk browse the young trees, although the plants are not a preferred food. Mammals including snowshoe hares, pocket gophers, voles, squirrels, porcupines, and black bears eat the inner bark. Grosbeaks, red crossbills, and nutcrackers extensively consume the seeds. Blue grouse and spruce grouse consume the seeds and also the needles. Lodgepole pine forests also provide shelter for many animals.

Serotiny (described in detail below) refers to the phenomenon of seed cones retaining their seeds for years. The pine or red squirrel (*Tamiasciurus hudsonicus*) is a major consumer of lodgepole pine seeds, and is particularly attracted to trees with serotinous cones, because they are where abundant seeds will be conveniently found. It has been discovered that in areas where the squirrel is absent, lodgepole pine cones are almost 100% serotinous, but in areas where the squirrel is present, the cones average less that 50% serotiny, indicating that the squirrels are causing local trees to produce cones that distribute their seeds quickly rather than retaining them. As noted below, serotiny is adaptive to regular occurrence of fire, but it appears that it is inadaptive to squirrel predation. (Reference: Benkman, C.W., and Siepielski, A.M. 2004. A keystone selective agent? Pine squirrels and the frequency of serotiny in lodgepole pine. Ecology 85: 2082–2087.)

Bark beetles of the genus *Dendroctonus* are serious pests of lodgepole pine, especially the mountain pine beetle (*D. ponderosae*) which is the most damaging agent of the tree. The beetles construct egg galleries in the phloem tissue, and the larvae girdle the trees. As a result of both girdling and fungi introduced by the beetles, the trees die. The larvae infesting the trees are an important food for woodpeckers. The beetles and the trees share an intimate, historical ecological cycle: by periodically infesting and killing off lodgepole pine forests, the beetles produce large amounts of fuel wood, that is eventually consumed by fire caused by lightning and people. This creates favourable conditions for regeneration of the pine, which otherwise would be eliminated by trees that are more competitive in shady conditions. Forest managers today have adopted burning of lodgepole stands as a deliberate means of controlling the mountain pine beetle and developing good stands. Mountain pine beetle is only one of many insects that feed on lodgepole pine. Others include several beetles which feed on leaves, roots, or branches, as well as scale insects and various moth larvae that feed on the needles.

Mountain pine beetle (*Dendroctonus ponderosae*). Photos by Klaus Bolte, Agriculture and Agri-Food Canada.

OH NO! —ANOTHER BEETLE!

Higher winter temperatures have allowed adult mountain pine beetles to survive over extensive areas where they could not previously. In many of these areas large amounts of mature woodland are available as a result of many years of fire control. The result is that the beetles have spread into higher elevation mature forests that were previously protected by cooler winters. Recently, huge areas of pine forests in south-central British Columbia and in the Rocky Mountains have been turning brown in what some refer to as "the largest known insect infestation in North American history". Is it really that serious? In fact major catastrophic events like fire, wind, floods, insect outbreaks and diseases are natural ecological processes that are a characteristic feature of many dynamic natural forests and contribute to the maintenance of high biodiversity. However, in a situation like this, where the insect may be invading new territory, the impact can be unusually severe, not unlike that of an invasive alien. In these circumstances ecologically sound management is required and both economic and environmental aspects have to be considered carefully. In Banff National Park, fire is being restored to the ecosystem. This will not only increase biodiversity—it will also reduce infestations of the beetle by thinning out mature trees. This in turn will reduce risk to commercial forestry operations outside the park. Parks Canada should be applauded for its management of this situation. See http://www.pc.gc.ca/canada/pn-tfn/itm2-/2005/2005-10-31_e.asp.

ECOLOGY (CONT'D)

Dwarf mistletoe (*Arceuthobium americanum*), a flowering plant parasite, is very common on lodgepole pine (a third of the trees of some populations may be infected), and can cause serious reduction in yield. At maturity, seeds of the mistletoe are forcibly ejected from the fruit for distances as great as 9 m (about 30 feet), the sticky seeds adhering to the foliage of the trees.

Pollination and Dispersal

Pines are wind-pollinated plants, pollen shedding occurring in early spring. The winged pollen accumulates at the base of a cone scale where it adheres to a sticky, secreted microdrop. It then floats upward or is carried by the evaporating drop into the ovule.

If pollen is taken into the ovule, fertilization can take place and no more drops are exuded; however, if no pollen is transported the drops continue to be exuded for up to several days until pollination is successful. In lodgepole pine, the seed cones tend to be found more often in the upper crown while the male cones are more frequently on the lower branches. Sometimes some trees bear mostly male cones and other trees mostly female cones. Both of the preceding phenomena serve to promote cross-fertilization and discourage self-pollination.

The seed cones of lodgepole pine are often serotinous—i.e., they are held closed by resin, which softens to release the seeds when exposed to the heat of a wildfire or from direct sunlight. Temperatures of 45–60 °C (113–140 °F) are required to melt the resin that binds the cone scales together; very severe fires may destroy most of the seed supply. Young trees tend to produce cones that open, releasing their seeds. Some trees produce non-serotinous cones for up to 60 years, and then transition to production of serotinous cones. On average, serotinous cones remain closed for 15 years (some do not open for 30 years), building up a large supply of seeds in an area. The seeds are long-lived, often viable for 80 years. Serotiny is an adaptation to areas in which fires often occur, and serves to repopulate a region in which the vegetation has been burned. The ash present as a result of fire is a natural fertilizer, encouraging rapid growth of seedlings. Individual trees in a population often differ with respect to serotiny, some with all or mostly serotinous cones, others with mostly cones that open at maturity. Most stands of var. *latifolia* are of fire origin, while var. *contorta* is less dependent on fire, and serotiny is much less evident, the cones more frequently releasing their seeds soon after maturing. Seed production may be as high as 2.43 million/ha (1 million/acre). The winged seeds are distributed mostly by wind, the majority falling within 60 m (200 feet) of the parental trees. Runoff from rain and small mammals also distribute some seeds. The seeds do not require stratification (i.e., a period of cold) in order to germinate, but do need light for optimum germination, and often germinate better in areas exposed to full sunlight.

Dwarf mistletoe (*Arceuthobium americanum*) on lodgepole pine. Courtesy of Brytten Steed, USDA Forest Service and Bugwood.org.

USES

The trunks of var. *latifolia* are extensively harvested for timber, employed as lumber in general construction and especially important for wood pulp. The trunks are also treated with preservatives (because they are especially susceptible to decay) and used for poles, railway ties, and mine timbers. The trunks are also used for fence posts and log houses. The young trunks are especially useful as corral rails, because of their small diameter and lack of taper. Lodgepole pine is the most widely distributed, harvested, and planted pine in British Columbia, and one of the most commercially valuable trees in Alberta and the northwestern U.S. It has been used to revegetate mine sites. The species is used in reforestation in Europe, especially in Norway and Sweden. As with other major forest trees, the value of lodgepole pine forests is immeasurable as protective cover for watersheds, as a natural element for the long-term maintenance of the local environment and ecosystem, and as sites for local recreation.

Indigenous people used flexible trunks 12–14 cm (4.7–5.5 inches) in diameter to construct tepees; explorers Lewis and Clark were among the first Europeans to have observed this, and have been credited with naming the tree "lodgepole" in recognition of the usage. Indians also used the poles to make horse-drawn travois (drag sleds). Great Plains Indians journeyed to the Rocky Mountains to obtain slender trunks. Resin from the trees was employed to waterproof canoes and baskets, and as chewing gum. Roots were braided to make ropes. The inner bark was sometimes boiled and eaten. The resin was extensively employed to treat a wide variety of illnesses; it was consumed to reduce tuberculosis, stomach pain, burns, and colds; and

applied externally for rheumatism, broken skin, heart problems, snow blindness, venereal diseases, muscle and joint aches, and facial blemishes. Boiled teas made with the bark or needles were used for these and other medical conditions.

Variety *contorta* is sometimes used locally as firewood, but because of its small size, limited trunk length, and relative infrequency, it is of negligible commercial value. The variety has been used to stabilize sand dunes. It is also considered to be useful for shelterbelts and for watershed stabilization (it grows well in moist soils).

TOXICITY

For most people, pines are not toxic. The pollen produced can contribute to hayfever. For some sensitive individuals, working with pine wood can cause dermatitis, allergic bronchial asthma, or rhinitis.

CULTIVATION

Lodgepole pine is a major North American forest tree, and there is a considerable literature on its commercial management. Several horticultural selections have been made, including 'Spaan's Dwarf' (a short-needled shrub), 'Taylor's Sunburst' (the young foliage is yellow, but matures to green), and 'Chief Joseph' (the young foliage is green but matures to a bright gold). Other ornamental cultivars include 'Asher', 'Frisian Gold', 'Pendula', 'Randolph', and 'Twister'.

CONSERVATION STATUS

Lodgepole pine is a common species, not in particular need of conservation measures over most of its range. The recent large-scale devastation of lodgepole pine forests by mountain pine beetles seems unlikely to threaten the species' existence; new young stands will develop following fires which burn the dead trees. Several plant associations in which lodgepole pine occurs as a dominant species have been described as vulnerable, imperiled, or critically imperiled. In New Zealand, where the species has been called "contorta pine", it has become a seriously invasive alien.

A trail going through an extremely dense lodgepole pine stand in southeast Washington. Source: U.S. Forest Service Historical Photo (date unknown).

MYTHS, LEGENDS, TALES, FOLKLORE AND INTERESTING FACTS

❋ In classical Greek mythology, Pitys was a beautiful nymph who was loved by Boreas (the north wind) and Pan (god of the forest, half goat half man, a fertility god believed to make goats pregnant; too ugly to make any of the nymphs fall in love with him, he contributed to elements of the Devil of Christianity). When she chose Pan, Boreas blew her over a cliff. Gaea (goddess of the Earth) took pity on her and turned her into a pine tree. It is said that when the north wind blows through the tree you can hear her weep. The resin of the pine was equated with the tears of Pitys. In another version of the story, Pan chased her and in order to get away from him Pitys turned herself into a pine tree. The tree then became holy to Pan, who made a wreath of pine branches to wear.

❋ Sinis was a mythological Greek robber and personification of the North Wind, who was also known as Pitokampes—"the pine-bender". This charming figure executed his opponents by tying their legs to two pine trees that he had forced down to the ground, and letting the trees fly apart, with the result that his victims would be torn to pieces. In a contest, the hero Theseus inflicted the same form of death on Sinis, and proceeded to marry his daughter. This mythological story reflects the early perception of the importance of pines in contests. The wreaths of victory in the earliest athletic competitions in Greece were in fact made out of pine branches.

❋ Druids (ancient Celtic priests of Wales and Ireland) used to light large bonfires of Scots pine at the winter solstice to celebrate the passing of the seasons and to draw back the sun, a practice that eventually gave rise to the Yule log. The trees were also decorated with candles and shiny objects, foreshadowing latter day Christmas tree customs.

❋ The New Jersey Pine Barrens or Pinelands is a unique natural area covering over 400,000 ha (over 1 million acres) of the Outer Coastal Plain in southern and central New Jersey. Fires were prevalent and the dominant tree is the fire-adapted pitch pine (*P. rigida*). Rich in diversity and having species found nowhere else, the global significance of the Pinelands is illustrated by the fact that it was selected as a United Nations International Biosphere Reserve in 1973. The legend of The Jersey Devil (no relation to the New Jersey Devils of the National Hockey League) began in the Pine Barrens. According to a popular version of the story, in 1735 mother Leeds already has 12 children, is expecting, and is fed up with motherhood. The thirteenth, a beautiful healthy baby boy appears one stormy night, and she exclaims "the Devil with you!" The baby turns into a hideous animal with wings, hooves, and a tail, and flies out the chimney. Ever since there have been sightings of the Jersey Devil, and numerous reports of grisly killings of sheep, chickens, and dogs. Strange hoofprints have been found on rooftops, and some have even observed the demon prancing on roofs. Dogs couldn't be used to pursue the creature because they refuse to follow his tracks. There are many strange encounters, and a police officer spotted him drinking from a horse's trough. Sightings sometimes created panic, especially in 1909, when terrified people refused to leave their homes, and factories and schools remained closed. During one week there were over 1,000 calls for help to the police. Numerous citizens have shot at the Devil, but so far he has magically escaped being wounded (not surprising since one early account told how he survived a direct hit from a cannonball without any damage). Keeping up with modern technology, the Devil appeared on television's popular X-files. Experts believe the beast resides in the huge preserved forest of the Pine Barrens.

❋ "Story sticks" were prepared from lodgepole pine by Blackfoot Indian elders. These were given to children in return for favours. The children were entitled to receive stories from the elders, who added a notch to the stick each time they told a story. Story sticks were sometimes employed to hang tepee doors.

❋ Petrified wood, common in gravel pits throughout Alberta, was adopted as the official stone of the province in 1977, due to the efforts of the Alberta Federation of Rock Clubs. Petrified wood was formed by the deposit of microcrystalline quartz in the pores and cells of fallen trees of the Cretaceous and Paleocene periods, 60 to 90 million years ago. Petrified wood has also been declared to be the official stone or fossil of six states: Alabama, Louisiana, Mississippi, North Dakota, Texas, and Washington.

Petrified wood. Courtesy of L. Hachey, Government of Alberta.

A BIODIVERSITY TREASURE

SOURCES OF ADDITIONAL INFORMATION

Baumgartner, D.M., Krebill, R.G., Arnott, J.T., and Weetman, G.F. (Editors). 1985. Lodgepole pine: the species and its management. Symposium proceedings. Cooperative Extension, Washington State University, Pullman WA. 381 pp.

Christensen, K.I. 2005. A morphometric study of the geographic variation in *Pinus contorta* (Pinaceae). Nordic J. Bot. 23: 563–575.

Fazekas, A.J., and Yeh, F.C. 2006. Postglacial colonization and population genetic relationships in the *Pinus contorta* complex. Can. J. Bot. 84: 223–234.

Horton, J.W. 1956. The ecology of lodgepole pine in Alberta and its role in forest succession. Tech. Note No. 45. Forest Res. Div., Forestry Branch, Dept. Northern Affairs and Nat. Resources, Ottawa, ON. 29 pp.

Koch, P. 1996. Lodgepole pine in North America. Forest Products Society, Madison, WI. 3 vols.

Kral, R. 1993. *Pinus. In* Flora of North America North of Mexico. *Edited by* Flora of North America Editorial Committee. Oxford University press, Oxford, U.K. Vol. 2. pp. 373–398

Lotan, J.E., and Critchfield, W.B. 1990. *Pinus contorta* Dougl. ex Loud. lodgepole pine. *In* Silvics of North America. Vol. 1. Conifers. *Edited by* R.M. Burns and B.H. Honkala. USDA Forest Service, Washington, D.C. pp. 302–315.

Lotan, J.E., and Perry, D.A. 1983. Ecology and regeneration of lodgepole pine. USDA Forest Service Ag. Handbook No. 606. Washington D.C. 51 pp.

Moss, E.H. 1949. Natural pine hybrids in Alberta. Can. J. Res. C, 27: 218–229.

Muir, P.S., and Lotan, J.E. 1985. Serotiny and life history of *Pinus contorta* var. *latifolia*. Can. J. Bot. 63: 938–945.

Owens, J.N. 2006. The reproductive biology of lodgepole pine. Forest Genetics Council of British Columbia Extension Note 07. 62 pp.

Rehfeldt, G.E., Wykoff, W.R., and Ying, C.C. 2001. Physiologic plasticity, evolution, and impacts of a changing climate on *Pinus contorta*. Climatic Change 50: 355–376.

Rweyongeza, D.M., Dhir, N.K., Barnhardt, L.K., Hansen, C., and Yang, R.-C. 2007. Population differentiation of the lodgepole pine (*Pinus contorta*) and jack pine (*Pinus banksiana*) complex in Alberta: growth, survival, and response to climate. Can. J. Bot. 86: 545–556.

Tackle, D. 1961. Silvics of lodgepole pine. Misc. Publ. 19. USDA Forest Service, Intermountain Forest and Range Expt. Station, Ogden, UT. 24 pp.

Wheeler, N.C. and Guries, R.P. 1982. Population structure, genic diversity, and morphological variation in *Pinus contorta* Dougl. Can. J. Forest Res. 12: 595–606.

Wheeler, N.C. and Guries, R.P. 1982. Biogeography of lodgepole pine. Can. J. Bot. 60: 1805–1814.

PINE POETRY

The elm lets fall its leaves before the frost,
The very oak grows shivering and sere,
The trees are barren when the summer's lost:
But one tree keeps its goodness all the year.
Green pine, unchanging as the days go by,
Thou art thyself beneath whatever sky:
My shelter from all winds, my own strong pine,
'Tis spring, 'tis summer, still, while thou art mine.
—*Augusta Davies Webster (1837–1894, English poet, novelist, and playwright)*

Is it the lumberman, then, who is the friend and lover of the pine, stands nearest to it, and understands its nature best? Is it the tanner who has barked it, or he who has boxed it for turpentine, whom posterity will fable to have been changed into a pine at last? No! no! it is the poet . . . . All the pines shudder and heave a sigh when that man steps on the forest floor.
—*Henry David Thoreau (1817–1862, American philosopher, author, and naturalist)*

Who leaves the pine-tree, leaves his friend,
Unnerves his strength, invites his end.
—*Ralph Waldo Emerson (1803–1882, American essayist, poet, and philosopher)*

"My apple trees will never get across
And eat the cones under his pines", I tell him.
He only says, "Good fences make good neighbors."
—*Robert Frost (1874–1963, American poet)*

GRASS: ROUGH FESCUE

Rough fescue grassland dominated by *Festuca campestris,* in Nose Hill Park, a protected native prairie overlooking Calgary. Photo by Joseph Leung, reproduced by permission. (Nose Hill Park in northwestern Calgary is one of the largest municipal parks in North America. This natural environment preserve is said to have been named for the shape of the nose of a local Indian chief.)

SYMBOLISM

In addition to the economic and ecological importance of rough fescue grasses mentioned below, others have cited their hardiness (capable of surviving extremely cold winters as well as drought), persistence (capable of living for decades), resiliency, beauty, diversity, and adaptiveness as desirable qualities symbolic of Albertans and their province.

COMMENTS DURING THE LEGISLATIVE DEBATE TO ADOPT ROUGH FESCUE AS THE ALBERTA PROVINCIAL EMBLEM

"The gold heads of the rough fescue, standing tall, waving in the wind with roots that are deep, tenacious, and adapted to our prairie climates, reflect the heart and grit, the strength of the province and our people."—*R. Danyluk*

"Ecologically, it would be hard to argue for a better grass than rough fescue to represent the province of Alberta. Fescue grasslands are symbolic of natural and human-based systems and host a rich range of contrasting elements that do indeed reflect the diversity of the province."—*D. Coutts*

"You may ask, 'Why a provincial grass?' to which I would respond: rough fescue is a very worthy symbol of our prairie heritage of rich grasslands and fertile soil, soil that was the gift of the grasslands to the first homesteaders and remains a gift to our farmers and our ranchers today. The prairie and foothills grasslands sustained the buffalo and Plains Indians for thousands of years before the ranchers and homesteader arrived . . . . These grasslands were the builders of the soil which sustains Alberta agriculture to this day. I believe that it is fitting to recognize a suitable grass species such as rough fescue to help Albertans understand the importance of native grassland as an ecological unit, unique its own right, and a grassland which is of major cultural and economic value to our province . . . . No other state or province in North America has designated rough fescue as its official grass, and Alberta today has the largest remaining rough fescue grassland, which, while not endangered, is at risk. Making rough rescue our provincial grass emblem, would, I believe, be an appropriate step to help Albertans recognize the importance of native grassland that is worthy of our respect and to preserve it for future generations." — *D. Tannas*

All three individuals are or were MLA's in the Legislative Assembly of Alberta; comments were recorded in Alberta Hansard, February 24, 2003.

NAMES

Latin Names
Festuca altaica Trin. (*Altaica* in the scientific name is a Latin word referring to the Altai region of Russia, where plants were found that were used to first recognize and describe the species.)

F. campestris Rydb. (*Campestris* in the scientific name is based on the Latin *campus,* field, used to indicate that the species occurs on plains.)

F. hallii (Vasey) Piper (*Hallii* in the scientific name commemorates the California botanist Harvey Monroe Hall, 1874–1932.)

(The name *F. scabrella* Torr. ex Hook. has been widely misapplied to the above three North American fescue grasses. The name *F. altaica* has also been used in some older literature to include all three species.)

The genus name *Festuca* is based on the Latin *festuca,* meaning stalk, stem, or straw, a name used by the classical Roman botanist Pliny for some plant.

English Names
Rough fescue: a name applied collectively to the following three species. The leaf blades, rachis (central axis of the inflorescence) and lemma (explained below) of the species are scabrous (rough to the touch), hence the "rough" in the common name. The name "fescue" traces to the Latin *Festuca,* explained above.

F. altaica: northern rough fescue. Also: Altai fescue.

F. campestris: mountain rough fescue. Also: foothills rough fescue.

F. hallii: plains rough fescue. Also: Hall's fescue.

NAMES (CONT'D)

French Names

F. altaica: fétuque de l'Altaï.

F. campestris: fétuque des prés (a name also used for other species of *Festuca*).

F. hallii: fétuque de Hall.

(The name fétuque scabre has been used for *Festuca scabrella,* a name that has been misapplied to the above three fescue grasses. In some publications the name is used for one or more of the three fescue species. "Rough fescue" is translated as fétuque rude, a name applicable to the three species.)

View of the skyline of downtown Calgary, Alberta, from Nose Hill Park, showing fescue grassland dominated by *Festuca campestris.* Photo taken in 2001. Source: Wikimedia.

Rough fescue (*Festuca campestris*) in Alberta, courtesy of A. Bicknell.

A BIODIVERSITY TREASURE

HISTORY

Canada

In the late 1980s, a wide variety of educational, industrial, scientific, and conservation groups came together as the Prairie Conservation Forum of Alberta to promote sustainable use of grasslands. In 2001, this organization sent ballots to interested Albertans asking them to vote on which of five common native grasses should be chosen as the provincial grass emblem. A committee had chosen the five species (blue grama, green needlegrass, June grass, rough fescue, and western wheatgrass) from the more than 135 grass species of the province on the criteria that they should be widespread in Alberta; ecologically significant; culturally, socially, and economically important; attractive; easily recognized; and have socially acceptable common names. Over 2,000 Albertans voted, the largest number (36%) for rough fescue.

"Rough fescue" became the official grass emblem of Alberta in 2003: "the grass known botanically as *Festuca scabrella* and popularly known as 'rough fescue' is hereby adopted as the grass emblem of Alberta" (Emblems of Alberta Act, RSA 1980 cE-8 s4). As pointed out above, the name *Festuca scabrella* has been misapplied in North America to three different species, *F. altaica, F. campestris,* and *F. hallii.* The legislation recognizing the grass emblem of Alberta was proposed by Don Tannas, MLA for Highwood. In his proposal (recorded in Legislative Assembly of Alberta, Alberta Hansard, Feb. 24, 2003), Tannas stated the following:

"I'm honoured to move second reading of Bill 201, Emblems of Alberta (Grass Emblem) Amendment Act, 2003.

"Last February the Prairie Conservation Forum approached me to sponsor a private member's public bill to amend the Emblems of Alberta Act to have rough fescue designated as Alberta's provincial grass. I was asked in part because Highwood contains a considerable portion of the remaining rough fescue grassland, which includes both the plains rough fescue and foothills rough fescue. Today I'm asking all hon. members of this Assembly to support the Prairie Conservation forum and myself in amending the Emblems of Alberta Act to designate rough fescue, Latin name Festuca scabrella, as Alberta's provincial grass.

"This rough fescue complex may also be recognized as three varieties or, as some taxonomists would prefer, three separate species, known as plains rough fescue, which is Latin Festuca hallii; foothills rough fescue, which is Festuca campestris; or the third one, northern rough fescue, Festuca altaica. Alberta is the only area that is home to all three members of the rough fescue complex."

The above parliamentary and legislative information, as well as comments of others (recorded in Hansard, cited above) make it clear that in spite of the use of the misapplied and ambiguous scientific name *"Festuca scabrella"*, and in spite of the natural assumption of most people that a plant with a common name ("rough fescue" in this case) chosen as an emblem would be just one species, the "Grass Emblem of Alberta" is a complex of three species of *Festuca,* one of which (*F. altaica*) is barely present in Alberta, a second (*F. campestris*) which has relatively limited presence, and a third (*F. hallii*) which is common in the province. If it were considered desirable to recognize a single species as an emblem of Alberta, *F. hallii* would best meet the criteria listed above.

Foreign

Needle-and-thread grass (*Hesperostipa comata*) was chosen as the official grass of Saskatchewan in 2001 (see the chapter on Saskatchwan emblems). Seventeen U.S. states have official grasses (http://en.wikipedia.org/wiki/List_of_U.S._state_grasses).

Cattle grazing in British Columbia. Such western Canadian rangelands are of immense value to Canadian agriculture. Source: Thinkstock.

APPEARANCE

The rough fescues are "bunchgrasses", forming clumps with thick mats 13–50 cm (5–30 inches) in diameter, made up of persistent sheath and stem bases. Flowering stems are 30–140 cm (12–55 inches) high. The root systems are fibrous, sometimes reaching deeper than 120 cm (4 feet). The plants spread vegetatively by tillers (shoots that spring from the base of grasses) and sometimes by rhizomes (which are usually produced in *F. hallii,* short and inconspicuous in *F. altaica,* and rarely produced in *F. campestris*).

Pavlick and Looman (1984) provided the following information about the rough fescues: "Plants of *F. campestris* are relatively tall and form large clumps, 25–30 cm in diameter with as many as 25 culms [stems] that typically slant at an angle of 45–50° from horizontal; their leaf blades are grey green and often more or less explanate [spread out flat] for the lower one-third to one-half portion with the upper part loosely to tightly folded; their panicles are usually erect (sometime nodding) with more or less rigid, ascending lower branches; and their flowers are dull green to moderately anthocyanic [purplish or reddish]. Plants of *F. hallii* are relatively short (as compared with *F. campestris*) and grow in clumps 7–10 cm in diameter, with often 3–5 and rarely as many as 10 culms that typically are erect or slant at an angle of 70–80° from horizontal; their leaf blades are also grey green but narrower than those of *F. campestris* and are always tightly folded; their panicles are always erect, although shorter and narrower than those of *F. campestris,* and always with lower branches more or less stiffly ascending; their floret color is similar to that of *F. campestris.* Plants of *F. altaica* range in height from as short as *F. hallii* to about as tall as *F. campestris,* with about 5–10 culms; their leaf blades are yellow green and often explanate or loosely folded in their upper parts; their panicles are usually nodding, often secund [florets all on one side], with weak, often recurved branches, and their florets are usually lustrous and intensely anthocyanic."

The rough fescues can be confused with other tussock-forming species, and are best identified when inflorescences are developed.

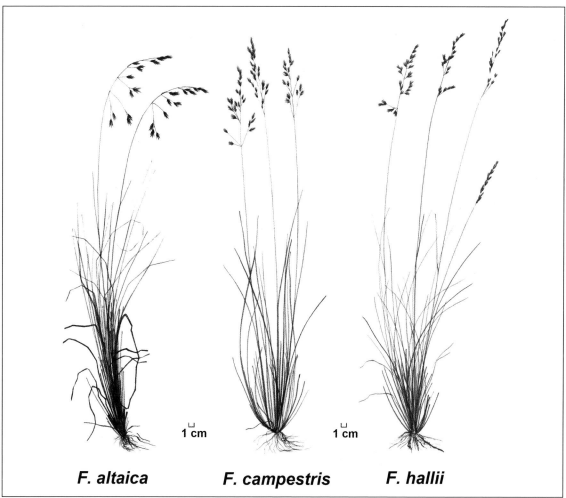

Rough fescue species. Source: Aiken and Darbyshire 1990.

F. altaica   F. campestris   F. hallii

1 cm   1 cm

APPEARANCE (CONT'D)

Key to the Species of Rough Fescue

(from Aiken and Darbyshire 1990)

1. Foliage yellow green to dark green; leaf blades in cross section with schlerenchyma only opposite veins. Panicle drooping (when mature), with branches flexuous and lax. Upper glume distinctly shorter than adjacent lemma. Lemmas laterally folded basally, usually red or purple with anthocyanin; lateral nerves more or les prominent. Plant of boreal and alpine grassland . . . . *F. altaica*

1. Foliage light green to gray green; leaf blades in cross section with sclerenchyma extending along abaxial side between veins. Panicle not drooping, with branches stiff, erect, or slightly spreading. Upper glume somewhat shorter than, to as long as, adjacent lemma. Lemmas dorsally rounded basally, usually green or stramineous; lateral nerves obscure. Plants of plains and montane grasslands 2

2. Plants strongly caespitose; shoots intravaginal. Culms (30-)40-90(-140) cm high. Spikelets with (3-)4-5(-7) florets, distinctly longer than glumes. Upper glume somewhat shorter than adjacent lemma. Lemmas (6-)7-8.5(-10) mm long. Plant of foothills and montane grasslands in western Alberta and British Columbia. . . . . . . *F. campestris*

2. Plants caespitose; shoots intravaginal and extra-vaginal forming creeping rhizomes. Culms (18-)20-65(-85) cm high. Spikelets with 2-3(-4) florets (3rd and 4th) usually sterile), scarcely if at all longer than glumes. Upper glume about equal to adjacent lemma. Lemmas 5.5-7(-9) mm long. Plants of western plains and parklands from western Ontario to Alberta . . . . *F. hallii*

Vocabulary for the above identification key

Abaxial: pertaining to position of a leaf, the "lower" side, i.e., pointing towards the base.

Caespitose: growing in dense clumps or tufts.

Extravaginal: branching in which the young shoot breaks through the base of the leaf sheath.

Glume: one of a pair of empty scales at the base of a grass spikelet.

Intravaginal: branching in which the young shoot grows up inside the leaf sheath, emerging at the shoot mouth.

Lemma: the lower of the two bracts enclosing the grass flower and together with the palea comprising a floret.

Panicle: in grasses, an inflorescence in which the primary axis bears branched axes with pedicillate spikelets.

Sclerenchyma: tissue with cells with thickened, rigid, secondary walls hardened with lignin, providing structural support.

Spikelet: the basic unit of a grass inflorescence; usually composed of two glumes and one or more florets on a rachilla (the central axis of the spikelet bearing the florets).

Sterile: lacking seeds.

Stramineous: straw-coloured.

CLASSIFICATION

Family: Poaceae (Gramineae; grass family).

Festuca is a genus of more than 500 species, which occur in alpine, temperate, and polar regions of all continents except Antarctica. Thirty-seven species are native to North America north of Mexico, eighteen of these native to Canada. The three rough fescue species discussed here have been placed in *Festuca* section *Breviaristatae*.

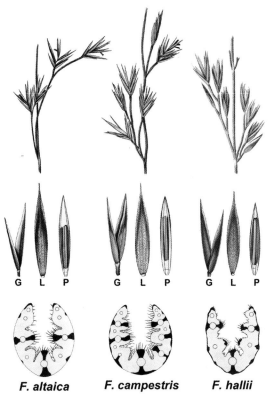

Key features of rough fescue species. Top row: inflorescences. Middle row: G = glume, L = lemma, P = palea. Bottom row: leaf cross sections; darkened areas are schlerenchyma (defined at left). Source: Aiken and Darbyshire 1990.

GEOGRAPHY

Festuca altaica is common in Alaska, Yukon, Northwest Territories, and northern British Columbia. The species occurs as localized populations in Quebec, western Labrador, Newfoundland, and Michigan. In the Old World it extends from the Bering Sea to the Altai region of central Asia.

Festuca campestris is found in southern Alberta, southern British Columbia, southwestern Saskatchewan, Washington, Oregon, Idaho, and Montana. *Festuca hallii* occurs mostly in the southern half of British Columbia and the southern half of Alberta. The species is rare in Ontario. In the U.S. it is found from Montana to North Dakota, south to Colorado. The distribution of *F. altaica* overlaps that of *F. hallii* in a limited region at about 51° N near the Alberta-British Columbia border, and likely elsewhere.

"Fescue prairie is the most typically Canadian of all the grassland associations, with only limited distribution in the United States" (Redmann, cited below). Today, rough fescue grasslands are merely remnants of pre-settlement distribution. Alberta has the largest area of rough fescue grassland in the world.

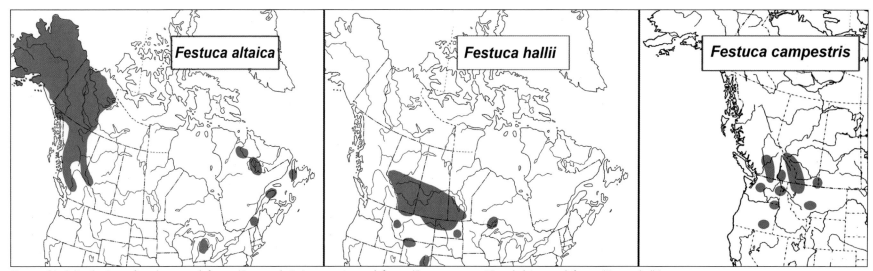

Geographical distributions of northern rough fescue (*Festuca altaica*), mountain rough fescue (*Festuca campestris*), and plains rough fescue (*Festuca hallii*).

ECOLOGY

Grasslands accumulate a layer of dead and decaying plant material called "litter". Litter is useful to the plants in serving as a kind of mulch, reducing moisture loss and the ability of competing plants to establish seedlings. When too much litter accumulates, growth of the grasses can be reduced and some low-growing species can be shaded out. Moreover, in the dry climate of grasslands, litter constitutes fuel for fires. In the early twentieth century, land managers were unaware of the beneficial effects of fire on grasslands, and often implemented fire suppression policies. By the late twentieth century, it was understood that periodic fires resulting from lightning strikes were a natural process that maintained many grasslands. (Aboriginal Peoples set prairie fires to improve grassland for forage and to drive game.) Fire retards the spread of alien plant species, reduces litter accumulation, and reduces competition, and the resulting ash acts as a fertilizer. Plants that are natural components of grasslands are adapted to these circumstances. The dense, tufted shape of the rough fescues assists them in resisting fire (as well as grazing). It has been estimated that in pre-settlement times, some areas of North American fescue grasslands burned as often as annually or as infrequently as once in 60 years (it has been suggested that rough fescues are naturally adapted to fire frequencies in the range of 5 to 10 years). Today, some areas have not been burned for more than 70 years because of fire suppression. Controlled burning is now considered to be an important management technique that promotes and maintains healthy prairie ecosystems. However, burning has to be done in a particular way, mimicking natural fires so as not to harm prairie fauna.

North American fescue grasslands were periodically grazed by herds of bison, elk, and other animals, many of which migrated seasonally. Dung from these animals fertilized the soil, and in some cases the animals distributed the seeds. The nomadic movements meant that heavy grazing tended to occur in different regions at different times. Prairie grasses in general and the grassland rough fescues in particular are adapted to withstanding such periodic grazing, but have suffered from overgrazing by cattle, which was once encouraged as a way to remove litter, leaving little to burn, and so reducing fires. Since the nineteenth century, European settlers have used North American grasslands as grazing pastures for cattle, and continuous, intensive grazing has degraded most of the grasslands. Moreover, many areas of grasslands with rich soil have been converted for the cultivation of crops.

Habitat

Early French explorers used the word "prairie" (for meadow) for the grasslands of North America. Today, many people use the word prairie as a synonym of grassland. By definition, grasslands are communities dominated by grasses, species of the Poaceae, of which there are about 10,000 in the world. Conditions that favour the development of grasslands include sandy soil, low moisture, fire, and wind. In relatively moist areas scattered trees may occur, but generally grasslands occur in climates too dry for tree growth.

The rough fescues are plants of open forests, montane and subalpine grass balds, and arctic and alpine tundra, but they are most significant as components of grasslands. Rough fescue grasslands in North America may contain over 150 species of plants. "Forbs" (perennial non-graminoid herbs) are often an important component, but shrubs typically occupy less than 10% of grasslands.

Festuca altaica has been recorded on sand plains in north-central Quebec and Michigan; gravel outwashes in western Newfoundland and Gaspé; serpentine barrens in western Newfoundland, Gaspé, and southern Quebec); limestone plains in Ungava; basaltic slopes in western in western Newfoundland; and alpine and subalpine areas, open forests, tree-less areas, rocky slopes, plateaus, meadows, and grasslands in Alaska, British Columbia, Yukon, and Northwest Territories.

Festuca campestris is a dominant species of several grassland associations in southern Alberta and British Columbia. It is common in foothills and in montane and subalpine grasslands at elevations up to 2,000 m (6,500 feet).

Festuca hallii is a major component of grasslands from the northern Great Plains to the boreal forest. In its southernmost range in Colorado it occurs in alpine meadows.

Inter-species Relationships

Bison and elk were major natural grazers of the Fescue Prairie in pre-settlement times. Thirty to sixty million North American bison once roamed the Great Plains. Other grazers include pronghorn antelope, mule deer, and bighorn sheep. In addition to the above-ground grazing by these ungulates, below-ground grazing is carried out by pocket gophers and prairie dogs.

Pollination and Dispersal

In western Canada, flowering of the three rough fescue species occurs during the times of maximum precipitation. *Festuca campestris* flowers in late May

ECOLOGY (CONT'D)

while *F. altaica* and *F. hallii* flower several weeks later. Like most grasses, the species are wind-pollinated.

There is little information on the agents of natural seed distribution of rough fescues. Gravity is an obvious factor, the seeds simply falling away from the maternal plants. Animals are perhaps the major means of distribution. The "seeds" (i.e., caryopses or grass fruits, including attached bracts) are rough, and so would tend to attach to fur and feathers (simple adhesion may also result from wetting). Possibly some seeds consumed by larger animals like bison might survive passage through the alimentary tract (such has not been demonstrated), but smaller animals would likely masticate the seeds, killing the embryos. Where seeds have been cached by animals, some often survive, and this may be true for the rough fescues.

ESSAYS ON ECOLOGY
"Sometime soon we will recognize the difference between going to a native grassland to sit and listen and learn from a microcosm of the World, to open ourselves to it for inspiration as to how best to live with it and minister to it, and going there with the intention of turning it into a source of recreation, into a show place for wild animals, into a landscape painting, into a pasture for cattle or—most terrible thought—into just another wheat field."
—*Stan Rowe (1918–2004, Canadian forester and eco-philosopher, in Home Place: Essays on Ecology, 1990; rev. ed. 2002)*

USES

The three rough fescue species are important native wild forage grasses. *Festuca campestris* and *F. hallii* are dominant species of grassland associations of central and southern Alberta, and accordingly are an important source of nutrition for native ungulates, as well as introduced horses and the large cattle herds of western Canada. The two species have high production potential and good forage quality after senescence; they cure on the stem, and as they remain more or less upright they are easily located by animals for winter grazing even when partly covered by snow. Snow becomes trapped in the clumps, moistening the dried-out plants, making them quite attractive to the animals.

Rough fescues are useful in landscape stabilization and roadside plantings because of their ability to form extensive fibrous root systems. Some ecologists have noted that the deep roots often developed by rough fescues (sometimes growing 3 m or 10 feet deep) decay slowly and represent considerable sequestering (storage) of carbon, thereby reducing carbon dioxide accumulation in the atmosphere and consequent warming of the planet. There have been recent attempts, sponsored by the oil and gas industries, to grow rough fescue specifically for the purpose of compensating for CO_2 emissions.

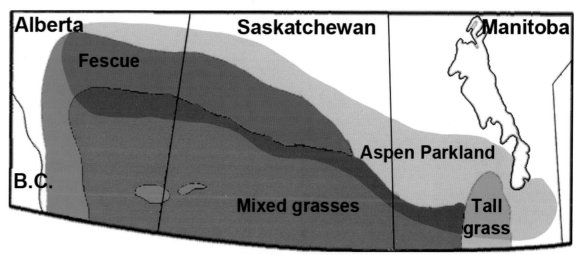

Distribution of major vegetation zones of the southern Prairie Provinces. Source: modified from Parks Canada/Exploring a grassland: http://www.pc.gc.ca/apprendre-learn/prof/sub/edukit/grassland/index_2_e.asp.

TOXICITY

No information about toxicity of rough fescues was found. However, tall fescue (*F. arundinacea*), an introduced European cool-season grass widely grown as turf and forage in North America, and established in southern Canada, is known to be susceptible to infection by the fungal endophyte, *Neotyphodium coenophialum* (formerly called *Acremonium coenophialum*) that is quite toxic to animals, and "fescue toxicosis" is a widespread concern for livestock operations. (For a review, see http://wiki.bugwood.org/Festuca_arundinacea.)

CULTIVATION

The rough fescues are not grown as crops, in pastures, or as ornamentals. They have been grown for seeds used to improve or rehabilitate wildlands, but most seed for these purposes is harvested from wild plants.

Buffalo (American bison) bulls quarreling over a patch of Alberta grassland. Source: Thinkstock.

CONSERVATION STATUS

Because of their importance for furnishing food, the prairies of North America have been called "the bread basket of the world". Unfortunately, they are among the most extensively exploited and altered landscapes. North American grasslands have suffered from several developments: fire control, domesticated animal overgrazing, land conversion for crops and urban development, drainage, extraction of water, oil, gas, and gravel, the introduction of invasive, non-native species, climate change, and poor management.

One-third of Canada's endangered species are found in the grasslands. In Alberta, 70% of all species at risk are in the grasslands, which cover only 14.5% (96,000 square km or 24 million acres) of the province.

Several invasive alien weeds, such as leafy spurge (*Euphorbia esula*), have invaded North American grasslands, displacing native species. Some of the aliens are Eurasian species deliberately introduced to increase grassland productivity and improve forage quality. Examples include smooth brome (*Bromus inermis*), crested wheat grass (*Agropyron cristatum, A. desertorum*) and timothy (*Phleum pratense*). All of these species have a deleterious effect on fescue grassland.

Fescue Prairie is one of several major grassland association of North America. It once formed an arc stretching from central Saskatchewan west to the foothills of the Rocky Mountains and south into Montana, Washington, and North Dakota. Elevation ranges from 500 m (1,640 feet) in central Saskatchewan to 1,400 m (4,600 feet) in the Cypress Hills of Saskatchewan. Temperatures can reach 40 °C (104 °F) in the summer and -40 °C (-40 ° F) in the winter, and mean annual precipitation ranges from 350 to 600 mm (14–24 inches), of which 50–60% occurs between May and August. *Festuca campestris* dominates in the Rocky Mountain foothills and Cypress Hills, and *F. hallii* dominates much of the remainder. Most of the fescue grasslands of Alberta and Saskatchewan are now used to produce cereals. Fescue grasslands have been described as endangered by Environment Canada, with only about 5% remaining in pre-settlement condition. There have been several studies of methods to restore fescue grasslands, with very limited success to date.

Due to global warming, a 3 °C (5.4 °F) increase in temperature has been predicted for the prairie region of western Canada. As the climate changes, migration and alteration of species ranges are likely, and the vegetation will tend to change somewhat to species that are more resistant of drought and higher temperatures. Pastures and rangelands are thought to be very sensitive to climate change, and so the fescue grasslands may be particularly threatened.

MYTHS, LEGENDS, TALES, FOLKLORE AND INTERESTING FACTS

❀ The grass family, Poaceae, with about 10,000 species, is the fourth largest family of flowering plants, exceeded only by the pea family (Fabaceae, with about 18,000 species), sunflower family (Asteraceae, with about 24,000 species) and orchid family (Orchidaceae, variously estimated to have 22,000–35,000 species).

❀ There are two widespread physiological classes of grasses that differ in the way they carry out photosynthesis (a third photosynthetic class, crassulacean acid metabolism, is present in many succulent plants of desert and semi-arid ecosystems, but not in grasses). About 60% of grass species are called C3 (Calvin cycle) plants because the first stable compound formed when carbon dioxide is processed is a three carbon compound, i.e., C3. Such plants typically grow best between 15–25 °C (59–77 °F) and produce maximum photosynthesis with only 20% of maximum sunlight. By contrast, about 40% of grass species are called C4 (dicarboxylic acid pathway) plants because the first organic compound incorporating CO_2 is a four carbon compound. C4 plants typically grow best between 30–40 °C (86–104 °F) and produce maximum photosynthesis only when light intensity reaches 100% of full sunlight. C4 plants also use water and nutrients more efficiently than C3 plants. Rough fescues are "cool-season grasses" that belong to the C3 class; indeed, most plant species of the northern prairies are dominated by C3 plants. By contrast, many tropical plants have the C4 type of photosynthesis, which allows for increased growth if temperature and light intensity are sufficiently high. Many tropical grass species are of the C4 type, accounting for the very high productivity of tropical and subtropical grasslands and savanna ecosystems. Many plant physiologists have concluded that C3 plants gain a competitive advantage at higher CO_2 levels, and predict that as climate change continues to increase CO_2 in the atmosphere, C3 plants will become more dominant.

❀ Samples of some fescue species growing almost 200 m (ca. 200 yards) apart in some pastures have proven to have identical genetic fingerprints, indicating that they can spread great distances by vegetative reproduction (reference: page 13 in Attenborough, D. 1995. the private life of plants. Princeton University Press, Princeton, NJ.). The resulting immense clones may be centuries old. When such clones are interpreted as "individuals", they are among the largest organisms in the world.

Rough fescue (*Festuca altaica*) in the Cariboo District of British Columbia. Courtesy of S. Darbyshire.

A BIODIVERSITY TREASURE

SOURCES OF ADDITIONAL INFORMATION

Aiken, S.G., and Darbyshire, S.J. 1990. Fescue grasses of Canada. Agriculture Canada Publ. 1844/E. Canadian Government Publishing Centre, Ottawa, ON. 113 pp.

Aiken, S.G., Dallwitz, M.J., McJannet, C.L., and Consaul, L.L. 1997. Fescue grasses of North America. Canadian Museum of Nature, Ottawa. (CD-ROM)

Darbyshire, S.J., and Pavlick, L.E. 2007. *Festuca. In* Flora of North America north of Mexico, vol. 24. *Edited by* M.E. Barkworth, K.M. Capels, S. Long, L.K. Anderton, and M.B. Piep. Oxford University Press, New York, NY. pp. 389–443.

Darbyshire, S.J., and Pavlick, L.E. 2007. *Festuca. In* Manual of grasses for North America. *Edited by* M.E. Barkworth, L.K. Anderton, K.M. Capels, S. Long, and M.B. Piep. Intermountain Herbarium and Utah State University Press, Utah State University, Logan. pp. 90–103.

Harms, V.L. 1985. A reconsideration of the nomenclature and taxonomy of the *Festuca altaica* complex (Poaceae) in North America. Madroño 32: 1–10.

Hill, M.J., Aspinall, R.J., and Willms, W.D. 1997. Knowledge-based and inductive modelling of rough fescue (*Festuca altaica, F. campestris* and *F. hallii*) distribution in Alberta, Canada. Ecological Modelling 103: 135–150.

King, J.R., Hill, M.J., and Willms, W.D. 1995. Growth response of *Festuca altaica, Festuca hallii,* and *Festuca campestris* to temperature. Can. J. Bot. 73: 1074–1080.

Pavlick, L.E., and Looman, J. 1984. Taxonomy and nomenclature of rough fescues, *Festuca altaica, F. campestris* (*F. scabrella* var. *major*) and *F. hallii,* in Canada and the adjacent United States. Can. J. Bot. 62: 1739–1749.

Redmann, R.E. (undated.) Grasses and grasslands, native. The encyclopedia of Saskatchewan. http://esask.uregina.ca/entry/grasses_and_grassland_native.html

Trottier, G.C. 2002. A landowner's guide. Conservation of Canadian prairie grasslands. Minister of the Environment/Canadian Wildlife Service. http://www.mb.ec.gc.ca/nature/whp/prgrass/df03s00.en.html

Rough fescue by a prairie roadside in Alberta. Source: Thinkstock.

BRITISH COLUMBIA

Provincial flag of British Columbia.

A BRITISH COLUMBIA LANDSCAPE: view of mountains in the alpine zone, with white pasqueflower (*Anemone occidentalis*) in the foreground.

FLORAL EMBLEM: PACIFIC DOGWOOD

Pacific dogwood (*Cornus nuttallii*) in flower. Source: Wikimedia (photographer: P. Schultz; Creative Commons Attribution 2.0 Generic license).

SYMBOLISM

Pacific dogwood is an excellent floral symbol for British Columbia. The province is the only part of Canada where the species grows naturally, and it can not easily be cultivated elsewhere in the country. The plant is fairly common in the southwestern part of the province, and well represents the widespread forest ecosystem of the West Coast of Canada. Pacific dogwood in flower is spectacularly beautiful and the brilliant red fall foliage is also very impressive. The species has been a useful economic plant for Indigenous Peoples of the province, and thus serves as a reminder of the native culture. Moreover, a dogwood blossom is on a flag representing Franco-Columbians (French speaking British Columbians) which was chosen in a contest in 1981 and first hoisted in 1982.

Silhouette of Pacific dogwood (*Cornus nuttallii*). Source: Farrar, J.L. 1995. Trees in Canada. Canadian Forest Service and Fitzhenry and Whiteside, Markham, ON, Canada. Reproduced with permission.

NAMES

Latin Names
Cornus nuttallii Audubon ex Torr. & Gray

The genus name *Cornus* is the Latin name for the (Eurasian) cornelian cherry, *Cornus mas* L., originating from the Greek *keras* and the Latin *cornus,* meaning "horn" (applied because of the hardness of the wood).

The specific epithet *nuttallii* in the name *Cornus nuttallii* honours Thomas Nuttall (1786–1859), a British-American botanist and ornithologist, the first to recognize Pacific dogwood as a new species, in 1834 at Fort Vancouver. His friend, the famous ornithologist John James Audubon, named the species after Nuttall. Nuttall was one of the most knowledgeable of early North American plant collectors. He made numerous, significant collections, and published extensively on these. Nuttall is noted for his encyclopedias: *The Genera of North American Plants, The North America Sylva,* and *Manual of Ornithology of the United States and Canada.* In addition to providing Audubon with specimens to illustrate, Nuttall contributed generously to the works of other naturalists. He is commemorated not only by *C. nuttalli,* but also in the names of several other birds and plants. For more on him, see Graustein, J.E. 1967. Thomas Nuttall naturalist—exploration in America 1808–1841. Harvard University Press, Cambridge, MA. 481 pp.

English Names
Pacific dogwood. Also: California dogwood, flowering dogwood (the phrase currently used in British Columbia legislation designating the floral emblem of the province, although this name is much more widely used for *C. florida* L.), mountain dogwood, mountain flowering dogwood, Nuttall's dogwood, Oregon dogwood, Pacific mountain dogwood, Western dogwood, Western flowering dogwood.

It has been suggested that the name "dogwood" arose in England where a boiled tea made from the bark was used to remove external parasites from dogs; or, from the words "daggerwood" or "dagwood", reflecting use of the hard wood as a dagger or skewer on which to cook meat. A third explanation which has been proposed is that the unpalatable fruits gave rise to the names "dogberry" and "dogwood"; this is consistent with an old tradition of using the word "dog" in reference to things of very limited value (e.g., as in the expression "not fit for a dog").

French Names
Cornouiller du Pacifique. Also: cornouiller de Nuttall.

Thomas Nuttall (in 1824), commemorated in the name *Cornus nuttallii.* This engraving was published in London in 1825.

HISTORY

Canada

The Pacific dogwood was adopted in 1956 as British Columbia's floral emblem, winning out over the columbine (presumably *Aquilegia formosa*). The dogwood was considered to be an unofficial emblem as early as 1931, when the Dogwood Protection Act was passed to prohibit cutting or picking its flowers on public land. During World War II, dogwood lapel pins were sold and the money was used to buy wool and other goods for British Columbian soldiers.

Foreign

In 1918, Virginia adopted the flowering dogwood (*C. florida*) as its official state flower, and in 1956 proclaimed it to also be the official state tree. In 1941 North Carolina adopted "dogwood" (generally interpreted as *C. florida*) as the official state flower. In 1951 New Jersey adopted *C. florida* as its official "state memorial tree". In 1955 Missouri adopted the same species as its official arboreal emblem. Although *C. florida* is mainly found in the U.S., it is also native to the southernmost part of Ontario.

Pacific dogwood (*Cornus nuttallii*) flower. Source: Wikipedia (photographer: P. Siegmund; Creative Commons Attribution-Share Alike 3.0 Unported license).

APPEARANCE

Pacific dogwood is a small to medium sized, multi-branched, deciduous tree, 6–25 m (20–82 feet) tall, sometimes appearing to be a shrub. In Canada it is typically 6–8 m (20–36 feet) in height, with a trunk 15–30 cm (6–12 inches) in diameter. The maximum trunk diameter (at breast height) reported is 61 cm (24 inches). The canopy of the larger trees sometimes spreads 6 m (20 feet). The bark is thin, smooth, and dark purple, in mature trees occasionally breaking into small rectangular plates. The tiny, dull-purple or green flowers are in dense clusters, surrounded by four to six (usually five, sometimes seven or eight), showy, creamy-white or (uncommonly) pinkish, petal-like bracts that are about 5 cm (2 inches) long. The clusters of flowers surrounded by the white bracts have the appearance of large flowers with white petals, and are widely interpreted as such. The clusters together with their bracts are often 10–13 cm (4–5 inches) across. The pinkish-red berries (technically drupes) are 1–1.5 cm (0.4–0.6 inch) in diameter, occurring in clusters of 30–40. The root system is typically deeply penetrating, often with a main taproot.

Pacific dogwood (*Cornus nuttallii*). Source: Canadian Heritage. 2002 (revised edition). Symbols of Canada. Canadian Heritage, Ottawa, ON. Reproduced with permission.

A BIODIVERSITY TREASURE

CLASSIFICATION

Family: dogwood family (Cornaceae).

The genus *Cornus* consists of several dozen species. The number of species is not clear because different authorities include different numbers of species. The plants are mostly deciduous shrubs and small trees of north temperate grasslands, woods, and swamps, but a few species are evergreen, some are perennial herbs, and one is native to the Southern Hemisphere. Ten species are native to Canada.

The bunchberries or dwarf cornels (*C. canadensis* and *C. suecica*), are familiar woodland herbs across Canada reaching 30 cm (1 foot) in height. Their flowers are very similar to those of the much larger Pacific dogwood and flowering dogwood, which are often trees. Despite the huge difference in size, the woodland herbs appear closely related to the trees, and recent molecular evolutionary studies have confirmed this close relationship. There are few other examples in the Canadian flora of trees and herbs so closely related as to be placed in the same genus.

Pacific dogwood (*Cornus nuttallii*). Source: Curtis's Botanical Magazine, 1910. Vol. 6. Lovell Reeve & Co., London, U.K. Plate 8311. 1, Flowering branch; 2, fruit cluster; 3, flower (the petals are above the sepals).

GEOGRAPHY

The Pacific dogwood is a native of the West Coast of North America, found in the coastal forest regions west of the Cascade Mountains, from southwestern British Columbia (including central and southern Vancouver Island) to southern California, with an isolated inland population in northern Idaho (considered to be in danger of extinction), and occasional populations in the mountains of San Diego and Los Angeles counties of California. The species usually occurs below 1,500 m (5,000 feet) in altitude over most of its range, generally below 300 m (1,000 feet) in Canada.

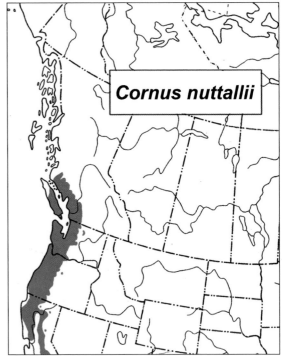

Canadian and adjacent United States distribution of Pacific dogwood (*Cornus nuttallii*).

ECOLOGY

Pacific dogwood occurs in the understory in low-elevation coniferous, hardwood, and mixed coastal forests. It develops best in Douglas fir (*Pseudotsuga menziesii*) forests and in the redwood forests of California. In southwestern B.C., Pacific dogwood associates with Douglas fir, grand fir (*Abies grandis*) and western hemlock (*Tsuga heterophylla*).

Habitat

The Pacific dogwood generally lives in the shade of forests, often along stream banks. It prefers moist but well-drained soils, and is both drought-tolerant and flood-tolerant. The soils occupied are typically deep (often more than 2 m or 6.6 feet), somewhat acidic (pH typically 5.5–6), range in texture from clay to sandy loam, and are often high in humus. Consistent with its mild, West Coast distribution, the species has limited frost tolerance.

Inter-species Relationships

Some deer species (especially mule deer) are known to graze regenerating sprouts of Pacific dogwood, but most mammals avoid eating the leaves (which have a bitter sap) and the branches. Bears, shrews, voles, and other small mammals, and many species of birds such as pigeons (especially the band-tailed pigeon shown here), quail, grosbeaks, hermit thrushes, and waxwings consume the fruits. Beavers will eat all above-ground parts of the plant. Pacific dogwood has been recommended as an appropriate garden plant to attract butterflies and hummingbirds.

Dogwood anthracnose (also called dogwood leaf blotch) is a disease caused by the fungus *Discula destructiva*, which has become a major threat to *C. nuttallii* and *C. florida* since the 1980s. It has been claimed that the fungus was imported to North America in shipments of Japanese dogwoods (*C. kousa*). Many wild and cultivated trees in North America have been affected. The disease begins with spots on the leaves, leading to the killing of branches which subsequently retain their dead leaves overwinter. This is followed by progressive dieback of the limbs, and the infected trees perish within two or three years. In parts of northeastern North America, the disease has become less virulent. Although the reasons for this are not understood, it is hoped that a similar trend of decreasing harm will occur in northwestern North America.

Pollination and Dispersal

Flowering plants employ different structures to create displays that attract pollinating insects. Most insect-pollinated plants have large, attractive petals. However, Pacific dogwood employs large white bracts (small leaves), which are actually not part of the flower, although they look like petals. The very conspicuous bracts surround a group of small flowers with small petals. What looks like a flower is actually an inflorescence, and the effect of many such inflorescences produces a very noticeable floral display. Pacific Dogwood is considered a pollinator friendly tree but little has been recorded about its pollinators. The closely related flowering dogwood of eastern North America is self-incompatible at least to a degree and its pollinators include bumble bees and honey bees. In British Columbia, flowering occurs from April to June, and fruits are ripe by September or October. Curiously, the species often flowers twice in a growing season, coming into bloom a second time in late summer or early fall. It regenerates both through seeds and by vegetative sprouting. The latter mode is common when the plants are damaged by fire or clearcutting. The fleshy fruits are likely dispersed by birds and small mammals.

Band-tailed pigeons (*Columba fasciata*) perched on a branch of Pacific dogwood (*Cornus nuttallii*). Source: Audubon, J.J. 1827–1838. The birds of America. Robert Havell Jr., London, U.K. Plate 367. Audubon based his painting of the birds on preserved specimens collected by explorer-biologists John Townsend and Thomas Nuttall during an expedition to the Pacific Northwest in 1834. In 1837 Audubon described the plant as a new species of *Cornus*, *C. nuttallii*, naming it in honour of Nuttall. The plant was painted by Audubon's assistant Maria Martin.

A BIODIVERSITY TREASURE

USES

The principal economic usage of Pacific dogwood is as an ornamental, widely employed in landscaping, notable for its showy flower clusters, bright red berries, and colourful fall foliage. However, the threat of dogwood leaf blotch has reduced new plantings. The wood is hard, heavy, whitish, and fine-grained, and wears smoothly. It has been used to make cabinets, piano keys, knitting needles, thread spindles, slingshots, golf club heads, mallet handles, and other tools requiring very hard wood that resists wear and repeated hammering. The berries are edible but bitter. Native peoples used the bark to make a brown dye, and medicinally as a general tonic and to treat a variety of ailments, including constipation, indigestion, and other stomach complaints. The wood was employed to make bows, arrows, harpoons, tools, and toys. The leaves were occasionally used for smoking, either directly or mixed with tobacco. Baby baskets were fashioned out of the twigs.

Antique golf club heads like these were often made of dogwood.

CULTIVATION

Pacific dogwood is used to some extent in revegetation, but is much more commonly planted as an ornamental. In Canada, the species is not hardy outside of its native area in the southwestern part of coastal British Columbia. In eastern Canada and parts of New England, it often fails to stop growing in time to harden for winter. Wild-growing trees are difficult to transplant, but nursery-grown stock can be easily established, preferably in well-drained soil. The foliage of plants grown in shade will be exposed to sunscald if the plants are moved directly to a sunny location. Once trees are established, natural summer rainfall is usually sufficient, and it is not necessary to provide water. Pruning the plant back to its base results in a proliferation of basal branches, and the development of a large shrub 2.4–3.7 m (8–12 feet) high. Fruits normally ripen in August and early September. The soft, outer pulp can be washed off in a pail of water, discarding any seeds that float (these are unlikely to germinate). The seeds need to be cold stratified to germinate. Seeds collected in the fall can be sown directly into soil outdoors, and during the winter the natural dormancy will be eliminated. The seeds can also be artificially stratified by storage in moist sand or peat moss in a refrigerator (0–4.5 °C, 32–40 °F) for 18 weeks. Professional horticulturists sometimes establish plants from softwood cuttings 5–7.5 (2–3 inches) long, from young, vigorous growth, rooting these in sand in a propagation case.

Cultivars of *Cornus nuttallii* include 'Barrick' (with large bracts and flower clusters), 'Boyd's Hardy' (a Tennessee selection), 'Colrigo Giant' (also known as 'Corrigo Giant' and 'Corego Giant'; named after the Columbia River Gorge where it was discovered, this has huge flower heads up to 15 cm (6 inches) across), 'Colrigo Wonder' (a variation of 'Colrigo Giant' with smaller flower heads), 'Eddiei' (discovered in 1918 by H.H. Eddie, a Vancouver nurseryman, the leaves have yellow blotches), 'Goldspot' (the leaves also have yellow blotches, and this may well be 'Eddiei' with a different name), 'Monarch' (a form with large flowers bracts and purplish young shoots), 'North Star' (has very large floral bracts, purple young shoots), 'Pilgrim' (a California selection with relatively small flowers), 'Portlemouth' (selected in England, this has large floral bracts), 'Vrughtman' (a selection with variegated white/green foliage), and 'Zurico' (an early flowering form). There are over 100 cultivars of *C. florida*, far more than of *C. nuttallii*, although the latter is one of the most widely cultivated species of the genus. The following cultivars are hybrids of *C. nuttallii* and *C. florida*: 'Ascona' (a small tree with pendulous branches), 'Eddie's White Wonder' (a sterile hybrid selected by H.H. Eddie, mentioned above), 'Ormonde' (with large flower bracts and almost fluorescent autumn foliage), and 'Pink Blush' (with pink flowers).

Cornus nuttallii has been hybridized with some of its close relatives in an attempt to produce superior cultivars. *Cornus florida* × *nuttallii* hybrids appear more like *C. nuttallii* than *C. florida*. *Cornus kousa* × *nuttallii* hybrids have been known to produce floral bracts 12.5–15 cm (5–6 inches) wide, occasionally up to 17.5 cm (7 inches). 'Venus' is a recently released cultivar of this hybrid.

Three exotic woody species of *Cornus* are occasionally planted in Canada. Kous dogwood resembles the eastern flowering dogwood but comes into flower two to three weeks later. The cornelian

CULTIVATION (CONT'D)

cherry (*C. mas*), is an early flowering species which produces many yellow flowers and has edible fruit. Red-branched dogwood (*C. sanguinea* L.) is notable for its dark red branches in winter. Similar to the last-mentioned is red osier, *C. stolonifera* Michx., a native of eastern North America that is widely cultivated.

Key to species of *Cornus* with showy bracts cultivated in Canada

1a. Plant a low herb . . . *C. canadensis* (bunchberry)
1b. Plant a tall shrub or tree 2

2a. Fruits joined into a globular, fleshy head (somewhat like a strawberry); leaves often narrow or long-pointed; Eurasian 3
2b. Fruits densely clustered but individually distinct; leaves usually oval and shortly pointed; North American 4

3a. Leaves ovate, thin, deciduous . . . . *C. kousa* (kousa dogwood)
3b. Leaves lanceolate, thin, partially evergreen . . . . *C. capitata* (Himalayan evergreen dogwood)
3c. Leaves narrowly elliptic, thick and evergreen . . . . *C. angustata* (Chinese evergreen dogwood)

4a. Bracts 4, emarginate (with a shallow notch) at the tip . . . . *C. florida* (flowering dogwood)
4b. Bracts 4–6, pointed to flat at the tip . . . . *C. nuttallii* (Pacific dogwood)

CONSERVATION STATUS

Cutting down or harvesting any part of the Pacific dogwood was prohibited in 1996 by the province of British Columbia, but the protective statute (The Dogwood, Trillium and Rhododendron Protection Act) was repealed in 2002. The recent threat posed by dogwood leaf blotch may necessitate reinstatement of protection for the species. In Idaho, Pacific dogwood is listed as a "Priority 1 species", with the indication that it is in danger of becoming extinct from the state in the foreseeable future. Because Pacific dogwood is fairly widely distributed in the western U.S., the future survival of the species is not threatened, but genetically distinct variations on the periphery of the range may require conservation measures.

Flowers of Pacific dogwood (*Cornus nuttallii*). Photo courtesy of Calvin Jones, Government of British Columbia.

MYTHS, LEGENDS, TALES, FOLKLORE AND INTERESTING FACTS

🍁 According to legend, the dogwood was once a huge forest tree. Because it was firm and strong, it was chosen as the timber for the Crucifixion of Christ. Distressed at this cruel usage, the tree decided to never again grow large enough to be used as an execution cross. To further express its regret, its blossoms took the form of a cross (evident in 4–bracted species).

🍁 The cornelian cherry, *Cornus mas,* a native of Eurasia, is reputed to have provided the wood used by Odysseus and his men to build the Trojan horse, a huge figure of a horse in which Greek soldiers hid. When the Greeks sailed away, the Trojans hauled the horse into the city of Troy, and subsequently the soldiers opened the gates to allow the entry of Greek forces which had sailed back under cover of night. It has been thought that the conflict was entirely fictitious, but some modern scholars have suggested that there may be a grain of truth to the legendary events, tracing back to the eleventh or twelfth century B.C. However, the small cornelian cherry is unlikely to have provided enough wood for a large Trojan horse.

🍁 The Thompson Indians used the flower heads of Pacific dogwood to wash the skin to treat "seven-year-itch", and a boiled tea made with bark strips to improve the lungs of hunters.

🍁 North American pioneers used boiled teas of both Pacific dogwood and eastern flowering dogwood as a substitute for quinine to treat malaria.

🍁 Dogwood species are often called arrowood (or arrowwood), a usage that also reflects the very hard wood of many of the species. The ancient Romans used the wood to make spears and arrows.

🍁 Dogwood timber is so hard that it was once used as a wedge to split other wood.

🍁 A "dogwood winter" is a phrase used in the southern United States (especially in Appalachia) to indicate a spell of cold weather in the spring (April and May) that coincides with the blooming period of local dogwoods. Such a period of cold is often the last harsh weather before summer. American journalist and poet W.J. Lampton (1859?–1917) wrote the following:

Now Jack Frost comes with his nipping airs
To take from the Spring his final toll;
He looks like Winter but he always wears
A dogwood blossom in his buttonhole.

How can you identify a dogwood? By its bark (rough-rough)! Prepared by B. Brookes.

Painting of the official flower of British Columbia, Pacific dogwood (*Cornus nuttallii*), from the Walter Coucill Canadian Centennial official flowers of Canada series (see Coucill 1966 cited in the first chapter of this book). Reproduced with the permission of the copyright holders, the Coucill family.

SOURCES OF ADDITIONAL INFORMATION

Andrews, S. 1991. *Cornus nuttallii* in cultivation. Kew Magazine 8(2): 71–78.

Cappiello, P., and Shadow, D. 2005. Dogwoods: the genus *Cornus*. Timber Press, Portland, OR. 224 pp.

Daughtrey, M.L., and Hibben, C.R. 1994. Dogwood anthracnose: a new disease threatens two native *Cornus* species. Ann. Rev. Phytopath. 32: 61–73.

Daughtrey, M.L., Hibben, C.R., Britton, K.O., Windham, M.T., and Redlin, S.C. 1996. Dogwood anthracnose: Understanding a disease new to North America. Plant Disease 80: 349–358.

Eyde, R.H. 1987. The case for keeping *Cornus* in the broad Linnaean sense. Syst. Bot. 12: 505–518.

Eyde, R.H. 1988. Comprehending *Cornus:* puzzles and progress in the systematics of the dogwoods. Bot. Rev. 54: 233–351.

Roof, J. 1951. Growing California's five dogwoods. J. Calif. Hort. Soc. 12(3): 50–58, 101–106.

Santamour, F.S., Jr., and McArdle, A.J. 1985. Cultivar checklists of the large-bracted dogwoods: *Cornus florida, C. kousa,* and *C. nuttallii.* J. Arboriculture 11(1): 29–36.

Witte, W.T., Windham, M.T., Windham, A.W., Hale, F.A., Fare, D.C., and Clatterbuck, W.K. Undated. Dogwoods for American gardens. Agricultural Extension Service, The University of Tennessee. 32 pp. www.utextension.utk.edu/publications/pbfiles/PB1670.pdf

The Coat of Arms of British Columbia. The crowned lion at the top is wearing a collar of Pacific dogwood flowers. At the base, flowers of Pacific dogwood also entwine the Latin motto "Splendor sine Occasu", meaning "splendour without diminishment".

Pacific dogwood (*Cornus nuttallii*) in flower. Source: Wikipedia (photographer: S. Shebs; GNU Free Documentation license).

TREE: WESTERN RED CEDAR

West coast temperate rainforest with western red cedar (*Thuja plicata*) trees. Source: Thinkstock.

SYMBOLISM

The western red cedar is an appropriate symbol of British Columbia given its current importance as a commercial source of lumber, and its key historical roles in the lives of West Coast Aboriginal Peoples. The towering trees are breath-taking, and their groves are as spiritually symbolic as cathedrals, providing mesmerizing havens for biodiversity, and representing the precious rainforest ecosystem of Canada's West Coast.

Silhouette of western red cedar (*Thuja plicata*). Source: Farrar, J.L. 1995. Trees in Canada. Canadian Forest Service and Fitzhenry and Whiteside, Markham, ON, Canada. Reproduced with permission.

NAMES

Latin Names

Thuja plicata Donn ex D. Don

The genus name *Thuja* traces to the Greek *thyia*, referring to a kind of resinous tree or a juniper, and the Latin *thyia*, an allusion to a citrus-tree. The specific epithet *plicata* is based on the Latin *plicare*, to fold, to plait (like a fan), a reference to the overlapping scale-like leaves.

English Names

Western red cedar. Also: British Columbia cedar, British Columbia red cedar, canoe cedar, cedar, giant arbor-vitae (= giant arborvitae, a name used in the American horticultural trade), giant cedar, giant redcedar, Pacific red cedar, shinglewood, western arbor-vitae ("arbor-vitae" is Latin for "tree of life").

"Red" in the name refers to the wood colour, which is pale to dark red. The name "cedar" is inappropriate (although it was originally applied because of the cedar-like appearance), since true cedars belong to the genus *Cedrus*. There have been attempts to avoid confusion by referring to *T. plicata* as "redcedar" instead of "red cedar". "Red cedar" (or eastern red cedar) is also the name of *Juniperus virginiana* L., and there have been similar attempts to call it "redcedar".

French Names

Cèdre de l'Ouest. Also: cèdre rouge de l'Ouest, cèdre, thuya géant, thuya de l'Ouest.

HISTORY

Canada

The British Columbia Tree Council was formed in 1987 to recommend a tree symbol for the province. The selection process also involved public nominations (British Columbians were given a list of 25 species, including western red cedar), and an essay contest for students. The western red cedar was adopted as the arboreal emblem of British Columbia on February 18, 1988.

Foreign

Thuja species are not recognized as official symbols of any political region outside of British Columbia. "Yellow cedar" or yellow elder (*Tecoma stans*), the official flower of the U.S. Virgin Islands, is quite unrelated to *Thuja*.

Seed cones of western red cedar (*Thuja plicata*). Source Wikipedia (photographer: W. Siegmund; GNU Free Documentation license).

APPEARANCE

Western red cedars are evergreen coniferous trees, generally 21–30 m (70–100 feet) at maturity, usually with a trunk 0.6–1.2 m (2–4 feet) in diameter; very large trees have reached 75 m (246 feet) tall and 7 m (23 feet) in trunk diameter. The western red cedar is one of the most colossal trees in the world. However, the inland trees (see distribution, below) are smaller than the coastal trees, and at high altitudes the plant may be reduced to a shrub. In harsh sites, stunted or distorted trees sometimes occur. The base of the tree is buttressed (swollen and fluted). Old trees often have many dead major limbs in the crown, and many leader limbs. The reddish brown or grayish brown, stringy, ragged bark is relatively thin (up to 25 mm or 1 inch thick), and is finely vertically ridged and furrowed. The bark is easily peeled off in long strips. The evergreen foliage is composed of small, scale-like leaves, 1.5–3 mm (0.05–0.1 inch) long, in opposite pairs with successive pairs at 90° to each other. The leaves are displayed in flat sprays. Male and female cones occur on the same trees. The male cones are very small (about 2 mm or 0.08 inch long) and inconspicuous. The seed cones are ellipsoid, 10–20 mm (0.4–0.8 inch) long, and clustered near the ends of twigs. Some trees live more than 1,000 years, and a few have been dated at almost 1,500 years of age.

CLASSIFICATION

Family: Cupressaceae (cypress family).

The genus *Thuja* has five species, two native to North America and three to eastern Asia. Several studies of genetic variation have concluded that *T. plicata* is a fairly uniform species, with limited evidence that subspecies or varieties deserve to be recognized. Northern white cedar (*Thuja occidentalis* L.) is the only other species of *Thuja* in North America. It has leaves that are dull yellowish-green above and below and the seed-cone scales are minutely mucronate (ending in a sharp point). In western red cedar the leaves are white-striped below (when fresh) and glossy green above and the seed-cone scales have a triangular projection near the tip.

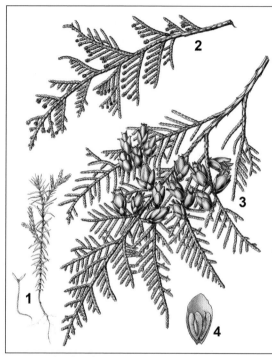

Western red cedar (*Thuja plicata*). 1, seedlings; 2, flowering branch (flowers scarcely apparent); 3, fruiting branch; 4, scale of a fruit, showing seeds. Source: Sargent, C.S. 1896. The silva of North America. Vol. 10. Houghton, Mifflin and Company, New York, NY. Plate 533.

Foliage of western red cedar (*Thuja plicata*). Photo courtesy of Chris Schnepf, University of Idaho and Bugwood.org.

GEOGRAPHY

Thuja plicata has two major distribution areas: (1) a Coast Range/Cascade Range, including the coastal mountains in southeast Alaska, British Columbia, Washington, Oregon, and northwestern California, and (2) in the Rocky Mountains, including southeastern British Columbia and southwestern Alberta, northeastern Washington, northern Idaho and northwestern Montana. The trees occur at altitudes from sea level to 1,500 m (5,000 feet), rarely to 2,300 m (7,500 feet).

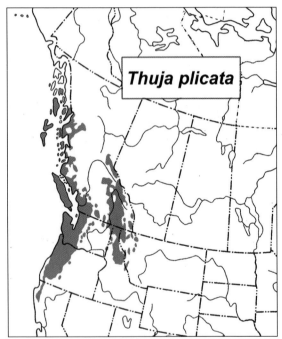

Canadian and adjacent United States distribution of western red cedar (*Thuja plicata*).

ECOLOGY

Western red cedar grows in mixed coniferous forests, rarely in pure stands. In its geographic area, it has been estimated that it covers about 20% of the vegetation. In Canada it usually associates with Douglas fir and western hemlock (two species that Pacific dogwood, also associates with, as noted earlier). As well as growing in forests, the species also occurs on rocky slopes, in forested swamps, and along streams. The trees are susceptible to frost, especially in late spring and early autumn.

A major requirement for regeneration from seed is disturbed mineral soil. Seeds will also germinate on rotting wood in old groves but replacement in these situations may more often result from vegetative reproduction. Although western red cedar is usually considered a climax or near climax species, the fact that seed development may be best on disturbed mineral soil raises the interesting question of whether it should also be considered a pioneer. Slash burning favours this tree by increasing mineral soil surfaces in cutover areas.

Habitat

Western red cedar is adapted to cool montane habitats in the foothills of the Rockies, and to maritime coastal climates with cool, cloudy summers and wet, mild winters. The trees generally occur in moist areas (including swamps, wet ravines, and poorly drained depressions), and occupy a variety of types of soil, preferring acidic, well-drained substrates (but tolerating alkaline soils). Western red cedar is quite shade-tolerant, and is able to reproduce under dense shade. Although the species is usually associated with coastal rainforests, the inland sites in the Rocky Mountain foothills may be better called "snow forests" because of the very heavy snow accumulation.

Inter-species Relationships

Deer, elk, and rodents browse on western red cedar seedlings and saplings, sometimes causing extensive damage. Near the coast, deer consume the foliage year-round, and in the northern Rocky Mountains the leaves are a major food for big game. Black bears have been observed to remove the bark and feed on the exposed sapwood. The trees provide cover for numerous birds and mammals. Western red cedar is host to many insects, some specific to it, but severe damage is not common. A gall midge fly (*Mayetiola thujae*) sometimes seriously damages the seeds. Although 200 fungi have been reported on western red cedar, it is less susceptible to pathological attack than other conifers. Over the long life of the trees fungi detoxify heartwood chemicals that provide decay resistance. As a result the accumulated decay in living trees is greater than for any other major conifer in British Columbia and hollow trees are common.

Western red cedar forests on the offshore islands of Haida Gwaii (Queen Charlotte Islands) evolved for a thousand years in the absence of large mammal browsing. Black-tailed deer (*Odocoileus hemionus sitkensis*) were introduced in 1901. Recent field experiments have suggested that the chemical defenses of plants from Haida Gwaii are less effective than those of mainland plants, possibly because of the lower need for protection in historical times.

"Nurse logs" are trees that have fallen on the forest floor and decompose, providing nutrients for young

ECOLOGY (CONT'D)

plants to grow rapidly. Fallen trees leave openings in the canopy allowing sunlight to penetrate, accelerating growth. Western red cedar decays

Western red cedar (*Thuja plicata*). Source Wikipedia (photographer: Abdallahh; Creative Commons Attribution 2.0 Generic license).

extremely slowly, so it releases nutrients slowly. Nevertheless the species has considerable value in nurturing the growth of other plants, as is evident by the fact that many plants, including young Pacific yew seedlings and saplings, grow well for decades on top of the fallen trees, finally growing around or through the trunks to contact the soil. Often one sees a row of trees with stilt-like roots, an indication that there was once a fallen tree upon which the trees became established. The moist environment in which western red cedar grows results in fallen trees becoming covered by mosses, which greatly facilitates the development of a substrate on which seedlings can become established.

Western red cedar is the predominant feature of some old-growth forests with rare and significant species and high biodiversity. At a site near Prince George (east-central B.C.), it has been estimated that there are about a thousand species of lichens and fungi. The northern spotted owl (*Strix occidentalis caurina*) is just one of hundreds of species that occur in remnants of the once extensive old growth red cedar forest of southwestern B.C.

Pollination and Dispersal

Western red cedar sheds windborne pollen in early spring (February to April), individual trees releasing pollen for one to two weeks. The species is self-fertile, but a moderate degree of cross-fertilization normally occurs. Western red cedar produces abundant, tiny, winged seeds, which are distributed by the wind, generally no farther than 122 m (400 feet) from the parent tree. The cones are mature in October, and seeds are distributed in October and November (occasionally some seeds are retained in the cones and are shed gradually during the winter). In coastal forests seed production may be as high as 2.5 million seeds/ha (1 million seeds/acre). The plants also propagate vegetatively, by layering (attached branches contacting the soil and developing into new shoots), and by branches that break off the trees, producing roots where they contact the ground. The trees are often windthrown in wet environments, and branches from the fallen trees can produce new shoots.

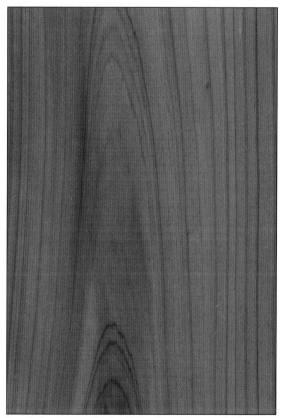

Board of western red cedar (*Thuja plicata*). Source: Thinkstock.

A BIODIVERSITY TREASURE

USES

North American Indians, especially those living along the coasts of British Columbia and Washington, used western red cedar extensively. Some coastal tribes called themselves "People of the Red Cedar" because of their dependence on the tree. Large trunks were carved into totem poles, hollowed out to produce huge, ocean-going whaling canoes (some capable of holding more than 60 people), and split into wide planks used in large, timber frame longhouses that sometimes extended more than 30 m (100 feet). The wood was used to make many objects, including paddles, religious masks, and utensils. The bark of young trees was fashioned into thatch, clothing (including rain-capes, skirts, and complete dresses), mats, blankets, ropes, and baskets. Finely shredded inner bark was once used by Northwest Coast Indians for use as an absorbant in diapers and as cradle padding. The inner bark was also employed as a slow match to carry fire from camp to camp. Flexible slim twigs were woven into baskets and whaling ropes. Thicker branches were used to make arrows. Roots were used for fishhooks. Boiled teas of various parts of the trees were used to treat a wide variety of illnesses.

Western red cedar is a major lumber tree of the West Coast of North America. In addition to the harvest of wild trees, it is cultivated to a small extent as a lumber tree in North America, western Europe, and New Zealand. British Columbia is the largest supplier, followed by the states of Washington and Alaska. In order of importance, the trunks are turned into lumber, shingles and shakes, and logs, these accounting for 90% of the harvest. In British Columbia, considerable cedar is used for fence posts, poles, pilings, and pulp. Manufactured

University of Northern British Columbia student Dave Radies in an ancient western red cedar rainforest 130 km east of Prince George. Photograph by Robert van Adrichem, September 28, 2007. Photo reproduced with permission.

USES (CONT'D)

products include veneer and plywood, rough lumber, decking, boards, siding, panelling, and fence and furniture products. The wood is often used for guitar sounding boards. In some years British Columbia has produced more than half of the world's demand for shakes and wooden shingles. Cedar leaf oil extracted from the leaves and twigs is used in perfumes, veterinary soaps, shoe polishes, deodorants, and other products. The pungent, aromatic wood is employed to line closets and chests in the widespread belief that the odour repels moth and carpet beetle larvae that can damage wool and other natural fibres. (There appears to be no reliable evidence that western red cedar is actually effective in this regard, although there is some evidence that eastern white cedar may have a small protective effect. Bee hives have been made from western red cedar, suggesting that the toxicity to insects may be limited.)

Possibly the earliest commercial manufacturing of western red cedar products was in 1825 in Fort Vancouver (in Washington, near Portland, Oregon), where the Hudson's Bay Company employed people to hand-split cedar into shakes. A "shake" is a wooden shingle made by splitting logs, usually not by sawing (although "tapersawn shakes", which are thicker at their butt ends, are made partly or wholly by sawing). Shakes can be used for various purposes (e.g., for siding), and are especially used to cover roofs. Originally shakes were not tapered, while shingles were often tapered (to promote run-off of rain). In early times all shakes were made by hand, but almost all are now produced with machinery. Wooden shingles (which are usually used to cover roofs) are always made by sawing wood on all six sides (in which case they are usually not shakes). Shakes are somewhat thicker than shingles, and since they are rougher in appearance they give a more rustic look when installed. Today, there are many kinds of products that are intermediate between shakes and shingles, and the distinction between them has become imprecise. The ease with which western red cedar wood can be split makes it particularly useful for preparing shakes and shingles, and 95% of these products sold in North America are made from western red cedar. Unfortunately, the ease with which breakage and splitting occurs is a disadvantage for structural uses, such as in beams and posts. The wood is also soft and extremely sensitive to marring. However, it has few knots, does not exude resin like many other conifers, has a beautiful, reddish appearance, takes stains well, possesses a pleasant aroma, is light in weight, and has very good insulating properties. Stainless-steel nails and fasteners are recommended for use with western red cedar, although hot-dipped galvanized and aluminum nails can be used. Regular galvanized nails and other kinds of metal fasteners react adversely with the oils in the wood, resulting in stains or streaks on the wood, and deterioration of the metal.

Western red cedar is favoured for outdoor uses where conditions promote decay. The wood is very resistant to insects as well as to fungi (a fallen tree may remain intact for a century), and is well suited for external uses such as siding, shingles, shakes, decking, shutters, outdoor furniture, arbours, gazebos, pergolas, trellises, sheds, greenhouses, planters, fences, gates, and utility poles. The wood is also in demand for indoor uses where high humidity is common, such as with saunas and hot tubs. Although western red cedar shingles can cost several times as much as standard asphalt shingles, they can last 100 years on a roof. Western red cedar is one of the preferred woods for boats and canoes, and is the principal veneer for covering racing shells (i.e., boats propelled by oarsmen in racing contests). The decay resistance is due to the presence of toxic chemicals called tropolones that are concentrated in the heartwood. Certain tropolone derivatives called thujaplicins are potent anti-fungal and anti-bacterial compounds.

The sweet smell and attractive, lacy foliage make branches of western red cedar ideal for use in flower bouquets and decorative floral arrangements.

A canoe constructed of western red cedar by Salish people of Washington State. Photographed about 1914 (public domain photo available on Wikipedia).

TOXICITY

Workers in the lumber, furniture, and cabinetry industries, and some wood carvers, have experienced asthma, rhinitis, or irritation of skin and eyes from exposure to the sawdust of *Thuja plicata*. "Western red cedar asthma" is a significant occupational hazard, and those diagnosed with the condition have often been forced to find other careers. Plicatic acid from wood has been shown to be the chief cause of the asthma. Cedar sawdust and shavings have occasionally been used in plant mulches, soil conditioners and animal litter, but acceptance is limited because of the known toxicity of the dust associated with these materials. However, western red cedar bark is widely employed as a long-lasting mulch. The wood is commonly used in outdoor furniture and play structures, suggesting that contact dermatitis is not a major problem for most people.

IS THE WESTERN RED CEDAR A "FLAGSHIP SPECIES"?

A flagship species is one that has been chosen to represent an environmental cause, such as an endangered ecosystem. Such species are not only vulnerable, but are photogenic, charismatic, and distinctive, thereby inspiring public action for their preservation. They are valuable in leveraging support for conservation of entire ecosystems. Examples of flagship species are the Asiatic lion of India, the giant panda of China, the mountain gorilla of Central Africa, and the northern spotted owl in Western North America. Western red cedar has been a focus of attention in attempts to protect old growth forests in Western Canada. The spectacular, old trees are vulnerable and diminishing. The species is distinctive and well-known as a provincial emblem. The huge size, soft foliage, and pleasant fragrance are appealing. There is also a mystical appeal associated with the tree, associated with images of rugged coasts with totem poles rising from the mist. There is now widespread public sympathy for the preservation of the vulnerable, ancient groves of towering, old trees. Although the species is not endangered, western red cedar serves all the purposes of a flagship species.

A large western red cedar (*Thuja plicata*) tree in Washington state. Source: Wikipedia (photographer: J. Werther; Creative Commons Attribution 2.0 Generic license).

CULTIVATION

Western red cedar is easily established from seeds, most samples not requiring cold stratification to germinate well. However, most cultivated plants raised for ornamental purposes are clones, established in containers from rooted stem cuttings, facilitating transplanting. The species is widely grown as a park tree, and often also as a hedge. The trees are used to some extent to revegetate disturbed sites and in erosion control. There are many ornamental cultivars, including: 'Atrovirens' (a slow-growing pyramidal plant with shiny green foliage), 'Canadian Gold' (a tree to 21 m or 70 feet tall, with golden foliage), 'Cuprea' (a dwarf, globe form with deep green leaves tipped with yellow), 'Green Giant' (a hybrid of *T. plicata* and *T. standishii,* with deep green foliage and a pyramidal habit), 'Grovpli' (a hardy tree about 6 m or 20 feet high), 'Hogan' (a tree about 6 m or 20 feet tall, with a densely columnar silhouette), 'Sunshine' (with golden foliage), 'Stoneham Gold' (an upright shrub with golden new growth that turns green), 'Virescens' (a narrow form, growing to about 9 m or 30 feet, with dark green foliage), and 'Zebrina' (a pyramidal form with variegated yellow foliage, growing to about 9 m or 30 feet).

CONSERVATION STATUS

British Columbia is one of the most biologically and ecologically diverse regions of Canada, with grasslands, oak parklands, desert-like steppes, dry pine forest, boreal black spruce muskegs, tundra, and alpine meadows. Two-thirds of the province is covered by forest land. The western red cedar occurs in the temperate rainforest along the Pacific Coast, and in an interior rainforest. Temperate rainforests are rare globally, and the Pacific Coast rainforest is the largest. British Columbia is the world's most important exporter of forest products, and the forests are critical to the province's economy, with perhaps one in every five jobs depending on forestry. The western red cedar is one of the most important forestry trees in the province, and its impressive stature and delicate habitat have led to conflicts among the forest industry, government, Indigenous Peoples, and conservationists. Western red cedar is a common tree, not requiring protection of its genetic resources, but the old growth ecosystem and biodiversity it represents are fragile and likely to continue to be the subject of debate between proponents of short-term resource exploitation and advocates of environmental protection.

"SUSTAINABLE DEVELOPMENT"—AN OXYMORON?

"Sustainable development" has become the key phrase that indicates the ideal compromise between mankind's use of planetary resources and the future welfare of the planet. Google this phrase together with "oxymoron" and you will get over 20,000 responses, suggesting there is something fundamentally wrong. American ecological economist Herman Daly (1938–) is credited with first calling sustainable development an oxymoron. Oxymorons are rhetorical figures in which incongruous or contradictory terms are combined (e.g., deafening silence, giant shrimp, natural makeup, a little pregnant, alone together, Hell's Angels). Certainly there is a contradictory element in the phrase "sustainable development": sustainable means to maintain, develop means to change. Nevertheless, in this practical world, does "sustainable development" at least point the way to a better world? The phrase was initiated in a 1987 report of the World Commission on Environment and Development (Brundtland Commission, *Our Common Future*), which defined sustainable development as "development that meets the needs of the present without compromising the ability of future generations to meet their own needs". We can't really judge what future generations need, but we can assume that it is desirable to limit the continuing deterioration of the planet's resources, biota, and atmosphere. Numerous analyses have been advanced recently by economists and ecologists arguing that good business practices are inherently respectful of the environment, and accordingly there is no fundamental disagreement between economic development and sustainability of the natural world (so sustainable development is not an oxymoron). Certainly it is true that pollution and depletion of natural resources injure businesses directly dependent on those resources: fishermen, farmers, foresters, and many others are harmed by water pollution, soil contamination, depletion of biodiversity, and atmospheric degradation. But in the short run it is almost always much easier in this extremely competitive world to maximize profit by using present technologies and practices, irrespective of the associated harm to the planet. The simple fact is that in most cases doing good for the future of the environment requires sacrifice, and most people are unable for a variety of reasons to sacrifice much. Elected governments invariably reflect the general will of the people, homogenizing the different viewpoints of all interested parties. Of course, some interests, especially large corporations, tend to be more equal than others. We conclude that "sustainable development" is a nice phrase, but that each of us needs to make whatever contributions we can to limit the overuse of resources, and to urge our elected officials to do the same. We recommend a visit to a grove of western red cedars by our political representatives, in the way that Indigenous People have congregated for millennia, to contemplate how best to carry on their lives; perhaps the emotional experience would be of greater benefit to Canada in the long run than a similar visit to the boardrooms of the corporate elite.

MYTHS, LEGENDS, TALES, FOLKLORE AND INTERESTING FACTS

✤ In pre-Columbian times, Native peoples of the West Coast lacked sharp metal tools that could be used as axes or saws to cut down the huge Pacific red cedars needed for canoes and totem poles. Felling of large trees was initiated with stone or mussel-shell adzes, and wedges and mauls made of antlers, bones, stones, or other local materials, creating a circumferential triangular cut. The cut was filled with tinder and small kindling, and lit. Wet moss and clay were packed above and below the cut to prevent the trunk from catching fire. Workers keeping the fire going were rotated day and night for several days until the trunk was burned through.

✤ The leaves of western red cedar have been shown to last about 11 years in the lower third of the canopy in forest trees, and about 7 years in the upper third, apparently because of the greater stresses there.

✤ With heights of up to 75 m (246 feet) and trunk diameters up to 7 m (23 feet), western red cedars are among the largest plants on earth. However, they are by no means the largest trees. The world's **tallest standing tree species** is the coast redwood (*Sequoia sempervirens*) of California. One of these, the "Hyperion", discovered in 2006, has been measured at 115.5 m (379.1 feet) in height, with a diameter at breast height of 3.14 m (10.3 feet). However, some trees of the species are thought to have grown taller than this, and a *Eucalyptus* tree of Australia is claimed to have been over 150 m (492 feet) tall. The world's **heaviest tree** is the giant sequoia (*Sequoiadendron giganteum*) of California (another "redwood"). One of these, the "General Sherman", which (at 83.8 m or 275 feet) is one of the tallest trees in the world, has been estimated to weigh 5,595 metric tons (6,167 tons). It has been calculated that the wood in the tree could be used to make 30 trillion matches! At breast height the tree has a diameter of 8.8 m or 28.9 feet (at ground level the circumference is 31.1 m or 102.6 feet), accepted by some to be greater than any other known tree in the world. However, the tree with the **largest girth** appears to be a Montezuma cypress (*Taxodium mucronatum*) called "El Arbol del Thule" in Oaxaca, Mexico, which has a circumference of 36 m (118 feet) at breast height (54 m or 178 feet at ground level). Some researchers have suggested that this tree might actually be a clonal colony of genetically identical individuals.

✤ Plants obtain water from the soil, and the water is moved upward through vascular tissues to the top of the plant. Water can be transported to considerable heights in very narrow, stiff-walled tubes, such as found in the xylem tissue of plants. Transpiration (water loss through the leaves) generates a gradient of pressure that pulls the water up from the roots, but in tall trees the pressure required can be enormous, especially during dry spells. The problem can be compared to getting water up very tall skyscrapers (normal city water pressure cannot adequately supply more than six floors, so pumps, and tanks on top of the buildings are necessary). In view of this, how can the redwood species described above and the western red cedar grow so tall? The fact that these species grow in humid environments is an essential consideration. The leaves seem to be adapted to condensing water droplets out of the air, facilitating hydration of the upper parts of the plant. (Reference: Limm, E.B., Simonin, K.A., Bothman, A.G., and Dawson, T.E. 2009. Foliar water uptake: a common water acquisition strategy for plants of the redwood forest. Oecologia 161: 449–459.) As fog moves in from the sea, the leaves of the trees also serve to condense moisture out of the air, raining water droplets down to the roots, additionally reducing water stress on the trees. (Reference: Dawson, T.E. 1998. Fog in the California redwood forest: ecosystem inputs and use by plants. Oecologia 117: 476–485.)

Totem poles in Stanley Park, Vancouver, British Columbia. Source: Thinkstock.

Totem poles at Kisegukla, a 1912 painting by Emily Carr (see discussion of her in the legend on the next page); Vancouver Art Gallery. Totem poles last a long time because western red cedar resists decay, but many that Emily Carr saw as on-site relics of a remarkable past culture have now fallen and others have been cut down and sold for museums and public parks. The few surviving ancient poles are compelling art forms that arouse the imagination to thoughts of what it was like in their special places only a few hundred years ago. Fortunately totem poles are not a bygone art form. Some painted by Emily Carr have been re-carved. In 1972 a totem pole was raised at the town of Kispiox at the junction of the Skeena and Kispiox Rivers in northern British Columbia. Two poles outside the Vancouver airport were carved in 1990. Of course this art is dependent on the preservation of declining primeval cedar forests.

Western red cedar (*Thuja plicata*). Source: Thinkstock.

A BIODIVERSITY TREASURE

Emily Carr (1871–1945), at left, was born in Victoria, British Columbia. She travelled widely training as an artist but it was not until 1928 that she gained recognition when Lawren Harris of the Group of Seven said to her, "you are one of us". It appears that her favourite trips were along the coast of British Columbia and her subjects were often sites of abandoned native villages with totem poles, and also scenes of the western forest. Her painting of a western red cedar (at right) has curves and waves characteristic of her style. She was an artist of stunning originality and strength, but was also an accomplished writer receiving the Governor-General's Award for her first book published in 1941. She was one of the first Canadian artists to capture the wild landscape of Canada in an impressionistic style.

SOURCES OF ADDITIONAL INFORMATION

Boyd, R.J. 1965. Western redcedar (*Thuja plicata* Donn). *In* Silvics of forest trees of the United States. *Compiled by* H.A. Fowells. U.S. Department of Agriculture, Agriculture Handbook 271, Washington, D.C. pp. 686–691.

Chambers, K.L. 1993. *Thuja. In* Flora of North America North of Mexico. *Edited by* Flora of North America Editorial Committee. Oxford University press, Oxford, U.K. Vol. 2. pp. 410–411.

Chan-Yeung, M. 1993. Western red cedar and other wood dusts. *In* Asthma in the Workplace. *Edited by* L. Bernstein, M. Chan-Yeung, J. Malo, and D.I. Bernstein. Marcel Dekker, New York, NY. pp. 503–531.

Harlow, B.A., Duursma, R.A., and Marshall, J.D. 2005 Leaf longevity of western red cedar (*Thuja plicata*) increases with depth in the canopy. Tree Physiology 25: 557–562.

Gonzalez, J.S. 2004. Growth, properties and uses of western redcedar (*Thuja plicata* Donn ex D. Don.) Second edition. Forintek Canada Corp., Vancouver, B.C. 42 pp.

Hess W.J. 1993. Western red cedar *Thuja plicata.* Morton Arboretum Quart. 29(4): 56–59.

Krueger, K.W. 1963. Compounds leached from western red cedar shingle tow found toxic to Douglas fir seedlings. Pacific Northwest For. and Range Exp. Sta., Publ. PNW-7. 12 pp.

Lowery, D.P. 1984. Western redcedar. Revised edition. Forest Service, U.S. Dept. of Agriculture, Washington, D.C. 7 pp.

Massie, M.R.C. 1987. Utilization opportunities for western red cedar: a review. Canadian Forestry Service, Victoria, B.C. 23 pp.

Minore, D. 1990. *Thuja plicata. In* Silvics of North America, vol. 1, conifers. *Edited by* R.M. Burns and B.H. Honkala. USDA Forest Service Agric. Handbook 654. Washington, D.C. pp. 590–600.

Nelson, J. Undated. A vanishing heritage: the loss of ancient red cedar from Canada's rainforests. 31 pp. www.davidsuzuki.org/files/Forests/cedarreport2.pdf

O'Connell, L.M., Ritland, K,M., and Thompson, S.L. 2008. Patterns of post-glacial colonization by western redcedar (*Thuja plicata*, Cupressaceae) as revealed by microsatellite markers. Can. J. Bot. 86: 194–203.

Stewart, H. 1984. Cedar: tree of life to the Northwest Coast Indians. Douglas & MacIntyre, Vancouver, B.C. 192 pp.

Vedal, S., Chan-Yeung, M, Enarson, D., Fera, T, Maclean, L., Tse, K.S., and Langille, R. 1986. Symptoms and pulmonary function in western red cedar workers related to duration of employment and dust exposure. Archives Environ. Health 41: 179–183.

Wenny, D.L., and Dumroese, R.K. 1990. A growing regime for container-grown western redcedar seedlings. Station Bulletin of the Idaho Forest, Wildlife and Range Experiment Station. 1990. 8 pp.

Western red cedar (*Thuja plicata*). Source: Nicholson, G. (*Editor*). 1889. The illustrated dictionary of gardening. Vol. 4. L. Upcott Gill, London, U.K.

A BIODIVERSITY TREASURE

Base of a huge western red cedar (*Thuja plicata*) tree. Source: Wikipedia (photographer: J.-P. Grandmont, Creative Commons Attribution-Share Alike 3.0 Unported license).

MANITOBA

Provincial flag of Manitoba.

A MANITOBA LANDSCAPE: American bison grazing in a prairie field.

FLORAL EMBLEM: PRAIRIE CROCUS

Prairie crocus (*Anemone patens*), on a relict grassland at Pelly Crossing in central Yukon. Photo by P.M. Catling.

SYMBOLISM

The prairie crocus is one of the earliest common and showy spring flowers in cool areas of central northwestern North America. It is very hardy, and sometimes the emerging flowers are surrounded by snow. Prairie crocus is regarded as a beautiful but exceptionally tough harbinger of spring and a symbol of compatibility with cold, northern climates.

Prairie crocus (*Anemone patens*), in fruit at left, in flower at right, by Lavonia R. Stockelbach (1874–1966). A collection of her paintings of Canadian provincial and territorial official flowers is associated with the herbarium of Agriculture and Agri-Food Canada in Ottawa.

NAMES

Latin Names

Anemone patens L. var. *multifida* Pritzel

The genus name *Anemone* has been interpreted as being based on the Greek *anemone* (or *amona*), a combination of the Greek roots *mon,* to be red and *damu,* blood. The name is possibly from *Naaman,* a Semitic name for Adonis, whose blood, according to myth, produced red anemones (*A. coronaria;* see Myths, below). An alternative explanation is that the name is from the Greek *anemos,* meaning wind, possibly a reference to the wind-dispersed seeds (equipped with long, feathery styles) or, less likely, to the early blooming of anemones during a windy season. According to the old saying, "March winds and April showers bring forth May flowers", but prairie crocuses often appear during the windy and rainy months of March and April.

The epithet *patens* in the scientific name is Latin for "spreading" or "outspreading". It has been speculated that this refers to the plant's habit of spreading over large areas and/or to the widely spreading petals or seed head.

The name *A. patens* var. *wolfgangiana* is used by some authors but *A. patens* var. *multifida* has priority. The epithet *multifida,* meaning many times divided, refers to the segments of the leaf. The illegitimate synonyms *Pulsatilla hirsutissima* and *P. ludoviciana* are often encountered, and the species is frequently listed as *P. patens* and *P. vulgaris,* and sometimes as *A. pulsatilla.*

English Names

Prairie crocus (prairie-crocus). Also: American pasqueflower, pasque flower (pasqueflower), prairie smoke (prairie-smoke), wind flower. Occasional local names include April fool, bleeding nose plant, crocus anemone, prairie anemone, ears of the earth, blue tulip, gosling, gosling plant, gosling weed, hartshorn plant. The name pasque flower reflects blooming during the Easter (Paschal) season, and pioneers used the mauve sepals ("petals") to dye Easter eggs. "Pasque" is from the Hebrew *paschal,* "relating to Passover", and in the Old World some anemones begin blooming as soon as the mountain snow melts, about the time of the Jewish holiday Passover. It has also been speculated that the word pasque is derived from the French *passer + fleur,* but this seems much less likely. "Crocus" is a misnomer applied by European immigrants to a plant that reminded them of the European crocuses (*Crocus* spp., of the Iridaceae or iris family), some of which bloom early in the spring and have flowers of similar size and colour. The name "wind flower" used for anemone species is probably based on the above explanation that the name *Anenone* is from the Greek *anemos,* wind. "Prairie smoke" is based on the plumed styles of the raised fruiting heads scattering light, creating a hazy, smoke-like appearance. The names "gosling", "gosling plant", and "goslin weed" are based on the furry appearance of the sepals, reminiscent of the downy appearance of goslings. "April fool" is based on the early appearance of the plant, which is sometime so "foolish" as to appear before the snow has melted.

French Names

Pulsatille. Also: anémone, anémone des prairies, anémone pulsatille, crocus des prairies, fleur de Pâques.

Painting of the official flower of Manitoba, prairie crocus (*Anemone patens*), from the Walter Coucill Canadian Centennial official flowers of Canada series (see Coucill 1966 cited in the first chapter of this book). Reproduced with the permission of the copyright holders, the Coucill family.

HISTORY

Canada

The prairie crocus was adopted as the floral emblem of Manitoba in 1906. Interest in the plant had been aroused by the Manitoba Horticultural Society, and by a vote among schoolchildren that put the prairie crocus in first place, the prairie lily second, and the wild rose third.

Foreign

The prairie crocus was adopted as the state flower of South Dakota in 1903. In Häme, a historical province of southern Finland, *A. patens* is considered to be the provincial flower. *Anemone vernalis* is the provincial flower of South Karelia, Finland.

Prairie crocus (*Anemone patens*). National Park Service (Yellowstone), U.S. Department of the Interior (photographer: J.W. Stockert).

APPEARANCE

Prairie crocus is a long-lived perennial herbaceous plant with a thick woody taproot and a woody base. The shoots are 5–40 cm (2–16 inches), sometimes as tall as 60 cm (2 feet), and are hairy. Individual plants may live for more than 50 years, occasional specimens becoming 30 cm (1 foot) across and producing more than 40 blossoms at a time. The basal leaves usually have slightly hairy blades 5–8 cm (2–3 inches) long, with petioles 5–10 cm (2–4 inches) long. The leaves are typically trifoliolate, with each leaflet dichotomously dissected. Flowering occurs in the spring and early summer. The flowers first appear near the ground at the bases of the newly expanding leaves. Usually there are three bracts under the singly-borne flowers, the bracts 2.5–4 cm (1–1.6 inches) long, hairy, and with dissected margins. The flowers are 2.5–10 cm (1–4 inches) across, with 5–8 sepals that are blue, light lavender, blue-purple, purple, or rarely white, 2–4 cm (0.8–1.6 inches) long, and quite wooly-hairy on the outer side. *Anemone patens* is unusual for the genus in having true petals; however, these are inconspicuous, gland-like bodies, resembling stamens, but smaller. The flowers have a central mass of 60–200 yellow stamens, as well as numerous pistils in a head. The flowers transform into heads of small, dry fertilized fruits (achenes or so-called seeds), each of which has a body 3–4(6) mm (about 0.3 inch) long and a curved extension ("beak", actually a persistent feathery style) 2–4 cm (0.8–1.6 inches) long. The peduncle (flower stalk) elongates during fruit development so that, at maturity, the tuft of silky-haired achenes is elevated for effective wind dispersal.

CLASSIFICATION

Family: Ranunculaceae (buttercup family).

The genus *Anemone* has about 150 species of perennial herbs, found nearly world-wide but primarily in cooler and arctic regions. Twenty-five species occur in North America north of Mexico, of which 16 are native to Canada. North American populations of *A. patens* have been assigned to var. *multifida*. At least three additional varieties are found in Eurasia.

Prairie crocus (*Anemone patens*). Source: Canadian Heritage. 2002 (revised edition). Symbols of Canada. Canadian Heritage, Ottawa, ON. Reproduced with permission.

GEOGRAPHY

In Canada, *A. patens* has been recorded in the Yukon, Northwest Territories, British Columbia, Alberta, Saskatchewan, Manitoba, and Ontario. The United States distribution includes Alaska, Colorado, Idaho, Illinois, Iowa, Minnesota, Montana, Nebraska, New Mexico, North Dakota, South Dakota, Utah, Wisconsin, and Wyoming. The species also occurs in Europe and northern Eurasia.

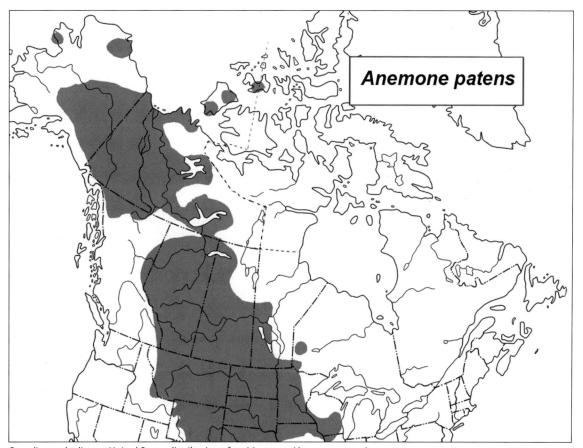

Anemone patens

Canadian and adjacent United States distribution of prairie crocus (*Anemone patens*).

Prairie crocus (*Anemone patens*). National Park Service (Yellowstone), U.S. Department of the Interior (photographer: R.G. Johnsson).

A BIODIVERSITY TREASURE

ECOLOGY

Habitat

Prairie crocus occurs in prairies, on open slopes, glacial moraines, burned-over ground, along railway rights of ways, in overgrazed pastures, and sometimes in open woods and on granite outcrops. The plants prefer well-drained conditions. The species is characteristic of the open, tall grass and mixed grass regions of North American western prairies, often thriving on exposed slopes and in dry, wooded areas. *Anemone patens* is known to grow well in areas that are regularly grazed, burned, or mowed.

Inter-species Relationships

Prairie crocus appears to thrive in overgrazed pasture lands, possibly because its toxic qualities discourage most herbivores. Moreover, the ground-level positioning of the crown of the plant with its vegetative and floral buds, and the frequent low position of the leaves, are considered to be adaptations making it difficult for grazers to damage the plants significantly. Nevertheless the species is consumed by some wildlife, including turkeys, rabbits, squirrels, deer, and elk, often because little else is available early in the season. For the same reason, floral-visiting insects often depend on the prairie crocus. Trampling by natural prairie grazers, such as the once-common buffalo, stimulates the development of deep-seated adventitious buds causing the production of small rosettes near the parent plant, and so encourages vegetative propagation.

Pollination and Dispersal

The prairie crocus is one of the earliest plants to bloom, this often occurring before the last winter snow has melted. Such early blooming is an adaptation to take advantage of available pollinators—bees (mostly smaller bees of the genus *Andrena*) and other insects. While the plants are self-fertile to some degree, they are primarily outcrossing. With early pollination the seeds may ripen by early summer, and if moisture is available they can germinate immediately. If the habitat becomes too dry, the seeds will become dormant, germinating during the following spring. Most other plants avoid such early flowering because occasional severe frosts (-10 to -5 °C or 14 to 23 °F) may destroy the season's seed crop.

Prairie crocus achenes ("seeds") are wind-distributed, the elongation of the flower stem after pollination being a mechanism to raise the achenes above the level of other plants in grazed grasslands, to expose them to the wind. However, distribution by wind is frequently not effective, as the achenes in a head often become entangled and some of the achenes are deposited close to the parental plants. It has been claimed that the achenes are self-planting, although this is disputed. Some have suggested that the long plume is "differentially hydrophyllic", composed of strands that imbibe water at different rates, so that when the tail gets wet or dries out, it twists, like a drill. The seeds are shaped like spears and are covered with backward pointing hairs, so that when twisted they drill into the earth. In addition to wind distribution, animals may also disperse the seeds through adhesion to wet fur, but this has not been well documented.

USES

The chief modern use of prairie crocus is as a garden ornamental, as detailed below. In the past, North American Indians used leaf poultices of the plant to treat rheumatism and neuralgia (but see Toxicity, below; although producing serious blisters, the resulting irritation may have functioned medicinally as a counter-irritant). The smell of crushed leaves was thought to cure headaches, and decoctions of the roots were employed for lung problems. Prairie crocus was listed in the U.S. Pharmacopaeia from 1882 to 1905 as a diuretic, expectorant, and uterine stimulant.

Prairie crocus (*Anemone patens*) in Botanical Garden, Hungarian Academy of Sciences. Source: Wikipedia (photographer: Pipi; released into the public domain).

TOXICITY

Handling the fresh plants can produce skin rash (contact dermatitis). A particularly severe reaction occurred when a 77-year-old woman treated her osteoarthritis of the knees with a compress of prairie crocus, resulting in an extreme dermatitis. About one hour after applying the compresses to her knees she developed a strong burning sensation, reddening and swelling, and the entire area of the knees became covered with large blisters. Open wounds were treated with saline compresses and steroid antibiotic ointment. Healing was gradual and required 14 days.

The vapours from the fresh juice of the plant can cause eye inflammation. Eating fresh material can produce irritation of the mouth, vomiting, and diarrhea. The toxicity is due to an acrid oil called protoanemonin, the result of an enzymatic breakdown product of the glycoside ranunculin, found in many species of *Anemone*. The oil in fresh leaves can cause severe topical (external) and gastrointestinal irritation (including acute inflammation of the gastric tract and kidneys, cramps, unconsciousness, and even death through respiratory failure), but is unstable and changes into harmless anemonin when plants are dried. In Russia, extracts were once used to poison arrow tips. There have been reports that the plant can cause mechanical blockages in the digestive tracts of sheep.

CULTIVATION

The prairie crocus is an excellent plant for sunny, perennial borders and rock gardens. Since the plants are toxic (see above), it is inadvisable to plant them in areas frequented by small children. The species should not be dug up from the wild, as it does not transplant well, and is an important component of biodiversity which supports other species. Garden-grown plants can be moved in late summer, preferably with a large clump of surrounding earth. Large clumps can be divided in late summer or early fall. Seeds can be collected from wild plants in late spring or early summer, but only small amounts should be taken to avoid reducing the natural capacity for propagation. Both plants and seeds can be purchased from various sources. Fresh seeds can be planted outdoors, or they can be stored in a cool place for planting in the following spring. If the seeds are allowed to dry out for a week or two they will become dormant, requiring stratification (several weeks of exposure to cool moist conditions) before they can germinate. Seedlings can be established by sowing seeds in a mixture of sand and peat moss as soon as they are ripe, and then transplanting to a protected location. Prairie crocuses grow best in sandy, well-drained soils in sunny locations. Seeds should be covered with about 1 cm (0.4 inch) of soil, and the soil packed down firmly, and watered regularly during dry spells. Established plants should not be watered during the summer unless the soil becomes very dry. The seeds are slow to germinate and the plants are slow growing. Flowering may occur at the start of the third growth season, but usually four to five years are required for a good floral display.

SOLAR HEATING IN FLOWERS

Saucer-shaped flowers often occur in plants of cool or cold regions, or in plants that develop at the coldest time of the year. Such flowers can function as solar heat collectors, much like parabolic dishes. In the case of the prairie crocus, highly-reflective sepals concentrate the heat in the centre of the flowers, where stamens and pistils are warmed, promoting fertilization and seed development. On a sunny day the temperature inside a prairie crocus flower can be as much as 10 °C (18 °F) warmer than the temperature of the surrounding air. In addition to the flowers concentrating the sun's warmth, the flowers of prairie crocus typically move to face the sun as it travels across the sky (a phenomenon called heliotropism or phototropism), such solar tracking maximizing the daily exposure to heat. Moreover, the flowers tend to close up at night. The warmth at the central part of the flower not only aids the development of pollen and seeds, but may also help insects survive and reproduce in cold climates, by providing warming stations on cool days. In arctic regions, such heat-accumulating flowers are adapted to a very short season; in cold-temperate regions, heat-accumulating flowers are an adaptation to reproducing sexually in the early spring, before other plants can attract available pollinators, and indeed before taller-growing, surrounding plants compete for light.

CONSERVATION STATUS

Both in North America and in Eurasia, there has been widespread reduction in populations of prairie crocus due to urbanization, agricultural activities, and decline of natural ecological processes, such as fire and grazing, that maintain the required habitat. In Manitoba and elsewhere in the Prairie Provinces, the plant has become significantly less common. A recent study has documented a gradual decline of prairie crocus due to invasion of alien grasses, particularly smooth brome (*Bromus inermis*). This may be an increasingly important threat to prairie crocus in North America. In much of Europe, the species is protected.

A SURVIVOR OF GLACIATION

Prairie crocus occurs on the relicts of tundra and grassland that dominated much of the unglaciated area called Beringia, which included parts of Yukon, the Northwest Territories, and Alaska. This region was dominated by steppe-tundra and prairie and had mammoths, horses, buffalo, antelope and two kinds of lions during a time more than 12,000 years ago when the rest of Canada was under mile-deep ice of the continental Wisconsin and Cordilleran glaciers. Prairie crocus probably survived glaciation in regions south of the ice front as well as in Beringia, and colonized the prairie region of central Canada as the glaciers receded about 10,000 years ago.

MYTHS, LEGENDS, TALES, FOLKLORE AND INTERESTING FACTS

❧ An all-steel, one-ton monument to the prairie crocus, fabricated by a local welder in 2000, is a chief attraction of Arden, in southern Manitoba (population ca. 150). The plants are 2.7 m (9 feet) tall and each of the three flowers is about 1.5 m (5 feet) wide. The monument stands on a municipally designated heritage area where there are numerous prairie crocuses. The village calls itself "the Crocus Capital of Manitoba" and holds an annual Crocus Festival (see http://www.ardenmb.ca/gallery.htm).

❧ According to Greek mythology, the handsome, young Adonis, while hunting, was stabbed by the tusks of a fierce boar. The goddess Aphrodite heard the cries of her lover and arrived to see him bleeding to death. Anemones sprang from the earth where the drops of his blood fell (or, alternatively, from Aphrodite's tears). One version of the story holds that anemones were white before the death of Adonis, whose blood turned them red. Christians later adopted red-flowered anemones as symbolic of the blood shed by Jesus Christ on the cross, and anemones sometimes appear in paintings of the Crucifixion.

❧ The Bible passage Matthew 6: 28–30 states "And why take ye thought for raiment? Consider the lilies of the field, how they grow; they toil not, nether do they spin: And yet I say unto you, That even Solomon in all his glory was not arrayed like one of these." Most authorities now regard the "lily of the fields" as the Palestine anemone, *A. coronaria*. (For more information, see: Moldenke, H.N., and Moldenke, A.L. 1952. Plants of the bible. The Ronald Press, New York, NY.)

❧ The Lakota Indian name for the prairie crocus is *hosi' cekpa*, translating as "child's navel", rather descriptive of the plump flower buds that look like a newborn's navel before it heals.

❧ The "Victorian language of flowers" was a secret coded language in Victorian times in England, with flowers and plants symbolic of certain messages, so when the flower or plant was mentioned in a letter those who knew the code could understand the hidden information. "Anemone" had the meanings sincerity, expectation, forsaken, and daintiness.

Prairie crocus monument in Arden, Manitoba, photographed February 18, 2006 by John Dietz, and reproduced with his permission.

SOURCES OF ADDITIONAL INFORMATION

Aaron, T.H., and Muttitt, E.L. 1964. Vesicant dermatitis due to prairie crocus (*Anemone patens* L.). Arch. Dermatol. 90: 168–171.

Bock, J.H., and Peterson, S.J. 1975. Reproductive biology of *Pulsatilla patens* (Ranunculaceae). Amer. Midl. Nat. 94: 476–478.

Dutton, B.E., Keener, C.S., and Ford, B.A 1997. *Anemone. In* Flora of North America North of Mexico. *Edited by* Flora of North America Editorial Committee. Oxford University press, Oxford, U.K. Vol. 3. pp. 139–158.

Kalliovirta1, M., Ryttäri,T., and Heikkinen, R.K. 2006. Population structure of a threatened plant, *Pulsatilla patens,* in boreal forests: modelling relationships to overgrowth and site closure. Biodiversity and Conservation 15: 3095–3108.

Lindell, T. 1998. Breeding systems and crossing experiments in *Anemone patens* and in the *Anemome pulsatilla* group (Ranunculaceae). Nordic J. Bot. 18: 549–561.

Ordway, E. 1986. The phenology and pollination biology of *Anemone patens* (Ranunculaceae) in western Minnesota. *In* The prairie: past, present, and future. Proceedings of the Ninth North American Prairie Conference, Moorhead, Minnesota, 1986. *Edited by* G.K. Clamby and R.H. Pemble. Tri-College University Center for Environmental Studies, Fargo, ND. pp. 31–34.

Röder, D., and Kiehl, K. 2006. Population structure and population dynamic of *Pulsatilla patens* (L.) Mill. in relation to vegetation characteristics. Flora 201: 499–507.

Wells, T.C.E. 1968. Land-use changes affecting *Pulsatilla vulgaris* in England. Biological Conservation 1: 37–43.

Wells, T.C.E., and Barling, D.M. 1971. Biological flora of the British Isles. *Pulsatilla vulgaris* Mill. (*Anemone pulsatilla* L.). J. Ecol. 59: 275–292.

Wildeman, A.G., and Steeves, T.A. 1982. The morphology and growth cycle of *Anemone patens.* Can. J. Bot. 60: 1126–1137.

Williams, J.F., and Crone, E.E. 2006. The impact of invasive grasses on the population growth of *Anemone patens,* a long-lived native forb. Ecology 87: 3200–3208.

Prairie crocus (*Anemone patens*) in New Mexico. Source: Wikipedia (photographer: J. Friedman; Creative Commons Attribution-Share Alike 3.0 Unported license).

A BIODIVERSITY TREASURE

Prairie crocus (*Anemone patens*) in Poland. Source: Wikipedia (photographer: J. Strzelecki; Creative Commons Attribution-Share Alike 3.0 Unported license).

TREE: WHITE SPRUCE

White spruce (*Picea glauca*) at Haines Junction, Yukon. Source: Wikimedia (photographer: I. Erskine-Kellie; Creative Commons 2.0 license).

SYMBOLISM

The white spruce is an appropriate choice as the arboreal emblem of Manitoba because of its extensive use by both early and modern societies of the province, by its aesthetically pleasing, distinctive appearance, its high economic value, and its occurrence throughout most of Manitoba. The tree is indeed symbolic of the valuable natural resources and cultural diversity of the province. The white spruce is also one of the hardiest of trees, capable of growing north to the limit of trees.

Coat of arms of Manitoba. The beaver at the top holds the provincial floral emblem, the prairie crocus. At the centre, seven prairie crocuses are symbolic of the diverse origins of the people of the province. At bottom right is a forest composed of the provincial tree, the white spruce.

NAMES

Latin Names
Picea glauca (Moench) Voss

The genus name *Picea* is based on the Latin word *pix* used for some species of pine, spruce, and fir, and also for the "pitch" (resin) of such trees. *Glauca* in the scientific name is a Latin word for glaucous (based on the Greek *glaukos,* meaning bright, sparkling, gleaming, grayish, bluish-green) and is a reference to the glaucous foliage, i.e., the bluish-green tint of the needles due to a whitish, waxy, covering layer.

English Names
White spruce. Also: Canada spruce, Canadian spruce, cat spruce, pasture spruce, skunk spruce, single spruce. For information on the derivation of the word "spruce", see the chapter dealing with the floral emblems of Newfoundland and Labrador. The names "cat spruce" and "skunk spruce" are based on the disagreeable odour produced by the needles when they are crushed. The name "pasture spruce" reflects recent establishment in pastures in eastern Canada. The obsolete name "single spruce" contrasts this species with the "double spruce", *P. mariana* (but why either species once had these names is obscure). See Classification, below, for information on the names Black Hills spruce, Porsild spruce, western white spruce, Alberta spruce, and Alberta white spruce. [For additional but obsolete or rare English and French names, see Plantes Vasculaires du Nouveau-Brunswick—Vascular Plants of New Brunswick http://www.cuslm.ca/foresterie/plantenb/pterigymnosyn.pdf]

French Names
Épinette blanche. Also épicéa glauque, épinette du Canada, épinette glauque, épinette grise, prusse blanche, sapinette blanche.

HISTORY

Canada
The white spruce was designated the provincial tree of Manitoba in 1991. The red spruce (*P. rubens*) was declared to be the provincial tree of Nova Scotia in 1988, and The black spruce (*P. mariana*) was made the provincial tree of Newfoundland and Labrador in 1991.

Foreign
Since 1947, the state tree of South Dakota has been the Black Hills variety of white spruce (the Black Hills are in South Dakota). The blue spruce (*P. pungens*) was made the state tree of Utah in 1933. Under the name Colorado blue spruce, it was proclaimed the state tree of Colorado in 1939. Alaska declared its state tree to be the Sitka spruce (*P. sitchensis*) in 1962. The Serbian spruce (*P. omorika*) is one of the national trees of Serbia (the "oak" is the other national tree).

APPEARANCE

Spruce species are evergreen, coniferous (cone-bearing) shrubs and trees with short (generally less than 2.5 cm or 1 inch), stiff, needle-like leaves with pointed but not dangerously sharp tips. White spruce often grows up to 25 m (82 feet), sometimes to 50 m (164 feet) in height, and the trunk diameter at breast height may be as large as 1 m (39 inches). It produces a crown that is broadly conic to spire-like, although near the treeline the plants may be reduced to shrubs (often called "krummholz"). Open-grown trees develop a pyramidal crown that extends nearly to the ground, making the tree attractive as an ornamental. The bark is thin, light grayish-brown, and produced in irregular, thin, scaly plates. The branches droop slightly. The needles occur singly on all sides of the twig, but are often crowded on the upper side; they are usually 1.5–2 cm (about 0.5–1 inch) long, blue-green, 4-angled, often inwardly curved, and sharp-pointed. Trees produce both male and female cones. The seed cones are light brown at maturity, usually 2.5–8 cm (1–3 inches) long, ellipsoid-cylindrical, and pendent, with scales that are thin, flexible, and rounded.

White spruce commonly grows from 100 to 250 years of age if protected from fire (stands older than 200 years are rare because of fire in the mostly drier habitats where they occur). As with other conifers, trees in stressful sites (at the extreme north of their range, or at elevational treelines) can become quite old, and specimens 500–1,000 years old have been reported.

Seed cones of white spruce (*Picea glauca*). Source: Wikimedia (Photographer: Chefranden; Creative Commons 2.0 license).

BURLS

"Burls" are rounded, often tumour-like growths on the sides of branches or trees, and may be caused in a variety of ways. They are valued by woodworkers for making bowls. Burls sometimes occur in specific circumstances. An example of this is white spruce on the seashore cliffs of Mount Desert Island, Maine, where the trees in a narrow coastal belt have numerous burls unlike the trees inland. A similar, remarkably high incidence of burls within and among white spruce trees occurs in parts of coastal New Brunswick and Cape Breton. This has been attributed to a number of factors, including seashore salt spray. One of the largest burls in the world was cut from the base of a 351-year-old Sitka spruce in 1976 at Port McNeill on northern Vancouver Island, British Columbia. This burl was 6 m (20 feet) in diameter and was estimated to weigh 30 tons.

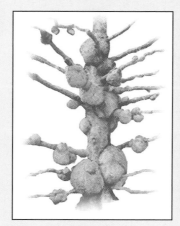

Numerous burls on a white spruce tree on a small island beside Mount Desert Island, Maine. Based on a photo in: White, P.R. and Millington, W.F. 1954. The distribution and possible importance of a woody tumor on trees of the white spruce, *Picea glauca*. Cancer Research 14: 128–134.

5 mm

Winged seed of white spruce (*Picea glauca*). Photo by S. Hurst, U.S. Department of Agriculture.

CLASSIFICATION

Family: Pinaceae (pine family).

There are about 35 species of *Picea*, including seven that are native to North America north of Mexico, five of which are native to Canada.

White spruce is notably variable throughout its range, and several varieties have been recognized taxonomically, including the following. Western white spruce (also sometimes called Alberta spruce and Alberta white spruce) refers to var. albertiana (S. Brown) Sargent of the Canadian Rocky Mountains. Porsild spruce refers to var. *porsildii* Raup of Alaska. Black Hills spruce refers to var. densata Bailey of the Black Hills of South Dakota and adjacent Wyoming. These variations are not clearly separated, and may be the result of environmental modification or hybridization with other species. Many taxonomists today do not recognize these varieties.

White spruce and Engelmann spruce (*P. engelmannii* Parry ex Engelmann) hybridize and intergrade where they occur together (such hybrids are often called *P. glauca* var. *albertiana*). Hybrids occur from central British Columbia south to Washington and Yellowstone National Park. In this area, white spruce is common at low elevations, Engelmann spruce at high elevations, and the hybrids at intermediate locations. White spruce also hybridizes with Sitka spruce and black spruce. Hybrids with Sitka spruce occur where the two species are sympatric in northeastern British Columbia and southwestern Alaska. Hybrids between white spruce and black spruce are relatively rare.

In eastern Canada, white spruce is easily separated from the other two native eastern spruce species, the black and red, by its elongated cones and flexible cone scales; also, white spruce twigs lack hairs whereas the twigs of red and black spruce are covered with hairs. In western Canada, white spruce is found with Sitka spruce, which has longer cones, more elongate and pointed cone scales, and much flatter needles. The non-native Norway spruce (*P. abies*) is commonly planted in Canada, and sometimes escapes from cultivation to natural areas; it has cones that are much larger and longer than those of white spruce.

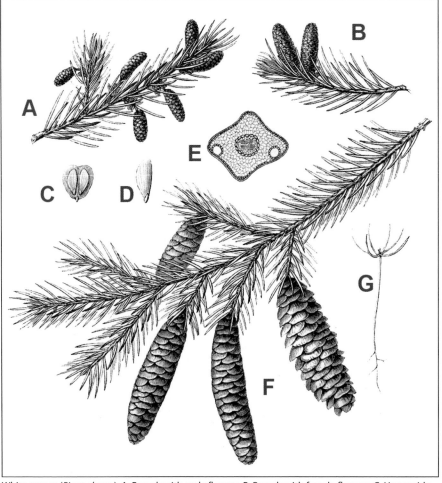

White spruce (*Picea glauca*). A, Branch with male flowers. B, Branch with female flowers. C, Upper side of a cone scale with seeds. D, Seed with attached wing. E, Cross section of a leaf. F, Fruiting branch. G, Seedling. Source: Sargent, C.S. 1898. The silva of North America. Houghton, Mifflin and Company, Boston, MA. Vol. 12, plate 598.

GEOGRAPHY

Picea glauca has a transcontinental distribution in North America, occurring from Alaska, Yukon, and British Columbia continuously eastward to Newfoundland and the northeastern United States, and sporadically in northern tier states (Montana, Wyoming, South Dakota, Minnesota, Wisconsin, and Michigan). The northern limit approximates the isotherm line of average 10 °C in July, and may form the limit of trees. (For more on treeline, see the chapters on the symbols of Newfoundland and Labrador, and Nunavut.) The southern limit corresponds to the average 18 °C July line, but there are many other factors. For example, the southern limit swings north of the 18 °C line in the prairie region due to severe, periodic drought.

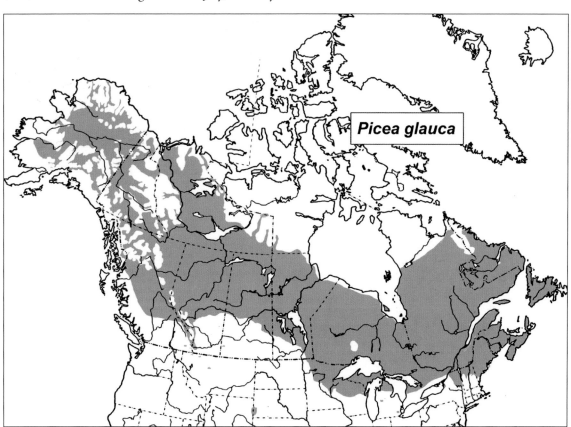

North American distribution of white spruce (*Picea glauca*).

Black Hills variety of white spruce (*Picea glauca* var. *densata*). Source: Herman, D.E. et al. 1996. North Dakota tree handbook (public domain photo).

A BIODIVERSITY TREASURE

ECOLOGY

White spruce is a dominant tree of interior boreal forests of Canada and Alaska, often occurring as an early colonizer. In British Columbia and Alberta, the species is often found on foothills and mountains ranging up to 1,500 m (5,000 feet) in altitude. In northeastern Alberta, there are open, parklike white spruce forests. In the west, white spruce is most common along rivers and lake shores. In eastern Canada and the northeastern United states, the species often occurs in coniferous and mixed coniferous-hardwood forests. In parts of eastern Canada, particularly Quebec (e.g., coastal portions of James Bay and Hudson Bay, and the Gulf of St. Lawrence), white spruce occurs in regions near treeline where fog occurs frequently (but may be replaced further inland by black spruce).

Habitat

White spruce is usually in drier sites, including well-drained upland, river terraces, and montane slopes, but it may also be found on floodplains, river banks, and in muskegs and bogs. The trees grow well on a wide variety of somewhat acidic or basic substrates, including gravel, sand, loam, silt, and clay. White spruce grows less well on sites with high water tables and/or permafrost. A permafrost lens often develops beneath a spruce tree in the north as a result of both the insulating effect of the thickened moss layer beneath trees in summer, and soil cooling in the winter due to a thinner insulating layer of snow beneath trees. Disturbance to the moss layer may result in melting of this lens, resulting in a space under the tree, which can lead to tipping over. The species is considered intermediate in shade tolerance. The seedlings are capable of germinating and growing well in the shade of spruce forests, but growth is best at full light intensity. The white spruce is quite susceptible to fire, but may rapidly colonize burned sites from seeds from unburned patches, partially burned trees, and edges of burned landscape.

Inter-species Relationships

Animals: White spruce is a significant but generally not a preferred food source for most wildlife. The spruce grouse feeds entirely on spruce needles in the winter. The seeds are consumed by chickadees, nuthatches, white-winged crossbills, pine siskins, and many other birds, as well as small mammals such as deer mice, red-backed and meadow voles, and chipmunks. Red squirrels feed on the buds in the spring, and also consume the seeds. Snowshoe hares eat the needles, bark, twigs, and seedlings. Porcupines frequently eat the bark of young trees. Black bears are said to strip the bark to consume the sweet sapwood. The tree is also useful for wildlife as cover, especially as winter shelter for caribou.

Defoliation by the spruce budworm and the western spruce budworm may kill the trees if infestations continue for 2 or more years. Many other insects including gall flies, moths, and beetles feed particularly on white spruce. Spruce spider mites (*Oligonychus* spp.) may build up in large numbers

Red squirrel consuming white spruce seeds. The squirrel has an ear tag and an aerial (visible near the tail) for tracking purposes. Photo courtesy of Sebastien Descamps.

COMPETITION BETWEEN WHITE SPRUCE AND RED SQUIRRELS

Red squirrels (*Tamiasciurus hudsonicus*) in the southwest Yukon feed almost exclusively on the seeds of white spruce. Many tree species, including the white spruce, produce an extremely abundant crop of seeds once every few years, with limited crops in the intervening years. Good production years ("mast years") in white spruce may be 2–12 years apart. This is an advantage to the trees since herbivores are reduced in number during times of limited seed production, and thus unable to consume as many seeds during times of abundant seed production. Very curiously, red squirrels are somehow able to predict years when a bountiful crop is about to occur and the rodents produce a second litter to take advantage of the abundance of food about to arrive. [For additional information see: Boutin, S., Wauters, L.A., McAdam, A.G., Humphries, M.M., Tosi, G., and Dhondt, A.A. 2006. Anticipatory reproduction and population growth in seed predators. Science 314(5807): 1928–1930. Also see http://www.expressnews.ualberta.ca/article.cfm?id=8109.]

ECOLOGY (CONT'D)

during early spring and summer and are sometimes pests of young spruce trees in greenhouses.

Fungi: A number of fungi affect white spruce. One of these, *Ionotus tomentosus,* is a major cause of death of patches of white spruce over areas of up to 0.4 ha (1 acre) in parts of Saskatchewan. The infection is called "stand-opening disease" and is less common on alkaline soils.

Other plants: Black and white spruce co-occur over a wide range, and are natural competitors. White spruce outcompetes black spruce on well-drained mineral soils with deep or no permafrost, while black spruce is more tolerant of sites with permafrost, flooding, and high soil acidity. The dwarf mistletoe (*Arceuthobium pusillum*) is more often parasitic on black spruce and often does not kill trees, but it has been reported to kill white spruce in the Canadian Maritime Provinces. (For more on mistletoe, see the chapter on the symbols of Newfoundland and Labrador.) White spruce is known to be allelopathic, i.e., chemicals leach from the tree and suppress the growth of some understory species.

Pollination and Dispersal

Pollen is shed and distributed by wind in the spring and early summer (May to July, depending on location). Although seed can be produced by trees as early as 4 years of age, most seed production is by trees 30 or more years old. The cones ripen in August or September, and open to release the winged seeds, which are mostly dispersed by wind (some by animals, especially squirrels). The seeds remain viable for only 1 or 2 years. Most seeds fall close to the parent plant, rarely reaching more than 100 m (328 feet) away. Seeds sometimes travel much longer distances over crusted snow. Following seed dispersal, the old cones may fall off, or remain on the trees for one or two years. At the northern treeline, viable seeds are usually not produced, and reproduction is almost exclusively by layering (branches contacting the soil and growing into new shoots).

THE BEETLES ARE COMING

Increasing pests due to accidental introduction or to other factors such as climate warming are a major developing problem. In the western Yukon, the spruce beetle (*Dendroctonus rufipennis*) has developed into a major, continuous infestation as a result of climate warming and the affected area of over 350,000 ha (865,000 acres) of grey and dying forest is now the most extensive spruce beetle outbreak ever recorded in Canada. On the other side of Canada there is concern that the introduced brown spruce longhorn beetle (*Tetropium fuscum*) will advance into a stage of exponential expansion and affect spruce across the country within the next decade or two. It is believed to have arrived in Point Pleasant Park in Halifax in the 1990s in wood packing material. Substantial effort to eradicate it failed, and since it has recently spread to central Nova Scotia, the primary goal has shifted from eradication to control and containment.

Most of the insects that feed on the economically important white spruce are considered to be pests, but not all of them are common enough to do serious damage. The boreal spruce beetle (*Dendroctonus punctata*) is very similar to the spruce beetle but is much less common and less well known.

Garbutt, R., Hawkes, B., and Allen, E. 2006. Spruce beetle and the forests of southwest Yukon. Canadian Forest Service, Pacific Forestry Centre, Victoria, BC. 68 pp. http://dsp-psd.pwgsc.gc.ca/collection_2007/nrcan-rncan/Fo143-2-406E.pdf

Smith, G., and Hurley, J.E. 2000. First North American record of the Palearctic species *Tetropium fuscum* (Fabricius) (Coleoptera: Cerambycidae). Coleopterists' Bull. 54: 540. For additional information on *T. fuscum* see www.inspection.gc.ca/english/plaveg/pestrava/tetfus/bslbqueste.shtml.

The boreal spruce beetle (*Dendroctonus punctatus*). This specimen, in the E.H. Strickland Entomological Museum, University of Alberta, was collected at Aklavik on the MacKenzie River, Northwest Territories on September 5, 1930. Photograph by D. Jensen, used with permission of the E.H. Strickland Museum.

USES

The principal economic value of spruce is in its use as a softwood for construction lumber, plywood, and paper pulp. White spruce constitutes a quarter of Canada's softwood stock. The wood is also used for furniture, cabinets, boxes, crates, paletes, musical instruments (especially for pianos, guitars, and violins, and as organ pipes, because of its superb

Open-grown, young spruce tree, showing attractive, ornamental appearance. Source: Harter, J. (*Editor*). 1988. The plant kingdom compendium. Bonanza Books, New York, NY. 374 pp.

resonance and capacity to transmit vibrations), food containers (the wood has no distinctive odour or taste and does not contaminate food with resin), and paddles. Historically, the tree was important to Native Peoples, who used it for food, shelter, medicine, and fuel. Boughs were used for bedding, the wood for canoe frames and paddles, bark as roofing material, and leaf extracts as medicines. The tough, pliable roots were employed as rope, lace for birchbark canoes, and to make woven baskets. Spruce trees are often used as Christmas trees, and the white spruce is suited for this, with excellent foliage colour, short, stiff needles that are retained well (but not as well as some other trees), and a good natural shape. (For more on Christmas trees, see the chapter on the symbols of New Brunswick.) The tree also is useful for stabilizing soil, establishing shelterbelts, revegetating mine spoils, and promoting recreation.

Spruce trees are used as ornamental and shade trees, sometimes as hedges, and there are more than 30 cultivars. The cultivar 'Conica' (called dwarf Alberta spruce or dwarf white spruce) is thought to be the best known and most widely sold dwarf conifer sold in the United States.

TOXICITY

White spruce is not considered to be a toxic species. In times of famine, native peoples sometimes ate the young sapwood and young cones, or prepared beverages using the foliage; it is not clear whether such consumption is risky, and in any event the limited palatability of white spruce reduces the likelihood of significant human consumption.

CULTIVATION

White spruce is frequently planted for forestry purposes, and extensive information is available in this regard. For horticultural purposes, most propagation is by seed, although layering and grafting have also been employed, especially with rarer cultivars. For ornamental purposes, the tree is best planted in a moist, well-drained soil in full sun, but it will withstand poorer soils and light shade. The tree transplants well from containers or when ball-and-burlapped, but digging up and moving field-grown or wild trees is much less successful. Cultivars differ in their susceptibility to insects, disease, heat, drought, and winter desiccation.

CONSERVATION STATUS

In Canada, white spruce is a widespread and locally abundant tree that seems unlikely to be in danger of population decline that would threaten its future survival. However, as a result of expanding insect pests in some parts of Canada, vast white spruce forests are being destroyed and more widespread loss of mature forests is a possibility in the near future. Because white spruce is a critical forestry species, there are collections of seeds preserved for breeding purposes, and recommendations that some stands should be protected as potential genetic resources.

MYTHS, LEGENDS, TALES, FOLKLORE AND INTERESTING FACTS

✤ Canada is the world's largest exporter of forest products, amounting to tens of billions of dollars annually. The United States is Canada's major customer. The forest sector directly employs hundreds of thousands of people, and hundreds of communities depend on forestry. More than half of the industry is located in British Columbia, followed by Ontario, Alberta, Quebec, New Brunswick, and Saskatchewan.

✤ Girls of the Koyukon Indians of North America placed branches of black spruce and white spruce on the tracks of animals before crossing them. Like crossing the path of a black cat, without this ceremony hunters of the tribe who were pursuing the animals would have had bad luck. The Koyukon also believed that sleeping beneath white spruce trees provided protection from evil spirits, and that the branches could be used as good luck charms, especially if they had golden needles. To cure the sick, Koyukon shamans brushed them with the tops of black spruce trees and ceremoniously burned the pitch of white spruce.

✤ An old wives' tale that has survived down to modern times in Nova Scotia holds that carrying a small chunk of wood from a white spruce tree will prevent rheumatism, arthritis, and leg cramps.

✤ On December 17, 1903, at Kitty Hawk, North Carolina, the 1903 Wright brothers "Flyer" became the first powered, heavier-than-air machine to achieve controlled, sustained flight with a pilot aboard. The airplane was constructed of spruce and ash covered with muslin. The spruce has been identified as "giant spruce", a name for Sitka spruce, a west-coast species, and presumably lumber was transported to North Carolina.

✤ The "Spruce Goose" was not made of spruce. Billionaire Howard Hughes (1905–1976) holds the record for flying what to this day is the largest aircraft, in terms of wingspan, ever to take flight. His plane has a wing span of 97 m (320 feet), a tail fin height of 24 m (80 feet), and a gross weight of 181 tonnes (200 tons), and was intended to carry up to 750 fully equipped troops, or two Sherman class tanks (a total maximum payload of 59 tonnes or 65 tons). The plane was three times larger than any other aircraft built to that time. The "Flying Boat" as it was known made only one flight, on November 2, 1947, lifting 10 m (33 feet) off the surface of Los Angeles Harbour, and flying about a mile in about a minute. The project was intended to save metal by building a wood plane during the Second World War, but the war ended so that the original purpose was no longer relevant. When it was completed in 1947, the U.S. government had spent $22 million (huge by the standards of the day), and Hughes had spent $18 million of his own money. A disgruntled U.S. Senator dubbed the plane the "flying lumberyard", which led to the nickname "The Spruce Goose". However, the giant airplane was constructed of birch, not spruce. The plane is now at the Evergreen Aviation Educational Center in McMinville, Oregon.

✤ In 2008, it was reported that "the world's oldest tree" is a Norway spruce (*P. abies* (L.) Karst), discovered in 2004 growing at 900 m (3,000 feet) in Dalarna Province, Sweden. However, the trunk of this tree was found to have a lifespan of only about 600 years, a new trunk emerging from the root stock whenever the old trunk dies. Ancient remnants of the roots of the tree were radiocarbon dated at 9,550 years, which indicates that the plant started growing not long after ice sheets retreated from Sweden after the last glaciation, 11,000 years ago. However, it has been pointed out that it is not quite fair to compare plants that reproduce clonally from basal portions, as is the case above, with individual, whole plants, with persistent above-ground parts. The "oldest tree" in the latter sense is a bristlecone pine dated at about 5,000 years. For a comparison of the world's oldest trees (separately treating individual plants and clonally reproducing plants), see http://en.wikipedia.org/wiki/List_of_oldest_trees. The oldest authoritatively dated spruce was an Engelmann spruce from Colorado that was felled about 1994, and was found to be 852 years old.

Silhouette of white spruce (*Picea glauca*). Source: Farrar, J.L. 1995. Trees in Canada. Canadian Forest Service and Fitzhenry and Whiteside, Markham, ON, Canada. Reproduced with permission.

SOURCES OF ADDITIONAL INFORMATION

(Also see the literature cited for black spruce in the chapter on the symbols of Newfoundland and Labrador; and for red spruce in the chapter on the symbols of Nova Scotia.)

Daubenmire, R. 1974. Taxonomic and ecologic relationships between *Picea glauca* and *Picea engelmannii*. Can. J. Bot. 52: 1545–1560.

LaRoi, G.H., and Dugle, J.R. 1968. A systematic and genecological study of *Picea glauca* and *P. engelmannii*, using paper chromatography of needle extracts. Can. J. Bot. 46: 649–687.

Little, E.L., Jr., and Pauley, S.S. 1958. A natural hybrid between black and white spruce in Minnesota. Am. Midl. Nat. 60: 202–211.

Nienstaedt, H., and Zasada, J.C. 1990. *Picea glauca. In* Silvics of North America. Vol. 1. Conifers. *Edited by* R.M. Burns and B.H. Honkala. USDA Forest Service, Agric. Handbook 654. Washington, D.C. pp. 204–226.

Taylor, R.J. 1993. *Picea. In* Flora of North America North of Mexico. *Edited by* Flora of North America Editorial Committee. Oxford University press, Oxford, U.K. Vol. 2. pp. 369–373.

Website: The U.S. Silvics Manual website provides a great deal of useful and authoritative information on this species. http://www.na.fs.fed.us/spfo/pubs/silvics_manual/Volume_1/picea/glauca.htm.

White spruce (*Picea glauca*) in winter. Source: Thinkstock.

NEW BRUNSWICK

Provincial flag of New Brunswick.

A NEW BRUNSWICK LANDSCAPE: mixed forest in the autumn along a fast, rocky stream.

FLORAL EMBLEM: PURPLE VIOLET (MARSH BLUE VIOLET)

Purple violet (*Viola cucullata*), in West Cape, Prince Edward Island. Courtesy of S. Blaney.

SYMBOLISM

With the violet as the official provincial flower, New Brunswick has become associated with the finest of human sentiments. The violet is a prevailing symbol of love. The symbolism of violet flowers includes: blue = faithfulness, fidelity, and love; white = purity of sentiment; small white = candour and innocence; sweet violet (*V. odorata*) = modesty and humility (in general violets were considered a symbol of humility because they grew close to the ground). By the Victorian era violets represented the qualities of an ideal wife: humility, faithfulness, and modesty.

Purple violet (*Viola cucullata*), by Lavonia R. Stockelbach (1874–1966). A collection of her paintings of Canadian provincial and territorial official flowers is associated with the herbarium of Agriculture and Agri-Food Canada in Ottawa.

The famous romance of Queen Victoria (1819–1901) and Prince Albert (1819–1861) was associated with violets. She wore a posy of violets on her dresses. He never walked through the gardens at Windsor Castle without picking a bunch of violets.

An even more celebrated love story that was intimately associated with violets concerns Napoleon Bonaparte (1769–1821) and Josephine (1763–1814). Napoleon's favourite flower was the violet, perhaps because it reminded him of his childhood in the woods of Corsica. He met Josephine at a ball, where she wore a coronet of violets and carried a bouquet of violets, which she threw to him from her carriage while departing. In memory of this, she wore a wedding gown embroidered with violets, and he gave her violets on each anniversary of their wedding. When he was sentenced to live out his days on the island of Elba, he told his followers that he would return in the spring, with violets. Napoleon's supporters sometimes determined people's political views by asking "Do you like violets?" In 1815, Napoleon returned to the royal palace in Paris, showered by violets. Accordingly, he was called by his followers *Caporal Violette* ("Corporal Violet") and *Papa-Père la Violette* ("Daddy Violet"), and the violet was adopted as the emblem of the Imperial Napoleonic party. After Josephine's death, Napoleon had her grave covered with violets. He kept some of them along with a lock of Josephine's hair in a locket near his breast until he died. Napoleon's life-

long grief over the loss of Josephine, however, did not prevent his remarriage to Eugenie, who he first saw at a ball, wearing a violet gown and violets in her hair. Like Josephine, she carried violets at her wedding and received bouquets of them at her anniversaries. When the French monarchy was restored, the wearing of violets was banned, and until 1874 French governments forbade any reproduction showing a violet, the symbol of Bonaparte supporters. Nevertheless, the violet flourished in the early days of the French Republic. France was flooded with postcards picturing innocent-looking violets with Napoleon's portrait cleverly hidden among the flowers.

In southern Germany during the Middle Ages, the violet was a symbol of spring. The discovery of the first violet to emerge triggered rejoicing. It was tied to a stake and a festival was held in its honour.

Purple violet (*Viola cucullata*). Source: Wikipedia (photographer: B. Gordy-Stith; Creative Commons Attribution-Share Alike 2.0 Generic license).

NAMES

Latin Names
Viola cucullata Aiton

The genus name *Viola* traces to the old Latin word for the plant, *viola,* which is based on the Greek word for violet, *ion* or *vion.* Io or Ione was a nymph in Greek mythology, a mistress of Zeus who, to protect her from the jealousy of his wife, turned Io into a white cow. To console her and sweeten her diet, he turned her tears into violets for her to graze on. The epithet *cucullata* in the scientific name is Latin for hooded, descriptive of the young leaves, which take the shape of a hood with inrolled basal lobes.

English Names
The purple violet is also known as blue marsh violet, hooded blue violet, long-stemmed marsh violet, marsh blue violet, marsh violet, and meadow violet. Although the most widely used name is marsh blue violet, we use the name purple violet because this name is used in provincial legislation and it is the name used in discussions of the floral emblem.

French Names
Violette cucullée.

HISTORY

Canada
The purple violet was selected as the floral emblem of New Brunswick in 1936, as a result of lobbying by the Provincial Women's Institute and schoolchildren. The early statutes used the common name only, but *Viola cucullata* has long been generally accepted as the species, and it is cited in recent provincial legislation.

Coat of Arms of New Brunswick. The floral base is made up of purple violets and fiddleheads (*Matteuccia struthiopteris,* a fern with edible young leaves, common in New Brunswick). At the summit, a crowned Atlantic salmon leaps from a coronet of gold maple leaves. The golden lion is symbolic of ties to England. The white-tailed deer at the left carries the Union Jack, the deer at the right has fleurs de lis, respectively indicating the province's British and French backgrounds.

Foreign
The violet is the national symbol of Poland, and the regional symbol of North Portugal. The state flower of Wisconsin is the wood violet (*V. papilionacea;* "wood violet" is more commonly applied to an Old World species of violet). This species is native to a large area of North America, including of course Wisconsin. The wood violet was nominated for state flower by school children in 1908, and in 1909 was named Wisconsin's unofficial state flower. In 1948 during Wisconsin's Centennial celebration it was adopted as the official Wisconsin flower (taking effect in 1949). The state flower of New Jersey is the common meadow violet (*V. sororia*), a native species widespread in North America. This violet was first unofficially designated as such by a resolution of the Legislature in 1913, but was not officially recognized until 1972. The native American violet, *V. palmata,* was adopted in 1968 as the state flower of Rhode Island. Illinois adopted the "blue violet" as its state flower in 1908. As there are at least eight native blue-flowered violet species in the state, no particular species can be identified. The most common of these is the dooryard violet (*V. sororia*), but then Rhode Island and New Jersey would have the same emblem.

APPEARANCE

The purple violet is a perennial herb that grows from a fleshy, branching rhizome (underground stem). The plants spread vegetatively to some extent, the rhizomes often splitting and developing several crowns. *Viola cucullata* lacks an above-ground branching stem, and the flowers are produced on long stalks arising from the ground. The plants develop a clump of basal leaves, and are usually 12–25 cm (5–10 inches) tall. The petioles (leaf stalks) tend to be longer than the leaf blades, which are up to 10 cm (4 inches) long. The leaf blades are usually more or less acutely pointed at the tip, and often heart-shaped at the base, while the edges have round teeth or are almost smooth. The slender flowering stalks are produced from early spring to late summer, each bearing one usually deep blue-violet flower about 2 cm (0.8 inch) wide. The flowers may also be white, pale lilac, or rosy pink, and they lack fragrance. After fertilization they develop into cylindrical-ovoid, green, fruiting capsules 10–15 mm (about 0.5 inch) long, containing black, spherical seeds.

Violets on an antique cup and saucer set. Source: Thinkstock.

CLASSIFICATION

Family: Violaceae (violet family).

Violets are species of the genus *Viola,* of which there are 400 to 500 in the world, including about 80 native to North America, about 40 of these in Canada. With so many species, many of which hybridize, identification can be difficult. *Viola cucullata* can usually be recognized by the following combination of characteristics: heart-shaped, unlobed leaf blades as broad or broader than long; smooth leaf surfaces with fine hair only on the upper side of the basal lobes; lack of an aerial stem (flowers and leaves arising directly from the rootstock at ground level); blue flowers carried above the leaves; pointed sepals; and club-shaped hairs on the inside of the lateral petals. Similar species are moderately or densely pubescent or have flowers at the same level as the leaves and tend to have the sepals blunt or obtuse instead of sharply pointed. The similar *V. nephrophylla* has hairs on the spur petal, unlike *V. cucullata,* and its first leaves are kidney-shaped.

Viola cucullata var. *microtitis* has sepals with basal auricles ("ears") that are relatively short (about 2 mm long), in contrast to var. *cucullata* in which the auricles measure up to 6 mm in length. Plants with white flowers have been called forma *albiflora,* while plants with blue and white mottled petals have been called forma *thurstoni.* The purple violet hybridizes with the wooly blue violet (*V. sororia*), the hybrids having hairy leaves and sepals with cilia (hairs), unlike purple violet (which may have leaves that are slightly pubescent). *Viola cucullata* also hybridizes with ten other species of violets based on literature reports.

Hybrids involving *Viola cucullata;* followed by the meanings of the epithet (the word following the first × in the line).

V. ×*bissellii* House (*cucullata* × *papilionacea*); after Charles Humphrey Bissell 1857–1925.

V. ×*insessa* House (*cucullata* × *nephrophylla*); meaning "fixed".

V. ×*consocia* House (*cucullata* × *affinis*); meaning "interrelated".

V. ×*conturbata* House (*cucullata* × *sororia*); meaning "confused".

V. ×*melissaefolia* Greene (*cucullata* × *septentrionalis*); meaning "Melissa-leaved".

V. ×*porteriana* Pollard (*cucullata* × *fimbriatula*); after Thomas Conrad Porter, 1822–1901.

V. ×*festata* House (*cucullata* × *sagittata*); referring to festive attire.

V. ×*greenmani* House (*cucullata* × *triloba*); after Jesse Moore Greenman, 1867–1950.

V. ×*ryoniae* House (*cucullata* × *palmata*); after Angie M. Ryon, 1867–1948.

V. ×*notabilis* Bicknell (*cucullata* × *brittoniana*); meaning "notable".

V. *cucullata* × *viarum* (not a named hybrid, i.e., merely designated by this combination).

GEOGRAPHY

Viola cucullata is native in Canada from Newfoundland to northwestern Ontario. It also occurs in the eastern U.S., from Minnesota and Nebraska south to North Carolina, Georgia, Tennessee, Missouri, and Arkansas.

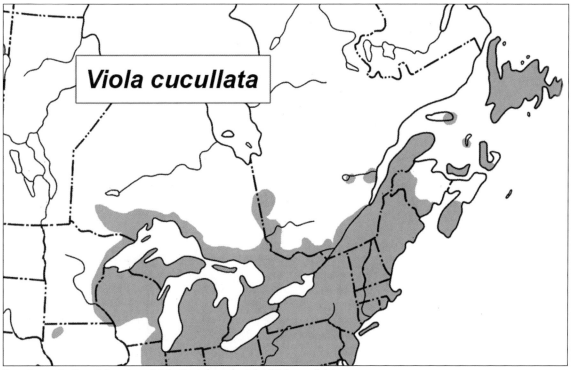

Canadian and adjacent American distribution of purple violet (*Viola cucullata*).

Purple violet (*Viola cucullata*) in Fairmont, Nova Scotia. Courtesy of S. Blaney.

ECOLOGY

Habitat

The purple violet can occupy dry hillsides but is more often found in wet meadows and woodlands, bogs, marshes, and swampy, shaded woods or forests. It usually roots in muck soils in low, wet areas, the roots generally submerged in water or in saturated humus. The pH of the soil is 4.6–6.6 (strongly acidic to slightly acidic). The plants prefer a cool climate, and do well in partial or deep shade.

Inter-species Relationships

Violets bloom early in the season, furnishing nectar for bees and butterflies. They are often grown in butterfly gardens, not just for the nectar, but also because the foliage is consumed by some caterpillars, notably fritillaries, which are large, attractive orange and brown summer butterflies sometimes confused with monarchs and viceroys.

Purple violet (*Viola cucullata*), by Brad Morrison. Reproduced with the permission of Communications New Brunswick.

Pollination and Dispersal

Many species of *Viola* produce normal, showy, cross-pollinated (*chasmogamous*) flowers in the early spring, and also closed, self-pollinating (*cleistogamous*) flowers that lack petals throughout the summer. This phenomenon occurs in at least 56 families of plants. In most such species open flowers are large and showy, attracting insects for cross-pollination, whereas the closed flowers are much smaller and produce seeds by self pollination and fertilization within the flower buds as insurance against the possibility that insects will not be available for pollination, with the result that seeds will not be produced. The showy flowers are advantageous in producing variable offspring, some of which will be more adapted than their parents, especially to changing conditions. In some cases the fruits of the purple violet are produced mostly from cleistogamous flowers.

The lower pair of petals in the cross-pollinated flowers are joined and form a spur (a hollow, tubular extension). Nectar is secreted into the base of the spur from the bases of the lowest two stamens. In trying to reach the nectar, insects brush against the stigma, often transferring pollen to it that has been acquired from previous visits to other flowers.

The purple violet, like many other species of *Viola*, has two special methods for distributing its seeds. First, there is a short-distance dispersal method, by which seeds are explosively ejected from the capsules. As the valves of the capsule dry, an elastic tension is produced and they suddenly open lengthwise, catapulting the seeds up to a few metres (several yards). The plants also have a long-distance dispersal method, based on a mutually beneficial relationship with ants. The violet seeds have nutritious, pale coloured, oily attachments that attract the ants, which carry the seeds back to their underground nests. Seeds that the ants lose along the way or that become buried in the ants' tunnels, often germinate far away from the parent plants. Violet seeds may also be distributed over great distances by birds.

Purple violet (*Viola cucullata*). Source: Canadian Heritage 2002 (revised edition). Symbols of Canada. Canadian Heritage, Ottawa, ON. Reproduced with permission.

USES

The common phrase "shrinking violet", applied to shy people, draws attention to the inconspicuous nature of the plants. Nevertheless their subtle beauty is extremely attractive. They were among the first flowers grown commercially, with nurseries established in Greece about 400 BC. The purple violet is often grown as an ornamental. There are numerous cultivars (e.g., 'Alba', 'Bicolor', 'Priceana', 'Queen Charlotte', 'Red Giant', 'Royal Robe', 'Rubra', 'White Czar'), including one with the curious name of 'Freckles', which has blue-flecked white flowers.

"Pixies in violets", from an old children's colouring book. Coloured by R. Brookes.

North American Indians employed purple violet roots in remedies for senility, urinary disorders, and other ailments; and the leaves as a poultice to treat headaches and as infusions or "teas" for colds and coughs.

The use of violets as food is ancient, although very limited, extending back to early Greek and Roman times, when violets were used to flavour butter, oil, vinegar, and wine. Violet-flavoured sherbet has been a favourite concoction of Asia Minor and other parts of the Middle East since very early times, some considering this the national drink of Syria and Turkey. In the fifteenth century, violets were often used in sauces and soups, and to make fritters, and some members of the Royalty in Great Britain during the Victorian era were extremely fond of violet preparations.

The young leaves of purple violet are rich in Vitamins A and C, and can be added to salads. The flowers are also edible, raw or cooked. The leaves can be added to soup as a thickener, much like okra (the leaves of wild violets were used as a substitute for okra in the South during the American Civil War). The flowers are sometimes made into a jam reputed to soothe indigestion, and a syrup said to suppress a cough.

TOXICITY

The seed pods, rhizomes and roots of *Viola* species can be poisonous in large doses, causing severe gastroenteritis, nervousness, and respiratory and circulatory depression. These parts of the plant are strong laxatives, and can induce nausea and vomiting. Violets should not be used for culinary purposes unless one is certain that they have not been sprayed with insecticides, herbicides, or fungicides.

The New Brunswick/Purple violet coin issued in 2007. This is part of the provincial and territorial symbols gold coin series (0.99999% gold), initiated in 1998 and completed in 2011 (see the first chapter of this book. This coin has a face value of $350 but, reflective of its value to collectors, the purchase price is over $1,500 Coin image© courtesy of the Royal Canadian Mint.

CULTIVATION

The following comments are from our colleague Larry Sherk's out-of-print "Growing Canada's Floral Emblems" (Canada Dept. Agric. Publication 1288, 1967): "This violet, like many others, is quite easy to grow in the garden provided the soil is not too rich. Plants in well-fertilized soil soon grow luxuriant but flower poorly. A soil rich in humus, kept reasonably moist, and shaded by tall trees or shrubs is best. If the soil is heavy or sandy, work in some leaf mould and peat moss and keep it slightly acid by mulching with well-rotted leaves. Be sure to gather seeds before the capsules split open. Sow seeds, as soon as they are ripe, in a moist shaded seedbed, in a seed pan, or in a shallow pot. Plants will likely self-sow in most gardens so they can become weedy if not controlled. These violets can be transplanted at most times if a good ball of soil is taken with the plants. To be sure of getting the right species, mark the plants when they are in bloom."

CONSERVATION STATUS

The purple violet is a common species, not in particular need of conservation measures. However, its wetland habitats are subject to numerous threats, particularly draining and infilling for agricultural and urban development.

MYTHS, LEGENDS, TALES, FOLKLORE AND INTERESTING FACTS

❦ The Greek dramatist Aristophanes (about 450–388 BC) referred to Athens in one of his plays as the violet crowned city because the king was named Ion, which meant violet. According to legend, Ion, the founder of Athens, led his people to Attica where they were welcomed by naiads, water nymphs who could inspire men and who gave them violets as signs of their good wishes. The violet has been emblematic of Athens for many years. In the ancient Athenian games the first prize was an award in the shape of a golden violet. Ancient Athenian houses, alters, statues, and brides were decorated with violets.

❦ Violets have long been used in love potions. The classical Greeks chose violet as their flower of fertility. In seventeenth century Europe, candied violets were eaten as an aphrodisiac.

❦ Although not used in modern medicine, violets have been thought to have curative properties since antiquity. In classical Roman times violets were prescribed for gout and spleen disorders. As well, it was common practice in Roman times to relate herbal treatments to gods, and since Jupiter was the supreme god, and the head is the supreme part of the body, violets were used to treat headaches and memory loss. Violets contain a chemical that is related to salicylic acid, the chief ingredient in aspirin, so that use for headache had some justification. The medieval herbalists used violets as an antiseptic, to soothe pain, and even for malignant tumours.

❦ In Medieval Europe, it was thought to be unlucky to bring bouquets of less than thirteen flowers into a church or house. However, this problem was eliminated if one of the flowers was a violet.

❦ According to legend, 7 centuries ago in England Robin Hood and Sir Richard dined on stewed violets gathered in the woods.

❦ Before litmus (which is obtained from lichens) became widely employed to indicate pH, syrup of violets was used (it turns red with acids, green with alkalies).

❦ Like the rose, the violet has been adopted as a colour because it is so well known. Of course, roses come in other colours than red, and violets come in other colours than blue.

❦ Ionine, the major chemical found in violet fragrance, is thought to have the ability to dull the sense of smell within a very short time, and this is why the sweet violet (*Viola odorata*) seems to lose its fragrance. The fragrance returns when the nose is rested. Shakespeare was aware of this when he wrote in *Hamlet:* "A violet in the youth of primy nature, Forward, not permanent; sweet, not lasting. The perfume and suppliance of a minute. No more."

❦ Many species of violet turn their flowers toward the ground at night or when it's cloudy.

Painting of purple violet (*Viola cucullata*) in its natural setting, from the Walter Coucill Canadian Centennial official flowers of Canada series (see Coucill 1966 cited in the first chapter of this book). Reproduced with the permission of the copyright holders, the Coucill family.

SOURCES OF ADDITIONAL INFORMATION

Baird, V.B., and Mathews, F.S. 1942. Wild violets of North America. University of California Press, Los Angeles, CA. 225 pp.

Ballard, H.E., Jr., Sytsma, K.J., and Kowal, R.R. 1998. Shrinking the violets: phylogenetic relationships of infrageneric groups in *Viola* (Violaceae) based on internal transcribed spacer DNA sequences. Syst. Bot. 23: 439–458.

Bernhardt, P. 1978. The wily violets: schemes for survival. Garden J. (New York) 2(3): 18–21, 32.

Brizicky, G.K. 1961. The genera of the Violaceae in the Southeastern United States. J. Arnold Arbor. 42: 321–333.

Brown, K., Hoffman, M., and Ringer, N. 1999. An herbalist's guide to growing & using violets. Storey Communications, Pownal, VT. 32 pp.

Coon, N. 1977. The complete book of violets. Thomas Yoseloff, London, U.K. 147 pp.

Gil-Ad,-N.L. 1997. Systematics of *Viola* subsection *Boreali-Americanae*. Boissiera 53: 1–130.

Klaber, D. 1976. Violets of the United States. A.S. Barnes, South Brunswick, NJ. 208 pp.

McKinney, L.E. 1992. A taxonomic revision of the acaulescent blue violets (*Viola*) of North America. SIDA, Botanical Miscellany No. 7. Botanical Research Institute of Texas, Fort Worth, TX. 51 pp. + plates.

Russell, N.H. 1965. Violets (*Viola*) of central and eastern United States: an introductory survey. Sida 2: 1–113.

Wetherbee, A. 1986. History of violets. The Herbarist 52: 14–19.

Zambra, G.L. 1950. Violets for garden & market. Revised edition. Collingridge, London, U.K. 79 pp.

Purple violet (*Viola cucullata*), in Nutby Mountain, Nova Scotia. Courtesy of S. Blaney.

TREE: BALSAM FIR

Balsam fir (*Abies balsamea*) in the Adirondack Mountains of New York. Source: Wikipedia (photographer: Tony; Creative Commons Attribution-Share Alike 2.0 Generic license).

SYMBOLISM

Fir trees have been associated with a winter solstice celebration since ancient pagan times in Europe, when the ritual of decorating a conifer represented tribute to the rebirth of the sun god. Gradually the custom was taken up by Christians, and at least since the 16th century in Europe small fir trees have been used to decorate houses at Christmas time. In Europe, the silver fir (*Abies alba*) has long been the fir of choice for Christmas trees. In North America, the balsam fir has been the most desirable Christmas tree for many years. Since New Brunswick is a major producer of Christmas trees, and the balsam fir is also important to the area's forest and tourist industries, the tree is an excellent choice as the official provincial emblem.

Balsam fir (*Abies balsamea*), by Brad Morrison. Reproduced with the permission of Communications New Brunswick.

NAMES

Latin Names
Abies balsamea (L.) Mill.

The genus name *Abies* is based on the Latin *abies*, a word used by the classical Romans to refer to the silver fir of Europe. Alternatively, the name is said to be based on the Latin *abire*, to rise up, referring to the great height of some of the species. *Balsamea* in the scientific name is Latin for balsamic, referring to resinous, aromatic, plant substances with a characteristic odour (often from benzoic or cinnamic acid) and frequently used medicinally as a soothing ointment. When crushed, the needles exude the smell of balsam.

English Names
Balsam fir has also been called American silver fir, balm of fir, balm of Gilead, balm-of-Gilead fir, balsam, blister fir, blister pine, Canada balsam, Canadian balsam, Canadian fir, eastern fir, fir balsam, fir pine, fir tree, silver pine, and white fir. Variety *phanerolepis* has been called bracted balsam fir. The word "fir" in modern English is restricted to the genera *Abies* and *Pseudotsuga*. The term "double balsam" is often encountered in the horticultural trade, and has several meanings: a) a form with naturally very crowded leaves; b) a form with abnormally dense branching due to pathology; c) Fraser fir (*A. fraseri*); d) *A. balsamea* var. *phanerolepis*. Both the names "double balsam" and "double fir" are employed in the Christmas tree trade to refer to kinds of older trees with somewhat twisted branches and thick, dense, brushlike needles, and perhaps short internodes. These terms have marketing value, since for "double the fir" one may expect to pay double the price.

French Names
Sapin baumier, sapin blanc, sapin rouge, sapin. Variety *phanerolepis* = sapin phanérolépide.

HISTORY

Canada
The balsam fir was adopted on May 1, 1987 as the provincial tree of New Brunswick. The closely related subalpine fir (*A. lasiocarpa*) was chosen as the official tree of the Yukon in 2001.

Foreign
No species of *Abies* appears to have been adopted as a symbol of any geographical area outside of Canada.

Silhouette of balsam fir (*Abies balsamea*). Source: J.L. Farrar 1995. Trees in Canada. Canadian Forest Service and Fitzhenry and Whiteside, Markham, ON, Canada. Reproduced with permission.

APPEARANCE

Balsam fir trees are usually 12–18 m (40–60 feet) high with a diameter (breast height) of 30–45 cm (12–18 inches). The tree can grow up to 23 m (75 feet) in height, with a trunk diameter up to 86 cm (34 inches). It is considered to be one of the most symmetrical of northeastern conifers, producing a narrow, pyramidal crown often capped by a spire-like tip. The branches tend to develop in whorls of four or five around the trunk. The bark is gray, thin, and smooth except for numerous raised resin blisters. The bark often breaks into irregular brownish scales as the trees mature. The leaves (needles) are usually 1.2–2.5 cm (0.5–1 inches) long (occasionally as long as 3 cm or 1.2 inches), flattish in cross section, shiny dark-green above and silvery-banded below, and lacking stalks. Needles on lower branches sometimes have a slight notch at the apex. The needles are spirally arranged on the twigs, but those on the lateral branches are twisted at the base, giving them a distinctive two-ranked arrangement (a phenomenon called "transverse heliotropism", that results in maximum exposure to sunlight on lower leaves, which usually receive less light). By contrast, the needles on upper shoots are oriented in all directions. Starting between twenty and thirty years of age, the plants bear both male cones (reddish, purplish, bluish, greenish, or orange at pollination, and smaller than the female cones) and female (seed) cones on one-year-old branches. The seed cones stand erect on the branches. At maturity they are oblong-cylindrical, 3–10 cm (1.2–4 inches) long and 1.5–3 cm (0.6–1.2 inches) wide, producing winged seeds. The seed scales detach gradually from the cones, leaving bare central axes that often remain attached to the branches for years, and are sometimes called "candles".

Balsam fir (*Abies balsamea* var. *phanerolepis*) in Vermont. Source: Wikimedia (photographer: Dvs; Creative Commons Attribution 2.0 Generic license).

CLASSIFICATION

Family: Pinaceae (pine family).

There are about 40 species of *Abies,* distributed in north temperate regions of the world, as well as in Mexico, Central America, and North Africa. Five species are native to Canada (considering *A. lasiocarpa* and *A. bifolia* as separate species).

Two varieties of balsam fir are often recognized; in var. *balsamea* the seed bracts are included inside the cones; in var. *phanerolepis* Fernald they extend slightly outside of the main body of the cones. Variety *balsamea* occurs across Canada and in the U.S. Variety *phanerolepis* tends to occur from Newfoundland to Ontario (but not west of Ontario), as well as in the U.S.

In Alberta, there are hybrids of balsam fir and Rocky Mountain alpine fir (*A. bifolia,* also called Rocky Mountain subalpine fir). It has also been claimed that in the Canadian Rockies, where their ranges overlap, balsam fir hybridizes with subalpine fir (*A. lasiocarpa,* also known as alpine fir). However, there has been some confusion regarding the separation of *A. bifolia* and *A. lasiocarpa,* some authorities treating the former as part of the latter. Some of the most recent taxonomic work has reported that *A. balsamea* and *A. lasiocarpa* are not morphologically distinct over a broad zone of overlap extending from Saskatchewan to British Columbia. It has been suggested that both are best treated as subspecies, but there is still disagreement over their rank, and we follow most recent authors in treating them as species.

Balsam fir is closely related to Fraser fir (*A. fraseri*), a species of North Carolina, Tennessee, and Virginia.

There are thought to be hybrids between the two in Virginia. Some authorities have recognized Fraser fir as a variety of balsam fir, *A. balsamea* var. *fraseri.*

The balsam fir can be distinguished from species of spruce (*Picea*) by its flat needles and erect cones (spruce needles are roundish and the cones are pendulous). It can be distinguished from eastern hemlock (*Tsuga canadensis*), the only Canadian species of *Tsuga* that grows in the same locations, by the absence of stalks on the needles (eastern hemlock has small stalks). The leaves of balsam fir are also similar to those of Canada yew but are whitened instead of green beneath and not as strongly pointed.

KEY TO NATIVE SPECIES OF *ABIES* IN CANADA

Note: Cone features are usually necessary for identification. Since the cones scatter their seed scales slowly while still attached to the trees, and cones are usually only on upper branches that can not be reached from the ground, it is often necessary to collect seed scales from beneath the trees. Do not confuse cone scales with the smaller bracts under the scales.

1. Leaves with white stomatal lines only on lower surfaces 2
  2. Cone scales 1.0 to 1.5 cm wide; resin canals near margin in leaf cross-section . . . *A. balsamea*
  2. Cone scales 2.0 to 3.0 cm wide; resin canals near centre in leaf cross-section 3
    3. Basal bud scales slightly pubescent or glabrous . . . . *A. grandis*
    3. Basal bud scales densely pubescent . . . . *A. amabilis*

1. Leaves with white stomatal lines on upper and lower surfaces 4
  4. Basal bud scales equilaterally triangular, margins crenate or dentate . . . . . . *A. lasiocarpa*
  4. Basal bud scales isosceles triangular, margins entire . . . . *A. bifolia*

Balsam fir (*Abies balsamea*) trunk. Source: BugwoodImages/ForestryImages (photographer: K. Kanoti; Creative Commons Attribution 3.0 license).

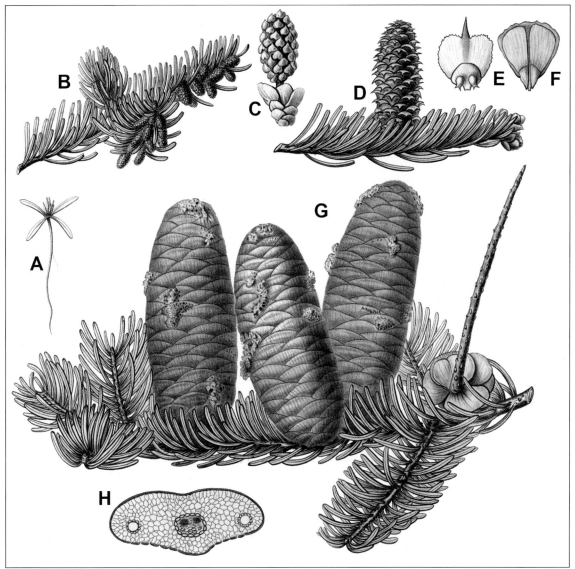

Balsam fir (*Abies balsamea*). A, seedling; B, branch with male cones; C, a male cone; D, a branch bearing a young female cone with flowers; E, upper side of a young cone scale with female flowers, showing the bract and ovules; F, upper side of a mature cone scale with its winged seeds; G, a branch with fruit (three intact cones are shown, while the one at the right has mostly shed its seed-bearing scales); H, cross-section of a leaf. Source: Sargent, C.S. 1898. The silva of North America. Houghton, Mifflin and Company, Boston, MA. Vol. 12, plate 610.

Balsam fir (*Abies balsamea*) in winter. Courtesy of J. O'Brien, United States Department of Agriculture Forest Service.

A BIODIVERSITY TREASURE

GEOGRAPHY

Abies balsamea is native to all provinces of Canada except British Columbia. The species is not indigenous to the three northern territories. It is most abundant in the Gulf of St. Lawrence region, including parts of Quebec, Newfoundland and Cape Breton; in this area it comprises more than 30% of the forest, thriving in the cool, moist, maritime environment. In the U.S., the tree ranges from Minnesota to New England, with local stands in Virginia, West Virginia, and northeastern Iowa. The best stands occur in southeastern Canada and the northeastern U.S. In the western part of its range, from James Bay and Lake Superior to the Athabaska River in Alberta, stands become increasingly scattered and more restricted to stream valleys and north-facing slopes. Balsam fir is the only native Canadian species of *Abies* growing east of Alberta.

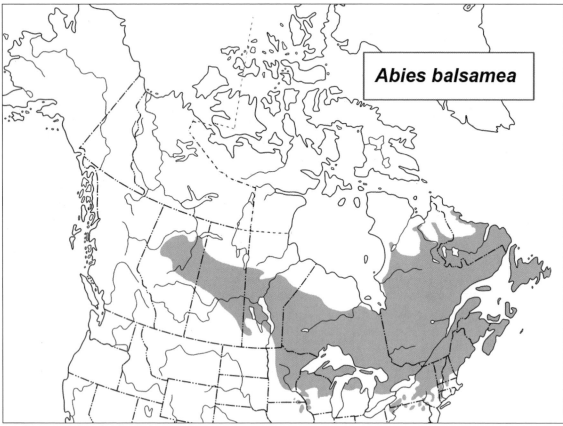

Distribution of balsam fir (*Abies balsamea*).

ECOLOGY

Balsam fir occurs extensively in boreal and northern forests, both in pure and mixed stands. It is often a dominant species or forms pure stands in Newfoundland, Ontario, and Quebec, and is also a principal tree of boreal mixed stands in Canada. In the northeastern U.S., balsam fir more often occurs in mixed stands than as a forest dominant. The trees can survive as long as 200 years, but rarely live longer than 125. The thin bark makes them susceptible to damage and tree rots. The generally shallow root system (especially on wet sites) makes the trees susceptible to windstorms and, during periods of drought, to drying out and fire damage. Fire is extremely detrimental, because most trees and seeds are killed.

Although fire kills balsam fir trees and seeds, it is a natural rejuvenating event that contributes to the development of new stands. Indeed, the boreal forest ecosystem is characterized by periodic catastrophic events that destroy large areas of tree cover, and the flora and fauna are adapted to such changes.

The status of balsam fir over large areas of Canada can change very quickly. For example, the volume of balsam fir doubled in the Gaspé peninsula of Quebec around 1950 due to the destruction of white spruce by European spruce sawfly and loss of birch due to birch dieback. While it increased in Gaspé, it declined over equally large areas elsewhere.

Habitat
The tree grows under a wide range of soil and climate conditions, but is most common on cool, moderately moist sites with acidic soils (pH 5.1–6.0). Well drained but moist, moderately deep sandy soils

ECOLOGY (CONT'D)

are preferred. Best growth occurs at about 50% of full sunlight, but the tree can withstand many years of suppression in dense shade, and an understory of balsam fir seedlings is common in many forest types; seedlings will survive for years on only 10% of full sunlight.

Inter-species Relationships

The spruce budworm moth (*Choristoneura fumiferana*) is the most damaging agent of balsam fir and the most damaging defoliator in North America's boreal forests. Despite its name, it prefers the balsam fir to spruce (it has been suggested that it should be called balsam fir budworm). The caterpillars feed on the buds and needles. Depending on provincial legislation, control measures sometimes involve aerial spraying of chemical insecticides or the bacterium *Bacillus thuringiensis,* both of which can be injurious to the natural ecosystem. The bacterium is a naturally occurring pathogen that affects budworm larvae, but also a host of other, non-injurious butterflies and moths. The many non-target insects affected play important roles as pollinators and food sources in the forest ecosystem. The responses to spruce budworm infestations have been quite different in New Brunswick and Nova Scotia (see Sandberg and Clancy 2002 for a review). In the former, intense and widespread application of insecticides was advocated, whereas the latter attempted a more varied and localized adoption of control measures. Today, there is less polarization and a growing trend toward a general appreciation of the value of letting nature take its course, where possible. Nevertheless, there will be continuing controversy about the best approaches, especially because "industrial forests" (i.e., those used by the forest industry) are often adjacent to parks and protected areas. Since the use of insecticides and bacteria to control periodic infestations continues to be controversial, a variety of other practices are increasingly being applied.

In New Brunswick, for example, in recent decades jack pine and black spruce have often been planted instead of balsam fir, since these are somewhat less susceptible to the budworm.

WAS SMOKEY WRONG?
Should balsam fir, and forests generally, be protected from fire? Smokey thought so. It was about 1947 when Smokey the Bear became an icon (almost as well known as Santa Claus) assisting the U.S. Forest Service in their fire prevention campaign. With a shovel in one hand and pointing a finger with the other, he said "only you can prevent forest fires." The impression developed that fires are a very bad thing in all respects. Notice the bears looking after the deer in the poster. There are few well documented observations of this phenomenon! For decades there was extensive fire prevention and tree planting. This had a negative impact on biodiversity. It now seems remarkable that attitudes involving fairy-tale-like images were so pervasive and influential only a very short time ago.

In fact fires resulting from lightning strikes are a natural process in forests. Fire is now considered to be an important management tool. Fires often burn in a mosaic so that the result is a patchwork of unburned forest and patches in various stages returning to forest. The patches increase overall biodiversity, and provide essential and improved habitat for wildlife (including deer). Much flora and fauna is dependent upon fires. Prevention of natural fires increases fuel in forests resulting in fires that are much more dangerous and difficult to control. Fires sometimes need to be controlled but often it is much more beneficial to let them burn.

United States Department of Agriculture Forest Service 1953 poster of Smokey the Bear.

ECOLOGY (CONT'D)

An interdependence has evolved between the spruce budworm and balsam fir forests. A cycle seems to exist in which mature fir stands become vulnerable and, every 35 years or so, the insect devastates the forest. Once a budworm outbreak develops, balsam fir trees start to die after three to five consecutive years of severe defoliation. Budworm outbreaks attract many insect-eating birds, especially warblers and woodpeckers. Woodpeckers in turn produce tree cavities which are employed by various wildlife species as homes. Spruce budworm is one of more than a hundred different insects that feed on balsam fir. Among the other important insects are various aphids (*Cinera* spp., *Mindarus abietinus, Adelges piceae*), balsam fir sawfly (*Neodiprion abietis*), balsam gall midge (*Paradiplosis tumifex*), balsam fir seed chalcid (*Megastigmus specularis*), balsam shootboring sawfly (*Pleroneura*

Adult (moth, above) and larva (caterpillar, below) of the spruce budworm. This insect is the most serious defoliator in North America's boreal forests. It particularly attacks balsam fir, and during uncontrolled outbreaks can kill almost all the trees in mature stands. On the positive side, it is an important food source for many inhabitants of the boreal forest, including birds, mammals, and other insects. Photos by Klaus Bolte.

brunneicornis), eastern black-headed budworm (*Acleris variana*), hemlock looper (*Lambdina fiscellaria*) and various weevils (*Hylobius* spp.).

Balsam fir provides important habitat for birds and mammals, especially as winter cover. Moose, white-tailed deer, caribou, and snowshoe hares browse on young plants. Mice and voles feed on the bark of saplings. Black bears sometimes strip the bark off mature trees, and have been observed licking the sap and gum from the inner bark. The buds are eaten by birds such as the spruce grouse and by squirrels. The needles are eaten by spruce and ruffed grouse. Mice, voles, and birds eat the seeds. Many animals often use fir stands for protection from weather or predators. For example, fir stands are frequently used by deer and moose with calves during severe winter months, because the snow is relatively shallow. Young balsam fir plants provide cover for small mammals and birds. With the presence of so many herbivorous animals in balsam fir forests, it is not surprising that several carnivorous mammals also are often found there, some of these rare or threatened. They include the timber wolf, pine marten, fisher, Canada lynx, and bobcat. Balsam fir is considered desirable along trout streams because its shade keeps the water cool, and relatively few trees are felled by beaver for building dams. This in turn reduces beaver dams which lower the quality of trout streams.

Pollination and Dispersal

Balsam fir is wind-pollinated and wind-distributed. Good seed crops occur every two to four years, with light crops in intervening years. Seeds begin to drop from the trees in late summer, most falling in autumn, but some continuing to be distributed until

early spring. The wings on the seeds act like sails to transport the seeds some distance away. Most seeds fall within 25–60 m (80–200 feet) of the parental tree, but some travel as far away as 160 m (525 feet). Germination occurs mainly from early spring to early summer. Most balsam fir seed germinates in less than a year, the ungerminated seeds rarely surviving for more than 1 year. The trees reproduce vegetatively to some extent by layering (lower branches becoming buried in the soil and producing new trees), but this is only important in some high-elevation trees in the U.S. where reproduction by seeds is rare.

A balsam fir Christmas tree. Source: Thinkstock.

USES

The unusually long wood fibres of balsam fir contribute to good pulping properties and the tree is a staple of eastern Canada's pulp industry. The wood is very low in decay resistance, so is not well suited for posts. It is low in nail-holding ability, and relatively soft, so it is widely used for applications not requiring structural strength, such as interior knotty panelling, crates, and millwork. Because the wood lacks taste and odour, it is used for fish box construction. The trees are used extensively for cabin logs. Canada, mainly Quebec and the Maritime provinces, produces much more balsam fir lumber than the U.S.: about 180 million board feet annually, or about 3% of total Canadian lumber production. The high production of balsam fir lumber in eastern Canada is due to the larger size, higher quality, and greater abundance of trees than elsewhere in North America.

The balsam fir is an extremely popular Christmas tree, and indeed a major source of income for New Brunswick. Boughs are also harvested for making wreaths. Balsam fir is ideal for these purposes because of its attractive conical shape, deep green colour, dense appearance, pliable branches (this enables the trees to be packed closely together for transportation), pleasant unique balsam fragrance, and especially its prolonged needle retention (needles are usually retained even after several weeks indoors). Still another advantage is that they respond well to shearing, so young trees in plantations can be improved. The balsam wooly aphid (*Adelges piceae*) is an important insect pest of the balsam fir, and a particular concern to growers of Christmas trees as it deforms or kills the trees.

In Canada the most popular Christmas trees in decreasing order are: balsam fir, Fraser fir, Scots pine, and white spruce. Forty million live Christmas trees are sold in North America every year; about six million of these grown in Canada. Canada exports almost 2.5 million trees annually, worth about $35 million, most of these to the U.S. The value of farm cash receipts for Christmas trees in Canada is about $75 million annually. The largest producers are (in decreasing order) Quebec, Nova Scotia,

ARE ARTIFICIAL CHRISTMAS TREES BETTER FOR THE ENVIRONMENT?

The first artificial tree was manufactured in Germany in the nineteenth century, to prevent deforestation. Most real Christmas trees sold today are harvested from tree farms. These farms have replaced natural habitats, so that there is still an environmental impact. Artificial trees are typically made of polyvinylchloride or polyethylene. Although they can be used for many years, their production requires non-renewable resources and energy, and they are usually non-recyclable, ending up in landfills. Genuine trees are used only once, but can be mulched and recycled. Further, live trees reduce the amount of carbon dioxide in the atmosphere. Also, trees grown as a crop frequently provide habitat for wildlife. On the other hand, Christmas tree crops usually are grown with heavy applications of pesticides and herbicides, which are not good for the environment. Organically grown Christmas trees are sometimes available. All things considered, real trees are probably environmentally preferable.

"The Queen's Christmas tree." This famous illustration shows the Christmas celebration of Queen Victoria and Prince Albert at Osborne House, the Royal Family's retreat on the Isle of Wight. The drawing was first published in December 1850 in Godey's Lady's Book. It was widely circulated in Britain and overseas, and served to popularize the use of a decorated fir tree during Christmas.

USES (CONT'D)

New Brunswick and Ontario. Canadians spend about $50 million annually on artificial Christmas trees, most of these imported from China.

It has recently been estimated that 98% of the Christmas trees sold commercially in Canada are grown on tree farms. However, it appears that more balsam firs are harvested from the wild than other kinds of Christmas trees. There are two reasons for this. First, the excellent tree quality commands a higher price which makes it makes the effort worthwhile. Second, the tops of larger trees can be used, so that harvest is not confined to a particular age class.

Although balsam fir is not considered to be a particularly suitable ornamental, it is grown to a small extent. It is probably unmatched for use as a natural outdoor Christmas tree. The ornamental use of balsam fir is more extensive in Europe than in North America, and often dwarf forms are grown in rock gardens and as foundation plants. Dwarf cultivars include 'Compacta', 'Prostrata', and 'Nana' (which has been described as "a nice Christmas tree for Lilliputians"). Cultivar 'Andover' is low, compact and spreading; 'Columnaris' is tall and columnar; 'Denudata' and 'Nudicaulis' produce a single, unbranched trunk. Several cultivars develop particular colours: 'Coerulea' is rather silvery, 'Coerulescens' is silver-blue, and 'Lutescens' is yellow to bronze.

Blisters on the bark of balsam fir yield Canada balsam, a sticky resin used for permanently mounting specimens on microscope slides. This feature of the bark has given rise to the name "blister fir". Canada balsam is also used as a cement for various parts of optical systems, because its refractive index, like that of ordinary glass, results in a minimum dispersion of light. Upon exposure to air balsam becomes thick, yellowish, and dries to a resinous mass, that is however completely soluble in ether. In the past, Canada balsam was also used in medicines, soaps, glues, candles, perfumes, and deodorizers.

Most commercial products with "pine" odours are really scented with essential oil distilled from the foliage of fir trees native to Russia. It has been suggested that a similar oil could be obtained from balsam fir. Early pioneers used balsam fir needles to stuff pillows, which retained a pleasant fragrance.

The inner bark of balsam fir can be used to make bread. It can even be chewed raw as an emergency food, but chewing should be thorough to avoid wood slivers being lodged in the throat. Bark was important in the diet of native North Americans and it is said that the Adirondack Indians owe their name to the Mohawk term for tree-eaters.

CULTIVATION

Balsam fir is cultivated in nurseries for Christmas trees and for ornamental plants. In North America, the first attempt at such cultivation took place in Ottawa about 1900. For information on growing balsam fir for Christmas trees, see the references below by Estabrooks (1987) and Smith et al. (1983). Over the last century there has been some development of agri-forestry of balsam fir, i.e., growing it in plantations, but today there is limited interest in this. By contrast, there is considerable management of natural stands. This may include "reforestation", i.e., seeding or planting of seedlings in areas that have been harvested or devastated by natural forces such as the spruce budworm; however, often other tree species are preferred to balsam fir for reforestation.

CONSERVATION STATUS

The balsam fir is a common species in Canada and the northeastern U.S., and not in particular need of conservation measures. In the highlands of West Virginia where it reaches its southern limit, extensive logging has reduced the habitat, and the tree is also threatened by large populations of white tailed deer and infestations of the balsam wooly aphid. Concerned groups in West Virginia are attempting to conserve the balsam fir there. Some of the isolated stands elsewhere south of the boreal forest in Iowa, New York, Pennsylvania and Virginia are genetically depauperate and threatened by climate change.

MYTHS, LEGENDS, TALES, FOLKLORE AND INTERESTING FACTS

❦ Christmas trees dry out very rapidly indoors if their cut ends are not placed in water. Experiments with balsam fir showed that when the butts of the tree were placed in water, the trees remained completely resistant to fire after 3 weeks indoors, but when not provided with water, they became extremely flammable in about 2 weeks.

❦ *Abies guatemalensis* is an endangered Central American endemic found only in dwindling pockets in mountainous regions of Guatemala. Risking 10 years in jail, poachers illegally harvest the lemon-smelling branches, and poor street vendors staple them to poles for sale as Christmas trees. The species is also used for charcoal production and as timber. It is feared that it will become extinct within a few decades.

❦ A "witches' broom" is an abnormal tufted growth of small branches on a tree or shrub. A very conspicuous witches' broom of balsam fir is caused by the rust fungus *Melampsorella caryophyllacearum*. Witches' brooms on large trees have been observed to be used as homes by fishers, and as nesting sites by long-eared owls. Several dwarf cultivars have originated by propagating young trees discovered to have been dwarfed by the rust fungus.

Balsam fir (*Abies balsamea*) forest in Jacques-Cartier National Park, Quebec. Source: Wikimedia (photographer: Cephas; Creative Commons Attribution-Share Alike 3.0 Unported license).

A BIODIVERSITY TREASURE

SOURCES OF ADDITIONAL INFORMATION

Estabrooks, G.F. 1987. Growing balsam fir Christmas trees in field and forest. Canadian Forestry Service (Maritimes), Information Report M-X-164. Canadian Forestry Service, Fredericton, NB. 25 pp.

Bakuzis, E.V., and Hansen, H.L. 1965. Balsam fir. *Abies balsamea* (Linnaeus) Miller. A monographic review. University of Minnesota Press, Minneapolis, MN. 445 pp.

Hunt, R.S. 1993. *Abies. In* Flora of North America, vol. 2. *Edited by* Flora of North America Editorial Committee. Oxford University Press, Oxford, U.K. pp. 354–362.

Johnston, W.F. 1986. Manager's handbook for balsam fir in the North Central States. U.S. Dept. of Agriculture, Forest Service, North Central Forest Experiment Station [Saint Paul, MN], General Technical Report NC-111. 27 pp.

Lester, D.T. 1968. Variation in cone morphology of balsam fir, *Abies balsamea*. Rhodora 70: 83–94.

Sandberg, L.A., and Clancy, P. 2002. Politics, science and the spruce budworm in New Brunswick and Nova Scotia. J. Canadian Studies 37: 164–191.

Smith, C.C., Newell, W.R., and Renault, T.R. 1983. Common insects and diseases of balsam fir Christmas trees. Dept. Environment, Canadian Forestry Service, Publication 1328. 60 pp.

Balsam fir (*Abies balsamea*) at treeline in the White Mountains of New Hampshire. Source: Wikimedia (photographer: Muffinman71xx; Creative Commons Attribution-Share Alike 2.0 Generic license).

NEWFOUNDLAND AND LABRADOR

Provincial flag of Newfoundland and Labrador.

A NEWFOUNDLAND AND LABRADOR LANDSCAPE: a beautiful lake shore.

FLORAL EMBLEM: PITCHER PLANT

Clump of pitcher plants (*Sarracenia purpurea*). Source: Thinkstock.

SYMBOLISM

The pitcher plant is an excellent choice as the provincial floral emblem of Newfoundland and Labrador, in view of the long historical association with the region, as pointed out below, but also in that it is superbly adapted to and abundant in the widespread bogs and barrens. It has a unique appearance that reflects well the unique character of the province. A true carnivorous (meat-eating) plant, it has remarkable leaves that trap and digest insect prey. The fact that animal-eating plants are sometimes considered gruesome does not seem to have ever detracted from the favourable image of the plant.

Pitcher plant (*Sarracenia purpurea*). Source: Canadian Heritage. 2002. Symbols of Canada (revised edition). Canadian Heritage, Ottawa, ON. Reproduced with permission of Canadian Heritage and Public Works and Government Services Canada.

NAMES

Latin Names

Sarracenia purpurea L.

The genus *Sarracenia* commemorates French naturalist and surgeon Michel Sarrazin (1659–1735), who has been called the "Founder of Canadian Science". French botanist Joseph Pitton de Tournefort (1656–1708) coined the genus name in recognition of Sarrazin after the latter sent him the first collections of *S. purpurea* from Quebec, where he held the post of surgeon-major. The specific epithet *purpurea,* purple, points out the strong anthocyanin colouration usually evident in the species. The name *Sarracenia purpurea* has been "conserved", a legalistic procedure that maintains names even though older names normally get precedence (Taxon 49: 262. 2000; also see citations below).

English Names

Common pitcher plant, pitcher plant, northern pitcher plant (in the Canadian and northern parts of its range), southern pitcher plant (in the southern part of the range), purple pitcher plant. Pitcher plants take their name from the pitcher-like shape of their leaves (although some species have leaves shaped like urns or trumpets). Because the plants are so interesting, numerous names, now obsolete, were also employed, for example: Adam's cup, devil's cup, dumbwatches (used in the New Jersey Pine Barrens, so-named because of the resemblance of the style and sepals to old-style watches with a star-shaped pattern on the cover, "dumb" because the flowers really couldn't keep time), flytrap, forefather's cup, frog's britches, huntsman's cap, sidesaddle flower and sidesaddle plant ("sidesaddle" is an apparent reference to the peculiar umbrella-liked expansion of the style), and whippoorwill's boots.

French Names

Sarracénie pourpre. Archaic Quebec names include petits cochons (apparently based on the next name), oreille de cochon ("pig's ear," for resemblance to the pitcher-leaf), and herbe-crapaud ("toad-herb", based on the idea that this herb, like toads, eats insects).

HISTORY

Canada

The pitcher plant was adopted as the floral emblem of Newfoundland in 1954. Prior to 1947, it was depicted on the island's one-cent coin, the choice having been made by Queen Victoria (from 1834 until Confederation in 1949, Newfoundland issued its own coinage and bank notes).

Foreign

No other political area on Earth appears to have employed the purple pitcher plant as an official emblem. In 2005, the Venus' flytrap (= Venus flytrap, *Dionoea muscipula*) was proposed (Senate Bill 116) as North Carolina's "Official Carnivorous Plant".

A Newfoundland coin showing the pitcher plant. Queen Victoria chose it to be engraved on Newfoundland coins.

APPEARANCE

Pitcher plants are bizarre herbaceous perennials, individual plants living for up to 50 years. They produce a low rosette of unique, hollow, tubular, pitcher-shaped leaves, called "pitchers", as well as leaves of more conventional appearance. The latter, called "phyllodia", have much reduced pitchers and appear more leaf-like. The plants have a round, horizontal underground stem (rhizome or rootstock), and lack an above-ground stem (except for the flower/fruit stalk). Rhizome extension spreads the plant vegetatively.

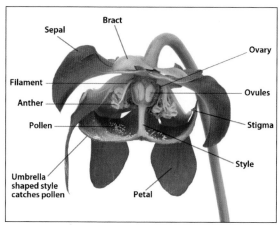

Long section of a pitcher plant flower showing its structure. Image by N. Elhardt, released into the public domain on Wikipedia.

Pitcher plant (*Sarracenia purpurea*) in Gros Morne National Park, Newfoundland and Labrador. Source: Wikipedia (photographer: D.G.E. Robertson; Creative Commons Attribution-Share Alike 3.0 Unported license).

A BIODIVERSITY TREASURE

CLASSIFICATION

Family: Sarraceniaceae (pitcher plant family).

The pitcher plant family is a small group of low-growing perennial herbs of bogs and wet savannas of the New World (there is also an unrelated Old World pitcher plant family, the Nepenthaceae). The largest genus, *Sarracenia,* has eight or nine species, and these occur in the Atlantic coastal regions of North America. Species of *Sarracenia* hybridize freely, and natural hybrids between *S. purpurea* and *S. flava* (the yellow pitcher plant) are common where their ranges overlap.

There is considerable variation within *S. purpurea,* and disagreement about how infraspecific groupings should be accepted. Generally, two subspecies are recognized: subsp. *purpurea* which is found in Canada, the Midwestern states and the northeastern states, and subsp. *venosa* (Raf.) Wherry, which occupies the southern part of the distribution range. The geographical boundary between the two subspecies is in southern Delaware and northern Maryland, and reflects the southernmost extent of the Pleistocene glaciation. Subspecies *purpurea* grows in formerly glaciated areas whereas subspecies *venosa* grows only in unglaciated areas. The subspecies are distinguished by shape of the pitcher hood, ratio of pitcher length to diameter of pitcher opening, presence or absence of hairs on the outside of the pitcher, and flower colour. However, a recent paper by Ellison et al. (2004) concluded that "there is no obvious way to distinguish these subspecies on morphological grounds alone." Alternative to treating the two groupings as subspecies, they have also been recognized as varieties: *S. purpurea* var. *purpurea* and *S. purpurea* var. *venosa* (a disconcerting technical difficulty with these names was circumvented in 2000; see Cheek et al. (1997) and Brummitt (2000)).

Subspecies *venosa* is often split into three varieties: var. *montana* Schnell & Determann in the southern Appalachians of Georgia and the Carolinas; var. *venosa* on the Atlantic coastal plain from Delaware and Maryland through Virginia and into the Carolinas, as well as occasionally rare occurrences in southern Georgia; and var. *burkii* Schnell in the Gulf coastal plain from the Florida panhandle into Louisiana (this is increasingly being recognized as a separate species, *S. rosea* Naczi, Case & Case).

In the distribution range of subsp. *purpurea,* a variation of the pitcher plant that lacks red colouration is often recognized as forma *heterophylla* (Eaton) Fernald. Such plants have been collected in various parts of the range, and presumably are based on mutations that prevent accumulation of anthocyanin pigments as occurs in normal plants. Other variants have been proposed but not accepted. The forma *incisa* Rousseau and Rouleau, described from Lac Albanel in Quebec, has the pistil disc deeply five-lobed. Variety *ripicola* Boivin, described from marly fens of the upper Great Lakes has numerous small, red pitchers but has been shown to develop fewer, larger green pitchers with red veins when transplanted to acid bog conditions, thus suggesting that its features are a consequence of habitat and unworthy of taxonomic recognition. The Nova Scotian forma *plena* Klawe was apparently based on a single floral freak and is also unworthy of recognition. Although several hybrids between *S. purpurea* and other species of *Sarracenia* have been recorded, none of these are in Canada; the parents of these hybrids occur further to the south.

Pitcher plant (*Sarracenia purpurea*). Source: Trail, C.P. and Fitzgibbon, A. 1868. Canadian WildFlowers. John Lovell, Montreal, Canada.

GEOGRAPHY

Sarracenia purpurea is the most widespread species in the pitcher plant family. It occurs from the sub-Arctic to the subtropics, ranging from Labrador to Great Slave Lake, and southward to Georgia, Florida, Alabama, Mississippi, and possibly Louisiana. Its wide geographic range includes much of Canada east of the Continental Divide, the northern United States westward through the Great Lakes region, New England, and the entire coastal plain of the eastern United States.

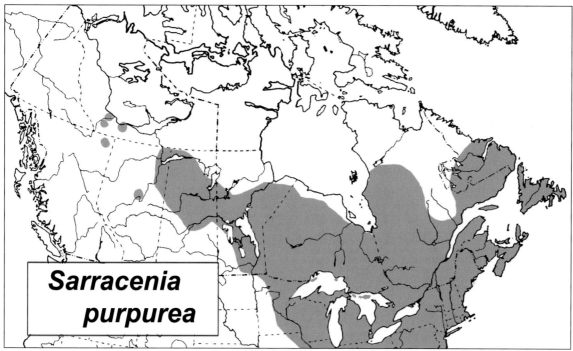

Canadian distribution of the pitcher plant (*Sarracenia purpurea*).

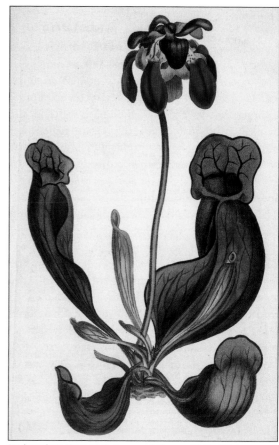

Pitcher plant (*Sarracenia purpurea*). Source: United States Department of Agriculture Research Service.

A BIODIVERSITY TREASURE

ECOLOGY

Habitat

Pitcher plants commonly occur in wet habitats, especially *Sphagnum* (peat moss) bogs in Canada and the northern part of their American range, but also in poor fens, seepage swamps and pine savannas, and even in the fast-flowing mountain streams of Georgia. The soils are saturated with water (acidic or alkaline as noted in the text box), and deficient in nitrates and phosphates. In sphagnum bogs, the base of the pitcher leaves are often buried in sphagnum.

Inter-species Relationships

There are relatively few flowering plants that digest flesh. Since insects are the main prey, such plants used to be called "insectivorous", but "carnivorous" has become the term of choice, because animals other than insects are also consumed. Pitcher plant leaves are remarkably constructed passive pitfalls designed to entrap insects and other tiny prey that have been lured to the mouth of the leaf by a light-reflecting patch and a trail of nectar-secreting glands extending from the lip of the pitcher down into it. Downward-pointing (retrorse) hairs in the lip of the throat of the pitcher help to prevent climbing upward to escape. The hairs are too dense to crawl between and are like a wall of spears. A hairless polished area in the steepest part of the throat acts like a greased slide, causing the exhausted prey to fall into accumulated rainwater at the bottom of the pitcher, where they drown. Digestive enzymes secreted from the polished area of the throat occur in the liquid. Both the enzymes as well as bacteria in the liquid serve to digest the trapped animals, and the odour of decay is often noticeable (it has been suggested that this may attract flies to the plants). Ants are the commonest insects trapped, but additionally there are often flies, wasps, spiders,

crickets and, less commonly, frogs, salamanders, and lizards are captured. In a Newfoundland study, slugs and snails were 20% of the prey. Indigestible parts of the animals accumulate in the pitchers, but older leaves eventually die and disintegrate.

The significance of the carnivorous habit in pitcher plants has been debated and there are several research studies, cited below, that deal with this. There is a general consensus that nitrogen compounds digested from the trapped animals are important to the plants which grow in habitats deficient in nitrogen. Trapped animals probably also serve as a source of phosphorus. While animals are a significant source of nitrogen, in some studies only about 10% of the plant's nitrogen budget comes from trapped animals. The roots are also quite inefficient at obtaining nitrogen from the substrate, obtaining as little as 5% of the plant's supply. Nitrogen-fixing bacteria have been found in the pitcher fluid, and these likely serve to increase the supply of nitrogen available to the plant. Rainwater (containing dust) and excretions from visiting (non-trapped) organisms that are present in the pitchers are also sources of nitrogen for the plants. As noted earlier, there are two kinds of leaves: insect-trapping pitchers and leaf-like phyllodia. Increased available nitrogen leads to fewer pitchers and more of the leaf-like phyllodia, thus supporting the interpretation that insect-trapping is important to supplement nitrogen.

Unlike the other species of the genus, the pitcher-leaves of *S. purpurea* do not have a hood that covers the opening, and this allows rain to freely enter the pitcher cavity. Also unlike most of the other species, the leaves of *S. purpurea* do not die back at the end of the growing season (i.e., they are evergreen), and

can survive freezing of the liquid inside the pitcher cavities. Leaves that have turned red in the fall may become green in the spring. The leaves usually last only 1 to 2 years, but young (pitcher) leaves, no older than 1 month, are known to trap most of the animals caught by the plants, and pitcher leaves older than 1 year have very low rates of photosynthesis.

In addition to pollinators, some animals are adapted to using the pitchers of pitcher plants as sources of food and/or shelter. Some of these insects have become so adapted to life in pitcher plant leaves that they cannot survive elsewhere. Three kinds of flies occur commonly

---

TWO DIFFERENT HABITATS: WHY?

In Canada, pitcher plants live in two very different kinds of habitats: acid, rain-fed ("ombrotrophic") bogs and alkaline groundwater-fed ("minerotrophic") fens. Bogs are dominated by sphagnum mosses and leathery-leaved shrubs of the heath family; they are irrigated by rainwater which is much like pure distilled water, i.e., without any nutrients, and they become progressively acidic. Fens are usually dominated by a sparse cover of grass-like plants; they are irrigated by ground water and often develop high concentrations of calcium and high alkalinity. These remarkably different habitats have one very important feature in common: low levels of macronutrients (nitrogen, phosphorus, potassium), so plants that capture and digest insects and other small organisms to supplement the few nutrients in their environment have an advantage. Indeed, both bogs and fens are host to a variety of other insectivorous plants.

ECOLOGY (CONT'D)

in pitcher plant leaves and they coexist by a spatial partitioning of the habitat and resources. Larvae of a midge fly (*Metriocnemus knabi*) feed on insect remains that accumulate at the bottom of the pitcher. Larvae of a sarcophagid fly (*Blaesoxipha fletcheri*) feed at the top of the pitchers on floating prey. Larvae of the pitcher plant mosquito (*Wyeomyia smithii*—see text box) live in the water, between the surface and the bottom. These inhabitants increase the rate of release of nitrogen from the decomposing prey and, to the benefit of the insects, the plant removes potentially toxic substances such as ammonia from the pitcher water and increases its oxygen content. The adults of these flies are able to fly in and out of the pitchers without being captured, and the larvae produce secretions that protect them against the digestive enzymes of the plant. Several species of moths feed on pitcher plants. One of these (*Exyra fax*) eats a hole in the leaves, draining the pitcher contents. It then feeds on the leaf tissue and passes the winter in cocoons inside the empty pitcher. The caterpillars of another moth (*Papaipema appassionata*) bore down the flower stems to eat the rootstock, often killing the entire plant. Both of these moths are evidently unique to pitcher plants. Birds sometimes slit pitchers to get at the insects. In all, the pitchers are home to about 20 kinds of insects, several species of mites, at least 25 genera of algae, at least 40 species of protozoa, and numerous other microorganisms.

Pollination & Dispersal

Pitcher plants produce flowers in early summer. The anthers shed their pollen onto the inverted umbrella-like style, where ants, beetles, and especially bees pick up the grains. Although self-pollination can occur, the flowers are basically outcrossing, and the pollen matures first, so that fertilization occurs primarily when pollinators transfer the grains to an older flower of another plant. Seeds are produced late in the season, with of the order of 1,000 seeds in a capsule. The seeds do not have specializations for distribution, but it has been suggested that they may be dispersed by flotation in water or by adhesion to wet fur or feathers.

USES

Pitcher plants are of minor economic importance. Indians in Newfoundland once used the roots to treat smallpox, a treatment that became popular for a brief period in the nineteenth century in England. A proprietary liquid extract of the roots was once used by physicians to treat neuralgia.

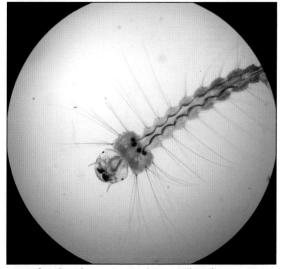

Larva of pitcher plant mosquito. Source: Wikipedia (photographer: Rkitko; Creative Commons Attribution-Share Alike 3.0 Unported license).

LIVING IN A PLANT'S STOMACH

While the leaf of the pitcher plant is a deadly trap for many insects, some species have adapted to life in it. The pitcher plant mosquito, *Wyeomyia smithii,* is one of the most interesting of 80 species of mosquitoes found in Canada. It appears to be totally dependent on the pitcher plant for survival. All Canadian mosquitoes have their larval stages in water but the larvae of this one have only been found in the water-filled leaves of the pitcher plant. Here, with their very specialized mouth parts, they filter bacteria and protozoa from the water. They can be found in the leaves at all times of the year. They can even spend several months encased in the core of ice that develops in the leaves overwinter. Their closest relatives occur in tropical regions of Central and South America where the larvae live in the water that collects in the leaf bases of epiphytic bromeliads (pineapple relatives) of wet rainforest and high elevation cloud forest. The pitcher plant mosquito differs from all others in Canada in that the sexes cannot be readily distinguished by differences in the antennae. While females of most Canadian species require a blood meal in order to develop eggs, the females of the pitcher plant mosquito do not take blood. Males of all of the 80 kinds of Canadian mosquitoes feed only on nectar from flowers.

Painting of pitcher plants (*Sarracenia purpurea*) in their natural setting, from the Walter Coucill Canadian Centennial official flowers of Canada series (see Coucill 1966 cited in the first chapter of this book). Reproduced with the permission of the copyright holders, the Coucill family.

CULTIVATION

For centuries, pitcher plants have been cultivated as curiosities. They make interesting, perennial ornamentals, both outdoors and indoors. As with most carnivorous plant species, growing conditions require acidic, wet soil (sphagnum peat and/or coarse sand should make up most of the substrate), good exposure to light is essential, and elevated humidity (60–90% has been recommended). Use of a loosely covered terrarium is one way to promote high humidity. Plastic pots are preferable to unglazed clay, and wide pots are best to accommodate the reclining pitchers. Fertilization should be avoided or at least extremely limited. Most people who have acquired carnivorous plants are tempted to feed them with leftover scraps of hamburger and the like—a mistake. Providing freshly killed insects in moderation is more likely to ensure survival.

CONSERVATION STATUS

Although *S. purpurea* is so widespread that it is not endangered in most of its range, the area occupied is decreasing, due mostly to habitat destruction and changes in water table levels. In Georgia, *S. purpurea* is considered to be Endangered. Several public and private organizations have attempted to restore a population of *S. purpurea* subsp. *venosa* var. *montana* in Georgia. Several southern U.S. endemic species of *Sarracenia* also have federal and/or state endangered status, and are protected by legislation. There is a large appetite for carnivorous plants in the horticultural trade, and unfortunately *Sarracenia* species are often simply collected from the wild and sold. Another factor that bears on conservation of *Sarracenia* is their restriction to wetlands, especially bogs, which are often the target of conversion for agriculture or other purposes.

Pitcher-like leaves of pitcher plant (*Sarracenia purpurea*). Source: Thinkstock.

MYTHS, LEGENDS, TALES, FOLKLORE AND INTERESTING FACTS

✤ A widespread myth about carnivorous plants is that, when grown in a house, they will catch all the flies present. They have also been recommended as a way of ridding a dwelling of cockroaches. However, it is mostly non-flying, small insects that are trapped, and carnivorous plants are not efficient enough to control household pests.

✤ Despite popular stories to the contrary, carnivorous plants are not capable of harming people. The largest prey—frogs, and rarely birds and small rodents such as rats—are sometimes captured by species of Southeast Asian *Nepenthes,* the vines sometimes reaching lengths of 15 m (50 feet), and the pitchers holding as much as 4 L (1 American gallon).

✤ The Sarraceniaceae family is considered native to the Americas. The first fossil plant belonging to the family, *Archaeamphora longicervia* Li, was recently reported from northeastern China. The fossil is quite reminiscent of *S. purpurea,* and its discovery suggests that flowering plants may have evolved much earlier than commonly believed. [See: Li, H. 2005. Early Cretaceous sarraceniacean-like pitcher plants from China. Acta Botanica Gallica 152: 227–234.]

SOURCES OF ADDITIONAL INFORMATION

Adams, R.M., II, and Barton, C. 1976. The flesh eaters: *Sarracenia purpurea,* the northern pitcher plant. Garden J. (U.S.A.) 26: 154–157.

Brummitt, R.K. 2000. Proposals to conserve or reject: report of the Committee for Spermatophyta: 49. Proposal 1316, to conserve *Sarracenia purpurea* with new type (Sarraceniaceae). Taxon 49: 262–263.

Chapin, C.T., and Pastor, J. 1995. Nutrient limitations in the northern pitcher plant *Sarracenia purpurea.* Can. J. Bot. 73: 728–734.

Cheek, M., Schnell, D., Reveal, J.L., and Schlauer, J. 1997. Proposal to conserve the name *Sarracenia purpurea* (Sarraceniaceae) with a new type. Taxon 46: 781–783.

Cody, W.J., and Talbot, S.S. 1973. The pitcher plant *Sarracenia purpurea* L. in the northwestern part of its range. Can. Field–Nat. 87: 318–320.

Cruise, J.E., and Catling, P.M. 1971. The pitcher-plant in Ontario. Ontario Naturalist 9(1): 18–21.

Ellison, A.M., and Gotelli, N.J. 2002. Nitrogen availability alters the expression of carnivory in the northern pitcher plant, *Sarracenia purpurea.* Proc. Nat. Acad. Sci. U.S.A. 99: 4409–4412.

Ellison, A.M., and Parker, J.N. 2002. Seed dispersal and seedling establishment of *Sarracenia purpurea* (Sarraceniacae). Am. J. Bot. 89: 1024–1026.

Ellison, A.M., Buckley, H.L., Miller, T.E., and Gotelli, N.J. 2004. Morphological variation in *Sarracenia purpurea* (Sarraceniaceae): geographic, environmental, and taxonomic correlates. Am. J. Bot. 91: 1930–1935.

Giberson, D., and Hardwick, M.L. 1999. Pitcher plants (*Sarracenia purpurea*) in eastern Canadian peatlands. Ecology and conservation of the invertebrate Inquilines. *In* Invertebrates in fresh-water wetlands of North America: ecology and management. *Edited by* D.P. Batzer, R.B. Rader, and S.A. Wissinger. John Wiley & Sons, Inc., New York, NY. pp. 401–422.

Godt, M.J.W., and Hamrick, J.L. 1999. Genetic divergence among infraspecific taxa of *Sarracenia purpurea.* Syst. Bot. 23: 427–438.

Gotelli, N.J., and Ellison, A.M. 2002. Nitrogen deposition and extinction risk in the northern pitcher plant, *Sarracenia purpurea.* Ecology 83: 2758–2765.

Heard, S.B. 1998. Capture rates of invertebrate prey by the pitcher plant, *Sarracenia purpurea* L. Am. Midl. Nat. 139: 79–89.

Newell, S.J., and Nastase, A.J. 1998. Efficiency of insect capture by *Sarracenia purpurea* (Sarraceniaceae), the northern pitcher plant. Am. J. Bot. 85: 88–91.

Paterson, C.G. 1971. Overwintering ecology of the aquatic fauna associated with the pitcher plant *Sarracenia purpurea* L. Can. J. Zool. 49: 1455–1459.

Reveal, J.L. 1993. The correct name of the northern expression of *Sarracenia purpurea* L. (Sarraceniaceae). Phytologia 74: 180–184.

Schnell, D.E. 1979. A critical review of published variants of *Sarracenia purpurea* L. Castanea 44: 47–59.

Schnell, D.E. 2002. Carnivorous plants of the United States and Canada. Second edition. Timber Press, Portland, OR. 468 pp.

Wherry, E.T. 1933. The geographic relations of *Sarracenia purpurea.* Bartonia 15: 1–6.

TREE: BLACK SPRUCE

Black spruce (*Picea mariana*) in Grands-Jardins National Park, Quebec. Source: Wikipedia (photographer: Cephas; Creative Commons Attribution-Share Alike 3.0 Unported license).

SYMBOLISM

There are few parts of the province where black spruce is not a prominent feature of the landscape, and so black spruce is a very familiar reminder of home to the citizens of Newfoundland and Labrador. The tree flourishes in the cool maritime climate. To those "from away" the pointed spires give a somewhat harsh look but to residents they represent home. In many parts of coastal regions the plants develop dense, low and virtually impenetrable thickets known locally as "tuckamore". These low dense forests extend for miles over the coastal headlands and surround extensive boggy meadows with caribou and abundant moose. They offer valued shelter from strong coastal winds. Black Spruce has a history of economic and social importance to the province that makes it an excellent choice as the provincial tree.

Silhouette of black spruce (*Picea mariana*). Source: J.L. Farrar 1995. Trees in Canada. Canadian Forest Service and Fitzhenry and Whiteside, Markham, ON, Canada. Reproduced with permission.

NAMES

Latin Names
Picea mariana (Mill.) BSP.

The genus name *Picea* is based on the Latin word *pix* used for some species of pine and also for the "pitch" (resin) from coniferous trees. (The English word "pizza" comes from the Latin, *picea,* black ashes from the floor of the fireplace, which has nothing to do with the genus *Picea*.) *Mariana* in the scientific name *P. mariana* is Latin for "of Maryland". Miller (the "Mill." in the scientific name) considered "Maryland" to mean "North America". Actually, black spruce is not native to the state of Maryland. (In some other scientific names, *mariana* refers to the Virgin Mary, mother of Jesus Christ.)

English Names
Black spruce is also known as bog spruce, swamp spruce, and shortleaf black spruce. While not actually "black" as the common name suggests, the twigs, cones, and bark are a darker brown than in related species. The word "spruce" has been explained as a modification of the old French *Pruse* (corresponding to the German *Preussen*), referring to Prussia, so named because in Europe spruces were associated with Prussia, particularly for making spruce beer. However, exactly the same explanation has been given for "spruce" in the sense of "neat and smart-looking" because, it has been argued, in the sixteenth century Prussian leather was used to make neat, smart-looking garments. An alternative explanation for the word spruce (as a tree) holds that the word comes from the German name of the tree, *Sprossenfichte,* literally "sprouts-fir".

French Names
Épinette noire; also épicéa glauque, épicéa marial, épinette à bière.

HISTORY

Canada
Black spruce was proclaimed to be the provincial tree of Newfoundland and Labrador in May of 1991.

Foreign
Picea mariana does not appear to have official emblem status elsewhere, although species of *Picea* have been widely designated as official trees in northern areas. Red spruce (*P. rubens* Sarg.) is the provincial tree of Nova Scotia, and white spruce (*P. glauca* (Moench) Voss) is the provincial tree of Manitoba. The blue spruce (*P. pungens* Engelm.) was made the state tree of Utah in 1933. Under the name Colorado blue spruce, it was proclaimed the state tree of Colorado in 1939. Alaska declared its state tree to be the Sitka spruce (*P. sitchensis* (Bong.) Carrière) in 1962.

APPEARANCE

Black spruce is a small to medium-sized evergreen tree. Especially near the tree line (alpine or boreal), black spruce grows as dwarf shrubs or stunted forest ("krummholz"). The dwarf shrubs have been named as varieties or forms (e.g., *P. mariana* f. *semiprostrata* (Peck) Blake). The trunk of normal trees is characteristically straight, with limited taper. The bark is scaly, unlike that of the similar balsam fir (*Abies balsamea* (L.) Mill.). The branches are typically short, drooping, with upturned tips. Dead branches often remain on the tree for several years. The lower branches, frequently having been strongly depressed by snow, often layer (i.e., they take root and produce new plants), so that a ring of young plants may form around an established tree (an arrangement referred to as a "candelabrum"). Through much of its range black spruce averages 9–15 m (30–50 feet) in height and 15–25 cm (6–10 inches) in diameter, occasionally growing to 30 m (100 feet) and 1 m (3 feet) in diameter. The trees are smaller—up to 20 m (66 feet) high and 30 cm (1 foot) in diameter—on poorly drained sites. The roots are shallow and widespreading. The leaves are needle-like, stiff, and sharp-pointed, dark bluish-green, generally coated with a whitish powder, and spirally arranged on the twigs. They are square in cross section, rather than flat as in balsam fir and hemlock (*Tsuga canadensis* (L.) Carrière). When crushed, the fresh foliage produces a strong scent of balsam or lemon balm. The cones (fruits) are 1.5–3 cm (0.6–1.2 inches) long, smaller than most other spruce species, and persist in the upper crown for several years.

In its range, black spruce could be mistaken for white spruce (*P. glauca*) or red spruce (*P. rubens*). The cones of white spruce are much longer (about 5 cm or 2 inches). Rarely, white spruce hybridizes with black spruce to produce plants called Rosendahl spruce. Red spruce, a native of eastern Canada and the eastern United States, frequently hybridizes with black spruce where their ranges overlap, and it is often very difficult to distinguish the two species.

Characteristically persisting cones of black spruce (*Picea mariana*). Photo by P.M. Catling.

APPEARANCE (CONT'D)

The following table (based on Morgenstern and Farrar 1964) points out key differences.

Differences between black spruce and the very closely related red spruce

Character	Black spruce *(Picea mariana)*	Red spruce *(Picea rubens)*
Male flowers	Dark red, subglobose	Bright red, oval
Immature cones	Purplish green to deep purple	Green to purplish green
Mature cones	Dull, gray-brown to brown, short-ovoid, persistent for 20–30 years, 2–4 cm long	Lustrous reddish brown, ovoid-oblong, falling within one year, 3–5 cm long
Cone base	Gradually narrows to strongly incurved stalk	Narrows more abruptly to less incurved stalk
Cone scales	Irregularly toothed on margins	Entire or slightly toothed on margins
Seeds	Very dark brown, about 882,000 to the kg	Dark brown, about 309,000 to the kg
First season seedlings	Number of cotyledons 2–7, predominantly 4	Number of cotyledons 4–8, predominantly 6
Needle shape and length	Slightly incurved above middle, 6–12 mm long	More strongly incurved above middle, 10–16 mm long
Needle colour	Bluish green, dull	Dark yellowish green, shiny
Number of lines of stomata on one lower surface	Mostly 3–4	Mostly 1–2
Buds, old trees	Ovoid, minutely pubescent	Ovoid, acute; reddish brown
Bud colour, young trees	Dull, grayish brown	Shiny, dark reddish brown
Twig surface shape	Decurrent ridges to which needles are attached are flat	Decurrent ridges are round
Twig pubescence	Twigs pubescent; hairs tipped with glands, crooked	Twigs more or less pubescent; hairs without glands, straight and conical
Twig colour, mature trees	Cinnamon-brown or blackish-brown	Orange-brown
Twig colour, four- to ten-year-old open grown trees	Yellowish brown with a purplish tinge	Straw-yellow
Bark	Grayish brown, flaky scales; inner layers somewhat olive-green	Predominantly reddish brown, firm scales; inner layers reddish grown
Form of crown in older stands	Open, irregular-cylindrical; branches drooping, turning up at ends	Broadly conical; middle and upper branches at right angles to trunk, then turning up at ends, often giving a pagoda effect

CLASSIFICATION

Family: Pinaceae (pine family)

There are about 35 species of the genus *Picea,* including seven that are native to North America. The plants are evergreen, coniferous (cone-bearing) shrubs and trees with short (generally less than 2.5 cm or 1 inch), needle-like leaves.

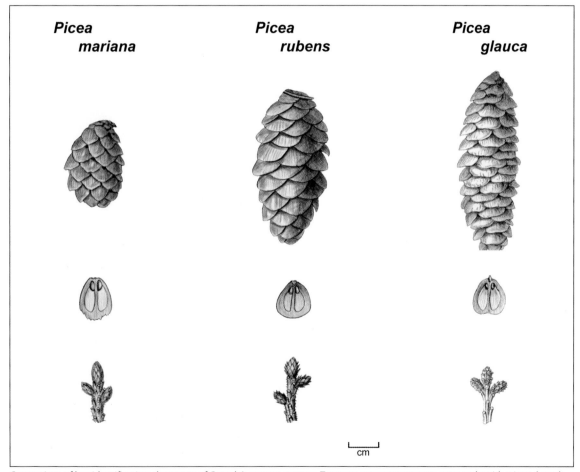

Comparison of key identification characters of Canada's eastern spruces. Top row: cones; centre row: cone scale with winged seeds; bottom row: Twigs (needles removed) showing winter buds. Source: Sargent 1898 (cited above), plates 596, 597, 598.

Black spruce (*Picea mariana*) tree trunk. Source: BugwoodImages/ForestryImages (photographer: K. Kanoti; Creative Commons Attribution 3.0 license).

A BIODIVERSITY TREASURE

GEOGRAPHY

Black spruce is widely distributed in North America, from Newfoundland to Alaska, north to the tree line, south to British Columbia and Minnesota, and east to Rhode Island and Massachusetts.

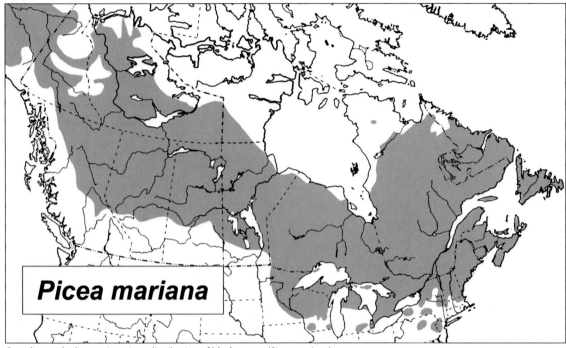

Picea mariana

Canadian and adjacent American distribution of black spruce (*Picea mariana*).

Young female cones of black spruce (*Picea mariana*). Source: Wikimedia (photographer: Clarity; Creative Commons Attribution 2.0 Generic license).

DOES BLACK SPRUCE FORM THE CANADIAN POLAR TREE LINE?

A frequently asked question is which tree extends the furthest north to form the "polar tree line". Throughout most of Canada the northernmost of the trees (even when they may not be more than several inches tall) is white spruce (*Picea glauca*) but black spruce does form the treeline in continental Nunavut and in parts of Ungava. In much of Europe, treeline is formed by Norway spruce (*Picea abies*) and Scots Pine (*Pinus sylvestris*), whereas in Siberia, Dahurian larch (*Larix dahurica*) and dwarf Siberian pine (*Pinus pumila*) form the polar treeline and no species of spruce comes close. For a more detailed discussion of treeline, see Hustich (1953) in Arctic 6(2): 149–162, and the information in the chapter on Nunavut.

ECOLOGY

Habitat

Black spruce is a dominant component of boreal forests of North America, where it grows in a variety of climates, on both organic and mineral soils. It is most commonly found on poorly drained, acidic peatlands. The species does best in a cool, subhumid climate, and in the southern parts of its range it is restricted to cool swamps and subalpine forest zones of the higher mountains. Black spruce is moderately shade-tolerant. The tree usually produces pure stands only on shallow, poorly drained, cold, organic soils where competition is limited. On the thinner soils and where there is a high water table, black spruce is very susceptible to windthrow because of the shallow root system.

Inter-species Relationships

Since black spruce is a dominant species in much of the boreal forest region, it should not be surprising that many organisms depend upon it. The needles are a major food of the spruce grouse, especially during the winter months when the intestinal tract of the birds elongates to enable digestion of such tough food. Many birds including chickadees, nuthatches, crossbills, grosbeaks, and pine siskins eat the seeds as do a variety of mammals including red squirrels, snowshoe hares, mice, voles, shrews, and chipmunks. The dense growth provides cover for many species including moose, deer, and caribou. Numerous birds nest in the trees, among them the ruby-crowned kinglet, magnolia warbler, Cape May warbler, and ovenbird.

Among the many insects associated with black spruce, two are particularly noteworthy. Why the bog elfin (*Callophrys lanoraieensis*), a tiny brown butterfly, is rare and local is a mystery since the only food plant of the caterpillars is the widespread black spruce. The young caterpillars burrow in the spruce needles. The adult butterflies, a little larger than houseflies with a wingspan of 2 cm (0.8 inch), often fly among the tops of the spruces. If not quite the smallest butterfly in Canada, this is certainly the most difficult to observe. Adults of the spruce budworm moth (*Choristoneura fumiferana*) are about the same size. The larvae actually feed more on balsam fir than spruce, but black spruce is particularly susceptible where it is mixed with the fir. Despite natural control by a number of tiny parasitic wasps and flies, spruce budworm can be devastating to large areas of forest. As a result, it is a target for control in areas of commercial black spruce harvest. Other insects that defoliate trees causing extensive damage include European, yellowheaded, and greenheaded spruce sawflies.

The crown of black spruce trees is often deformed near the top by red squirrels (*Tamiasciurus hudsonicus*). The tips of cone-bearing branches at the top are chewed off by the squirrels, resulting in a characteristic dense mass of small branches with many cones at the top of the tree (often called a "club" or a "crow's nest") and a bare portion of trunk just below.

ESSENCE OF THE BOREAL FOREST

Black Spruce is the most prominent tree of the Boreal Forest, an ecosystem that extends as a nearly continuous subarctic belt across North America and Eurasia and represents one third of the planet's forests. The Canadian Boreal Forest is a relatively recent development. It occupies a vast territory that was glaciated only 10,000 years ago and occurs in a cold continental climate where winters are severe. Black spruce is well adapted to these conditions. The narrowly conical shape of the tree allows snow to be shed without damage to branches. The needle-like leaves have a low surface area to volume ratio which dramatically reduces moisture loss when the ground is frozen and trees cannot replenish their water supply from the roots. The evergreen habit allows photosynthesis as soon as temperatures in the short growing season permit, thus avoiding delay for leaf growth.

The wilds of the Boreal Forest are home to fur-bearing animals that were the basis of early trade with Europe; beaver, muskrat, mink, ermine, fisher, marten, wolverine, lynx and others. They brought the voyageurs and the Hudson's Bay Company. Although the boreal forest region is almost uninhabited compared to the rest of Canada, it is no longer a pristine wilderness. To the contrary, it is riddled with development related to logging, mining, and hydroelectric development, which represent a threat to northern species, such as the woodland caribou. It is hoped that with a major planning effort, the biodiversity of the Boreal Forest and the associated traditional lifestyles of first nations such as the Cree, Innu, Métis, Dene, Gwich'in and Athabascan can be protected.

ECOLOGY (CONT'D)

Somewhat similar dense masses of branches called "witches' brooms" are formed where dwarf mistletoe (*Arceuthobium pusillum*), a parasitic flowering plant, grows on the branches. The parasite obtains most of its nutrients through root-like structures that penetrate the host branch. This particular species of mistletoe, the only one found in eastern Canada, is indeed tiny, with the leaves reduced to scales and the plant less than 2 cm (0.8 inch) in length. It is most often found on black spruce but also grows on white spruce, red spruce, blue spruce, balsam fir, tamarack, and on white, red and jack pine. Although these mistletoe plants are very small, they can discharge the seeds with an explosive mechanism up to 16.5 m (55 feet), but more often 1.5–6 m (5–20 feet) and at a speed of 80 kph (50 mph). The seeds are sticky and attach to whatever they hit. Birds may carry the seeds long distances on their feet. A fungus, spruce broom rust (*Chrysomyxa arctostaphylii*), also produces witches brooms in the trees but these lack the characteristic cups on the branches which indicate where the male flowers of mistletoe infection were shed. The mistletoe can do substantial damage, and is often subject to control in areas of commercial production.

With devastation by fire and infestations of insects, the boreal forest is subject to short-term, cyclical change, unlike some of the ecosystems further to the south that develop sustained climax forests. Although periodic fires and infestations are alarming, in fact they are to some extent natural processes to which the flora and fauna are adapted.

Pollination & Dispersal
Pollen and seeds are both carried by the wind. The seeds are equipped with a prominent wing to assist in wind transport. The species reproduces both by seed and by layering following cutting or fire. The trees are easily killed by fire, but the cones are serotinous—adapted to releasing seeds following fire. (Most seeds are released from 2 months to 3 years following a fire, but viable seeds may be dispersed from a given cone for more than 25 years.) Because fire often occurs (every 50–150 years) in black spruce habitats, the stands are often made up of even-aged trees. However, ages up to 300 years have been recorded (a longevity of 500 years has been claimed).

Black spruce (*Picea mariana*) stand. Source: Thinkstock.

USES

The principal economic value of spruce is as a north-temperate softwood tree used for construction lumber and paper pulp. Spruce trees are often used as Christmas trees, and while black spruce was often cut down for this purpose in the past, it is now rarely employed (the needles tend to fall off the cut tree fairly quickly). Most black spruce is used for pulpwood, and the species is highly valued by the pulp and paper industry, especially in Canada where it is the leading pulpwood source. Some black spruce is used for construction framing, general millwork, boxes, crates, and piano sounding boards (thin spruce boards have exceptional resonance qualities; see use in violins, below). Because of the relatively small size of the trees, spruce lumber is of secondary importance.

North American Indians prepared a string from the long roots and employed this to stitch together bark for canoes, to sew baskets, and for similar uses. They also used pitch (resin) from the trunk to seal the hulls of their canoes. Pitch from the trunk or branches was used by Native Peoples for a variety of medical problems, both externally (for burns, wounds, and various skin conditions), as a gargle (for sore throats and toothaches), and internally (for coughs, diarrrhea, and other conditions). Spruce resin is used today to a very minor extent for medicinal salves.

Although not particularly appealing, some spruce trees have been used as food. It has been said (tongue in cheek) that Christmas trees are edible. Amerindians used the exuded resin of several North American spruce species as a chewing gum, and spruce gum was quite popular in the early eighteenth century among European settlers. The first commercial chewing gum in North America, manufactured in Maine about 1850, was made with spruce resin. Indians used the bark or twigs of several species to make tea or flavour other beverages. Black spruce was used to brew a beer by the Anticosti Indians of North America. The inner bark in the spring and early summer, and the stripped young shoots have been consumed as emergency food. "Spruce tips" is a phrase occasionally used in North America to refer to young branches of black or white spruce. These are used for ornamental purposes in bouquets and floral arrangements, but also for flavouring purposes, for examples: like capers in fish dishes, chopped fine into a sauce, or used directly in salads. Spruce wood is almost tasteless and odourless, and is the preferred wood for food containers.

SPRUCE BEER

Spruce beer is manufactured in North America and Northern Europe. Now considered a weird beverage, it was popular in the United States and Canada during colonial times. Spruce leaves are rich in vitamin C, and spruce beer was a favoured remedy for scurvy, a common malady of the immigrants, soldiers, and sailors. Daily rations of spruce beer (typically a pint or a quart) were widely given to soldiers in Canada and the northern United States and to sailors until the value of citrus fruits to prevent scurvy became appreciated. "Chowder beer" is a beverage made by boiling black spruce twigs in water and mixing in molasses. This concoction is virtually unknown today, but in past times in the New World it was prepared as a palatable anti-scurvy drink (spruce providing the vitamin C). An alcoholic version of this, "callibogus" (calabogus, calibogus, calibougas; usually pronounced kahl-ee-boh-gahs), made of molasses, rum, and spruce beer, was a favourite drink of the admirals of North American colonial days. Today, it is essentially known only in Newfoundland, where it is also called "quick-call-an-ambulance"! Newfoundlanders make this brew with "screech" (a Newfoundland term for cheap, potent Jamaican rum, tracing to an early twentieth century British term for harsh whiskey). Genuine spruce beer (as distinguished from soft drinks with this name) is beer flavoured with spruce twigs or spruce extract.

Recipe for Spruce Beer used in the Eighteenth Century at the Fortress of Louisbourg
(from The Louisbourg Institute website)

Bring 4 gallons of water to a boil, add a bundle of spruce twigs (approximately 20" in diameter, using only the last 6" of the tips of the boughs) and bring to a boil again. Boil for one hour, longer for a stronger spruce flavour. Strain twice through a piece of fine (tightly woven, not cheesecloth) white cloth, into a container. When the liquid is lukewarm, add molasses (approximately 2 quarts, or to taste) and a package of dried yeast, proofed in ½ cup molasses and 3 cups warm (body temperature) water; mix well. Cover loosely with cloth and allow 3–4 days to ferment. Skim the foam lightly from the top frequently; do not stir or disturb the beer. When the bubbles cease to rise, strain through a cloth again. It can be bottled at this point or drunk immediately. If it is bottled, leave about 3" of space at the top of each bottle. Do not tighten the caps for at least 12 hours.

CULTIVATION

Black spruce is easily grown in tree nurseries, and is often planted for harvest of timber and pulp. Although not considered exceptional for ecological planting, black spruce is used in mixed plantings intended for erosion control and windbreaks. Breeding, or at least selection of superior genotypes, has been conducted in federal and provincial forestry departments. Black spruce is one of the main species used for reforestation in Canada. Experimental plantations for timber have even been established in northern Europe. Although black spruce is rarely grown as an ornamental tree, there are several ornamental cultivars, including a dwarf form known as 'Nana'.

Spruce beer sellers in Jamaica. Spruce beer (originating from North America) was popular with sailors in old times as the high vitamin C content prevented scurvy. Source: Harper's Monthly Magazine 22: 169 (Jan. 1861).

CONSERVATION STATUS

Black spruce is one of the most widespread and abundant species in North America, and therefore there is little risk of its becoming endangered. Although there has been very limited taxonomic subdivision of *P. mariana,* it is possible that at its distribution limits in northern Canada the species has developed genes specialized for survival in extreme stress, and such unique plants may be useful in the future for forestry and agriculture. While black spruce is not in need of special conservation measures, because it is a principal forest resource for Canada and is quite slow-growing in its natural habitats, it requires wise management policies. The tree is intolerant of atmospheric pollution, and its health can be seriously affected by acid rain. The species is naturally adapted to the extremely widespread boreal regions of Canada, and climate change therefore represents a considerable potential future threat, especially to isolated occurrences near the southern range limit, such as in southern Ontario.

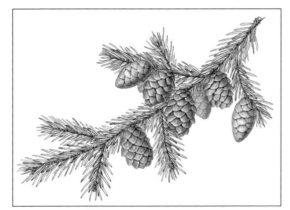

Fruiting branch of black spruce (*Picea mariana*). Source: Sargent, C.S. 1898. The silva of North America. Houghton, Mifflin and Company, Boston, MA. vol. 12, plate 596.

Seedling and winged seed of black spruce (*Picea mariana*). Source: Sargent, C.S. 1898. The silva of North America. Houghton, Mifflin and Company, Boston, MA. vol. 12, plate 596.

MYTHS, LEGENDS, TALES, FOLKLORE AND INTERESTING FACTS

🍁 French explorer and navigator Jacques Cartier (1491–1557) discovered the St. Lawrence River in 1535. During his second voyage in 1536, he decided to overwinter in the river, and his ship became frozen in the icy waters near Quebec City. By March, twenty-five of his crew had died of scurvy, and only a handful of healthy sailors were left. At the time, the need to supply vitamin C to prevent scurvy was unknown. Cartier then sought help from tribal chief Dom Agaya, who brought branches of an evergreen tree he called *annedda,* and instructed that the branches should be ground up, boiled into a tea, and drunk every 2 days. The cure worked, because conifer needles, including those of spruce, pine, balsam fir, hemlock and cedar, yield three to five times the vitamin C of oranges. *Annedda* has not been identified, but it would seem probable that it was spruce.

🍁 The Italian Antonius Stradivarius (1644?–1682) is considered to be the greatest of all violin makers, and alpine spruce was one of the woods he favoured for his instruments. The rich resonance of his instruments remains a secret, but has often been attributed to some special varnish or wood treatment. An article by H. Grissino-Mayer and L. Burckle in the July 2003 issue of the scientific journal Dendrochronologia hypothesized that the superior sound was due to exceptionally dense wood developed in alpine spruce as it grew very slowly because of very cool conditions that prevailed in Europe before and during the time of Stradivarius.

🍁 The chopsticks provided at fast food restaurants in the Far East are frequently made of black spruce wood.

Black spruce (*Picea mariana*) stand. Source: United States Fish and Wildlife Service.

A BIODIVERSITY TREASURE

SOURCES OF ADDITIONAL INFORMATION

Begin, C., and Filion, L. 1999. Black spruce (*Picea mariana*) architecture. Can. J. Bot. 77: 664–672.

Fraser, D.A. 1966. Vegetative and reproductive growth of black spruce (*Picea mariana* (Mill.) BSP.) Can. J. Bot. 44: 567–580.

Gordon, A.G. 1976. The taxonomy and genetics of *Picea rubens* and its relationship to *Picea mariana*. Can. J. Bot. 54: 781–813.

Great Lakes Forest Research Centre. 1975. Black spruce symposium. Canadian Forestry Service, Dept. of the Environment, Sault Ste. Marie, ON. 289 pp.

Haavisto, V.F., Cameron, D.A., and Crook, G.W. 1995. Bibliography of black spruce literature published by the Canadian Forest Service—Ontario, Great Lakes Forestry Centre 1965–1995. Great Lakes Forestry Centre, Sault Ste-Marie, ON. 34 pp.

Hawley, G.J., DeHayes, D.H., and Badger, G.J. 2000. Red and black spruce introgression in montane ecosystems in New England and New York. J. Sustain. For. 10: 327–333.

Heinselman, M.L. 1957. Silvical characteristics of black spruce (*Picea mariana*). Lake States Forest Experiment Station, Forest Service, U.S. Dept. of Agriculture, St. Paul, MN. 30 pp.

Jaramillo-Correa, J.P., and Bousquet, J. 2003. New evidence from mitochondrial DNA of a progenitor-derivative species relationship between black spruce and red spruce (Pinaceae). Am. J. Bot. 90: 1801–1806.

Jaramillo-Correa, J.P., Beaulieu, J., and Bousquet, J. 2004. Variation in mitochondrial DNA reveals multiple distant glacial refugia in black spruce (*Picea mariana*), a transcontinental North American conifer. Molec. Ecol. 13: 2735–2747.

Johnston, W.F. 1977. Manager's handbook for black spruce in the north central states. North Central Forest Experiment Station, Forest Service, U.S. Dept. of Agriculture, St. Paul, MN. 18 pp.

Lamhamedi, M.S., and Bernier, P.Y. 1994. Ecophysiology and field performance of black spruce (*Picea mariana*): a review. Ann. Sci. Forest. (France). 51: 529–551. (In French)

Larsen, E.L. 1939. Pehr Kalm's description of spruce beer. Am. Agric. 22: 142–143.

Morgenstern, E.K., and Farrar, J.L. 1964. Introgressive hybridization in red spruce and black spruce. Forest Research Branch Contribution No. 608. Forest Research Branch, Department of Forestry, Canada. 46 pp.

Morgenstern, E.K., and Fowler, D.P. 1969. Genetics and breeding of black spruce and red spruce. Forest Chron. 45: 408–412.

Pereg, D., and Payette, S. 1998. Development of black spruce growth forms at treeline. Plant Ecol. 138: 137–147.

Perron, M., and Bousquet, J. 1997. Natural hybridization between black spruce and red spruce. Molec. Ecol. 6: 725–734.

Peterson, E.B., and Peterson, N.M. 1994. Synopsis of information on white, Engelmann, and black spruce natural regeneration in North America. Forestry Canada and Alberta Land and Forest Services, Edmonton, AB. 221 pp.

Rajora, O.P., Pluhar, S.A. 2003. Genetic diversity impacts of forest fires, forest harvesting, and alternative reforestation practices in black spruce (*Picea mariana*). Theor. Appl. Genet. 106: 1203–1212.

Vincent, A.B. 1965. Black spruce: a review of its silvics, ecology, and silviculture. Canadian Forestry Service, Ottawa, ON. 79 pp.

THE NORTHWEST TERRITORIES

Flag of the Northwest Territories.

A NORTHWEST TERRITORIES LANDSCAPE: northern lights over scattered spruce woodland.

FLORAL EMBLEM: MOUNTAIN AVENS

Mountain avens (*Dryas integrifolia*) in Great Whale River area, northern Quebec, July 12, 1969. Photo taken by S. Brisson and provided by J. Cayouette.

SYMBOLISM

Mountain avens is an excellent symbol of the Northwest Territories. The species provides a creamy white floral carpet over many gravel flats and rocky terrain, bringing impressive beauty to the landscape. It reflects the hardiness of the people in adapting to the stressful climate in one of the most extensive (and last) regions of wilderness in the world. The species is a dominant plant of the arctic tundra, and thus has an impact on many other arctic species. It is also a popular plant with First Nations people, and so reflects their important presence.

Mountain avens (*Dryas integrifolia*) by Lavonia R. Stockelbach (1874–1966). A collection of her paintings of Canadian provincial and territorial official flowers is associated with the herbarium of Agriculture and Agri-Food Canada in Ottawa.

NAMES

Latin Names
Dryas integrifolia Vahl

The genus name *Dryas* is based on a Greek word (*druas*) for dryad. Dryads were mythological female spirits of nature (nymphs) who presided over groves and forests. They were particularly associated with oak woods, and the genus name was based on a resemblance of the tiny leaves of one of the European species to the foliage of Mediterranean region oaks. However, *Dryas* species are not inhabitants of woods. *Integrifolia* in the scientific name is Greek for entire-leaved, i.e., having leaves with margins that are not lobed or serrated.

English Names
Mountain avens. Also: arctic dryad, entireleaf arctic avens, entireleaf mountain-avens, white dryad, white mountain avens.

The names white dryad and white mountain avens are also applied to the closely related *D. octopetala* (alpine dryad). "Avens" is the usual name for species of the genus *Geum*, the word tracing through Old French *avence* to Medieval Latin avencia, and interpreted as a kind of clover.

French Names
Dryade de montagne. Also: dryade à feuilles entières.

Inuit Names
There are numerous Inuit names for the species, many referring to the plant at different seasons, or to specific parts of the plant. The name *malikkaat* indicates significant seasonal occurrences. The word *isurramuat* refers to the fact that the flowers follow the path of the sun. The name *piluit* for the plant is also the name for a dye and seeds from it. Names for the leaves, *qasilinnait* and *atungaujat*, are also used for the plant, which is also known as "the plant that numbs the tongue". For additional information, see Aiken et al. (2007), and Mallory and Aiken (2004, which also includes informative text in Inuktitut), cited below.

HISTORY

Canada
Dryas integrifolia was selected as the floral emblem by the Council of the Northwest Territories on June 7, 1957. The choice was made on the advice of A.E. Porsild, Chief Botanist of the National Museum of Canada and a distinguished Arctic explorer, who had noted that the plant was extremely common in the Arctic. Numerous websites erroneously state that the floral emblem is *D. octopetala*, a very similar species. The Floral Emblem Act stated: "The flower known botanically as the *Dryas integrifolia* and popularly known as the mountain avens is adopted as the floral emblem of the Northwest Territories." In anticipation of the splitting off of Nunavut from the Northwest Territories (which occurred on April 1, 1999), a Special Committee was established in 1998 to advise on the continuing status of the official symbols, and it was suggested that mountain avens be retained as the floral symbol of the new, reduced Northwest Territories. This recommendation was followed.

Foreign
Dryas octopetala was chosen as Iceland's national flower in 2004 by the country's parliament, after a nationwide public opinion poll.

APPEARANCE

Mountain avens is a dwarf or low-growing, long-lived shrub, usually 5–15 cm (2–6 inches) high, often trailing or forming low mats 10–100 cm (4–39 inches) in diameter. The branches often take root in the soil. The more or less smooth-edged leaves are spade-shaped, leathery, usually wooly on the undersides, small (5–25 mm or 0.2–1 inch long), and often remain green overwinter (the foliage has been variously and contradictorily described as "evergreen", "deciduous", and "tardily dehiscent"). Flowering occurs from June to July. The flowers are bowl or saucer shaped, and have 8–10 white or creamy yellow petals. The flowers occur singly on stalks that are 2.5–15 cm (1–6 inches) long. After flowering, the styles of each flower become long and feathery, each attached to a single-seeded fruit. The fruits are dry, brown or straw-coloured, and 2–5 mm (0.08–0.2 inch) long. When immature or damp, the long, feathery, plume-like styles are twisted together so the fruits are massed in a tight head. As the fruits mature and dry out their styles unravel (giving the head of fruits the appearance of a feather duster) and the individual single-seeded fruits are scattered by the wind.

Mountain avens (*Dryas integrifolia*) in Ukkusiksalik National Park, Nunavut. Photo taken on July 7, 1999, courtesy of Ansgar Walk.

Mountain avens (*Dryas integrifolia*). Source: Department of the Secretary of State of Canada. 1967. The arms, flags and floral emblems of Canada. Reproduced with permission.

A BIODIVERSITY TREASURE

CLASSIFICATION

Family: Rose family (Rosaceae).

Six species of *Dryas*, one with two varieties, have been recognized in the Northwest Territories. The most widespread in Canada and the Northwest Territories is *D. integrifolia*. A key to the species of Canada (all of which are in the Northwest Territories) follows, and indicates where they occur in the territory.

1a. Flowers yellow, nodding with petals forming a bell shape; filaments hairy near the base; leaves wavy-edged from base to near tip. . . *D. drummondii* (no varieties recognized, occurs in the west or in the east)
1b. Flowers white or whitish-yellow, erect with petals spreading; filaments smooth near the base; leaves wavy-edged or wavy edged only in the basal half 2

2a. Leaves wavy-edged only in the basal half, non-glandular with simple hairs on the underside . . . . *D. integrifolia* . . . 3
2b. Leaves wavy-edged from base to near tip, glandular or not and with hairs on the underside that are simple, feathery, and/or scale-like. 4

3a. Leaves linear, with revolute margins and pointed tips . . . . . . *D. integrifolia* subsp. *integrifolia* (widespread)
3b. Leaves oblong, with flat margins and rounded tips. . . . . . . *D. integrifolia* subsp. *sylvatica* (local in the west)

4a. Leaves bearing feathery hairs, especially on abaxial midribs and petioles . . . . . *D. octopetala* var. *kamtschatica* (occurs in MacKenzie Mountains)

4b. Leaves bearing mostly or entirely simple hairs (gland-tipped or not) 5

5a. Midvein on undersurface of leaf without stalked glands but often densely hairy. . . . . *D. crenulata* (occurs on mountains in MacKenzie Valley)
5b. Midvein on undersurface of leaf with gland-tipped hairs 6

6a. Leaves thinly hairy between the nerves. . . . . *D. alaskensis* (occurs in the Richardson Mountains in the northwest)

6b. Leaves densely hairy between the nerves. . . . . *D. hookeriana* (occurs in southern MacKenzie Valley)

Hybridization is thought to be common where species overlap and this may lead to difficulties in identification. Hybrids with *D. octopetala* have been reported in parts of the range. There are also two named natural hybrids: *D. ×sundermannii*, a hybrid between *D. octopetala* and *D. drummondii*, recorded in Alberta; and *D. ×wyssiana*, a hybrid between *D. integrifolia* and *D. drummondii* found in Quebec.

Mountain avens (*Dryas integrifolia*). Photo courtesy of United States Fish and Wildlife Service.

GEOGRAPHY

Mountain avens is a common, widespread, Arctic species, native to the northern half of North America, especially the Canadian Arctic Archipelago, as well as Chukotka in Beringia, and the coastal areas of Greenland and Alaska. Isolated collections have been made in Maine, Montana, and New Hampshire. In Canada the species extends from the north of Ellesmere Island down through the Canadian Arctic Archipelago to southern Nunavut, the Labrador-Ungava Peninsula, the Gaspé Peninsula, Quebec, Jasper Park in Alberta, western Newfoundland, along the north shore of Lake Superior, and on the coasts of James Bay, Hudson Bay, and Yukon. When most of Canada was covered by mile-deep ice more than 10,000 years ago, mountain avens occupied refugial, unglaciated areas including Beringia (parts of Alaska, Yukon, and western Northwest Territories) and the High Arctic.

Mountain avens (*Dryas integrifolia*) in Quttinirpaaq National Park. Photo by A. Walk, Creative Commons Attribution license).

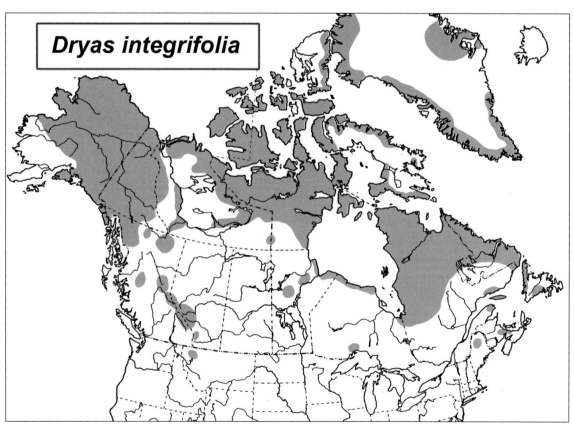

Dryas integrifolia

North American distribution of mountain avens (*Dryas integrifolia*).

ECOLOGY

Mountain avens is a pioneer species, adapted to colonizing open areas. It is often found on marine beaches and gravelly regions, both habitats that are very deficient in plant nutrients. Northern gravel sites also often provide limited moisture. Such sites are difficult for most plant species to colonize, and mountain avens is unusually tolerant of the stresses presented in these situations. *Dryas integrifolia* has several adaptations suiting it to its harsh, short-season environment. The low stature is protective against drying in the wind (wind speed is considerably reduced near ground level), and also lowers abrasion from sand-blasting. The wooliness and downward curving of the leaf margins reduces moisture loss from the tissues, and the taproot grows down to obtain moisture. The semi-evergreen nature of the leaves is a way of taking advantage of the short season during which photosynthesis can occur, since many leaves are present on the plant in early spring as soon as the warming temperature revives the plants.

Habitat

Dryas integrifolia occurs in meadows, tundra, slopes, ridges, and river terraces. It is found on both moist and dry areas, and is most abundant on calcareous (limestone), barren, rocky or gravelly ground.

Root nodules of the related *Dryas drummondii* plants have been demonstrated to contain the symbiotic nitrogen-fixing bacterium *Frankia*, and the same has been claimed for *D. integrifolia*. Plant species adapted to nutrient-poor soils often are associated with nitrogen-fixing microorganisms, because of the advantage in acquiring nitrogen, the most important soil element in plant productivity. However, the evidence for nitrogen fixation in *D. integrifolia* is weak.

Inter-species Relationships

Caribou eat large amounts of *D. integrifolia;* this is not surprising since it is a dominant plant on the tundra. Muskoxen, the other major ungulate species in the arctic environment, eat lesser amounts. The immature fruits are consumed by numerous species of small rodents as well as several species of birds.

Pollination & Dispersal

Dryas flowers are often heliotropic, turning towards the sun as it moves across the horizon. However, the degree of heliotropism has been found to differ somewhat, depending on location, and often not all flowers of a plant follow the sun. Frequently when the flowers are not heliotropic, they nevertheless tend to be oriented towards the mid-day sun. The bowl or saucer shape of the flowers of *Dryas* and many other arctic plant species is commonly interpreted as a sort of parabolic satellite dish that focuses the rays of the sun at the centre of the flower where the seed develops. This arrangement appears to be an adaptation to collect solar heat, promoting faster development of the seeds in an environment that is quite cold. In fact, in *D. integrifolia* it has been found that flowers oriented directly towards the sun are about 4 °C (7 °F) warmer than ambient temperatures. Moreover, insects often bask in the concentrated heat generated in the flowers, and it has been found that mountain avens flowers facing the sun are more likely to be visited by pollinators. Although the species can self-pollinate, cross-pollination has been found to produce larger seeds, and plants are dependent on insects for maximum seed set. Several species of flies are important pollinators of mountain avens, but so are workers of the bumble bee *Bombus polaris.*

The fruits are single-seeded, attached to the persisting style of the flower, which is feathery and serves as a sail or parachute for seed distribution by wind. Lemmings are thought to distribute some of the seeds. Seed production is often very irregular. Lateral rooting of branches coupled with fragmentation of mats is a form of vegetative reproduction that assists somewhat in spreading the plant.

USES

Mountain avens is occasionally grown as a rock garden ornamental. First Nations people sometimes obtained a bright green dye from the flowers and seed heads. Several researchers have commented that it seems to be a good candidate for purposes of revegetating northern landscapes.

Mountain avens (*Dryas integrifolia*). Source: Canadian Heritage. 2002 (revised edition). Symbols of Canada. Canadian Heritage, Ottawa, ON. Reproduced with permission.

CULTIVATION

There are a few cultivars (such as 'Greenland Green') of *Dryas integrifolia*, but most cultivated plants are simply identical to the wild plants. Instructions on how to grow mountain avens, from former Central Experimental Farm horticulturalist and co-worker Larry Sherk, are reproduced in the following, from his popular but out-of-print (1967) guide (cited in the first chapter of this book) to growing Canada's floral emblems: "If you want to grow the plant in the warmer southern areas, be sure to plant it in a rock garden or among pebbles where there is good drainage but enough moisture to keep the soil from becoming too dry. The plants need shade from the hot afternoon sun, but sun for the rest of the day. Use a well drained soil with some added peat moss or leaf mold. Large plants usually do not survive transplanting. Because this plant has a taproot, even young seedlings in the wild must be moved carefully. Cuttings taken in August can be rooted in moist sand. To start the plants from seed, sow the seed as soon as it is ripe in seed pans in a well drained, sandy soil mixture. Sow older seed in the same way, but first stratify it at 40 °F (5 °C) for at least 2 months. Transplant seedlings into individual pots rather than flats to reduce the shock of transplanting them later in the garden. Plants grown from seed take several years to flower."

CONSERVATION STATUS

Dryas integrifolia is a widespread plant, not currently in need of conservation. Climate change is altering the Arctic environment, and this could result in a reduction of the species in some regions.

Mountain avens (*Dryas integrifolia*), in flower, photographed near Upernavik, Greenland on June 28, 2007. Photo courtesy of Kim Hansen.

MYTHS, LEGENDS, TALES, FOLKLORE AND INTERESTING FACTS

✤ The "Younger Dryas" (ca. 10800–9500 B.C.E.; also called "The Big Freeze") and the "Older Dryas" (occurring about 1,000 years before the Younger Dryas, and lasting only about 3 centuries) are cold geological periods (but not as cold as ice ages) that affected at least the Northern Hemisphere. These periods were named after *Dryas octopetala* plants in Ireland that flourished during those times, and are used as fossil indicators of the periods.

✤ The Inuit employed the degree of maturity of mountain avens as a seasonal indicator. The untwisting of the tangled styles in the seed head was interpreted as the best time to move inland to hunt caribou. When the seed heads are tightly twisted, caribou skins were considered too thin to make clothing. As the seed heads untwisted, the skins were considered suitable for women's clothing, and when the seed heads fully expanded, caribou skins were then believed to be suitable for men's clothing.

✤ *Dryas octopetala* (which occurs in the highlands of Scotland) is the badge of the Scottish clan MacNeil.

✤ Patches of mountain avens that are only 0.5 m² (1.5 square feet) in area, formed by vegetative reproduction, can be hundreds of years old, although no existing part of the plant is that age (the oldest recorded age of part of a living plant is 68 years).

Mountain avens (*Dryas integrifolia*), photographed near Upernavik, Greenland on July 16, 2007. The Plant is mostly in flower but a few fruiting heads are developing. Photo courtesy of Kim Hansen.

Painting of the official flower of the Northwest Territories, mountain avens (*Dryan integrifolia*), from the Walter Coucill Canadian Centennial official flowers of Canada series (see the first chapter of this book). Reproduced with the permission of the copyright holders, the Coucill family.

A BIODIVERSITY TREASURE

SOURCES OF ADDITIONAL INFORMATION

Aiken, S.G., Dallwitz, M.J., Consaul, L.L., McJannet, C.L., Gillespie, L.J., Boles, R.L., Argus, G.W. Gillett, J.M., Scott, P.J., Elven, R., LeBlanc, M.C., Brysting, A.K., and Solstad, H. 1999 onwards. Flora of the Canadian Arctic Archipelago: descriptions, illustrations, identification, and information Retrieval. Version: April 29, 2003. http://www.mun.ca/biology/delta/arcticf/.

Au, R., and Tardif, J.C. 2007. Allometric relationships and dendroecology of the dwarf shrub *Dryas integrifolia* near Churchill, subarctic Manitoba. Can. J. Bot. 85: 585–597.

Hart, G.T., and Svoboda, J. 1994. Autecology of *Dryas integrifolia* in Alexandra Fiord lowland habitats. *In* Ecology of a polar oasis: Alexandra Fiord, Ellesmere Island, Canada. *Edited by* J. Svoboda and B. Freedman. Captus University Publications, Toronto, ON. pp. 145–156.

Hultén, E. 1959. Studies in the genus *Dryas*. Svensk Botanisk Tidskrift 53: 507–542.

Kevan, P.G. 1972. Insect pollination of High Arctic flowers. J. Ecol. 60: 831–847.

Krannitz, P.G. 1996. Reproductive ecology of *Dryas integrifolia* in the high Arctic semi-desert. Can. J. Bot. 74: 1451–1460.

Mallory, C., and Aiken, S. 2004. Common plants of Nunavut. Nunavut Dept. Education, Nunavut Wildlife Management Board, Canadian Museum of Nature. National Printers, Nepean, ON. 400 pp. (200 in English, 200 in Inuktituk).

Markham, J.H. 2009. Does *Dryas integrifolia* fix nitrogen? Botany 87: 1106–1109.

Philipp, M., and Siegismund, H.R. 2003. What can morphology and isozymes tell us about the history of the *Dryas integrifolia* complex? Molec. Ecol. 12: 2231–2242.

Porsild, A.E. 1947. The genus *Dryas* in North America. Can. Field-Nat. 61: 175–192.

Rouleau, E. 1956. The genus *Dryas* (Rosaceae) in Newfoundland. Contributions de l'Institut Botanique de l'Université de Montréal 69: 5–23.

Tremblay, N.O., and Schoen, D.J. 1999. Molecular phylogeography of *Dryas integrifolia:* glacial refugia and postglacial recolonization. Molec. Ecol. 8: 1187–1198.

Wada, N. 1998. Sun-tracking flower movement and seed production of mountain avens, *Dryas octopetala* L. in the high arctic NY-Ålesund, Sfalbard. Proc. NIPR Symp. Polar Biol. 11: 128–136.

Mountain avens (*Dryas integrifolia*), photographed near Upernavik, Greenland on July 11, 2007. The upper photo show a plant in flower, the lower photo shows a plant developing a fruiting head. Photos reproduced by courtesy of Kim Hansen.

TREE: TAMARACK

Tamarack (*Larix laricina*) in fall colouration. Photo by J. O'Brien, United States Forest Service.

SYMBOLISM

The tamarack is a very suitable choice as the official tree of the Northwest Territories, because: it is exceptionally attractive, noted for its conical shape and striking golden autumn colouration; its hardiness epitomizes the ability of the inhabitants to thrive in a difficult climate; First Nations people used the tree extensively, and so it reflects their contributions and presence; the tree is common in the territory.

Silhouette of tamarack (*Larix laricina*). Source: Farrar, J.L. 1995. Trees in Canada. Canadian Forest Service and Fitzhenry and Whiteside, Markham, ON, Canada. Reproduced with permission.

NAMES

Latin Names

Larix laricina (DuRoi) K. Koch

The genus name *Larix* is the classical Latin name for the larch tree (the word has been claimed to translate as "fat", a reference to the tree's resin). *Laricina* in the scientific name is Latin for larch-like, the word used because the species was once considered to be a pine, with the name *Pinus larix* L.

English Names

Tamarack. Also: American larch, black larch, eastern larch, hackmatack, larch, larch hackmatack, red larch, tamarack larch. The inappropriate name "juniper" is sometimes used in the Maritime Provinces.

The name "tamarack" is a French Canadian modification of the Abenaki (of the Algonquian Native American group) name for the species, *akemantak*, meaning "wood used for snowshoes". "Hackmatack" (which is also occasionally applied to balsam poplar, *Populus balsamifera*), may also trace to the same Abenaki term. The English word "larch" traces back to the Latin *larix*, probably through the German *Lärche*. "Alaska larch" refers to L. *laricina* var. *alaskensis* (Wight) Raup, an isolated central Alaskan variety that most taxonomists have concluded does not merit recognition. The name "red larch" (and the French épinette rouge) points out the often reddish colour of the underbark (several *Larix* species frequently have a vivid reddish-purple inner bark).

French Names

Mélèze laricin. Also: épinette rouge, fausse épinette rouge, mélèze, mélèze d'Amérique, tamarac, violon.

The French name *mélèze* is probably based on *miel*, honey, a reference to the bittersweet resin secreted by the tree. The French word *épinette* normally means spruce, but its use for the tamarack reflects the practice of the first French settlers in Canada to apply *épinette* to several species of conifers.

HISTORY

Canada

In anticipation of the splitting off of Nunavut from the Northwest Territories (which occurred on April 1, 1999), a Special Committee was established in 1998 to examine the continuing status of the official symbols, and it was recommended that tamarack replace jack pine as the official tree of the reduced territory. The tamarack was named as the official tree on September 9, 1999.

Foreign

The Northwest Territories is the only large political area that has adopted a species of *Larix* as an official emblem.

APPEARANCE

Well-developed tamarack trees are generally 15–23 m (49–76 feet) tall, with a diameter at breast height of 36–51 cm (14–20 inches). However, the trees are often stunted on poor soils, in the far north, and on mountains. The bark is thin, smooth when young and rough and scaly on older trees. The needle-like leaves are soft, flexible, and mostly 1–2.5 cm (0.4–1 inch) long. The ends of the branches bear single, distinctly separated needles. Farther back on the regular branches the needles occur in clusters or tufts of 10–20 on very short, stubby, "spur branches". The leaves are deciduous, unlike the foliage of most other coniferous plants, turning from light green in summer to yellow before they are shed in the autumn. (Bald cypresses, *Taxodium* species, are other examples of the very few conifers that are deciduous.) After the leaves have fallen, a knob is left on the regular branch (the remnants of the spur branch), and the knobby regular branches of tamarack are very characteristic of the species. Both male and female cones occur on the same tree, the female cones maturing their seed within the season they are produced. The male cones have the appearance of small mounds (less than 5 mm or 0.2 inch wide), and are made up of brown to yellowish pollen sacs with papery scales at their base. They occur along the branches, especially in the lower part of the crown. The male cones develop in early spring, shed their pollen, and wither. The seed cones are 1–2.3 cm (0.4–0.9 inch) long, bright red or green when young but turning brown with maturity; they contain 12–25 seed scales, each bearing 2 seeds. After shedding their seeds in late summer and fall, the cones often remain on the tree for 2 to 5 years. The seeds are 2–3 mm (about 0.1 inch) long, excluding their wings. The trees rarely live as long as 200 years.

Tamarack (*Larix laricina*) trees in their fall foliage on October 31, 2008 in Barre town, Vermont. Photo by Linda Baird-White, released into the pubic domain on Wikimedia.

A BIODIVERSITY TREASURE

CLASSIFICATION

Family: Pinaceae (pine family).

Larix is a genus of about ten species of the northern hemisphere, three occurring in North America. In addition to *L. laricina*, *L. occidentalis* (western larch) and *L. lyallii* (alpine larch) occur in southern British Columbia and southern Alberta; both of the latter species also are native to the northwestern United States. The following key identifies the larches commonly found in Canada.

1a Scales of fruiting cone pubescent on the outside . . . . *L. decidua* (introduced)
1b Scales of fruiting cone smooth on the outside 2

2a Twigs smooth; seed cones 1–2 cm long, with bracts shorter than the scales . . . . *L. laricina*
2b Twigs hairy, at least when young; seed cones 2–5 cm long, with bracts longer than the scales . . 3

3a Twigs densely hairy; scale margins with rough, irregular edges . . . . *L. lyallii*
3b Twigs sparsely hairy; becoming smooth; scale margins with straight edges . . . . *L. occidentalis*

Tamarack (*Larix laricina*). A, Seedling. B, Flowering branch. C, cross section of a leaf. D, Fruiting branch. E, Branchlet in winter. F, Lower side of cone scale. G, Upper side of cone scale with its two seeds. Source: Sargent, C.S. 1898. The silva of North America. Houghton, Mifflin and Company, Boston, MA. Vol. 12, plate 593.

GEOGRAPHY

Larix laricina is distributed widely through the boreal forest of North America from Alaska to Newfoundland, extending from the tree line in the north slightly into the deciduous forest to the south. The southern limit includes northeastern British Columbia and central Alberta, southern Minnesota, Wisconsin, northeastern Illinois, and New England, with isolated populations in western Ohio, Pennsylvania, West Virginia, western Maryland, Long Island, and Rhode Island. *Larix laricina* occurs in every province and territory of Canada.

A number of maps fail to show the distribution correctly in northern Yukon, where tamarack occurs west of the Richardson Mountains. and north to the Porcupine River. The ranges of western larch, alpine larch and tamarack come close to each other in southwestern Alberta but may not overlap. It appears that tamarack does not occur south to the Bow Valley and Kananaskis regions where western larch is well established. Alpine larch does occur in the Kananaskis country but at higher elevations than western larch. The occurrence of western larch in Alberta is completely omitted from some recent maps.

Genetic studies have revealed a general east to west pattern of variation in tamarack, although the trees are not known to differ morphologically. Similarly, the trees of the Great Lakes region are distinctive genetically, but have not been shown to differ externally. On the other hand, trees from Alaska differ slightly in morphology from the trees of the northern Yukon, and this is thought to have resulted from different origins.

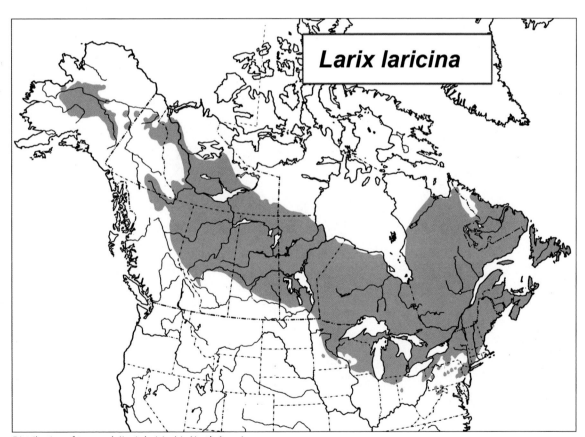

Distribution of tamarack (*Larix laricina*) in North America.

Young cones of tamarack (*Larix laricina*). Photo courtesy of Steven Katovich (USDA Forest Service) and Bugwood.org.

A BIODIVERSITY TREASURE

ECOLOGY

Larix laricina is mostly a species of cold climates, found in northern forest stands bordering the tundra. It has the widest range of any North American coniferous tree, growing farther north than white and black spruce, both of which become shrub-like in areas where tamarack is still able to grow as a tree. *Larix laricina* is a pioneering species, often the first tree to invade open bogs and swamps, and burned peatlands. Tamarack is frequently associated with black spruce (*Picea mariana*). In much of Canada the tree forms extensive pure stands, but in most of the U.S. this is uncommon.

Habitat

Tamarack usually occurs in cold, wet, poorly drained sphagnum bogs and muskegs, and in these conditions it is often stunted. The soils are usually acidic. In addition to these organic soils, the species is also found on moist but well-drained upland mineral soils, and then it often grows extremely well, often better than all other northern conifers. Tamarack is also found in swamps, and on the margins of streams and lakes. It is very shade-intolerant.

Inter-species Relationships

Tamarack cones provide seeds for some birds (including pine siskin and crossbills), and small mammals (such as squirrels, mice, voles, and shrews). The twigs are browsed to a small extent by snowshoe hares and grouse, but deer, moose, and caribou avoid tamarack or consume very small amounts. Porcupines fed on the inner bark. Because tamarack sheds its leaves, it does not provide good winter cover for most animals. The larch sawfly (*Pristiphora erichsoni*) is the most destructive pest of tamarack, periodically defoliating stands and killing many trees. On the positive side, outbreaks of this insect provide food for other species of insects, as well as birds and mammals. The sawfly was first recorded in North America in 1880, and is believed to be an invasive alien which originated in Europe.

Pollination & Dispersal

Tamarack is wind-pollinated. Like numerous other tree species, good crops are produced in cycles, usually once every 3 to 6 years in *L. laricina*. A large tree can produce 20,000 cones with 300,000 seeds in a good season. Squirrels distribute some of the seeds, but most are dispersed by the wind. The majority of the seeds fall within a distance of two to three times the height of the tree. At the northern limit of the species range seed production is very limited, but the lower branches of the dwarfed trees occasionally take root and produce new trees.

Tamarack (*Larix laricina*) branch with larvae of the larch sawfly, *Pristophora erichsonii*. Photo courtesy of Steven Katovich (USDA Forest Service) and Bugwood.org.

USES

Because tamarack is adapted to short-season, cold, wet habitats, it has potential for reforestation in such situations, although it currently is not extensively planted. Wild stands are managed for forestry purposes, but *L. laricina* is not a leading commercial tree. Tamarack wood is heavy, durable, and decay-resistant, and is employed to a limited extent for railway ties, pilings, posts, poles, mine timbers, rough lumber, boxes, crates, and fuelwood. However, the lumber is of limited commercial value because of insect (especially larch sawfly) and disease problems. The wood is used for pulp, mainly in the United States, but has poor pulping properties because of the high resin content. In the past, tannin extracted from the tree was employed for tanning leather. Indigenous Peoples used tamarack for a very wide range of tools and medicinal uses, and a few food uses. Northern First Nations craftspeople, especially the Cree (the largest group of First Nations people in Canada, with over 200,000 people), are highly respected for fashioning bundles of tamarack twigs into sculptures of geese, and elegant, lifelike goose hunting decoys.

Arabinogalactan, a carbohydrate (polysaccharide) extracted from the resin of *Larix* species (including *L. laricina*), is approved in some jurisdictions as a food additive or dietary fibre for use in digestive health products. Advantages alleged (but requiring verification) are that it stimulates the immune system, fights cancer, and helps grow beneficial bacteria in the digestive tract.

"Tamarack geese" prepared by Cree in the James Bay area, and sold as collector's items at prices ranging up to $500. Photo courtesy of Chichester Inc.

TOXICITY

Sawdust from the wood has caused dermatitis in some sensitive people, but tamarack is not considered to be a toxic plant.

CULTIVATION

Larch species, especially the European larch (*L. decidua*), are often planted for forestry purposes, but *L. laricina* is infrequently planted in this regard. As noted above, however, it has potential for cold, wet, northern habitats. *Larix laricina* is grown occasionally as an ornamental tree, especially in cold climates, but the European larch is usually cultivated in preference to it. There are several ornamental cultivars of *L. laricina*, mostly selected for dwarf form and/or for foliage colour. Cultivars include 'Beehive', 'Blue Sparkler', 'Craftbury Flats', 'Diane', 'Deborah Waxman', 'Eidelweiss WB', 'Lanark', 'Nana', 'Newport Beauty', 'Steuben', 'Stubby', and 'Therandt'. *Larix laricina* is very popular as bonsai.

CONSERVATION STATUS

Tamarack is a very widespread species, not considered in need of special conservation measures. For forestry purposes, the widespread damage inflicted by the larch sawfly is of concern, since this has greatly limited the commercial value of the species.

Tamarack (*Larix laricina*) trained for 26 years as bonsai. Photo by Nick Lenz, released into the public domain on Wikimedia.

MYTHS, LEGENDS, TALES, FOLKLORE AND INTERESTING FACTS

❧ The natural crooks in the stumps and roots of large tamarack trees were used by eighteenth and nineteenth century boatwrights in constructing small ships because they are naturally curved as much as 90°, and so could be used to join ribs to deck timbers. A section of trunk attached to a lateral root was termed a "knee", one part used to support the deck, the other to tie beams to the boat's hull.

❧ Early American settlers employed tamarack needles for stuffing pillows and mattresses, but the fragrant needles of balsam fir may have been more popular for this purpose.

❧ Before 1917 in Alberta, surveyors used tamarack posts as markers of the northeast corner of Sections of Townships, because the wood is very rot resistant and readily available. (A township measures 6 miles × 6 miles, and contains 36 sections, each 1 mile square.)

❧ The Gwich'in First Nation people (of Alaska, Yukon, and the Northwest Territories) so respect the tamarack that tradition calls for leaving an offering, such as tea or sugar, each time part of a tree is collected.

❧ The northernmost tree in the world, extending into Eastern Siberia, is Dahurian larch (*L. gmelinii*). It is considered to be the most cold-hardy tree on Earth (reaching 72° 31' N), and can tolerate temperatures of -70 °C (-94 °F). According to Encyclopedia Brittanica, the northernmost tree in North America is said to be white spruce (*Picea glauca*) growing along the Mackenzie River delta, near the shore of the Arctic Ocean. However, tree-sized feltleaf willows (*Salix alaxensis*), which are up to 2.4 m (8 feet) tall and 81 years old, exist in sheltered ravines at the head of Minto Inlet (71° 34' N), in western Victoria Island, NWT. Here they are disjunct from more continuous occurrence along near-treeline floodplains several hundred kilometres to the south. These may be interpreted as the northernmost trees in North America. (See "What is a tree?" in the chapter on Nunavut.)

Tamarack (*Larix laricina*) in fall colour in Blaine, Minnesota. Photo courtesy of Steven Katovich (USDA Forest Service) and Bugwood.org.

SOURCES OF ADDITIONAL INFORMATION

Brunton, D.F. 1984. The status of western larch, *Larix occidentalis*, in Alberta. Can. Field-Nat. 98: 167–170.

Tamarack (*Larix laricina*) in fall colouration, on the South Saskatchewan River bank in Saskatoon. Photo (online on Wikimedia) by SriMesh, Creative Commons Attribution-Share Alike 3.0 Unported license.

Edlund, S.A., and Egginton, P.A. 1984. Morphology and description of an outlier population of tree-sized willows on Western Victoria Island, District of Franklin. Current Research, Part A. Geological Survey of Canada Paper 84-1A: 279–285.

Graham, C.M., Farintosh, H.L., and Linhart, Y.B. (Editors). 1983. Larch symposium. Potential for the future. (Nov. 9, 1982). Fac. Forestry, Univ. Toronto and Ont. Min. Nat. Res., Toronto, ON. 175 pp.

Johnston, W.F. 1990. *Larix laricina*. *In* Silvics of North America, Vol. 1. Agric. Handbook 654, R.M. Burns and B.H. Honkala (Technical Coordinators). USDA For. Serv., Washington, D.C. pp. 141–151.

Johnston, W.F., and Carpenter, E.M. 1985. Tamarack. USDA Forest Service, Washington, D.C. 7 pp.

MacGillivrary, H.G. 1969. Larches for reforestation and tree improvement in Eastern Canada. For. Chron. 45: 440–444.

Parker, W.H. 1993. *Larix*. *In* Flora of North America, vol. 2. *Edited by* Flora of North America Editorial Committee. Oxford University Press, Oxford, U.K. pp. 366–368.

Parker, W.H., and Dickinson, T.A. 1990. Range-wide morphological and anatomical variation in *Larix laricina*. Can. J. Bot. 68: 832–840.

Roe, E.I. 1957. Silvical characteristics of tamarack, *Larix laricina*. United States Dept. of Agriculture, Forest Service No. 52LS. Lake States Forest Experiment Station, St. Paul, MN. 22 pp.

Schmidt, W.C., and McDonald, K.J. (Compilers) 1995. Ecology and management of *Larix* forests: a look ahead. Proceedings of an International Symposium, Whitefish, Montana, October 5–9, 1992. GTR-INT-319. USDA For. Serv., Inter-mountain Research Station, Ogden, UT. 521 pp.

Semerikov, V.L., and Lascoux, M. 1999. Genetic relationship among Eurasian and American *Larix* species based on allozymes. Heredity 83: 62–70.

Zoltai, S.C. 1973. The range of tamarack (*Larix laricina* (Du Roi) K. Koch) in northern Yukon Territory. Can. J. Forest Research 3: 461–464.

NOVA SCOTIA

Provincial flag of Nova Scotia.

A NOVA SCOTIA LANDSCAPE: a river running through a forest in the autumn.

FLORAL EMBLEM: MAYFLOWER

Mayflower (*Epigaea repens*). Photograph courtesy of M. Munro, Nova Scotia Museum.

SYMBOLISM

In the spring, the Mayflower produces delicate pink flowers in the forests and heathlands (open shrubby places) of Nova Scotia, signalling the retreat of winter and the promise of warmth. Not surprisingly, early residents of the province adopted the plant as a symbol suggesting high achievement in the face of adversity. As early as 1820, the Mayflower was employed as a native patriotic emblem. It was praised by songwriters and poets, showcased on early stamps and coins of the province before Confederation, and represented on the decorative brass of the militia and on the Lieutenant Governor's chain of state. The Mayflower also was adopted as the name of at least two Nova Scotian newspapers. While Nova Scotia was a colony of Great Britain, it was granted a Coat of Arms in 1625 (the oldest Coat of Arms outside of Great Britain), but this was not used after 1867 when Nova Scotia joined Confederation. In 1929 the original Coat of Arms was re-adopted, with the addition of the Mayflower.

Mayflower (*Epigaea repens*) from Canadian Heritage. 2002. Symbols of Canada (revised). Canadian Heritage, Ottawa, ON. Reproduced with permission of Canadian Heritage, Public works and Government Services Canada.

NAMES

Latin Names
Epigaea repens L.

The genus name *Epigaea* is based on the Greek *epi* "upon" and *gaia* "the earth", referring to the creeping habit. The epithet *repens* is Greek for trailing or creeping, also referring to the habit.

English Names
The name Mayflower is usually interpreted as being based on the early spring flowering of the plant (with this in mind, we capitalize the M in the name, although "mayflower" is also commonly found). It is often claimed that the name was given to the plant by the Pilgrims who emigrated to Massachusetts, who not only noticed that the plant flowered in the spring but were sensitized to the name Mayflower because it was the name of the ship that brought them to Plymouth Rock. However, this is likely a contrived explanation; the name Mayflower was applied by the English of then and now to species of hawthorn (*Crataegus*), as well as to a number of other plants. In fact, more than a dozen species are called Mayflower, and this name can be ambiguous. The famous Harvard botanist, M.L. Fernald commented (in the Preface of the eighth edition of Gray's Manual of Botany), "such a name as 'Mayflower' is used in so many senses as to be essentially meaningless outside restricted areas." The names "creeping Mayflower" and (rarely) "Plymouth Mayflower" are sometimes used for *E. repens* to avoid ambiguity. "Canada Mayflower" is sometimes applied to *Maianthemum canadense*, a widespread herb in Canada. Another spring-flowering Canadian herb, *Cardamine pratensis*, is also occasionally known as Mayflower. *Epigaea repens* is also known as trailing arbutus, this name deriving from the small size

in comparison with the trees and shrubs of the genus *Arbutus*. The latter, also in the heath family, has fourteen species of which *A. menziesii*, called arbutus and madrona (or madrone in much of the United States), is a Canadian native, occurring in southwestern British Columbia. Obsolete names for Mayflower (which apply to other species as well) include gravel plant or gravel weed (so-named because of early medical use to treat "gravel", i.e., kidney stones), shadflower (shad are important food fishes of Europe and North America, especially the Atlantic coast; spring runs of the fish in North America have led to the application of "shad" to various spring-flowering plants), ground laurel, moss beauty, mountain pink, winter pink, and crocus.

French Names
Fleur de mai (fleur-de-mai), épigée rampante, épigée fleur de mai.

Nova Scotia's Coat of Arms with Mayflower at the bottom.

HISTORY

Canada

The Mayflower was officially declared the Provincial Flower of Nova Scotia in 1901 (the Legislature stated that the flower has been the floral emblem of the province "from time immemorial").

Foreign

The Forest Potawatomi Indians of Wisconsin have long considered the Mayflower to be their tribal flower, and indeed believe that it is divine, having come directly from kîtci' manîtowiwîn, their divinity. The state of Massachusetts declared the Mayflower to be its floral emblem in 1925.

Nova Scotia and Massachusetts have much more in common than the same floral symbol. The province and state share a great deal in terms of history, geography, and commercial and family ties (see the discussion of red spruce, later in this chapter).

Mayflower (*Epigaea repens*). Source: Wikipedia (photographer: Nancy; Creative Commons Attribution 2.0 Generic license).

APPEARANCE

The Mayflower is an exceptionally attractive flowering plant—"probably the best beloved of all the wild flowers of the eastern United States" according to Coville (1911). However, after flowering in the early spring it is inconspicuous and easily overlooked, despite the fact that it is a fairly common plant in much of its range. The Mayflower is a prostrate, sprawling, dwarf shrub that forms patches. It has scarcely woody, thin, vinelike branching stems up to 40 cm (16 inches) long (occasionally up a metre), the surface sometimes slightly shredded. The aboveground stems arise from a short rhizome (underground stem) which is 2–4 cm or about an inch in length, up to 1.5 cm (0.6 inch) in diameter) and often twisted and knobby, producing a strongly branching root. The above-ground stems bear evergreen, leathery, alternate leaves up to 7.5 cm (3 inches) long. Adventitious roots are developed at the nodes. Rust-coloured hairs occur on the stems and petioles, and also often on the lower surfaces of the leaves. The flowers are in groups of three to five (occasionally more) on the ends of branches. The trumpet-shaped flowers have a waxy appearance, and are about 12 mm (0.5 inch) long, with five white to pink or rose-coloured petals (the latter sometimes fading to white) and a spicy fragrance. Plants usually bear only male or only female flowers. Female flowers usually have stamens, but these are reduced

Mayflower (*Epigaea repens*). Based on a postcard of a water-colour painted by Maria Morris Miller, supplied courtesy of M. Munro, Nova Scotia Museum.

in size compared to those of the male flowers, and do not produce functional pollen. The male flowers have abortive pistils so they cannot produce seeds. Depending on location, flowering occurs from March to May (in many places where it is found, the Mayflower is the earliest wildflower to bloom). The berry-like fruit is a small, globular capsule appearing like a large purple or pale yellow-orange pea (4–5.5 mm or about 0.2 inch in diameter). The five chambers of the fruit are filled with numerous tiny dark brown seeds in a white pulp. The plant is often concealed by leaf litter, and often only its leaves are visible. The species can be easily identified by its prostrate growth habit; stems with brown hairs; leathery, ovate, often heart-shaped leaves; and white, fragrant flowers.

CLASSIFICATION

Family: Ericaceae (heath family)

Epigaea repens is one of three species of *Epigaea*. *Epigaea asiatica* Maxim. occurs in Japan and Taiwan, and *E. gaultherioides* (Boiss. & Bal.) Takht. is native to the Caucasus of Georgia and northwestern Turkey (Asia Minor).

Several varieties and/or forms of *E. repens* have been recognized on the basis of floral colour and presence of hairs on the foliage. Canadian plants are often assigned to var. *glabrifolia* Fern., which develops limited hairs on the leaves. Forma *plena* Rehd., which is rare, has doubled flowers.

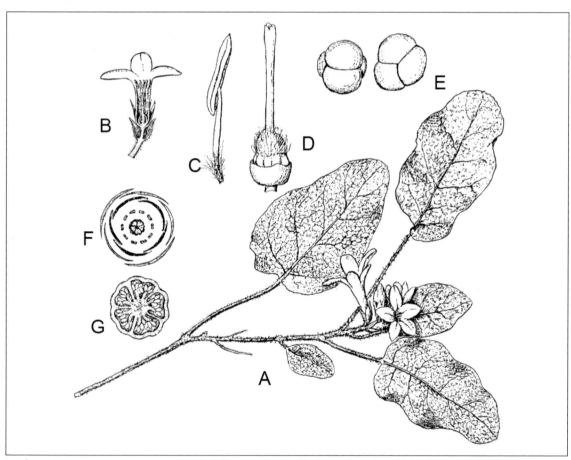

Mayflower (*Epigaea repens*). A, lowering branch; B, flower cut longitudinally; C, anther viewed laterally; D, pistil; E, pollen grains; F, floral diagram; G, cross-section of ovary. From Bastin (1895).

THE MAYFLOWERS

O sacred flowers of faith and hope,
As sweetly now as then
Ye bloom on many a birchen slope,
In many a pine-dark glen.

Behind the sea-wall's rugged length,
Unchanged, your leaves unfold
Like love behind the manly strength
Of the brave hearts of old.

So live the fathers in their sons,
Their sturdy faith be ours,
And ours the love that overruns
Its rocky strength with flowers.

But warmer suns ere long shall bring
To life the frozen sod;
And, through dead leaves of hope, shall spring
Afresh the flowers of God!

—Extracted from *The Mayflowers* by John Greenleaf Whittier (1807–1892, American poet).

GEOGRAPHY

Epigaea repens occurs from Newfoundland to Manitoba and Wisconsin, south to Kentucky and Florida. In the U.S., it has been recorded from 29 states, including all of those east of the Mississippi River. *Epigaea repens* is one of about 3 dozen herbaceous genera of plants that have one species in eastern North America and a very closely related species in eastern Asia. These plants are thought to be survivors of an ancestral deciduous forest (the Arcto-Tertiary Forest) that formed a continuous band around the northern hemisphere 15 to 20 million years ago (see Li, H.-L. 1952. Floristic relationships between Eastern Asia and Eastern North America. Trans. Am. Phil. Soc. (N.S.) 42: 371–429.)

Mayflower (*Epigaea repens*). Courtesy of M. Munro, Nova Scotia Museum.

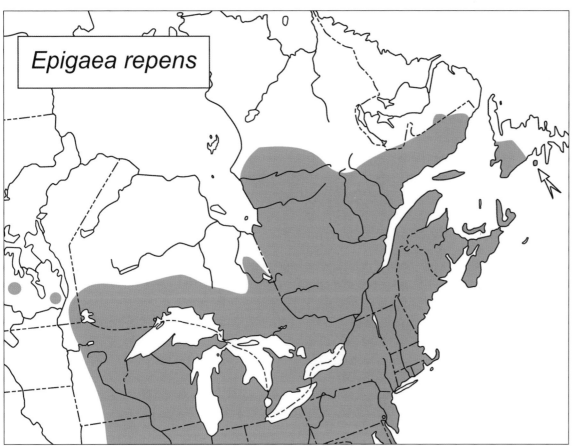

Canadian and adjacent American distribution of Mayflower (*Epigaea repens*). Arrow indicates presence on the French islands of St. Pierre and Miquelon.

A BIODIVERSITY TREASURE

ECOLOGY

Habitat

In Nova Scotia and elsewhere, Mayflower occupies a moderately wide range of habitats. It is frequently found in open shrubby places, including barrens and bogs, as well as in deciduous and coniferous forests, and rocky pastures. Mayflower is adapted to shade, but does not flourish in deep shade, and is more common at the edge of forests. It is most common on acidic, dry, sandy and coarse well-drained soils, frequently on slopes. It occurs occasionally in rich woods or on pond margins in deeper, peaty soils. It is sometimes on cliffs and headlands where strong winds prevent the growth of taller plants. In Newfoundland, the Mayflower is a characteristic inhabitant of the Southern Long Range subregion, where it is a "snow-bed species". Such species occur in areas where snow does not completely melt until late in the growing season (completion of melting does not occur until the middle of June in Newfoundland).

Inter-species Relationships

Chipmunks and small animals may eat the fruits of Mayflower, but the plant is not an important food source for wildlife. *Epigaea repens* does not have root hairs, which in most plants absorb nutrients and water from the soil; instead, it has a mutualistic association with a mycorrhizal fungus that serves to increase absorption of nutrients to the plant.

Pollination and Dispersal

The flowers of Mayflower are pollinated by a variety of ants and flying insects (including bumblebees). Fruits ripen 4 to 5 weeks after pollination, turning from green to red or purple, then split open, exposing the seeds which are embedded in a sweet, sticky pulp. When the fruit splits open, the force may eject some of the seeds over short distances. Ants have been reported to be the principal distributors of the seeds. The ants gather the sugary pulp for food use and while transporting it back to their nest they drop seeds along the way in places that are often suitable for germination. The seeds also likely adhere to birds and mammal that come in contact with the fruit, and thus may be distributed over great distances.

USES

First Peoples of North America employed leaf infusions or decoctions of Mayflower for a variety of ailments, including diarrhea, indigestion, abdominal pains, labour pains during childbirth, rheumatism, and kidney problems. Some of these uses were adopted during colonial times in the U.S., but primarily the plant was a remedy for urinary problems. The foliage contains the chemical arbutin that acts as a urinary antiseptic. However, Mayflower is now thought to have harmful properties, because arbutin hydrolyzes, i.e., reacts with water, to produce hydroquinone, which is toxic. Medical usage is considered obsolete today.

The spicy, aromatic flowers are sometimes eaten, and the fruits are said to be edible, but Mayflower is not considered to be a wild food plant. As noted below, Mayflower is sometimes cultivated as an ornamental, mostly in rockeries, and occasionally as a groundcover.

ANTS MOVE MAYFLOWERS

Seed dispersal by ants is called myrmecochory, and is widespread in northeastern North American woodlands. Plants that are assisted by ants in this way include many unrelated species (such as violets, goldenseal, bloodroot, sedges, claytonia, and Seneca snakeroot), suggesting that the ant-plant relationship has evolved independently on many occasions. In most cases, ant-dispersed seeds are relatively large and have a nutritious (often oily) appendage usually called an elaiosome. This contrasts to the tiny seeds of Mayflower, where the fruit pulp rather than any part of the seed is the attractant. Mayflower is the only ant-dispersed shrub in northeastern North America; the other ant-dispersed plants are all herbaceous perennials.

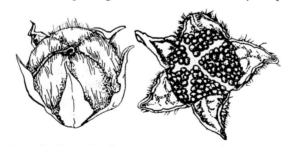

Berry-like fruits of Mayflower (*Epigaea repens*). Left: closed; right: opened by separation of five valves to show numerous seeds embedded in pulp. Prepared by B. Brookes.

Painting of Mayflower (*Epigaea repens*) in its natural setting, from the Walter Coucill Canadian Centennial official flowers of Canada series (see Coucill 1966 cited in the first chapter of this book). Reproduced with the permission of the copyright holders, the Coucill family.

A BIODIVERSITY TREASURE

CULTIVATION

Records show that the Mayflower has been cultivated for centuries in England and the U.S., but not frequently, because it is not an easy plant to grow. All three species of *Epigaea* are sometimes grown as ornamental plants in rockeries, where they require moist, acidic soil. A few ornamental cultivars of Mayflower and *E. ×intertexta,* a hybrid between *E. repens* and *E. asiatica,* are marketed for cultivation. Detailed instructions on how to grow Mayflower, from former Central Experimental Farm horticulturalist and co-worker Larry Sherk, are reproduced below from his popular but out-of-print (1967) guide to growing Canada's floral emblems.

"It is very hard to reestablish plants taken from their native habitats. If possible, use only nursery-grown plants or those raised in pots from cuttings or seed.

Take cuttings 3 to 5 inches [7.5–12.5 cm] long either in spring soon after flowering or in early fall. In a large pot or flat, put a mixture of one part ground peat moss and one part sharp clean sand. Stick all of the cuttings except the top leaves into the mixture and keep them moist but not wet. Mist beds are not satisfactory for rooting this plant. Cuttings root in 2 or 3 months. Pot up spring cuttings in early fall if they are well rooted, but leave fall cuttings until the next spring, protecting them over the winter in a cold frame.

To raise plants from seeds, follow these directions carefully. Seed capsules ripen and start to split 40 to 55 days after flowering. Watch them closely because ants soon remove the seeds. You may sow the seeds at once or store them overwinter in sealed jars in a refrigerator. For sowing the seeds, use seed pans or other shallow pots containing one part peat moss, two parts well-rotted oak leaves rubbed through an eighth-inch screen, and one part sand. Screen a thin layer of finely sifted sphagnum moss over the mixture and scatter the seeds evenly over it. To keep the seeds moist after sowing, cover the seed pan with a sheet of glass and plunge the pan in a larger pan or flat filled with damp peat moss.

The seeds germinate in 5 to 6 weeks. When the seedlings are 2 to 3 months old, transplant them to 2- or 3-inch pots, using the same soil mixture. Sink the pots in a flat of moist peat moss and keep them indoors until spring. The seedlings must be kept moist but not wet. In the spring, transfer the seedlings to a shaded cold frame. During the summer, transfer them to 3- or 4-inch pots or to their permanent location. If you leave young seedlings over the winter in a cold frame, mulch them with 3 or 4 inches [7.5–10 cm] of oak leaves.

The mayflower may be planted in a natural woodlot, or in an area in the garden that is shaded for part of the day. Because it is hard to keep the mayflower growing well in a garden, follow these recommendations carefully. Select a spot that will not be disturbed by the roots of aggressive trees and shrubs. Remove the soil to a depth of 18 inches [46 cm] and put down a 3-inch [7.5 inch] layer of small stones, cinders, or coarse sand. Then fill the hole to within 6 inches [15 cm] of the top with a mixture of equal parts of sand and peat moss. Fill the top 6 inches [15 cm] with a mixture of two parts oak-leaf mold, one part sand, and one part peat moss. If you have to keep out aggressive roots, sink a sheet metal or plastic barrier around the soil mixture. Water the plants well when you transplant them and often afterwards. A layer of pine needles also helps to keep the soil moist. Cover the plants with a 3- or 4-inch [7.5–10 cm] layer of oak leaves in the fall and remove the leaves gradually in the spring after danger of hard frosts is past. Plants may also be set out in the rock garden if the location is not too hot and dry in the summer."

The only aspects of cultivation to add to Sherk's very complete text, above, are: (1) Cold treatment improves germination. (2) Flowering tends to occur after rosettes have been exposed to cold (just above freezing suffices). (3) Using soil collected near well-established plants in soil mixtures is very desirable, as this introduces the mycorrhizal fungus that the plant needs for good growth (spores of the fungus also often seem to get attached to the seeds). The fungus appears to be essential for propagation from cuttings.

CONSERVATION STATUS

Although the Mayflower is considered common and secure through much of its range, there are many regions where it is rare. It is sometimes collected for winter decoration and wreaths, but because it is very slow growing, harvesting has eliminated or nearly eliminated it from some areas. It was extirpated from parts of Massachusetts, where it has been the floral emblem since 1925. A law dating from that time provides for a fine of up to $50 for harvesting the plant from private land without permission, but if done "in disguise or secretly in the nighttime" the fine may be up to $100. Once officially listed in Indiana as Threatened or Endangered, it is now ranked as a "Watch List species" there. The Mayflower is classified as "Endangered" in Florida. In New York it has been listed as "Exploitably Vulnerable".

MYTHS, LEGENDS, TALES, FOLKLORE AND INTERESTING FACTS

❦ According to legend of the Forest Potawatomi Indians and the Ottawa Indians, an old man living alone prayed that he would not succumb to the harsh winter. A beautiful maiden then entered his lodge, breathing a warm, fragrance that put the man to sleep. The maiden then transformed the man into a Mayflower, and as she retreated through the woods Mayflower plants grew in each of her footsteps.

❦ The "Victorian language of flowers" was a secret coded language in Victorian times (i.e., when Queen Victoria ruled, from 1837 to 1901), with flowers and plants symbolic of certain words or phrases, so when the flower or plant was mentioned in a letter those who knew the code could understand the hidden information. Mayflower stood for "budding".

❦ In 1959, Queen Elizabeth II conducted a 45-day tour of Canada. On August 1 at a banquet in the Nova Scotian Hotel in Halifax, she wore a grey silk organdie evening dress designed by Hardy Amies, with pink and white floral embroidery that included Mayflowers for the occasion.

❦ Studies in Nova Scotia have shown first flowering dates of Mayflower to be significantly later than they were a century ago, perhaps as a response to a cooling trend in the Maritimes. (Vasseur, L., Guscott, R.L., and Mudie, P.J. 2001. Monitoring of spring flower phenology in Nova Scotia: comparison over the last century. Northeastern Naturalist 8: 393–402.)

❦ Colours are notoriously difficult to define. According to Webster's Third International Dictionary, the colour "Mayflower" is "a moderate red that is yellower and paler than cerise, claret, or average strawberry and bluer and paler than Turkey red."

Mayflower (*Epigaea repens*). Source: plate 126, Walcott, M.V. 125. North American wild flowers. Smithsonian Institution, Washington, D.C. 5 vols.

SOURCES OF ADDITIONAL INFORMATION

Barrows, F.L. 1936. Propagation of *Epigaea repens* L.: 1. Cuttings and seeds. Contributions of the Boyce Thompson Institute 8: 81–97.

Bastin, E.S. 1895. Structure of *Epigaea repens*. Amer. J. Pharmacy 67(5): 1–6.

Blum, B.M., and Krochmal, A. 1974. *Epigaea repens* L., trailing-arbutus. In Schopmeyer C.S., Seeds of woody plants in the United States. Agric. Handbk. 450. USDA Forest Service, Washington, D.C. pp. 380–381.

Clay, K. 1983. Myrmecochory in the trailing arbutus (*Epigaea repens* L.). Bull. Torrey Bot. Club 110: 166–169.

Clay, K., and Ellstrand, N.C. 1981. Stylar polymorphism in *Epigaea repens*, a dioecious species. Bull.Torrey Bot. Club 108: 305–310.

Councilman, W.T. 1923. The root system of *Epigaea repens* and its relation to the fungi of the humus. Proc. N.A.S. 9: 279–285.

Coville, F.V. 1911. The use of acid soil for raising seedlings of the mayflower, *Epigaea repens*. Science 33(853): 711–712.

Coville FV. 1915. The cultivation of the mayflower. National Geographic Magazine 27: 518–519.

Dolan, R.W. 2004. Conservation assessment for trailing arbutus (*Epigaea repens* L.). USDA Forest service, Eastern Region. 17 pp. http://www.fs.fed.us/r9/wildlife/tes/ca-overview/docs/Epigaea%20repens2.pdf

Lemmon, R.S. 1935. The trailing arbutus in home gardens. Horticulture 13: 101–102.

Lincoln, W.C. Jr. 1980. Laboratory germination of *Epigaea repens*. Newslett. Assoc. Official Seed Analysts 54: 72–73.

Sherk, L.C. 1967. Growing Canada's floral emblems. Canada Dept. Agric. Publication 1288. unpaginated (28 pp.). (Also available in French.)

Sugiura, S., and Yamazaki, K. 2005. Seed dispersal of *Epigaea asiatica* (Ericaceae) by ants. Bull. Forestry, Forest Products Res. Inst. 4(3): 201–205.

Mayflower (*Epigaea repens*). Photograph courtesy of M. Munro, Nova Scotia Museum.

TREE: RED SPRUCE

Red spruce woodland. Source: Wikimedia (photographer: Forestgladesiwander, Creative Commons Attribution-Share Alike 2.0 license).

SYMBOLISM

The red spruce has played an important role in the history of Nova Scotia. Red spruce tea, with its high content of vitamin C, helped the pioneers fight off scurvy. In the early days of shipbuilding when white pine was scarce, red spruce became an important mainstay of the industry. In justification of the choice of the red spruce as its provincial tree, the following admirable qualities have been cited to show that the tree represents the strength and versatility of the people of Nova Scotia: (1) The species can thrive in a variety of places, from bogs to rocky shallow soils. (2) Red spruce can grow to an impressive height, sometimes more than 30 m (100 feet) in the province. (3) The tree is a remarkable survivor, capable of living for a century under dense shade and rebounding once it is provided with good light. (4) Red spruce is the leading sawn lumber species of the province, and second in pulpwood, hence a mainstay of the economy.

Silhouette of red spruce (*Picea rubens*) tree. Source: J.L. Farrar 1995. Trees in Canada. Canadian Forest Service and Fitzhenry and Whiteside, Markham, ON, Canada. Reproduced with permission.

NAMES

Latin Names
Picea rubens Sarg.

The genus name *Picea* is derived from the Latin word *pix*, which refers to some species of pine, and also for the "pitch" (resin) of coniferous trees. *Rubens* in the scientific name is Latin for reddish. The bark is light reddish brown, and the cones and buds are also reddish-brown.

English Names
Red spruce has also been called Adirondack spruce, Canadian spruce, Canadian red spruce, double spruce, Eastern spruce, he-balsam, West Virginia spruce, and yellow spruce. The curious name "he-balsam" was applied by residents of Appalachia to contrast the red spruce and Fraser fir, which often occur together in that region. Because of the red spruce's rough bark and prickly needles, like a man's beard, the tree was referred to as a "he". By contrast, the smooth-barked Fraser fir (*Abies fraseri* (Pursh) Poir.) with its flat, less prickly needles, was called "she-balsam".

French Names
Épinette rouge. Obsolete names: épicéa rouge, épicéa rouge du Canada, épinette jaune, prusqueur rouge, sapinette rouge, sapinette rouge du Canada.

HISTORY

Canada
The red spruce was declared to be the provincial tree of Nova Scotia in 1988.

Foreign
Spruce tree species are widely employed as symbols of political regions, but the red spruce is officially recognized as a symbol only in Nova Scotia.

Branch of red spruce (*Picea rubens*). Source: BugwoodImages/ForestryImages (photographer: K. Kanoti; Creative Commons Attribution 3.0 license).

APPEARANCE

Red spruce is monoecious (male and female flowers occur on the same plant). Both male and female flowers are aggregated in separate strobili (cones). The male flowers are pendant and bright red, while female flowers are erect and bright red, pinkish-purple, or green tinged with purple. The cone buds form in mid summer, but the male and female cones are difficult to distinguish until September, and pollination and fertilization do not occur until the following spring. The female cones are receptive to pollen when they are fully open, a period lasting only a few days. The female cones and their seeds mature in the fall and become pendant. At maturity, these are cylindrical with rounded ends, 2.3–5 cm (0.9–2 inches) long, light reddish brown (or orange-brown), glossy, with rigid, rounded scales that are frequently slightly toothed on the edges.

Under low light, red spruce can survive for more than a century as a dwarfed plant (growth may be as little as 2.5 cm (1 inch) annually), but once the canopy opens up the plant can develop into a substantial tree. Red spruce rarely, if ever, reproduces vegetatively by layering (rooting of branches). The trees grow from 21–35 m (70–115 feet) in height (rarely as tall as 46 m or 151 feet), and develop trunk diameters of 30–60 cm (1–2 feet), rarely as thick as 1.3 m (4.3 feet). In stands, self-pruning occurs, with shedding of the lower branches that receive limited light. The crown of the tree is conical. The ends of the main branches are characteristically upturned. The root system is quite shallow, and subject to windthrow. The needle-like leaves are yellow-green to dark green (not glaucous, i.e., with a bluish, whitish, or grayish waxy coating), (8)12–15(30) mm (0.3–1.2 inches) long, four-sided, curved, with a sharp point, extending from all sides of the twig. The thin, scaly bark is gray-brown on the surface, red-brown on the inside. The trees are long-lived and, in the absence of fire or other catastrophe, often survive 250–350 years.

Red spruce (*Picea rubens*) trees. Source: Wikimedia (photographer: Bobistraveling; Creative Commons Generic Attribution 2.0 license).

A SYMBOL OF HOPE AND SHARING

Every December the people of Nova Scotia send a large Christmas tree to the City of Boston. The Nova Scotia Department of Natural Resources requires that the tree be a red spruce, white spruce, or balsam fir (all Canadian provincial trees), and at least 13.7 m (45 feet) high. The gift expresses gratitude for the assistance of Bostonians to Haligonians in the aftermath of a terrible explosion in Halifax Harbour in 1917. The yearly lighting of that tree in downtown Boston combines the symbolism of Christmas as a time of hope and sharing, with a reminder that neighbours working together can rise above extreme misfortune and adversity.

The Halifax explosion resulted from the collision of a French munitions ship with a Norwegian relief vessel. The munitions ship caught fire and exploded, killing an estimated 2,000 people and injuring over 9,000, many permanently blinded. The explosion caused a tsunami wave in the harbour, and a pressure wave of air that snapped trees, bent iron rails, demolished buildings, grounded vessels, and carried fragments of the ship for kilometres. It was the largest artificial explosion until the first atomic bomb test in 1945 and remains one of the largest artificial non-nuclear explosions. 1,630 homes were completely destroyed and over 6,000 people were left without shelter from the extremely cold weather that followed. The people of Halifax were destitute and in shock. The prompt and extremely generous assistance from Boston made a huge difference.

CLASSIFICATION

Family: Pinaceae (pine family)

Red and black spruces are closely related, and hybridize where their ranges overlap. In the chapter on the emblems of Newfoundland and Labrador, an extensive table is presented comparing the characteristics of the two species. At least ten other species of *Picea* have been crossed experimentally with red spruce in breeding studies, but in nature hybrids with these other species are uncommon.

Picea rubens forma *virgata* (Rehd.) Fern. & Weath. has long, slender branches almost without branchlets, and is encountered most frequently in cultivation.

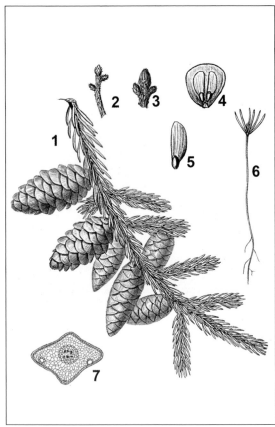

Red spruce (*Picea rubens*). 1, fruiting branch; 2, branch with winter buds; 3, winter buds showing bracts at base; 4, cone scale with seeds; 5, seed with attached wing; 6, seedling; 7, cross section of leaf. Source: Sargent, C.S. 1898. The silva of North America. Houghton, Mifflin and Company, Boston, MA. Vol. 12, Tab. 597.

Red spruce (*Picea rubens*) in mixed vegetation. Source: Wikimedia (photographer. M. Sprague; Creative Commons Attribution Generic 2.0 license).

GEOGRAPHY

Red spruce is a native of eastern Canada and the eastern United States, as well as St. Pierre and Miquelon (France). It ranges from Newfoundland (an isolated population) west to Maine, southern Quebec and southern Ontario, south to New York, Pennsylvania, New Jersey, and Massachusetts. It also occurs south along the Appalachian Mountains to North Carolina, at higher elevations (2,000 m, 6,600 feet). Red spruce is common over much of the Maritime Provinces, but is uncommon in south-central Ontario and in Quebec north of the St. Lawrence River.

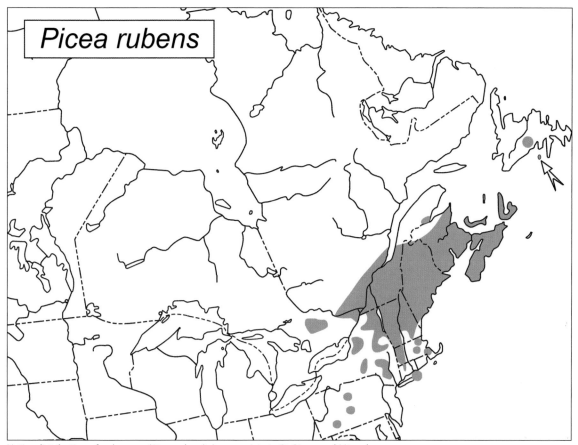

Picea rubens

Native distribution of red spruce (*Picea rubens*). Arrow points to St. Pierre and Miquelon.

Red spruce (*Picea rubens*). Source: Wikimedia (photographer. C. Powers; Creative Commons Attribution Generic 2.0 license).

A BIODIVERSITY TREASURE

ECOLOGY

Habitat

Red spruce occurs as pure stands and in mixed forests along with other coniferous and deciduous trees. In its Appalachian range, it extends into montane and subalpine forests. Red spruce is adapted to a cool, moist climate. It grows on a wide variety of well-drained soils, including shallow till soils, and organic soils covering rocks, but usually the pH ranges from 4.0–5.5. Sites occupied include steep rocky slopes and wet bottomland; however, it does not thrive on poorly drained soils. It is susceptible to damage from air pollution, and this is believed to be a factor in its decline in the Appalachian region. In the northern part of the range the trees must withstand heavy snow cover. Along the Appalachian Mountains, red spruce occurs at higher elevations.

Red spruce seedlings can become established under light intensities as low as 10% of full sunlight, but require intensities of 50% or more for optimum growth. The species competes moderately well with other trees, but will be outcompeted by hardwoods that produce heavy shade, like beech and maple. Balsam fir, which is comparably shade-tolerant, is a major competitor.

Inter-species Relationships

Red spruce is a major component of many forests, and it provides important food and cover for numerous species. Some of the insect species that consume it destroy the trees and are considered serious pests by the forest industry. The spruce budworm (*Choristoneura fumiferana*) is the most significant herbivore of red spruce. However, because the tree opens its buds later in the year than balsam fir or white spruce, the latter two species are more vulnerable. The eastern spruce beetle (*Dendroctonus rufipennis*) damages mature red spruce trees. The European spruce sawfly (*Diprion hercyniae*) and the native yellowheaded spruce sawfly (*Pikonema alaskensis*) cause severe defoliation in some areas. The eastern spruce gall adelgid (*Adelges abietis*) is sometimes also a serious pest on spruce. Eastern dwarf mistletoe (*Arceuthobium pusillum*), a parasitic plant, occasionally infects red spruce and causes reduction of growth, mortality, and degradation of wood quality. Mice and squirrels consume the seeds. Spruce grouse browse the twigs and leaves. Birds (especially crossbills or grosbeaks) eat the terminal buds of young trees, as do red squirrels, porcupines, bears, snowshoe hares, and rarely deer. Red spruce provides important winter cover for deer, moose to a lesser extent, snowshoe hare and other furred animals, ruffed grouse, woodcock, and many song birds.

Pollination & Dispersal

Red spruce is wind-pollinated. The wind also distributes the seeds, the attached wings acting as sails. Seed production begins when the trees are about 15 years of age. Rodents (especially mice, voles, squirrels and chipmunks) and birds consume the seeds, and to some extent also serve as distribution agents.

As in numerous other trees, seed production varies from year to year, with very good seed crops occurring once every 3 to 8 years with light crops during intervening years. These "mast years" of very high production have been interpreted as an adaptation against herbivores that consume the seeds. In a year of high production, herbivore populations are likely to be lower because the preceding years have provided only small amounts of seeds. Most red spruce seeds germinate the spring following dispersal, and sometimes they germinate in the fall soon after dropping from the parent tree.

THE IMPORTANCE OF NOVA SCOTIA'S FORESTS

Nova Scotia is situated in the Acadian Forest Region, which includes Prince Edward Island and much of New Brunswick, as well as Maine. The Acadian Forest is unique in its composition of softwood and hardwood species. Softwoods include red, white, and black spruce, balsam fir (the foundation of Nova Scotia's Christmas tree industry), eastern white and red pine, and eastern hemlock. Hardwoods include red and sugar maple, white and yellow birch, trembling and large tooth aspen, and beech. The adjoining Boreal Forest is dominated by fewer tree species, and softwoods are often predominant. Nova Scotia has been logged since the early 1600s, and forestry is still a key industry of the province, especially in rural areas, where nearly three quarters of the province's primary forest workers live, and where there are numerous sawmills and family-owned woodlots. Over 30,000 woodlot owners own almost half of Nova Scotia's productive forestland. Because the forests are essential for tourism, recreation, and clean air and water, and provide the habitats for considerable native biodiversity, sustainable management of the forest sector is essential.

USES

Red spruce is one of the most important commercially harvested coniferous trees of eastern Canada and the northeastern U.S. Its wood is soft, light in weight (with a specific gravity of 0.41, when dry), straight-grained, and resilient. A pale yellowish-white colour is characteristic and the heartwood is similar to the sapwood. The wood is used to produce pulp for paper, construction lumber, and musical instruments (including pianos, guitars, mandolins, violins, and organ pipes; thin red spruce boards have exceptional resonance). It is easily worked, and has moderate shrinkage and moderate strength. The wood holds paint well but rates low in holding nails. It has limited decay resistance and is difficult to inject with preservatives. Red spruce is employed to a minor extent as a Christmas tree, but other species have proven to have better qualities for this purpose. White spruce is a more common Christmas tree, but all Canadian spruces tend to shed their needles a few weeks after being brought indoors.

CULTIVATION

Red spruce is a major silvicultural species, of special concern to foresters. It is not usually cultivated as an ornamental tree, although a few horticultural varieties are available. For forestation purposes, there is considerable technical information available on seed collection, storage, and germination, and establishment and care of young trees. The species grows well in moist, acid, peaty or rocky soils.

CONSERVATION STATUS

Forest ecologists have noted a decline in red spruce throughout most of its geographic range. This has been attributed to: (1) Red spruce is a species adapted to late stages of succession; such plants have difficulty (in contrast to early-succession species like black spruce) in recovering from excessive harvesting, as has occurred); and (2) adverse environmental and climatic changes including warming over the last two centuries. (Projected increases of temperature from human activities may result in further decline, although parts of the range of red spruce may be less subject to increased temperature than other regions.) Increasing hybridization with black spruce may also result in the decline of red spruce. With extensive harvesting, the once continuous forests of red spruce become fragmented on the landscape, and black spruce becomes more abundant. "Genetic swamping" may then occur, i.e., the more frequent pollen of black spruce results in a reduction of pure red spruce seed.

Cones of red spruce (*Picea rubens*). Photograph provided by M. Munro, Nova Scotia Museum of Science.

A BIODIVERSITY TREASURE

MYTHS, LEGENDS, TALES, FOLKLORE AND INTERESTING FACTS

✹ Red spruce gum that exudes on trunk wounds was employed as a masticatory (chewing gum) by native Americans. During the last half of the nineteenth and the early twentieth centuries, red spruce gum was the basis for a flourishing chewing-gum industry in Maine. (To make your own gum, collect the sap, boil it until completely dissolved, and pour it onto a greased cookie sheet.)

✹ The famous acoustic guitar manufacturer, Martin and Company, made most of its guitar tops from red spruce from about 1900 to the mid 1940s. Like high-elevation spruce of Europe, the wood from Adirondack red spruce is prized for its extraordinary tone, projection, and clarity. With the recent decline of Appalachian red spruce, a good supply of such wood is no longer available.

✹ In 2005, it was reported that Mount Allison student Ben Phillips found a 445-year-old red spruce tree, along the Bay of Fundy coast in New Brunswick (see January/February 2006 edition of Canadian Geographic). This is the oldest reported *Picea rubens* tree based on a tree ring count. Despite its venerable age, the tree is only 30 cm (1 foot) in diameter. The oldest authoritatively dated species of *Picea* is an Engelmann spruce (*P. engelmannii* Parry ex Engelm.) from Colorado that was felled about 1994, and was found to be 852 years old.

✹ Sometimes when a single seed of red spruce is planted, several plants emerge. How does this happen? Among living things, sexual combination of a single male gamete with a female gamete produces just one individual. Polyembryony (equivalent to twinning in humans) is the production of more than one individual from a single fertilization, and it occurs occasionally among certain species, including animals such as the armadillo, and coniferous plants such as red spruce (Baldwin, H.I., and Percival, W.E. 1931. Polyembrony in red spruce. Science 74(1912): 203.). A polyembryonic seed produces several (usually genetically identical, or essentially so) independent plants. This may improve chances of germination and seedling establishment.

HAVE SEED, WILL TRAVEL
Stephen Hawking, one of the greatest physicists of all time, and author of the well-known (and occasionally read) book, *A Brief History of Time,* was warned by his publisher that every mathematical equation that he included would cut sales by half. However, this would never apply to people interested in plants! The following formula is useful in predicting dispersal distances of red spruce seeds. Knowing that red spruce seeds fall at a rate of 4.2 feet/sec in still air, the distance of travel can be calculated as follows:

$$D = S^h(1.47v)$$

where D = distance the seed will travel in feet, S = the time in seconds required for the seed to fall from height h (in feet) and v = the wind velocity in miles per hour.

Reference: Walter, L.C. 1967. Silviculture of the minor southern conifers. Stephen F. Austin State College School of Forestry, Bull. 15, Nacogdoches, TX. pp. 56–62.

A mature red spruce (*Picea rubens*) growing at Lays Lake, Halifax County, Nova Scotia. Photograph provided by E. Gratton, Nova Scotia Department of Natural Resources.

SOURCES OF ADDITIONAL INFORMATION

Cook, E.R., and Johnson, A.H. 1989. Climate change and forest decline: a review of the red spruce case. Water Air Soil Pollution 48: 127–140.

Eagar, C., and Adams, M.B. 1992. Ecology and decline of red spruce in the eastern United States. Springer-Verlag, New York, NY. 417 pp.

Gordon, A.G. 1957. Red spruce in Ontario. Sylva 13(1): 1–7.

Hamburg, S.P., and Cogbill, C.V. 1988. Historical decline of red spruce populations and climate warming. Nature (London) 331: 428–431.

Hart, A.C. 1959. Silvical characteristics of red spruce (*Picea rubens*). Northeastern Forest Experiment Station, Upper Darby, PA. 18 pp.

Keenan, R.E, and Maritato, M.C. 1985. The protection of red spruce from spruce budworm defoliation: a literature review. Maine Forest Service, Dept. of Conservation, Augusta, ME. 57 pp.

Major, J.E., Mosseler, A., Johnsen, K.H., Rajora, O.P., Barsi, D.C., Kim, K.-H., Park, J.-M., and Campbell, M. 2005. Reproductive barriers and hybridity in two spruces, *Picea rubens* and *Picea mariana*, sympatric in eastern North America. Can. J. Bot. 83: 163–175.

Manley, S.A.M. 1971. Identification of red, black, and hybrid spruce. Can. Dept. Environ., Can. Forest. Serv. Publ. No. 1301. 14 pp.

Mello, R.A. 1987. Last stand of the red spruce. Island Press, Washington, D.C. 199 pp.

Tomlinson, G.H. II. 1983. Die-back of red spruce, acid deposition, and changes in soil nutrient status—a review. *In* Effects of accumulation of air pollution in forest ecosystems: proceedings of a workshop held at Gottingen, West Germany, May 16-18, 1982. *Edited by* B. Ulrich and J. Pankrath. D. Reidel Pub. Co., Dordrecht, The Netherlands. pp. 331–342.

U.S. Department of Agriculture. 1917. The red spruce: its growth and management. U.S.D.A., Washington, D.C. 100 pp.

Red spruce (*Picea rubens*). Source: Wikimedia (photographer: Forestglandesiwander; Creative Commons Attribution Generic 2.0 license).

Red spruce (*Picea rubens*). Source: Wikimedia (photographer. Forestglandesiwander; Creative Commons Attribution Generic 2.0 license).

BERRY: LOWBUSH BLUEBERRY

Fruiting branches of lowbush blueberry (*Vaccinium angustifolium*). Source: S. Ferguson, Nova Scotia Department of Agriculture and Fisheries.

SYMBOLISM

The lowbush blueberry is an appropriate choice for Nova Scotia's provincial berry, given its importance to the province, its widespread occurrence, and its popularity. The area devoted to lowbush blueberry (13,355 ha; 33,000 acres) exceeds that of any other crop in the province, and the value (farm gate: $15,000,000; retail: $35,000,000 annually) exceeds that of any other fruit crop. There are about 1,000 blueberry growers in the province.

Lowbush blueberry (*Vaccinium angustifolium*) in flower. Photo courtesy of S. Darbyshire.

NAMES

Latin Names
Vaccinium angustifolium Ait.

Synonyms include *V. lamarkii* Camp and *V. pennsylvanicum* Lam.

The genus name *Vaccinium* is the classical Latin name for the blueberry. It is said to derive from the Latin *vaccinus,* of cows. English navigator and explorer Captain James Cook (1728–1779) noted that cows love the berries. The genus name has also been interpreted as originating from *bacca,* berry, for the prominent, numerous berries. *Angustifolium* in the scientific name is Latin for narrow-leaved, describing the characteristically narrow leaves of the plant.

English Names
The lowbush blueberry is also known as late lowbush blueberry, late sweet blueberry, low sweet blueberry, northern lowbush blueberry, sweet blueberry, and sweet-hurts ["hurts" is from the archaic West-Country (English) verb "to-go-a hurting", i.e., collecting berries; "hurts" and "hurtleberries" are used in parts of England to designate the bilberry, *V. myrtillus* L.]

The English name blueberry is named for the blue(-black) color of the fruit, and originates from the Scottish "blaeberry", used to denote related European species. The "blue" or "blae" traces to the Old High German word for blue, *blao*.

Blueberries (*Vaccinium* species) are known by many names, principally because early settlers observed that they resembled the European berries they knew as blaeberries, hurtleberries, trackleberries, whinberries, and whortleberries (the Scots associated them with the blaeberry, the Irish with whortleberries, the Danes with bilberries). "Whortleberry" is a dialectal variant of "hurtleberry", derived from Middle English *hurtilberi,* and is perhaps based on *hurt,* an azure-colored ball (from Old French *heurte*) + *berye,* berry. Other interesting names for blueberry species include deerberries, farkleberries, southern gooseberries, and sparkleberries.

French Names
Airelle à feuilles étroites, bleuet à feuilles étroites, bleuet nain, bleuet sauvage nain.

Lowbush blueberry (*Vaccinium angustifolium*). Artist: B. Flahey, Agriculture & Agri-Food Canada.

HISTORY

Canada

The "Nova Scotia wild blueberry" became Nova Scotia's "Provincial Berry" in 1996.

Foreign

The lowbush blueberry has not been adopted specifically as an official emblem outside of Nova Scotia. However, "blueberries" in general and other species of *Vaccinium* have been chosen as official emblems. In 2001, the blueberry (no particular species) became the official State Blue Berry of North Carolina (its official State Red Berry is the strawberry; red and blue are the official state colours of North Carolina). The blueberry muffin was made Minnesota's "State Muffin" in 1988. The "wild blueberry" (interpreted as *V. angustifolium*) was declared to be Maine's "State Berry" in 1991. The province of Benguet of The Philippines adopted the "native highbush blueberry" (identified by the local names ayosi and alumani) as its Official Provincial Fruit in 1987. Web documents produced by the government of Benguet identify the species by the names highbush blueberry (*V. corymbosum*) and mountain blueberry (*V. membranaceum*), species that are not native to The Philippines. The species appears to be *V. myrtoides* (Blume) Miq. (personal communication, D.A. Madulid, Philippines National Herbarium).

APPEARANCE

The lowbush blueberry is a depressed shrub, varying from 5–90 cm (2–36 inches) in height, generally about 30 cm (1 foot) tall. It typically produces extensive, dense colonies. The root system is usually shallow and fibrous, although occasionally a tap root as deep as 1 m (39 inches) is formed. The plants spread by slim (about 5 mm or 0.2 inch in diameter) woody rhizomes (underground stems) growing about 5 cm (2 inches) below the surface. The white or pinkish-white, urn-shaped, small (4–6 mm or about 0.2 inch long) flowers are borne in small clusters. The globular, bluish-black berries are 5–13 mm (0.2–0.5 inch), rarely 25 mm (1 inch) in diameter, and are sweet. The fruit contains up to several dozen tiny nutlets—so small that they are not objectionable to eat.

Lowbush blueberry (*Vaccinium angustifolium*) in fruit, in the Lac St. Jean area of Quebec. Source: Wikipedia (photographer: J. Dumais; Creative Commons Attribution-Share Alike 3.0 Unported license).

CLASSIFICATION

Family: Ericaceae (heath family)

Lowbush blueberry is extremely variable, and some taxonomists have recognized several distinctive kinds of plants, especially the following two. Widespread plants with green leaves and blue berries have been called *V. lamarckii* and *V. angustifolium* var. *laevifolium* House; several botanists have recognize this as forma *leucocarpum* (Deane) Rehder. Plants with whitish-green leaves and blackish fruit have been called *V. brittonii* and *V. angustifolium* var. *nigrum* (Wood) Dole; this has also been recognized as forma *nigrum* (A.W. Wood) Boivin. There is some evidence that f. *nigrum* increases more rapidly in stands that are burned regularly, but these two kinds of plant show little if any ecological separation, they interbreed freely, and they have not been accepted to be taxonomically distinct by most recent researchers. White fruit has been found to result from the expression of two independent genes. The characteristics associated with black (f. *nigrum*) fruit on the other hand are apparently influenced by a number of genetic factors.

Other minor variants have been recognized, including plants that have hairs on the veins of the lower surface of the leaves (var. *hypoplasium* Fern.) and plants with white berries (forma *leucocarpum* (Deane) Rehder).

Vaccinium angustifolium hybridizes with at least six other North American species, and hybrids are often difficult to identify. Cultivars 'Northblue' and 'Northcountry' are hybrids of *V. angustifolium* and *V. corymbosum*.

Lowbush blueberry is a distinctive species in northeastern North America, differing from the others as follows. It differs from cranberries (*V. oxycoccos*, *V. macrocarpon*) and northern mountain cranberry (*V. vitis-idaea*) in its erect (instead of prostrate) stems, blue (instead of red), berries and non-evergreen (instead of evergreen) leaves. Unlike the bilberry group (sometimes also called blueberries, including *V. cespitosum*, *V. uliginosum*, *V. ovalifolium* and *V. membranaceum*) the flowers and fruit are not single or in pairs in the leaf axils, but rather in crowded clusters. The highbush blueberry (*V. corymbosum*) has larger flowers, mostly over 6.5 mm long, is often taller, reaching 1 m, and does not form extensive low patches. The similar velvet-leaf blueberry (*V. myrtilloides*) has densely hairy twigs and leaves that are very hairy below, unlike lowbush blueberry which lacks dense hair. The dryland blueberry (*V. pallidum*) has the leaf margins without teeth (instead of serrated as in lowbush blueberry) and it is more southern, reaching Canada only in southern Ontario. The boreal and high elevation northern blueberry (*V. boreale*) is similar but is a dwarf shrub, not reaching 10 cm in height, and has leaf blades 3–5 mm wide, whereas lowbush blueberry is generally taller and has leaf blades 6–16 mm wide. Huckleberry (*Gaylusaccia*) bushes differ from lowbush blueberry in their resinous leaves (with shiny orange resin dots on the lower surface) and the fruits have much larger seeds, and are therefore less attractive to most people.

Fruiting branches of lowbush blueberry (*Vaccinium angustifolium*). Source: S. Ferguson, Nova Scotia Department of Agriculture and Fisheries.

GEOGRAPHY

The lowbush blueberry is native to eastern Canada and the northeastern United States. It grows from Newfoundland and Labrador west to southern Manitoba and Minnesota, and south to northern Illinois in the West and New England through the Appalachians to West Virginia and Virginia in the East.

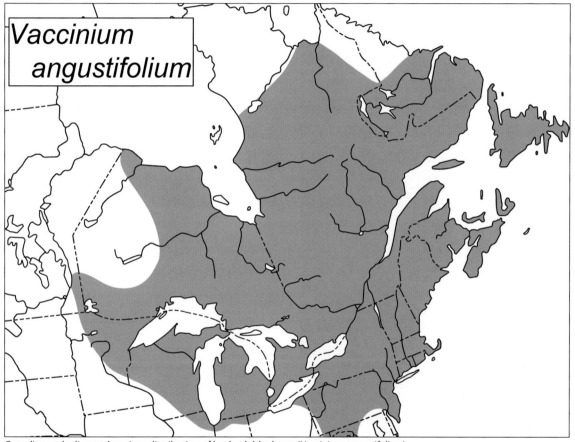

Vaccinium angustifolium

Canadian and adjacent American distribution of lowbush blueberry (*Vaccinium angustifolium*).

Lowbush blueberry (*Vaccinium angustifolium*) in flower. Photo courtesy of S. Darbyshire.

A BIODIVERSITY TREASURE

ECOLOGY

Lowbush blueberry typically occurs in both evergreen and deciduous forests, often dominating the understory vegetation. It is an important recolonizer of clearcuts, burns, fields, and pastures. Lowbush blueberry's tolerance of shade allows it to thrive in forests, but when the trees are removed the bushes usually expand vigorously by their spreading rhizomes, and produce a much larger crop of berries. The species is also tolerant of acid rain, and it has been speculated that its presence could increase in boreal forests affected by acid rain.

Habitat

Lowbush blueberry grows in a wide range of habitats. It is found in mixed conifer and hardwood forests, bogs, along sandy riverbanks, on exposed rocky outcrops, in abandoned pastures and clearcuts, and along roadsides. Wet habitats occupied included bogs, swamps, wet depressions, seepage slopes, and the margins of ditches, rivers, and lakes. Dry sites occupied include granite outcrops, sand hills, headlands, meadows, and parklands. The species is most frequent on well-drained loam and clay loams, often with high levels of organic material. The soil pH range is 2.8–6.6, optimally 4.2–5.2. The species occurs from sea level to 1,500 m (5,000 feet).

Some of the exposed plant communities where lowbush blueberry is common, such as outcroppings of the Canadian Shield in the Thousand Island region of Ontario, appear to change little in species composition or in the amount of lowbush blueberry over a 10-year period. However, an interesting spatial relationship has been observed between blueberry and spreading juniper (*Juniperus communis*). The blueberry plants are displaced by circular patches of spreading juniper, but then the blueberry invades the empty centre of the juniper patches. In the maritime region, lowbush blueberry is more commonly encountered in rapidly changing plant communities, such as old fields where it reaches peak abundance 10 to 25 years after abandonment.

Field of lowbush blueberry. Source: S. Ferguson, Nova Scotia Department of Agriculture and Fisheries.

ECOLOGY (CONT'D)

Inter-species Relationships
Lowbush blueberry occurs in association with a large number of other plant species, which become significant competitors under certain conditions. Among the most important competitors are the bracken fern (*Pteridium aquilinum*) and sheep-laurel (*Kalmia angustifolia*). Stem growth of the latter after fire exceeds that of lowbush blueberry.

The berries are consumed by dozens of species of birds (including robin, crow, eastern bluebird, and wild turkey) and mammals (including black bear, red fox, raccoon, fox squirrel, red squirrel, eastern spotted skunk, gray fox, chipmunks, red-backed vole, and mice). So important are the berries to black bears that when the blueberry crop is poor, it has been found in some areas that the rate of survival of bear cubs decreases. Flower buds are eaten by ruffed grouse during the winter. The foliage of lowbush blueberry is browsed by white-tailed deer, black bear, and eastern cottontail. As far as growers and harvesters are concerned, the most objectionable feeder is the blueberry maggot (*Rhagoletis mendax*). The adult of this insect is a fly, slightly smaller than a house fly, with black bands across the wings and white lines on the abdomen. It lays eggs beneath the skin of the fruit, and the larvae feed on the fruit, making it unusable for commercial purposes. Regular burning helps to control populations in commercial fields. At least 15 other insects are regarded as important pests.

Pollination and Dispersal
Pollination by insects is essential for good fruit set (some clones are self-fertile, others require cross-pollination). Several species of *Andrena* (solitary bees) and *Bombus* (bumblebees) have been reported to be important pollinators; notable pollinators include *B. terricola*, *B. ternarius*, *A. lata*, *A. carlini*, and *Dialictus cressoni*. Most insects visit the flowers to collect nectar, although bumble bees collect pollen. In some areas, widespread use of insecticides has decimated the supply of wild bees, and blueberry growers employ honeybees and alfalfa leafcutter bees to effect pollination.

The seeds are dispersed by birds and mammals. Deer, mice, chipmunks, and red-back voles have been found to be important short-distance dispersal agents, while the American robin and black bear are effective at long-distance distribution of the seeds. Seedlings are often observed in parts of the Maritime Provinces and in northern Maine, but are rare in eastern Ontario and other parts of the species' range. In many areas, reproduction is primarily vegetative. After fire or other disturbances, sprouts may appear from the stem base, from underground rhizomes, or from unburned belowground portions of aerial stems.

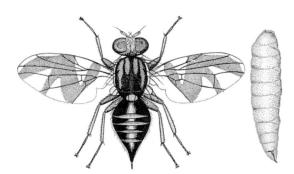

Adult female and larva of the blueberry maggot (*Rhagoletis mendax*), from Hall (1979).

MONEY IN THE GROWER'S POCKET
Wild bees do a better job of pollinating blueberry crops than managed bees (such as honey and leafcutter bees). They visit up to 6.5 times as many flowers in the time it takes a honey bee to visit one. They also carry more pollen and transfer more pollen. However they require adjacent natural habitats for nest sites and other food resources when crops are not available. Thus maintaining adjacent natural habitats not only protects biodiversity within an agricultural landscape—it puts money in the grower's pocket and helps the economy.

A native andrenid bee visiting a blueberry blossom in a cultivated blueberry crop in the Annapolis valley of Nova Scotia. Photo by Agriculture & Agri-Food Canada biologist Steve Javorek.

USES

Native North Americans in eastern Canada and the northeastern U.S. were the first to realize the value of lowbush blueberry. The berries were consumed fresh, preserved by drying, baked, added to soups, or mixed with venison and other meats. European settlers also collected the fresh fruit, and used it extensively to prepare jams, jellies, and preserves. With increasing culinary technology, the berries are now also canned, frozen, used to make wine, juice, and incorporated into numerous processed foods, including pastry mixes, ice cream, and yogurt. Blueberries have become the second most popular berry in the United States (strawberries are first). The lowbush blueberry is the second most important commercial blueberry species in North America, after the highbush blueberry (*V. corymbosum* L.).

The colour pigments of blueberries are chemicals called anthocyanins, and these include antioxidants. Antioxidants are needed by the body to fight compounds called free radicals that are formed as a byproduct of breathing, digesting and exercising. Free radicals are believed to be harmful, increasing the risk of cancer, heart disease, other diseases and premature aging. Blueberries were found to have the highest level of antioxidants in a study by the United States Department of Agriculture of 40 fruits and vegetables. Blueberries are very strongly recommended by nutrition experts.

In some parts of eastern Canada where wild blueberries are common, they are gathered by local people and sold at roadside stalls. The roadside vendors often also sell much larger (averaging twice the size) berries of the highbush blueberry, imported from New Jersey. Knowledgeable consumers will purchase the smaller and tastier wild berries, albeit at a higher price.

Blueberries ship well, and are a favourite fresh dessert eaten alone, topped with cream or liqueurs, mixed in fruits salads and cereals, and used as a topping for waffles and crêpes. As well, syrup, jams, jellies, ice cream, tarts, pies, muffins, cheesecakes, and dozens of other blueberry confections and breakfast pastries are widely enjoyed. Fungy (fungee) is a deep dish blueberry pie, popular for example in Nova Scotia. A "grunt" (also known as a slump) is a colonial American dessert, typically prepared with fresh fruit topped with biscuit dough and steamed in a closed container. Blueberry grunt is a specialty of Nova Scotia and adjacent regions, where wild blueberries grow. To prevent bleeding of the colour into other ingredients during cooking, blueberries should be added at the last minute, and stirred gently, to keep the skins from breaking. More than half of the commercial crop is processed by quick freezing. The fruit may also be canned and freeze-dried, and a pleasant wine can be manufactured. Blueberries are fragile and should be handled carefully. When purchased, they should be consumed promptly. If stored in a refrigerator, where they will keep for a few days, damaged berries should first be removed to prevent the spread of mould.

To a limited extent, lowbush blueberry is cultivated as an ornamental shrub and hedge. The cultivar 'Top Hat' is grown as an ornamental, sometimes as bonsai. Also to a small extent, the species has been used for land cover, notably to rehabilitate areas contaminated by mining and to prevent soil erosion on steep slopes.

Using a blueberry rake to harvest lowbush blueberry (*Vaccinium angustifolium*). Source: S. Ferguson, Nova Scotia Department of Agriculture and Fisheries.

Making blueberry jam. Source: Wikipedia (photographer: Quadell; Creative Commons Attribution 3.0 Unported license).

CULTIVATION

Lowbush blueberry can be easily propagated using seeds, cuttings, and transplanted rhizomes. However, it is often managed in wild stands, rather than being planted as a horticultural crop like the highbush blueberry (*V. corymbosum*). Although yield may be less for a few years, the cost of planting seedlings may be less than the cost of planting rooted cuttings. Indians in Maine apparently realized that the wild blueberry does not bear fruit well when overgrown with brush and weeds, and burned the area to encourage vigorous regrowth. Commercial fields are burned every second year, thus maintaining high fruit productivity. Lowbush blueberry plants are managed much like garden plants—they are fertilized and pests are controlled. Most lowbush blueberries are produced in Maine and eastern Canada (especially in Nova Scotia, but also in Ontario, New Brunswick, and Quebec). Only a few cultivated varieties are available. High-yielding clones of lowbush blueberry were developed by the Agriculture and Agri-food Canada research station at Kentville, Nova Scotia, and by the University of Maine. Cultivars developed at Kentville include: 'Augusta', 'Brunswick', 'Chignecto', 'Blomidon', 'Cumberland', and 'Fundy'.

Lowbush blueberries are often harvested in a single picking operation. They are picked by hand raking, using a metal rake that was invented by Abijah Tabutt of Maine in 1822. This looks like a dust pan, the bottom of which is made up of many close-set knitting needles. Most wild blueberries were hand picked using this device until recently, but mechanical pickers are now becoming popular.

A critical factor limiting flower and fruit development is late spring frosts. Temperatures cooler than -2.2 °C (28 °F) for 6 hours will reduce flowering and fruiting. Frosts may also reduce fruit set by limiting pollinators.

CONSERVATION STATUS

Lowbush blueberry is a widespread species that is not currently considered in need of conservation protection.

In some places, sandy barrens and open woodlands are special, restricted habitats that are home to rare species. Blueberry does well in these habitats, and they have been targeted for blueberry production. However, their conversion to commercial blueberry fields has threatened some rare species. For example, species of *Hudsonia* (sand heathers) have declined in the Annapolis Valley of Nova Scotia and in the Lac St. Jean area of Quebec.

Using a blueberry harvester to harvest lowbush blueberry (*Vaccinium angustifolium*). Source: S. Ferguson, Nova Scotia Department of Agriculture and Fisheries.

MYTHS, LEGENDS, TALES, FOLKLORE AND INTERESTING FACTS

❧ North American Indians preserved blueberries in various ways. In northern areas, the Inuit placed the berries in seal oil, or stored them in leather bags deposited in the permafrost. The berries were also dried in the sunshine or by a fire.

❧ Native peoples of North America used wild blueberries in spiritual ceremonies. The Maliseet valued the berries because they were believed to bring stamina, since they were the food of the bear. Native American Indians in what is now the northeastern United States observed that the stem end of the flower (the calyx) formed a perfect five-pointed star. These "star-berries" were said to have been sent to earth by the Great Spirit to relieve the children's hunger during a famine.

❧ Native North Americans taught European settlers how to prepare various blueberry dishes. In 1615, the French explorer Champlain observed Native Americans gathering wild blueberries to make a dish called "Sautauthig". The Native People would dry the wild blueberries and beat them into a powder that was added it to parched meat.

❧ Native American peoples used blueberries as a source of dye for colouring clothing and basketry.

❧ Early American colonists made grey paint by boiling blueberries in milk.

❧ The juice of blueberries is sometimes white.

❧ Blueberries will not ripen after they are picked.

❧ Blueberries are about 85% water.

Flowers of lowbush blueberry (*Vaccinium angustifolium*). Photo courtesy of D.L. Rubbelke.

SOURCES OF ADDITIONAL INFORMATION

Barker, W.G., Hall, I.V., Aalders, L.E., and Wood, G.W. 1964. The lowbush blueberry industry in eastern Canada. Econ. Bot. 18: 357–365.

Bertelsen, D.R., Harwood, J.L., and Zepp, G.A. 1995. The U.S. blueberry industry. United States. Dept. of Agriculture. Economic Research Service. Commercial Agriculture Division, Washington, D.C. 39 pp.

Boulanger, L.W., Wood G.W., Osgood, E.A., and Dirks C.O. 1967. Native bees associated with the lowbush blueberry in Maine and eastern Canada. Maine Agr. Expt. Sta. Tech. Bul. 26. 22 pp.

Camp, W.H. 1945. The North American blueberries with notes on other groups of Vacciniaceae. Brittonia 5: 203–275.

Caruso, F.L., and Ramsdell, D.C. (*Editors*). 1995. Compendium of blueberry and cranberry diseases. Amer. Phytopathological Soc. Press, St. Paul, MN. 87 pp.

Cuddy, J.D., and Cuddy, T.M. 2000. Growing blueberries: a guide for the serious gardener and commercial grower. 2nd edition. Rush River Publications, Maiden Rock, WI. 139 pp.

Darrow, G.M. 1957. Blueberry growing. U.S. Govt. Print. Off., Washington, D.C. 33 pp.

Eck, P. 1986. Blueberry. *In* CRC handbook of fruit set and development. *Edited by* S.P. Monselise. CRC Press, Boca Raton, FL. pp. 75–85.

Eck, P. 1988. Blueberry science. Rutgers University Press, New Brunswick, NY. 284 pp.

Eck, P., and Childers, N.F. (*Editors*). 1966. Blueberry culture. Rutgers University Press, New Brunswick, NY. 378 pp.

Eck, P., Gough, R.E., Hall, I.V., and Spiers, J.M. 1990. Blueberry management. *In* Small fruit crop management. *Edited by* G.J. Galletta and D.G. Himelrick. Prentice Hall, Englewood Cliffs, NJ. pp. 273–333.

Forney, C.F., and Eaton, L.J. (*Editors*). 2004. Proceedings of the ninth North American blueberry research and extension workers conference (Halifax, Nova Scotia). Food Products Press, Binghamton, NY. 452 pp.

Gough, R.E., and Korcak, R.F. (*Editors*). 1995. Blueberries: a century of research. Food Products Press, Binghamton, NY. 245 pp.

Hall, I.V. 1979. Lowbush blueberry production. Canada Department of Agriculture (Public. 1477), Ottawa, ON. 39 pp.

Hall, I.V., Aalders, L.E., Nickerson, N.L., and Vander Kloet, S.P. 1979. The biological flora of Canada. 1. *Vaccinium angustifolium* Ait., sweet lowbush blueberry. Can. Field-Nat. 93: 415–430.

Hancock, J.F. 1995. Blueberry, cranberry, etc. *In* Evolution of crop plants. Second edition. *Edited by* J. Smartt and N.W. Simmonds. Longman Scientific & Technical, Burnt Mill, Harlow, Essex, U.K. pp. 121–123.

Hutchinson, U. 1995. Blueberries. Amana Publications, Beltsville, MD. 39 pp.

ICON Health Publications. 2003. Blueberries: a medical dictionary, bibliography, and annotated research guide to internet references. ICON Health Publications, San Diego, CA. 112 pp.

Javorek, S., Mackenzie, K., and Vander Kloet, S.P. 2002. Comparative pollination effectiveness among bees (Hymenoptera: Apoidea) on lowbush blueberry (Ericaceae: *Vaccinium angustifolium*). Ann. Entomol. Soc. Am. 95: 345–351.

Kevan, P.G. 1977. Blueberry crops in Nova Scotia and New Brunswick: pesticides and crop reductions. Can. J. Agric. Econ. 25: 61–64.

Lavoie, V. 1968. La phytosociologie et l'aménagement des bleuetières. Nat. can. 95: 397–412.

Luby, J.L., Ballington, J.R., Draper, A.D., Pliszka, K., and Austin, M.E. 1990. Blueberries and cranberries (*Vaccinium*). *In* Genetic resources of temperate fruit and nut crops. *Edited by* J.N. Moore and J.R. Ballington, Jr. Int. Soc. Hort. Sci., Wageningen, The Netherlands. pp. 393–456.

SOURCES OF ADDITIONAL INFORMATION (CONT'D)

Maine Agricultural Experiment Station. 1950. Producing blueberries in Maine. Bull. 479. Maine Agricultural Experiment Station, Orono, ME. 42 pp.

Moore, J.N. 1994. The blueberry industry of North America. HortTechnology 4: 96–102.

Shutak, V.G., and Gough, R.E. 1982. Grow the best blueberries. Garden Way, Charlotte, VT. 32 pp.

Trehane, J. 2004. Blueberries, cranberries, and other vacciniums. Timber Press, Portland, OR. 256 pp.

Trevett, M.F. 1962. Nutrition and growth of the lowbush blueberry. Maine Agricultural Exp. Station Bull. 605. 151 pp.

Vander Kloet, S.P. 1978. Systematics, distribution, and nomenclature of the polymorphic *Vaccinium angustifolium.* Rhodora 80: 358–376.

Vander Kloet, S.P. 1988. The genus *Vaccinium* in North America. Research Branch, Agriculture Canada, Ottawa, ON. 201 pp.

Wild Blueberry Commission of Maine. 2002. Maine wild blueberries, America's native berry. Wild Blueberry Commission of Maine, Orone, ME. 62 pp.

Wood, G.W. 2004. The wild blueberry industry— past. Small Fruits Rev. 3(1/2): 11–18.

Yarborough, D.E. 2004. Factors contributing to the increase in productivity in the wild blueberry industry. Small Fruits Rev. 3(1/2): 33–43.

Lowbush blueberry (*Vaccinium angustifolium*) growing as an understorey shrub in a Jack pine (*Pinus banksiana*) forest in Neils Harbour, Nova Scotia. Source: Wikipedia (photographer: Mricon; Creative Commons Attribution-Share Alike 2.0 Generic license).

NUNAVUT

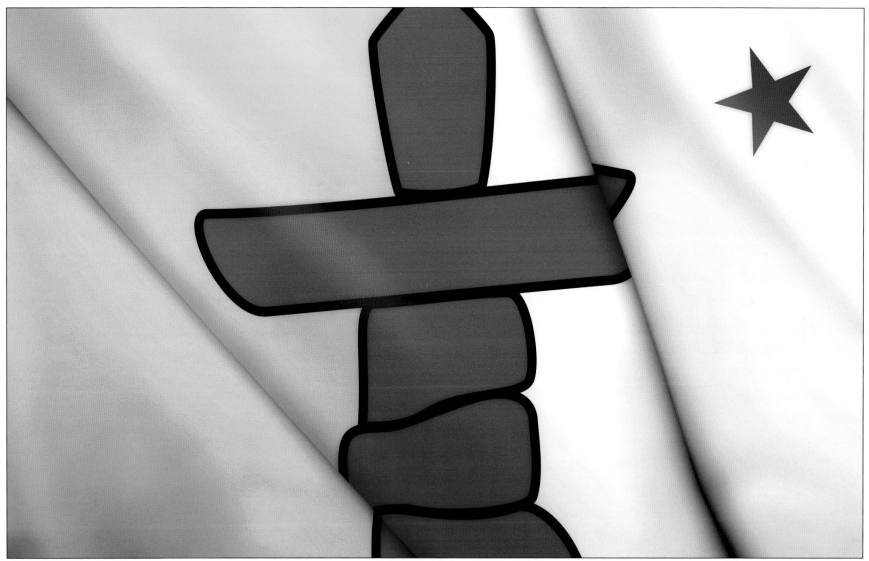

Flag of Nunavut.

A NUNAVUT LANDSCAPE: a valley in the mountains.

FLORAL EMBLEM: PURPLE SAXIFRAGE

Purple saxifrage (*Saxifraga oppositifolia*). Photo by P.M. Catling in May 2005, on the western Newfoundland coast.

SYMBOLISM

Purple saxifrage is exceptionally beautiful, brightening the sometimes bleak northern landscape. It is also very hardy and widespread in Nunavut, making it a fitting choice as the territorial floral emblem.

The Coat of Arms of Nunavut was granted by a warrant of the Governor-General of Canada on March 31, 1999, one day before the territory was created. The legislative description of it refers to the herbs below the caribou as "Arctic poppies, dwarf fireweed, and Arctic heather". The two patches of yellow-flowered plants appear to be arctic poppy (Papaver radicatum s.l., often split into several species). The purple-flowered clump nearest the right rear foot of the caribou appears to be dwarf fireweed (Epilobium latifolium). The patch with white flowers near the left rear foot of the caribou appears to be arctic heather (Cassiope tetragona). Although many websites state that one of the three wildflowers on the Coat of Arms is purple saxifrage, this is an error.

NAMES

Latin Names
Saxifraga oppositifolia L.

The genus name *Saxifraga* is based on the Latin *saxum*, a stone, and *frangere*, to break. This name was coined to apply to European species with granular bulblets, which were supposed to dissolve urinary concretions. By the "Doctrine of Signatures" of ancient medicine, plants were thought to signal their therapeutic value by some feature, and in this case the resemblance of the bulblets to urinary stones suggested that they could cure the condition. The "stone-breaker" in the name has also been ascribed to the fact that saxifrage species often grow on rocky ground, but this appears to be a misinterpretation. *Oppositifolia* in the scientific name is Latin for opposite-leaved.

English Names
Purple saxifrage. Also: French knot moss, opposite-leaved saxifrage, purple mountain saxifrage.

French Names
Saxifrage à feuilles opposées.

Inuktitut Names
Aupilaktunnguat. Also transliterated as aupilaktunnguaq.

The name translates as "resembling something red", presumably a reference to the floral colour and/or the leaf colour in winter.

Purple saxifrage (*Saxifraga oppositifolia*), photographed near Upernavik, Greenland, on 22 June 2007. Photos reproduced by courtesy of Kim Hansen (available on Wikimedia Commons, where copyright restrictions are noted).

HISTORY

Canada

The Nunavut Legislative Assembly's Floral Emblem Act of October 30, 2000 stated "The flower known botanically in Latin as the saxifraga oppositifolia and popularly known as the purple saxifrage is adopted as the floral emblem of Nunavut."

Foreign

Saxifraga oppositifolia is the official flower of county Londonderry in Northern Ireland.

APPEARANCE

Purple saxifrage is usually described as a herb, but its branches tend to become semi-woody, producing new growth annually at the tips, and such plants are often called sub-shrubs. Purple saxifrage is very low-growing, typically 3–5 cm (1.2–2 inches) in height. The plants are long-lived but grow very slowly; a clump only 10 cm (4 inches) wide is probably many decades old. The branches are creeping or trailing, and often tangle together, forming loose to dense mats or cushions 20–50 cm (8–20 inches) in diameter.

The root system is extensive, made up of a main tap root about 50 cm (20 inches) long and many side branches. The leaves are very small (2.5–4 mm or 0.1–0.16 inch long), triangular, leathery, fleshy, and gray-green. They overlap, somewhat like scales, and are arranged in opposite pairs, forming four rows along the stem. On the flowering stems, the leaves are more widely spaced, and often do not overlap. Bristle-like hairs occur on the leaf edges. The foliage turns red in the fall. Some of the leaves live through the winter and turn green again in the spring, others last only one season, hence the term "semi-evergreen" is applied. Each flowering stem bears a solitary flower, 1–1.5 cm (0.4–0.6 inch) across, and since there are often numerous flowering stems close together, a clump of plants appears to be covered with flowers. Although normally purple or lilac, the flowers are sometimes pink, pale red, or rarely white. Flowering begins in spring, and in some localities blooming occurs throughout the summer. The fruit is a brown or purplish-red dry capsule 5–7.5 mm (0.2–0.3 inch) long, which splits apart at the top to release the 50–100 tiny, smooth, brown seeds.

A sculpture of purple saxifrage, the territorial floral emblem, displayed in a glass case near the entrance to the legislative chamber of Nunavut. This work is about 15 cm (6 inches) wide. Photo courtesy of S. Aiken.

A BIODIVERSITY TREASURE

CLASSIFICATION

Family: Saxifrage family (Saxifragaceae).

Purple saxifrage is a very variable species. Two major evolutionary groups have been identified, one in East Asia and North America and the other in Eurasia. Within North America, some studies (including chloroplast DNA analysis) have supported the recognition of subsp. *glandulisepala* of much of western Canada and the arctic islands, and subsp. *oppositifolia* of eastern Canada and the southern range limit in the western mountains. However, the single morphological character separating them (glandular hair on the sepals of the former) is variable, and the most recent evaluation has recommended against recognition of subspecies in North America.

Purple saxifrage (*Saxifraga oppositifolia*). Photo by P.M. Catling.

Purple saxifrage (*Saxifraga oppositifolia*) ; A, B: flowering plants; C: petal; D: leaf with ciliate margin; E: calyx. Source: Sturm, J., and Krause, E.H.L. 1902. J. Sturms Flora von Deutschland. K.G. Lutz, Stuttgart, Germany. Vol. 7, plate 54.

GEOGRAPHY

The distribution of purple saxifrage is circumpolar, with plants in the arctic regions of both North America and Eurasia. The species is also alpine, occurring at altitudes up to 3,800 m (12,500 feet) in high mountains like the Alps and Pyrenees in the Old World, and in high alpine areas in British Columbia and Alberta. Purple saxifrage is found in the northernmost regions accessible to higher plants and is also among the flowering plants reaching the highest elevations in the Alps. In Canada, it grows from the Yukon to Ellesmere Island and from northern Quebec to Newfoundland. The species extends south to Washington, Oregon, Montana, Idaho, and Wyoming. In the southern parts of its range, it has persisted as a postglacial relict in the higher elevations of New England and in the Corney Brook gorge of Cape Breton in Nova Scotia where other arctic relicts are found.

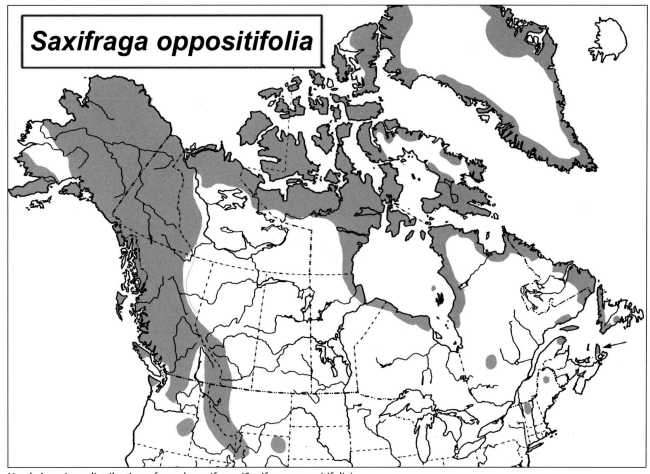

Saxifraga oppositifolia

North American distribution of purple saxifrage (*Saxifraga oppositifolia*).

Hybridization between *S. oppositifolia* and *S. biflora* to produce *S. ×kochii* has been reported in Europe but no hybrids are known in North America. Intermediates between the subspecies mentioned above might be interpreted as hybrids but have been treated most recently as continuous variation within the species. *Saxifraga ×nathorstii* from northern Greenland is thought to be a hybrid of *S. oppositifolia* and *S. aizoides*.

ECOLOGY

The arctic environment is extremely harsh and difficult for flowering plants, but purple saxifrage is so well adapted that it experiences very limited competition from other plants. It is abundant throughout much of its distribution area, and is one of the first colonizers after glacial recession. The arctic summer is very short, and temperatures infrequently rise above 10 °C (50 °F), requiring physiological adaptation to low temperatures and to intermittent freezing of tissues. The intertwined, hairy stems of purple saxifrage tend to act like a tent, providing a protected, relatively warm space that promotes growth. The reddish colour developed by the foliage of the plants in the fall has been observed to increase absorption of heat from the sun. The habit of growing close to the ground protects the plant from abrasion by wind-driven sand and snow, and protects the flower buds over the winter. The subsoil in the Arctic is permanently frozen, the uppermost part thawing annually. On sandy and gravely soil, on which purple saxifrage occurs, thawing is much deeper than on poorly drained peaty soil, on which only the top few inches may thaw. Soil movement due to thaw-freeze cycles and runoff of meltwater is another major problem for arctic plants. It has been observed that tufted species with moderately developed tap roots, like purple saxifrage, are much more resistant to soil movement than are plants with creeping rhizomes (horizontal underground stems). Because of the cold climate, short summer, and low soil temperatures, arctic soils are sterile. Bacterial decay is very limited, resulting in deficiencies of plant nutrients, especially nitrates. Purple saxifrage is particularly adapted to conditions of low nitrogen, and can grow on very infertile soil.

Habitat

Purple saxifrage grows in a wide array of habitats, including tundra, scree slopes, rock crevices, snow beds, moist calcareous gravels, ledges, cliffs, on the margins of ponds, streams, and lakes, and on seashores.

Inter-species Relationships

The principal pollinators of purple saxifrage include flies, bumble bees, moths, and butterflies. Various herbivorous animals consume the plant, one of relatively few that are common in the north. Seeds and probably flowers and flower buds are eaten by snow buntings, ptarmigan, and lemmings. Lepidopteran caterpillars also feed on the plants. Cushions of purple saxifrage provide refuge for a variety of insects.

Pollination and Dispersal

In the high arctic, there are two growth forms: some plants are prostrate and creeping while others develop cushions. Creeping plants sometimes layer, i.e., branches take root in the soil and produce new plants, a mode of vegetative rather than sexual reproduction. However, the new plants remain very close to the original plants. Creeping plants achieve longer distance vegetative reproduction by shoot fragments. The cushion form has advantages for sexual reproduction (e.g., more concentrated floral display).

Low temperatures in the Arctic limit the number of insect pollinator species, and reduce the activity of the species that occur there. The short summer and uncertain pollination result in quite variable seed set from year to year. However, a few studies have suggested that sexual reproduction is not affected by elevation in purple saxifrage, indicating that scarcity of pollinators is not necessarily a problem at high elevations. *Saxifraga oppositifolia* flowers very early in the spring, as soon as snow-melt exposes the plants. The flowering buds overwinter in an advanced state of development, so that they are ready to expand and open at the beginning of the warm season. Once the snow cover melts, the flowers mature in only five to sixteen days, and less than two months are required from flower opening to seed maturity. Outcrossing is promoted by flowers that are "protogynous", with the female parts appearing first and male parts of the same flower developing later, this reducing the likelihood of self-pollination. The species can self-pollinate, but many plants depend strongly on insect pollination for seed set, and they attract insects by their massive floral display and copious nectar production. Seeds are usually not released from the fruits until snow covers the ground. Wind easily pushes numerous seeds away over the smooth, frozen surface.

USES

The Inuit traditionally consume the sweet flowers of purple saxifrage with seal blubber, especially where berries are not abundant. The flowers are also eaten to relieve gastric problems, but eating too many can cause diarrhea. The stems and leaves are occasionally used to make tea. In the past, purple saxifrage stems and leaves were often added to tobacco. Green, gold, and cream-coloured dyes were sometimes made from the plant.

CULTIVATION

Purple saxifrage is a popular plant in alpine and rock gardens, but is relatively difficult to grow in warm climates. The plant requires conditions imitating its usual arctic or alpine environment. The soil should be gravelly and rapidly draining, but kept moist. If grown on a fertile soil like conventional garden plants, purple saxifrage develops many weak stems but does not flower. In rock gardens the plant should be provided with shade from the hottest midday sun, preferably a north-facing exposure. Several cultivars are available, especially from Europe. Recommended cultivated varieties include 'Wetterhorn', with large rose-red flowers; 'Ruth Draper', a vigorous, large-flowered cultivar; 'Theoden', with large rose-purple flowers; and 'Corrie Fee', a white-flowering variety.

CONSERVATION STATUS

Purple saxifrage is a widely distributed plant, not in need of particular conservation measures, although isolated populations at the extremes of the natural range are likely genetically distinctive and so deserving of protection. Concern has been expressed about the possible effects of global warming on the species, since experiments have shown that natural populations do not react well when artificially exposed to warmer temperatures. There is also concern about trampling of clumps of the species by visitors to the north, since the plants are fragile and recover from damage very slowly.

MYTHS, LEGENDS, TALES, FOLKLORE AND INTERESTING FACTS

🍁 Unlike animals, plants do not usually eliminate waste products, but usually store then inside their cells in sacs called vacuoles. However, some plants absorb or accumulate excessive amounts of some compounds (especially salt in saline habitats), and often they have "hydathodes", which are specialized secretory tissues that eliminate waste or absorbed products through a leaf pore. Hydathodes (usually one, sometimes up to three) are present on the leaf apex of purple saxifrage, and a white ring of calcium carbonate (as noted above, the soils occupied are calcareous) is frequently deposited around the pore, especially when the plants are growing on limestone rock.

🍁 The Inuit associate the full blooming of purple saxifrage with young caribou being born, and this knowledge is useful for determining times for hunting.

🍁 *Saxifraga oppositifolia* is one of four plant species growing on the northernmost site of plant growth on earth, Lockwood Island (83° 05' N) on the north coast of Greenland.

Hydathode-secreted calcite deposits on the surface of the end of the leaves of *Saxifraga oppositifolia*. Photo credit: ©Gary Steel, Cornwallis Island, Resolute Bay, Nunavut, from the publication Aiken et al. (2007).

SOURCES OF ADDITIONAL INFORMATION

Abbott, R.J., and Comes, H.P. 2003. Evolution in the Arctic: a phylogeographic analysis of the circumarctic plant, *Saxifraga oppositifolia* (purple saxifrage). New Phytol. 161: 211–224.

Abbott, R.J., Smith, L.C. Milne, R.I., Crawford, R.M.M., Wolff, K., and Balfour, J. 2000. Molecular analysis of plant migration and refugia in the Arctic. Science 289: 1343–1346.

Aiken, S.G., LeBlanc, M.C., and Boles, R.L. 2005. Growth forms and sepal hairs of the purple saxifrage (*Saxifaga opositifolia*: Saxifragaceae) in North America related to chromosome records and DNA information. Can J. Bot. 83: 1088–1095.

Aiken, S.G., Dallwitz, M.J., Consaul, L.L., McJannet, C.L., Boles, R.L., Argus, G.W., Gillett, J.M., Scott, P.J., Elven, R., LeBlanc, M.C., Gillespie, L.J., Brysting, A.K., Solstad, H., and Harris, J.G. 2007. Flora of the Canadian Arctic Archipelago: descriptions, illustrations, identification, and information retrieval. [CD-ROM] NRC Research Press, National Research Council of Canada, Ottawa.

Belland, R.J., and Schofield, W.B. 1993. *Salix vestita* Pursh and *Saxifraga oppositifolia* L.: arctic alpine species new to Nova Scotia. Rhodora 95: 76–78.

Gabrielsen, T.M., Bachmann, K., Jakobsen, K.S., and Brochmann, C. 1997. Glacial survival does not matter: RAPD phylogeography of Nordic *Saxifraga opositifolia*. Molec. Ecol. 6: 831–842.

Guglerli, F. 1997. Sexual reproduction in *Saxifraga oppositifolia* L. and *Saxifraga biflora* All. (Saxifragaceae) in the Alps. Int. J. Plant Sci. 158: 274–281.

Holderegger, R., and Abbott, R.J. 2003. Phylogeography of the Arctic-Alpine *Saxifraga oppositifolia* (Saxifagaceae) and some related taxa based on cpDNA and ITS sequence variation. Am. J. Bot. 90: 931–936.

Jones, V., and Richards, P.W. 1956. Biological flora of the British Isles: *Saxifraga oppositifolia*. J. Ecol. 44: 300–316.

Kume, A., Nakatsubo, T., Bekku, Y., and Masuzawa, T. 1999. Ecological significance of different growth forms of purple saxifrage, Saxifraga oppositifolia L., in the high Arctic, Ny-Ålesund, Svalbard. Arctic, Antarctic, Alpine Res. 31: 27–33.

Mallory, C., and Aiken, S. 2004. Common plants of Nunavut. Nunavut Dept. Education, Nunavut Wildlife Management Board, Canadian Museum of Nature. National Printers, Nepean, ON. 400 pp. (200 in English, 200 in Inuktituk).

Porsild, A.E. 1957. Illustrated flora of the Canadian Arctic Archipelago. Bulletin No. 146. National Museum of Canada, Ottawa, ON. 209 pp.

Savile, D.B.O. 1972. Arctic adaptations in plants. Research Branch, Canada Dept. Agriculture, Ottawa, ON. 81 pp.

Stenström, M., and Molau, U. 1992. Reproductive ecology of *Saxifraga oppositifolia:* phenology, mating system, and reproductive success. Arctic Alpine Res. 24: 337–343.

Stenström, M., Gugerli, F., and Henry, G.H.R. 1997. Response of *Saxifraga oppositifolia* L. to simulated climate change at three contrasting latitudes. Global Change Biol. 3(Suppl. 1): 44–54.

The Nunavut purple saxifrage coin issued in 2008. This is part of the provincial and territorial symbols gold coin series (0.99999% gold), discussed in the first chapter. This coin has a face value of $350.00 but, reflective of its value to collectors, the purchase price was $1,676.95. Only 1,400 coins were minted. Coin image © courtesy of the Royal Canadian Mint.

POTENTIAL SHRUB EMBLEM: ARCTIC WILLOW

Arctic willow (*Salix arctica*), photographed near Upernavik, Greenland, on June 22, 2007. Photo reproduced by courtesy of Kim Hansen (available on Wikimedia Commons, where copyright restrictions are noted).

THE TREELINE

Nunavut is largely above the treeline, a critical consideration with respect to the subject of an official tree for the territory. The Canadian Arctic includes all land surfaces north of the tree-line, which approximately includes the area of Canada north of the 10 °C (50 °F) isotherm for the warmest month of the year. To the west, in the delta of the Mackenzie, the tree line extends to 68° 40', almost reaching the shores of the Arctic Ocean. To the east, the tree line is deflected southeasterly. The northern Canadian tree line runs from the northwest in the Yukon Territory southeastward across the southern end of Hudson Bay, northeast across Quebec to Ungava Bay, and then more or less southeastward to the Labrador coast. The tree line is the boundary between the boreal forest to the south and the arctic tundra to the north. However, it is difficult to draw a sharp line where plants recognizable as trees stop growing, because of the irregular, scattered geographical occurrence of woodland patches and individual trees in protected sites where tundra predominates. Because of this, some biogeographers reject the concept of a "tree line", emphasizing that there is an "ecotone" (transitional area between vegetation associations) separating the boreal forest and the tundra. As concluded in the following paragraph regarding the definition of a tree, a treeline is somewhat difficult to define, but is nevertheless a well-established and useful concept.

LACK OF AN ARBOREAL EMBLEM

Nunavut does not have an arboreal emblem, although before it was split off from the Northwest Territories the arboreal emblem of the region was the jack pine (*Pinus banksiana*).

Note: Our colleague Jacques Cayouette has suggested that a cotton grass (of the genus *Eriophorum*, representing the sedge family) could be considered for status as an official plant of Nunavut. Species of the sedge family dominate the landscape of the Canadian arctic.

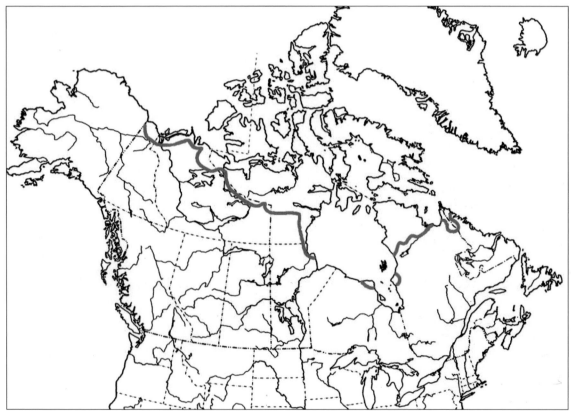

The northern treeline of Canada (in red).

AN ARBOREAL EMBLEM FOR NUNAVUT?

Balsam poplar (*Populus balsamifera*), perhaps the most northern broad-leaved tree of Canada, is present in Nunavut, and could be the most suitable choice as an arboreal emblem. It has not been adopted elsewhere. Four other cold-hardy trees are present in Nunavut, but have already been adopted as Canadian arboreal emblems: white spruce (*Picea glauca*, the provincial tree of Manitoba), white birch (*Betula papyrifera*, the provincial tree of Saskatchewan), black spruce (*P. mariana*, the provincial tree of Newfoundland and Labrador), and tamarack (*Larix laricina*, the official tree of the Northwest Territories). Jack pine (*Pinus banksiana*), the former official tree of the Northwest Territories, also occurs in southern Nunavut. Two additional species of birch (*B. neoalaskana* and *B. occidentalis*), and trembling aspen (*P. tremuloides*) may also occur in a more limited area of the territory.

As the only one of the thirteen provinces and territories of Canada lacking an official tree, the question arises whether or not Nunavut should adopt an official tree and, if so, which species is most suitable.

Trees of normal stature occur only in a small portion of the extensive land mass of Nunavut, much of which is north of the tree line. In the rest of Canada, and indeed in the rest of the world, official arboreal emblems representing political regions have been chosen because the trees have one or more of the following characteristics: 1) large stature; 2) visual impressiveness, especially in flower; 3) widespread presence in the area; 4) unique presence in the area (i.e., not present in other parts of the world); 5) current economic importance (especially for forestry); 6) strong support and lobbying by persuasive groups, such as school children, conservation groups, private industry, forestry organizations, and garden clubs; 7) possession of qualities that reflect well on the people of the region (such as resilience to an inhospitable climate); 8) a history of use and/or significance to indigenous people; 9) ecological importance (for example, as food and habitat for wildlife); 10) an absence of negative qualities (such as weediness, toxicity, association with negative mythology or historical events, or the subject of current serious attack by diseases); 11) freedom from possible legal complications or litigation problems (e.g., associated with conservation legislation or private industry trademarks); 12 not already adopted as an official symbol in other regions.

Of the above criteria, widespread presence in the area is a notable impediment to recognition of an official tree for Nunavut. Moreover, the very few trees of conventional size are located in a small southern part of the territory, and are not representative of the territory as a whole. Additionally, trees are absent from the most populated regions of the territory. For example, the capital Iqaluit is in the treeless tundra.

POTENTIAL SHRUB EMBLEM

The fact that Nunavut has only one official plant emblem while all other provinces and territories have at least two, suggests the desirability of recognizing an additional plant symbol. It should be noted that the official plant symbols of provinces and territories are not limited to trees and flowers. Saskatchewan and Alberta have official grasses and Nova Scotia has an official fruit. Nunavut is a unique region of Canada, and an additional symbol should reflect this uniqueness. We suggest that an "official shrub" rather than a tree would meet the need, and note a particularly interesting species for this role in the following.

Of the shrubs of the Canadian arctic, there are more species of willows (genus *Salix*) than of any other kind. At least 17 species of *Salix* have been recorded in Nunavut. Willows are particularly significant in Nunavut. The arctic willow is an important source of food for muskox, caribou, and other animals. The leaves and bark are commonly used medicinally (they contain aspirin-like chemicals). The wood can be used to make baskets, utensils, and tools, and is the only available fuel in some regions. Willows have even been used to monitor climate change. "Arctic willow" (*Salix arctica* Pall.) might be considered as an especially suitable plant for this role (judged by numbers 3 and 7–12 of the above criteria for an emblem). According to Wikipedia, "it is the northernmost woody plant in the world." According to *Vascular Plants of Continental Northwest Territories* by A.E. Porsild and W.J. Cody, it is "the most arctic of our willows, and in North America the only one ranging north beyond the eightieth parallel, and perhaps also the most adaptable as to habitat".

MYTHS, LEGENDS, TALES, FOLKLORE AND INTERESTING FACTS

❀ It has been observed that the warming climate of the north has resulted in some species of willows that previously grew very close to the ground suddenly became capable of growing more than a metre (about a yard) tall. This has enabled large predators (wolves and bears) to remain concealed and more easily ambush caribou.

SOURCES OF ADDITIONAL INFORMATION

Elliott-Fisk, D.L. 1983. The stability of the northern Canadian tree limit. Annals Assoc. Amer. Geographers 73: 560–576.

Arctic willow (*Salix arctica*) in Quttinirpaaq National Park, Nunavut. Source: Wikimedia (photographer: A. Walk; Creative Commons Attribution-Share Alike 2.5 license).

WHAT IS A TREE?
A "tree" is usually defined as a tall perennial plant with a woody main trunk. Some definitions try to be more precise, for example: "A tree is a woody plant with a single erect perennial trunk at least 3 inches (7.6 cm) in diameter at breast height (DBH). Most trees have definitely formed crowns of foliage and attain heights in excess of 13 feet (4 m). In contrast, a shrub is a small, low growing woody plant with multiple stems." Most species that are accepted to be trees when growing in southern parts of their distribution range are much smaller near the tree line or at their altitudinal limits, where they would not be "trees" in the above strict sense (indeed, many develop into shrubs). While the definition of a tree is somewhat arbitrary, all of the arboreal emblems of Canada normally grow into quite tall plants with large trunks, so that they clearly are trees.

Genera with species that are usually trees may have species that are, at best, "dwarf trees" in the arctic. While willows are familiar trees, Arctic willow (*Salix arctica*) is remarkably small in stature. It is typically a low shrub only 1–15 cm (0.4–6 inches) tall, although known to grow to 50 cm (20 inches) in height in the Pacific Northwest. Most birch (*Betula*) species are trees, but the arctic dwarf birch (*B. nana*) similarly is a low shrub, usually not much higher than 1 m (about a yard).

ONTARIO

Provincial flag of Ontario.

AN ONTARIO LANDSCAPE: an autumn forest reflected in a lake.

FLORAL EMBLEM: WHITE TRILLIUM

A large colony of white trillium (*Trillium grandiflorum*) in an Ontario woodland. Source: Thinkstock.

SYMBOLISM

In 1934, a committee was established by the Ontario Horticultural Association to study the issue of a provincial flower for Ontario. The 1935 report recommended the white trillium, stating (as cited in Pringle 1984):

"We have every right to be glad this flower occupies the place of honour in the minds of so many people. It possesses most of the qualities which should mark a floral emblem. It is democratic, blooming freely throughout a great part of Ontario, and known by its correct name to nearly everyone. It is of good size and graceful appearance. It is of simple structure, lending itself to decorative design, and is still so distinctive that it is unlikely to be mistaken for any other flower. The trillium is associated with the gladness, beauty and fresh hope of spring, and so is eminently suitable for our young country. Finally, while the plant and animal emblems of many other countries carry beaks, fangs, claws, spines and thorns, suggestive of the need of defence, the emblem selected for Ontario might well be entirely a blossom of peace, suggesting only healing and fruitfulness."

Christianity has sometimes employed the trillium as a religious symbol of the Trinity's three-in-oneness. The three leaves and three petals have been said to reflect the divine mystery of God as Creator, Son, and Spirit. The white trillium is occasionally called the "trinity lily". [Similarly, other plants that have been considered as bearing Trinity symbolism because of their three-petaled flowers include shamrock (*Oxalis acetosella*) and Virginia spiderwort (*Tradescantia viginiana*). In Europe the wild pansy (*Viola tricolor*) was once widely known as trinity flower for the three colours of the petals.]

NAMES

Latin Names
Trillium grandiflorum (Michx.) Salisb.

The genus name *Trillium* is based on the Greek root *tris*, meaning "thrice", reflecting the arrangement of leaves and floral parts, borne in three's. The epithet *grandiflorum* in the scientific name is Latin for "large-flowered".

English Names
White trillium. Also: bath flower, big white trillium, eastern white trillium, great white trillium, large-flowered trillium, large-flowered wakerobin, snow trillium (a name better reserved for *T. nivale*, and also applied to jack-in-the pulpit, *Arisaema triphyllum*), white wake-robin. The name "wake-robin" appears to reflect an 18th century belief that northern birds hibernated, and were awakened in the spring by the appearance of the flowers. The names "big white trillium" and "great white trillium" stand in contrast to "dwarf white trillium" (*T. nivale*). "Snow trillium" reflects the early appearance in the spring, when snow may still be present. The name "bath flower" is a corruption of "birth flower" or "beth flower", discussed below in relation to gynecological use.

French Names
Trille blanc. Also: trille à grande fleur, trille grandiflore, trillie à grande fleur. The name pâquerette (usually translated as "daisy") is sometimes mistakenly applied.

HISTORY

Canada
The white trillium was adopted as the floral emblem of Ontario in 1937. Tracing back at least to 1915, the species had been among several considered for the status of a "national flower" for Canada. The proposal that the trillium be chosen as a national emblem has been credited to James Burns Spencer (1866–1950), Chief of the Publications Branch, Dominion Department of Agriculture. However, it appears that increasing recognition of the maple leaf as a national emblem limited interest in the idea. In 1934, at the 28th convention of the Ontario Horticultural Association, referred to above, a committee that included Spencer was established to study the issue of a floral emblem for Ontario. Opinions were obtained from most of the high schools and collegiate institutes of Ontario, and this led to the association's backing of the white trillium, and eventually its adoption as Ontario's floral emblem. (For more detailed information, see Pringle 1984 and Dodds and Markel 1973.)

Foreign
Trillium grandiflorum was declared to be the "official wildflower" of Ohio in 1987. The deciding factor in this choice was the fact that it grows in every one of the state's 88 counties.

APPEARANCE

The white trillium tends to grow in colonies, and in some localities in Ontario the species forms extensive, dense stands that are spectacular in bloom. White trillium forms the largest populations of its genus in eastern North America, sometimes producing stands of over 10,000 individuals. As noted in Case and Case (1997), the species can reproduce clonally, i.e., vegetatively, despite statements in the literature that white trillium does not do so. The plants are 15–45 cm (6–18 inches) high, usually with a single flowering stem arising from a short, tuberlike rhizome that bears long, contractile roots. (These roots pull the rhizome downwards into the soil to compensate for it's tendency to grow up and out of the soil.) Generally one flower is developed annually per rootstock, and this is positioned at the top of the stem. Just beneath the flower, the stem bears a whorl of three "leaves" (the leaflike structures subtending the flowers are technically bracts, not leaves, but this distinction is academic since these structures are photosynthetic, like true leaves). The leaves lack petioles, and are 12–20 cm (5–8 inches) long. Trilliums usually require a minimum of 7 years to produce their first flower. White trillium often does not become reproductive for 15 years; the plants can survive for more than 30 years. The flowers are single, 8–10 cm (3–4 inches) in diameter, with three white petals 3–5 cm (1.5–2 inches) long and three green sepals up to 5 cm (2 inches) long. Each flower has two whorls of three stamens, one whorl opposite the petals, the other whorl opposite the sepals. White trillium blooms from late spring to early summer— from late April to late May or early June in Ontario (individual flowers are in bloom for 2 to 3 weeks). As the petals fade, they change to various shades of pink. Occasionally, flowers striped with varying degrees of green or completely double flowers (i.e., with extra petals) may be found (see below). Plants with flowers that are initially salmon-pink, called forma *roseum*, are also occasionally encountered. The fruit has been reported to be green, red, or blue-black, possibly depending on age and local variation. It is a more or less globose, six-angled, berry-like, fleshy capsule about 1.2–1.6 cm (about 0.5 inch) long, and matures in the summer. Typically a fruit will develop about sixteen small, brown seeds. Leaves completely deteriorate by mid-summer, and the plants are dormant until the next spring.

Characteristics of the common Ontario species of *Trillium*[1]

Character	White trillium (*T. grandiflorum*)	Nodding trillium (*T. cernuum*)	Painted trillium (*T. undulatum*)	Red trillium (*T. erectum*)
Petioles	Absent	Absent	Present*	Absent
Typical flower colour	White, fading to pink	White	White, with reddish-purple streaks at the base*	Dark red[2]
Petal margin	Not wavy	Not wavy	Wavy (undulate)*	Not wavy
Flower position	Erect	Nodding and hidden beneath the leaves*	Erect	Erect
Anther colour	Yellow	Pink	White or pink	Maroon to yellow

[1] The drooping trillium (*T. flexipes*) is represented in Canada only by two localized populations in southwestern Ontario (http://www.rom.on.ca/ontario/risk.php?doc_type=fact&lang=&id=9). Closely related to *T. cernuum*, it has drooping white or maroon flowers on long peduncles, and relatively broad leaves without petioles.

[2] A common misconception is that the red trillium is merely the white trillium with aging flowers. These species are often confused because there is a white-flowered form of the red trillium.

* Denotes a character that generally serves by itself to distinguish the species.

CLASSIFICATION

Family: Traditionally and still generally placed in the Liliaceae (lily family), and sometimes placed in its own segregate family, the Trilliaceae; more recently allocated to the Melanthiaceae on the basis of molecular evidence.

The genus *Trillium* has 43 species of perennial herbs, which occur primarily in North America, with a few in Asia. Of the six species native to Canada, five are found in Ontario, one in British Columbia.

Forms in White Trillium

In the past taxonomists frequently used the category of "forma" to describe minor variants. For example, white trilliums with green and white petals were named forma *striatum*. Today these are more often simply referred to as "green-striped forms". This is only one of numerous striking variants of trilliums. Indeed, the famous Harvard botanist Merritt Lyndon Fernald, who accepted eight formae in his revised edition of Gray's Manual in 1950, described white trillium as: "our handsomest, most fickle . . . species, with many scores of aberrant forms".

The green-striped forms, and some of the other variations in white trillium, are now known to be caused by infection by the bacterial genus *Mycoplasma*. Some of the anomalous forms reappear each year for at least several years. In some cases development of anomalous flowers in a population has been followed by gradual decline as would be expected from a pathological condition.

Although the Latin names of variants of white trillium are not widely used today, they are of interest as a record of what keen observers have documented. One of the best summaries is that produced by Dr. Jim Pringle who has provided some of the most authoritative information on trilliums in Ontario. Here we reproduce some of his text from the second (1976) edition of his "Trilliums of Ontario".

"Some plants are exceptional only in that their leaves and floral cycles are in two's [f. *dimerum* Louis-Marie] or in four's or more [f. *polymerum* Vict.]. Other plants have leaves and floral organs which are modified in their structure, sometimes extremely so. Among the more frequently encountered aberrations are those in which the leaves are definitely petioled and often borne lower on the stem [f. *lirioides* (Raf.) Vict.]; the leaves are lacking, their function being performed by greatly enlarged sepals [f. *chandleri* (Farw.) Vict.]; the petals are narrowly or broadly green-striped at the centre [f. *striatum* Louis-Marie]; or the petals are completely green and leaflike in texture [f. *viride* Farw.]. A remarkable extreme of the "lirioides" type of variation was reported in which the stem was completely suppressed, the peduncle and the long leaf petioles arising from below ground level. Small (1934) has reported a form with spiralled, overlapping petals. Forms with corollas which are pink when they emerge have also been reported for Ontario. One of these has been selected as the cultivar 'Rose Queen' f. *rhodanthum*, described as having petals which were pink when they first appeared, later turning white." [This may be the same as forma *roseum* Farw. that is frequent on the Blue Ridge Mountains of Virginia.]

Double Trilliums

Forms of *Trillium grandiflorum* with flowers that have the stamens and pistil replaced by additional petals (f. *polymerum*) are very attractive and prized by collectors. Since these relatively stable, double-flowered plants are sterile and must be propagated by asexual division, they are generally expensive. Some "double forms" have up to 40 petals.

White trillium (*Trillium grandiflorum*). Source: Canadian Heritage. 2002 (revised edition). Symbols of Canada. Canadian Heritage, Ottawa, ON. Reproduced with permission.

GEOGRAPHY

Trillium grandiflorum is native in Canada in Nova Scotia (where it is represented by an isolated population), Quebec, and Ontario. It grows around the Great Lakes, extending southward along the Appalachian mountain region through North Carolina and Tennessee, reaching to Georgia. The white trillium is a common wildflower across southern Ontario as far north as Lake Nipissing and extends into southwestern Quebec. It soon disappears from the woodlands as one travels north of Ottawa into the Gatineau hills, and has always been rare or absent through much of the New England states. Its centre of abundance is the southern Great Lakes region and the Appalachian Mountains.

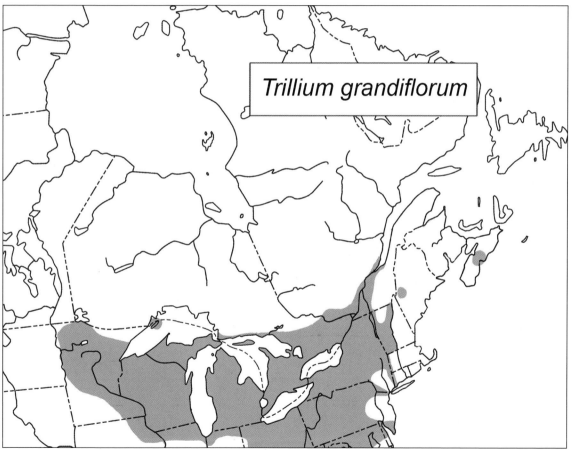

Trillium grandiflorum

Canadian and adjacent American distribution of white trillium (*Trillium grandiflorum*).

White trillium (*Trillium grandiflorum*) in a Quebec woodland.
Source: Thinkstock.

A BIODIVERSITY TREASURE

ECOLOGY

Habitat

The white trillium grows mostly as an understory herb in shady, rich, deciduous woods and mixed coniferous-deciduous upland woods and thickets, sometimes in floodplains and roadsides, on deep or rocky soils. The species prefers neutral to slightly acidic soils. In Ontario, it is common in deciduous woodlands (particularly maple and oak) of the southern part of the province, especially on non-granitic soils. By contrast, it is sporadic in much of the Canadian Shield.

Inter-species Relationships

Trilliums are spring ephemerals, developing rapidly after snow melt in the light available before overtopping deciduous trees produce a shady canopy. Deer are extremely fond of white trillium, and will feed voraciously on it, especially in early spring. Long-term management of deer populations (now without natural predators over much of Ontario) may be necessary for conservation of trillium and other understory herbs. Populations where 6–12% of the plants are browsed annually have been observed to decline by 3.6% per year. It has been shown that in areas where white-tailed deer feed extensively on white trillium, the plants are shorter.

Pollination & Dispersal

Insects are attracted to the flowers of white trillium by nectar secreted from sepal glands located between the ovary and stamen filaments. Unlike some other species of trillium that attract pollinators by smell, the flowers of white trillium have no discernible odour. Hymenoptera (particularly bumblebees of the genus *Bombus*, occasionally also honey bees) and (to a much lesser extent) Diptera (flies) have been recorded on the flowers, and have been observed collecting not just the nectar but also the pollen. The flowers are outcrossing, but self pollination is known in some populations.

The fruits drop from the plants at maturity in late summer. Trilliums generally have a weak region at the base of the fruit, which deteriorates at maturity, so that the seeds are released from the fallen fruit, much like a sack of apples that bursts at its bottom when dropped, to scatter the fruit. Many of the seeds remain close to the parent plants. Birds, mice, deer, chipmunks, wasps, and harvestmen (which are arachnids, i.e., related to spiders) are all thought to distribute the seeds of *T. grandiflorum*. However, the chief dispersal agents are ants. Ant dispersal of seeds is quite common, and is termed "myrmecochory". Each seed has an attached elaiosome—an edible, usually oil-rich, structure known to attract a variety of ant species and induce them to carry the seeds to their nests. Ants are so attracted by the elaiosomes that they have sometimes been observed cutting holes in immature capsules still on the plants, in order to extract the seeds. Ants generally carry the seeds only short distances (up to 10 m or 33 feet), but birds and mammals (by eating and defecating the seeds) can distribute them over much longer distances. It has been demonstrated that even short distance dispersal by ants is advantageous in promoting genetic differences among nearby plants.

Variation in petals of white trillium (*Trillium grandiflorum*). Photo courtesy of Fred W. Case.

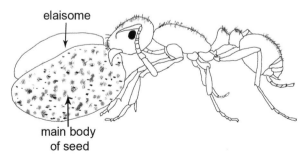

An ant dragging away a white trillium seed. Drawn by B. Brookes.

USES

The principal value of the trillium is as an extraordinarily attractive component of natural landscapes used for recreation. Millions of Ontarians love trilliums, and the pleasure and comfort of viewing them and photographing them in the spring woodlands reminds us of the importance of our natural landscapes for psychological well-being.

White trillium is grown as a cultivated, garden ornamental, particularly popular in native plant gardens, and indeed the species is the most widely cultivated *Trillium.* There are several cultivars, including 'Floro Pleno' (with doubled flowers) and 'Roseum' (with flowers pink from the time they open). Dwarf forms and forms with variegated leaves are also available.

Leaves of the white trillium have been used as food by Native People and occasionally by wild food collectors. The name "much-hunger" has been employed for trilliums in Maine, a reflection of their use primarily as an emergency food.

There are several, obsolete medicinal uses of white trillium. Chemicals called steroidal saponins in some species of *Trillium,* including *T. grandiflorum,* are uterine stimulants. These species are known as beth root and birth root because Native Americans used them to aid in birth, not just as a stimulant but also to stop excessive uterine bleeding. North American Indians applied decoctions of the root externally to treat sore eyes, joint pains, and external sores, and also used these preparations internally for menstrual irregularities, cramps, and to increase urination.

A woodland in Michigan carpeted with white trillium (*Trillium grandiflorum*). Photo courtesy of Fred W. Case.

TOXICITY

The fruits, seeds, and rhizomes of trilliums are generally considered to be poisonous (especially acting as an emetic). Although the plants are potentially harmful to livestock, deer are extremely fond of the above-ground parts.

EVOLUTION OF ONTARIO'S TRILLIUM SYMBOL

In 2006 the Ontario liberal government redesigned the original trillium logo (at a cost of several hundred thousand dollars). Since its introduction in 1964, the logo received minor modifications in 1972, 1994 (when it was coloured green), and 2002, but in 2006 there was a markedly new version that eliminated the surrounding box and added three abstract human figures. The new logo was thought by some to resemble poison ivy or holly more than a trillium (especially when reproduced at a small size), but expert botanists pointed out that it resembled neither. The modern trillium logo has been said to represent three people holding hands symbolizing unity and togetherness (as well as the trillium), but many have expressed the thought that it looks like three people in a triangular whirlpool bath.

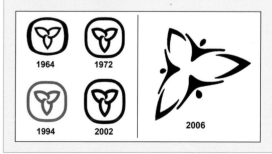

CULTIVATION

Detailed instructions on how to grow white trillium, from former Central Experimental Farm horticulturalist and co-worker Larry Sherk, are reproduced below from his popular but out-of-print (1967) guide to growing Canada's floral emblems (note also the comments below in the section Conservation Status).

"With a little preparation and care, the trillium is rather easy to maintain in the garden and is long-lived. The root is a thick tuber-like rhizome. The trillium can be transplanted [but not from protected areas] to the garden at any time of the year if a large enough ball of soil is taken and the roots are not disturbed. But it is best to mark the clumps in the spring and then move them in the late summer or early fall when the plants are dormant. At this time of year they can be transplanted with bare roots, but results are always better if a clump of earth is kept around the roots. Choose a location that has good drainage and shade from the hot afternoon sun in summer. Plant them in a neutral to slightly acid soil with some well-rotted leaf mould and peat moss added. Avoid heavy clay or sandy soils. If you plant bare-root material, set the roots 3 to 4 inches below the surface of the soil. To obtain seedlings, sow the seed as soon as it is ripe in a mixture of sand and leaf mould; choose a protected spot outdoors or a shaded location in the greenhouse. Seedlings appear the next year and take 3 to 5 years to flower. If you don't sow the seed as soon as it is ripe and if you let it dry out, germination will take at least 2 years."

As suggested above, seed that is not sown promptly becomes dormant. The seeds of white trillium are noted for their "double dormancy"—a requirement for two cold periods—but this can be circumvented by sowing seeds that are freshly harvested from the fruits, without being allowed to dry out. For additional excellent information on cultivation, see Case and Case (1997).

White trillium (*Trillium grandiflorum*), showing a white-flowered plant (top), pinkish, older-flowered plant (bottom right), and a plant with a bluish-black fruit (bottom left). Also notice the short, tuberlike rhizomes. Source: a set of drawings of Canada's floral emblems by Lavonia R. Stockelbach (1874–1966). A collection of her paintings of Canadian provincial and territorial official flowers is associated with the herbarium of Agriculture and Agri-Food Canada in Ottawa.

CONSERVATION STATUS

Urbanization and picking of wildflowers has resulted in the white trillium becoming rare in many of the heavily populated areas of Ontario. Although picking the above-ground part may not be fatal, it results in weakening the plant, and it may not flower again for 7 or 8 years. Harvesting the rhizomes for commercial, horticultural sale occurs very widely, and indeed some conservationists recommend not purchasing white trillium from nurseries, in case they were taken directly from the wild. However, habitat destruction and browsing by white-tailed deer, not picking of flowering stalks or harvesting of rhizomes, are considered to be the chief threats to the white trillium in Ontario. Trilliums are protected species in many U.S. states, including Michigan, Minnesota, New York, Oregon, and Washington. The white trillium is ranked as endangered in Maine. In British Columbia, it is illegal to pick the western trillium (*T. ovatum*). In Ontario the very rare drooping trillium (*Trillium flexipes*) is protected. However, the popular belief that there is a specific law preventing the picking of white trillium in Ontario is incorrect (although various legislation protects wildflowers in general). The white trillium is ranked as Vulnerable in Quebec and protected from unauthorized collection.

Fortunately white trilliums are protected in a number of natural areas. One of the best known is Trillium Woods Provincial Nature Reserve [http://www.ontarioparks.com/ENGLISH/tril.html] near the village of Sweaburg, protected specifically for its magnificent displays of white trillium.

Painting of the official flower of Ontario, the white trillium (*Trillium grandiflorum*), from the Walter Coucill Canadian Centennial official flowers of Canada series (see Coucill 1966 cited in the first chapter of this book). Reproduced with the permission of the copyright holders, the Coucill family.

MYTHS, LEGENDS, TALES, FOLKLORE AND INTERESTING FACTS

❧ The Iroquois Indians had several curious uses for trilliums. The dried root was carried for luck and for protection of teeth, and the root was also used to detect bewitchment.

❧ As noted above, white trillium flowers become pink with age, but occasionally are initially or permanently quite red. North American Indians sometimes interpreted red-flowered plants as most suitable for treating male illnesses, and white-flowered plants as best for female complaints.

❧ According to superstition, if you pick a trillium it will rain (it will also rain if you kill a snake, step on a beetle and, if you kill a spider in the morning, it will rain before noon).

❧ The chromosomes of *Trillium* are extraordinarily large, and the number of them is quite small—only five pairs in most species. Consequently, they are easy to observe and slides of *Trillium* chromosomes are frequently used in biology classes.

❧ The "Victorian language of flowers" was a secret, coded language in Victorian times in England (the period Queen Victoria reigned, 1837–1901), with flowers and plants symbolic of certain messages, so when the flower or plant was mentioned in a letter those who knew the code could understand the hidden information. The trillium represented "modest beauty".

A large colony of white trillium (*Trillium grandiflorum*). Source: Wikipedia (photographer: Director, Arc of Appalachia; public domain with attribution).

The Franco-Ontarian flag. The stylized trillium (right) is the floral symbol of Ontario, while the fleur-de-lys (left) represents French-Canadian heritage. The flag was officially recognized as an emblem in the Franco-Ontarian Emblem Act of 2001.

SOURCES OF ADDITIONAL INFORMATION

Case, F.W., Jr. 2002. *Trillium. In* Flora of North America North of Mexico. *Edited by* Flora of North America Editorial Committee. Oxford University press, Oxford, U.K. Vol. 26. pp. 90–117.

Case, F.W. and Case, R.B. 1997. Trilliums. Timber Press, Portland, OR. 285 pp.

Dodds, P.F., and Markel, H.E. 1973. Ontario's floral emblem. *In* The story of Ontario horticultural societies . . . 1854–1974. *Edited by* P.F. Dodds, H.E. Markel. et al. Ontario Horticultural Association, Picton. pp. 11–13, 15.

Kalisz, S., Hanzawa, F.M., Tonsor, S.J., Thiede, D.A. and Voigt, S. 1999. Ant-mediated seed dispersal alters pattern of relatedness in a population of *Trillium grandiflorum*. Ecology 80: 2620–2634.

Knight, T.M. 2004. The effects of herbivory and pollen limitation on a declining population of *Trillium grandiflorum*. Ecol. Applic. 14: 915–928.

Lamoureux, G. 200. Flore printanière. Fleurbec éditeur, Saint-Henri-de-Lévis, Quebec. [see pp. 48–53, 429–449.]

Nickerson, N.L., and Hall, I.V. 1978. Large-flowered trillium, *Trillium grandiflorum*, in Nova Scotia. Can. Field-Nat. 92: 291.

Pringle, J.S. 1984. The trilliums of Ontario. Royal Bot. Gard. (Hamilton, Ontario), Tech. Bull. 5, third edition. 27 pp.

Sage, T.L., Griffin, S.R., Pontieri, V., Drobac, P., Cole, W.W., and Barrett, S.C.H. 2001. Stigmatic self-incompatibility and mating patterns in *Trillium grandiflorum* and *Trillium erectum* (Melanthiaceae). Ann. Bot. 88: 829–841.

Soper, J.H. 1961. The distribution of Ontario's provincial flower. Bull. Fed. Ont. Nat. 92: 6–8.

Pink-flowered form of white trillium (*Trillium grandiflorum*). Source: Wikipedia (photographer: E. Hall; Creative Commons Attribution-Share Alike 2.0 license).

White trillium (*Trillium grandiflorum*). Source: Department of the Secretary of State of Canada. 1967. The arms, flags and floral emblems of Canada. Reproduced with permission.

A BIODIVERSITY TREASURE

White trillium (*Trillium grandiflorum*), courtesy of J. O'Brien (USDA Forest Service) and Bugwood.org.

TREE: EASTERN WHITE PINE

Eastern white pine (*Pinus strobus*), growing in the Ottawa Forest, Michigan. Photo courtesy of J. O'Brien, USDA Forest Service, and Bugwood.org.

SYMBOLISM

Eastern White Pine

Eastern white pine is a reminder of the importance of natural resources in commerce and trade since the days of the early pioneers when it was so important in shipbuilding. It is also a reminder of the rugged beauty of the rocky region of the Canadian Shield which is characteristic of so much of Ontario. To many, its wind-formed growth on the rocky shores of northern lakes evokes strength and endurance. The eastern white pine was considered to be a symbol of peace by eastern American Indians, because the needles grow in clusters of five and, after centuries of warfare, a peace treaty united five tribes (Cayuga, Mohawk, Oneida, Onondaga, and Seneca).

Other Pines

In the Old World, pine species have played extraordinary symbolic roles. In ancient Egypt, an image of Osiris, the god of agriculture, was ritually imprisoned each year in a hollow pine log, to be resurrected in order to ensure good crops. The stone pine (*P. pinea*) was sacred to the ancient Greek god Neptune, and pines were associated with the Greek goddess of the pine, Pitthea, the god of pine, Pittheus, and with the gods Dionysus and Bacchus. Dionysus was the most interesting of these. He was accompanied by the Maenads, wild women, inebriated with wine, shoulders draped with a fawn skin, carrying rods tipped with pine cones as a fertility symbol. The image of the pine cone has also been found as a symbol of fertility on ancient Greek amulets. Worshippers of Dionysus often wore foliage from pine trees (ouch!). In early Greece, wreaths of victory in athletic competitions were made out of pine branches. Ancient Romans regarded opened pine cones as symbols of virginity.

In China and Japan, the pine tree symbolizes longevity and immortality. The Chinese god of longevity is often shown sitting under a pine tree, with the crane, another symbol of long life, in the branches. Druids (ancient Celtic priests of Wales and Ireland) used to light large bonfires of Scots pine (*P. sylvestris*) at the winter solstice to celebrate the passing of the seasons and to draw back the sun, a practice that eventually gave rise to the Yule log. The trees were also decorated with lights and shiny objects, foreshadowing latter day Christmas tree customs. Groves of Scots pine in eastern Siberia were called "shaman forests", and were considered sacred by the Buriats, a Mongolian people living around the southern end of Lake Baikal. The groves had to be approached and entered in silence and reverence, respectful of the gods and spirits residing there.

Pines were also of great spiritual significance to North American Indians. The Santa Clara Tewa Indians of New Mexico interpret a very old pine as the oldest tree on earth, and indeed the one that produced the first food consumed by humans. The piñon pine (*P. edulis*) was an important part of the spiritual life of many Native Americans of the southwestern United Sates. The Navaho smeared pitch from the trees on corpses before burial. In December, before going outside, the Hopi applied a dab of piñon pitch to their foreheads as protection against sorcerers. Piñon gum was burned as incense in Navaho ceremonies, and selected branches from the piñon were used as ritual wands.

Silhouette of eastern white pine (*Pinus strobus*). Source: Farrar, J.L. 1995. Trees in Canada. Canadian Forest Service and Fitzhenry and Whiteside, Markham, ON, Canada. Reproduced with permission.

NAMES

Latin Names
Pinus strobus L.

The genus name *Pinus* is based on the Latin word for pine, *pinus*, which in turn comes from the Greek *pitys*, pine or fir tree. *Strobus* in the scientific name is the Latin word for pine cone, and originated from the Greek *strobilos*, meaning pine cone, and *strobos*, meaning whirling around, a reference to the cone scale arrangement.

English Names
Eastern white pine. Also: cork pine, majestic pine, northern pine, northern white pine, pattern pine, Quebec pine, soft pine, Weymouth pine, white pine, yellow pine. The "white" in the name white pine refers to the typically creamy-white wood. The name "Weymouth pine" is widely attributed to a Lord Weymouth who planted the eastern white pine on his estate at Longleat in England in the early 1700s, but the name could be based on Captain George Weymouth, who brought the species to Britain from Maine in 1605. The yellowish colour often exhibited by the heartwood is responsible for the name "yellow pine".

True pines belong to the genus *Pinus*, in the family Pinaceae, but the name pine is often applied to other plants. For example, the "Wollemi pine" is *Wollemia nobilis*, considered extinct for 65 million years before being discovered in 1994 growing in New South Wales, Australia. The Norfolk Island pine, *Araucaria heterophylla*, is a popular house plant, but is not a pine (the preceding two species are in the Araucariaceae, another family of conifers). Screw pines (so named because the long, flat leaves are spirally arranged) are members of the tropical family Pandanaceae, which is not coniferous.

French Names
Pin blanc. Also: pin blanc de l'est, pin blanc du nord, pin jaune, pin strobus, pin de Weymouth, pin du Weymouth, pin Weymouth, pin du Lord (the latter four names have been used in France; the "Lord" in "pin du Lord" is Lord Weymouth).

Base of large white pine (*Pinus strobus*). Source: Wikipedia (photographer: J.-P. Grandmont; Creative Commons Attribution 3.0 license).

HOW OLD IS A PINE TREE?
The main trunk of a young white pine tree develops a new whorl of branches each year. You can tell how old it is by simply counting the number of spaces between the whorls (from either the top of the tree to the bottom or from the bottom to the top). Old trees have to be cored for a count of annual growth rings. Research in some places, such as Algonquin Park, where there are trees up to 486 years old, has revealed that the thickest trees may not be the oldest. An old-growth white pine forest has been defined as one with more than ten white pine trees per hectare that are more than 140 years old.

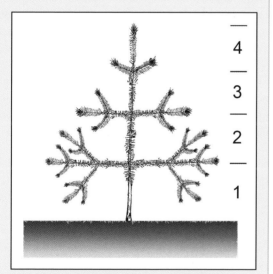

Determining the age of a young pine tree. The four segments between the base and the tip of the central stem indicate that this tree is 4 years old. Diagrammatic view prepared by B. Brookes.

A BIODIVERSITY TREASURE

HISTORY

Canada

The eastern white pine is the provincial tree of Ontario, designated in 1984. The lodgepole pine (*P. contorta*) was adopted as the provincial tree of Alberta in 1984. The jack pine (*P. banksiana*) was the official tree of the Northwest Territories of Canada, but was replaced by the tamarack (*Larix laricina*) in 1999.

Foreign

Pine species are official trees of twelve U.S. states. The eastern white pine (*P. strobus*) is the state tree of Michigan, so designated in 1955. The tree was the basis of lumbering in the state and, from 1870 to the early 1900s, Michigan led the U.S. in lumber production. Maine calls itself "the pine state" (or "pine-tree state") and also has adopted the eastern white pine as a state emblem. In 1895 it chose the white pine cone and tassel as its state flower, and in 1945 it designated the white pine as its state tree. The Western white pine (*P. monticola*) is the state tree of Idaho, adopted in 1935. The piñon pine (*P. edulis*) was declared to be the official state tree of New Mexico in 1948. The single-leaf piñon (*P. monophylla*) and bristlecone pine (*P. aristata*) are the state trees of Nevada, respectively designated in 1953 and 1987. The longleaf pine (*P. palustris*) was declared to be the state tree of North Carolina in 1963. The red pine (*P. resinosa*) was made the state tree of Minnesota in 1953. The southern longleaf pine (*P. palustris*) was adopted as the state tree of Alabama in 1997. The loblolly pine (*P. taeda*) was adopted as the state tree of Arkansas in 1939. The ponderosa pine (*P. ponderosa*) was designated the state tree of Montana in 1949. The Scots pine is the national tree of Scotland. The Bahama Pine (*Pinus caribaea* var. *bahamensis*) is the national tree of the Turks & Caicos islands, and is thought to be threatened with extinction.

APPEARANCE

The eastern white pine is the tallest evergreen tree in eastern Canada and the northeastern U.S. Before most large trees were cut down in past centuries, there were often specimens in virgin forests that reached 46 m (150 feet) in height and 100 cm (40 inches) in diameter at breast height, with rare trees claimed to have reached heights of 67 m (220 feet). Maximum (U.S.) records for eastern white pine trees that are still living are 2 m (5.4 feet) for trunk diameter at breast height and 56.7 m (185.9 feet) in height. Eastern white pine often reaches 200 years of age, sometimes exceeding 450 years. Most large trees seen in Canada today are less than 100 years old.

In the open, the trees have straight, uniform trunks with wide branches along the middle portion, and branches near the top curving upwards, producing an overall oval silhouette. In forests, the trunks are usually straight and free of branches for two-thirds or more of their height. The bark on younger trees is grey-brown or grey-green, becoming dark grey-brown or reddish-brown with age. On older trees the bark is deeply furrowed with vertical ridges and furrows. The roots spread widely and grow moderately deep, and the trees are not easily toppled by wind. The needles (leaves) are dark blue-green, straight, flexible, soft to the touch, 6–13 cm (2.5–5 inches) long, and clustered in fascicles of five leaves. Eastern white pine is the only five-needled pine native to eastern North America. The needles remain on the trees for 2 or 3 (sometimes 4) years before turning brown and falling off. The pollen cones are yellow, ellipsoid, 10–15 mm (0.4–0.6 inches) long, and occur near branch tips. The seed cones are more or less cylindrical when closed, 6–20 cm (2.4–7.9 inches) long, about 2.5 cm (1 inch) wide, and often curved. They hang singly or in groups from branches near the tops of the trees. The brownish seeds are made up of a body portion 5–6 mm (about 0.2 inch) long, with a wing 1.8–2.5 cm (0.7–1 inch) long.

Two large native eastern white pine trees, by Daicey Pond in Baxter State Park, Maine. Photo courtesy of C.J. Earle and The Gymnosperm Database (http://www.conifers.org/pi/pin/strobus.htm).

CLASSIFICATION

Family: Pinaceae (pine family).

There are about 100 pine species, almost all in north temperate areas of the world. Thirty-seven species are native to North America north of Mexico, and nine are native to Canada. Plants related to *P. strobus* that occur in the mountains of southern Mexico and neighbouring Guatemala are recognized as *P. strobus* var. *chiapensis*, *P. strobus* subsp. *chiapensis*, or *P. chiapensis*. The differences between this southern pine and *P. strobus* in its northern range are small (see Farjon and Styles 1997, and Gernandt et al. 2005), and its taxonomic rank is debatable.

Eastern white pine (*Pinus strobus*). Left, branch with male (staminate) cones. Right, branch with young female (pistillate) cone. Source: Sargent, C.S. 1897. The silva of North America. Houghton, Mifflin and Company, Boston, MA. Vol. 11, plate 538.

Eastern white pine (*Pinus strobus*). Top: mature female (pistillate) cones. Bottom, left to right: seedling, fascicle of leaves, cross section of leaf, lower side of cone scale, upper side of cone scale with two seeds, seed, seed with wing. Source: Sargent, C.S. 1897. The silva of North America. Houghton, Mifflin and Company, Boston, MA. Vol. 11, plate 539.

Cluster of five needles of white pine (*Pinus strobus*). Source: BugwoodImages/ForestryImages (photographer: B. Cook; Creative Commons Attribution 3.0 license).

A BIODIVERSITY TREASURE

GEOGRAPHY

Pinus strobus is native from Newfoundland west to southeastern Manitoba, south to the Great Lake States, down the Atlantic seaboard to New Jersey, and in the Appalachian Mountains to northern Georgia. Populations are also found in Iowa, Kentucky, Tennessee, and Delaware. In Canada, eastern white pine occurs particularly in the Great Lakes/St. Lawrence Forest area, extending into the Boreal, Acadian, and Deciduous Forest regions.

White pine has been introduced to many parts of Europe and in some cases it has escaped and spread onto the landscape. It is now naturalizing in the mountains of southern Poland and the Czech Republic.

A PINE LINE
Currently eastern white pines reach a rather definite northern geographical line. However, it appears that they were more common well north of this line in Ontario a few thousand years ago, based on the discovery of pollen and macrofossils in the older sediments of lake beds. Both the Great Lakes-St. Lawrence forest and white pines occurred at least 140 km (87 miles) north of their present position 3,000 years ago. The climate was warmer at the time. Subsequently it cooled, remaining more or less stable until about 1500, and from then to about 1850 there was another cooling episode, referred to as the Little Ice Age. Disjunct, isolated occurrences that exist today north of the boundary of continuous distribution are considered to be a result of the colder temperatures eliminating pines from all but the most optimal sites. With continued global warming we may (or may not) see white pine again crossing the northern pine line.

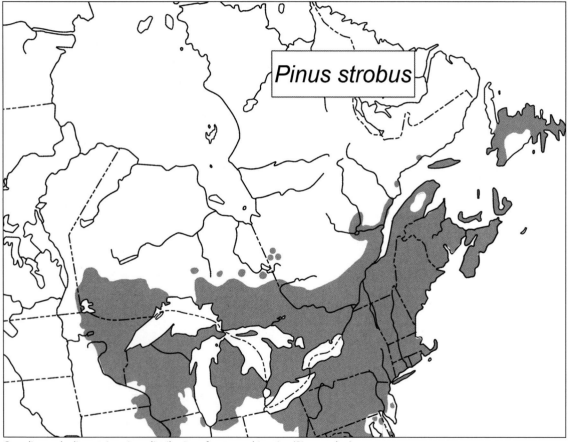

Pinus strobus

Canadian and adjacent American distribution of eastern white pine (*Pinus strobus*).

ECOLOGY

Eastern white pine is a dominant or co-dominant tree of northern, dryland pine forests. In mixed hardwood-conifer forests, occasional trees are found that tower above the rest of the canopy. While the species grows in association with many other trees, in pure stands of eastern white pine understory species may be scarce. Occasionally eastern white pine grows in bogs and swamps. It is a pioneer in disturbed sites (especially in post-fire mineral soils), and may persist for many years in climax mixed forests.

Habitat

The eastern white pine grows in many types of soil, tolerates moderate shade, and survives in a wide range of moisture availability. It is most competitive on fairly infertile, dry, sandy soils, but grows best on moist, loamy soils.

The eastern pine elfin butterfly, discussed in the text as one of the regular associates of the eastern white pine. Photographed May 2008 in the Burnt Lands Provincial Park, Ontario.

Inter-species Relationships

Several unusual vascular plants lacking chlorophyll grow well in the needle litter under white pine. Especially notable are pinesap (*Monotropa hypopithys*), pine-drops (*Pterospora andromeda*), and corral-root orchids (species of *Corallorhiza*). Birds and small mammals consume the seeds of white pine (a large seed crop is produced once every 3 to 5 years). Rabbits and white-tailed deer browse the foliage, and beaver and porcupines consume the bark. A variety of breeding birds nest among the branches, or occasionally in cavities in the trunk or larger branches (eagles are known to nest in particularly tall trees). The trees provide shelter for moose, bear, grouse, woodcock, and small mammals. The caterpillars of the eastern pine elfin butterfly (*Collophrys niphon*) feed on pine needles. The white pine weevil (*Pissodes strobi*) is the major insect pest, deforming trees by killing the terminal shoots. White pine blister rust (*Cronartium ribicola*) is a very damaging fungal disease, which relies on wild currants and gooseberries (of the genus *Ribes*) for part of its reproductive cycle. Accordingly, white pines are best grown away from most species of currants and gooseberries.

Pollination & Dispersal

Pinus strobus is wind-pollinated, the trees shedding pollen in the spring. While the pollen grains must enter the ovules within a short period or they will die, fertilization occurs more than a year after pollination, and seeds are dispersed in late summer and fall, more than 2 years following pollination. The seeds are mostly scattered by the wind, typically travelling up to 60 m (200 feet) within a stand and more than 200 m (700 feet) in the open. Squirrels, mice, and voles cache the seeds, thereby also serving to distribute them to a limited extent.

PINE WARBLERS

Pine warblers breed in open pine forests. In the northern part of their range the warblers most often build their nests and forage in white pines. There are dozens of warbler species in North America, most of which feed on insects. Pine warblers are one of the few species of warblers that eat large quantities of seeds, mostly pine seeds. Although the first warblers seen by most people in the spring are the yellow-rumped and the black and white, the pine warblers also arrive very early, but perhaps because they favour isolated pine groves with full foliage they are often overlooked, despite their very distinctive song.

Male pine warbler. Source: Audubon, J.J. 1827–1838. Birds of America. Havell, London, UK.

USES

The eastern white pine is the most valuable softwood timber species in eastern Canada and the northeastern U.S. The wood is of moderate strength, finishes well, and stains easily, and is employed for furniture, cabinets, panels, doors, mouldings, siding, and trim. In colonial times, large eastern white pines with a trunk diameter greater than 24 inches (61 cm) were reserved for Royal Navy ship masts (as a consequence, it is difficult to find old pine boards wider than 23 inches). The species has been widely used in reforestation. It is used as a landscape tree, but since it can grow as tall as a 15-storey building, full-sized trees are not suitable for small properties. Nevertheless, there are several horticultural varieties, including 'Contorta' (with twisted branches and needles), developed in Rochester New York in 1932; 'Fastigiata' (an erect, columnar clone), which traces to Germany in 1884; and 'Radiata' (one of many semi-dwarf forms, which usually grows wider than it is tall), which originated in England in 1923. Eastern white pine is occasionally used as a Christmas tree.

There are also a number of minor uses for eastern white pine. It has been employed in the eastern U.S. to stabilize strip-mine spoils. About a dozen pine species, not including the white pine, produce seeds that are sufficiently large, common, and tasty to be collected and sold commercially as "pine nuts", but for the most part these are marketed and consumed locally. Some Native Americans once consumed the inner bark (cambium) of eastern white pine as a famine food, and colonists used the inner bark as a component of cough remedies (extracts from the bark are still sometimes used for this purpose). Eastern white pine has occasionally been employed as a source of turpentine and rosin (the substance left after turpentine is removed from the resin, and used by violinists on their bows and by baseball players to get a better grip on their bats). However, turpentine, rosin, and indeed other resin extracts are mostly obtained from other pine species today.

"The White Pine" painted in 1957 by A.J. Casson (1898–1992), the youngest member of the "Group of Seven" Canadian artists (a group that originally had seven members, but went on to add three more; they were active as a group from 1919 to 1931). Paintings of the Canadian wilderness by these artists greatly influenced Canadian art, negating the viewpoint common up to World War II that the Canadian landscape was not a worthy subject for artists.

TOXICITY

Pine wood, sawdust and resin may cause dermatitis, allergic bronchial asthma, or rhinitis in some individuals. Pine pollen has sometimes caused hay fever and asthma. When used as a Christmas tree, the relatively limited aroma results in fewer allergic reactions than the more aromatic species. Consumption of pine nuts results in anaphylaxis in some people, but white pine nuts are so small they are rarely eaten.

CULTIVATION

As a principal forestry tree, there is an extensive literature on management of eastern white pine for timber production. White pine is also often grown for windbreaks and for landscaping. Heavy clay soils and poorly drained bottom lands are best avoided. Seeds should be planted in moderately dry places and in sandy soils without competition or shading from other plants. Young trees prefer similar conditions.

CONSERVATION STATUS

Eastern white pine is less frequent today than in early colonial times. The early pioneers found it to be one of the most abundant trees. The species was heavily logged in the eighteenth and nineteenth centuries. It has been estimated that only 0.4% of presettlement white pine stands remain. Compared to other trees, white pine appears to be relatively sensitive to air pollutants such as ozone, fluorides, and sulfur dioxide. Over large parts of eastern Ontario where large white pine trees grow in older woodlots, there is little or no recruitment of young trees in either the woodlands or nearby old fields. The pines there today may not be there a century from now. However, *P. strobus* is widespread and there is not concern about its survival over most of its natural range. The southern relative of *P. strobus*, *P. chiapensis*, has been extensively logged in Mexico and Guatemala, and has been assigned a conservation status of Vulnerable.

Possibly the largest pristine white and red pine landscape left in the world is in Ontario's Algoma Highlands, where in 1999 a portion was protected in Spanish River Provincial Park. Another place to see 300-year-old pines is the "Old Growth White Pine Trail" south of Temagami (trailhead at 46.71672 N, -79.81650 W) www.ontariotrails.on.ca/trails-a-z/old-growth-white-pine-trail/.

Foliage of white pine (*Pinus strobus*) covered by snow in winter. Source: Thinkstock.

WHITE PINE AT THE CENTRE OF CANADIAN COMMERCE

During the 1800s a huge industry developed around the exploitation of white pine for use in shipbuilding. The upper Ottawa River Valley was a major lumbering region. The pines were cut during the winter, and then pulled across lakes by boat, and floated on spring-flooded rivers to the Ottawa River. Here they were collected and squared, and then formed into large rafts that were steered down the Ottawa and St. Lawrence rivers to Montreal and Quebec City. Water transport was possible because softwood floats well. The industry was controlled by famous lumber barons such as J.R. Booth whose company supplied over a half million board feet in 1874. The thousands of people employed in lumbering required food, which was supplied by expanding, nearby agricultural communities. For a hundred years white pine was at the centre of growth and settlement in Canada.

MYTHS, LEGENDS, TALES, FOLKLORE AND INTERESTING FACTS

✤ In ancient China, accumulations of resin that were in the shape of dragons, formed at the bottom of large, old pine trees, were thought to give rise to dragons. Such resin was considered to have great medicinal value, enabling people to live for hundreds of years.

✤ Leonardo da Vinci (1452–1519) painted the Mona Lisa on a piece of pinewood measuring 77 × 53 cm (30 × 21 inches) in 1506.

✤ It was once said that eating a pine kernel from the very top of a pine tree would result in immunity from being shot. In Bohemia (an ancient kingdom, now in the Czech Republic), gathering cones on St. John's Day (June 24) and eating one kernel daily were thought to make one immune to gunshot—a practice that attracted thieves and robbers.

✤ A Scottish superstition cautioned about not felling pine trees for shipbuilding during the waning of the moon, as the tidal influence of the moon was said to affect the resin content (and hence the water resistance) of the wood. Modern research has established that the flow of sap in plants is to a very minor extent affected by the gravitational influences of the moon's cycles.

✤ "Pine drape" and "pine overcoat" are obsolete slang American expressions for a coffin (based on how commonly pine is used to make coffins).

✤ Floor cleaning products in Venezuela are fortified with ten times as much pine fragrance as North American floor cleaners. The much stronger scent is desired to send the message that the house is clean.

✤ Pine cones are excellent subjects for demonstrating the famous Fibonacci series, a type of arithmetic that describes how many living things develop. If you count the spiral rows of scales on a pine cone, you may find eight spirals winding up to the left and 13 spirals winding up to the right, or 13 left and 21 right spirals, or other pairs of numbers. These pairs of numbers are always adjacent numbers in the Fibonacci series: 1, 1, 2, 3, 5, 8, 13, 21. In this series, each number is the sum of the previous two numbers.

✤ The capercaillie (*Tetrao urogallus*, also known as capercailzie and cock o' the woods) is the largest game bird of the British Isles, where it became extinct in 1785, but was reintroduced. This member of the grouse family habitually feeds on the tops of young pine trees, giving its flesh a slight flavour of turpentine. Knowledgeable cooks remove the turpentine aroma by eviscerating the bird as soon as possible after it has been shot, stuffing it with potatoes, hanging it for five days, then discarding the potatoes.

✤ Artificial vanilla (vanilline) has been manufactured from a chemical (coniferine) found in pine lumber waste.

✤ "Retsina" is a unique Greek wine flavoured with the resin of the Aleppo pine, *P. halepensis* Mill. The association of wine and pine resin seems to trace to Greece of 3,000 years ago, when resin was employed to seal the large amphorae used to store wine. During transportation, the resin would come in contact with the wine and flavour it. It was wrongly believed that resin would help preserve the wine. The resin gives the wine a distinctively sappy, turpentine-like flavour—a taste that is acquired.

✤ "Pumpkin pine" refers to unusually coloured, old eastern white pine boards that are light yellowish-golden or reddish brown. The colour is thought to be associated with slow growth in virgin forests, which resulted in the accumulation of coloured products in the heartwood.

White pine (*Pinus strobus*). Source: Wikipedia (photographer: Botteville; released into the public domain).

Nineteenth century pine logging scenes. Upper left: cutting and sawing pine lumber. Upper right: pair of oxen pulling a skid with pine logs. Lower left: preparing logs for water transport. Lower right: breaking up a log jam. Source: The Minnesota Pineries. Harper's New Monthly Magazine, March, 1868.

White pine (*Pinus strobus*) cone and seeds. Source: Hempel, G. and Wilhelm, K. 1889. Die Bäume und Sträucher des Waldes in botanischer und forstwirthschaftlicher Beziehung, vol. 1. Wien, Austria.

A BIODIVERSITY TREASURE

SOURCES OF ADDITIONAL INFORMATION

Aird, P.L. 1985. In praise of pine: the eastern white pine and red pine timber harvest from Ontario's Crown forest. Petawawa National Forestry Institute, Chalk River, ON. 23 pp.

Critchfield, W.B., and Little, E.L. 1966. Geographic distribution of the pines of the world. U.S. Dept. of Agriculture, Forest Service, Washington, D.C. 97 pp.

Del Castillo, RF, and Acosta, S. 2002. Ethnobotanical notes on *Pinus strobus* var. *chiapensis*. Anales del Instituto de Biología, Universidad Nacional Autónoma de México, Serie Botánica 73: 319–327.

Farjon, A. 1984. Pines, drawings and descriptions of the genus *Pinus*. Backhuys, Leiden, The Netherlands. 220 pp.

Farjon, A., and Styles, B.T. 1967. *Pinus* (Pinaceae). New York Botanical Garden, New York, NY. 291 pp.

Farjon, A., and Styles, B.T. 1997. *Pinus* (Pinaceae). Flora Neotropica Monograph 75. The New York Botanical Garden, New York, NY. 291 pp.

Funk, D.T. 1986. Eastern white pine: today and tomorrow: symposium proceedings, June 12–14, 1985, Durham, New Hampshire. U.S. Dept. of Agriculture, Forest Service, Washington, D.C. 124 pp.

Gernandt, D.S., Geada López, G., Garcia, S.O., and Liston, A. 2005. Phylogeny and classification of *Pinus*. Taxon 54: 29–42.

Haddow, W.R. 1948. Distribution and occurrence of white pine (*Pinus strobus* L.) and red pine (*Pinus resinosa* Ait.) at the northern limit of their range in Ontario. J. Arnold Arb. 29: 217–226.

Kelleher, S. (Assembler). 1985. Eastern white pine (*Pinus strobus* L.), Ontario's arboreal emblem: a collection of papers on the growth and management of white pine. Ontario Forestry Association and Ontario Ministry of Natural Resources. 628 pp.

Mirov, N.T. 1967. The genus *Pinus*. Ronald Press Co. New York, NY. 602 pp.

Mirov, N.T., and Hasbrouck, J. 1976. The story of pines. Indiana University Press, Bloomington, IN. 148 pp.

Quinby, P.A. 1993. Definitions of old-growth eastern white pine and red pine forests for the Temagami region of eastern Ontario. www.ancientforest.org/flb3.html

Richardson, D.M. (*Editor*). 1998. Ecology and biogeography of *Pinus*. Cambridge University Press, Cambridge, U.K. 527 pp.

Wendel, G.W., and Smith, H.C. 1990. Eastern white pine. pp. 476–488 *in* Silvics of North America. Vol. 1, Conifers. *Edited by* R.C. Burns and B.H. Honkala. USDA Forest Service Agric. Handb. 654.

White pine (*Pinus strobus*). Source: S. Katovich, United States Forest Service.

PRINCE EDWARD ISLAND

Provincial flag of Prince Edward Island.

A PRINCE EDWARD ISLAND LANDSCAPE: the Trout River meandering through scattered mixed deciduous-coniferous woodland and farmland on rolling hills.

FLORAL EMBLEM: PINK LADY'S-SLIPPER

Pink lady's-slipper (*Cypripedium acaule*). Source Wikipedia (photographer: Magellan nh; Creative Commons Attribution-Share Alike 3.0 Unported license).

SYMBOLISM

In Chinese culture, orchids symbolize unity and modesty, while in the West they are often said to express love and affection, although there is no indication that these admirable sentiments played a role in an orchid becoming Prince Edward Island's floral emblem. A local naturalist was responsible for the choice of the lady's-slipper orchid as the provincial symbol of Prince Edward Island in 1947. There seems to be no particular historical reason for the choice, other than the fact that the plant is widely considered to be one of the most beautiful of wildflowers. Like the Islanders, it inspires admiration without ostentation. The alternative name "mocassin flower" serves as a reminder of Prince Edward Island's original native inhabitants, the Micmac.

Pink lady's-slipper (*Cypripedium acaule*). Source: Canadian Heritage. 2002. Symbols of Canada (revised). Canadian Heritage, Ottawa, ON. Reproduced with permission of Canadian Heritage, Public works, and Government Services Canada.

NAMES

Latin Names

Cypripedium acaule Aiton

The genus name *Cypripedium* is based on a combination of two Greek words: *kypris*, a name of Aphrodite (equivalent to the Roman goddess Venus) which was once used on the island of Cyprus, and *pedilon*, a slipper, referring to the shape of the flowers. The epithet *acaule* in the scientific name is Latin for "stemless" (or apparently so, since the plant does have a subterranean stem). The scape (flower stalk) is leafless, and therefore presumably this was not considered to be a "stem" when the epithet was adopted. *Cypripedium acaule* is the only species in its genus that has leaves that are only basal.

English Names

Pink lady's-slipper (the hyphen is used in most authoritative works, but is frequently omitted elsewhere), pink ladyslipper, small pink lady's-slipper, lady's-slipper, lady's-slipper orchid, common lady's-slipper, stemless lady's-slipper, two-leaf lady's-slipper, two-leaved lady's-slipper, mocassin flower, pink mocassin flower, American valerian, nerve root, shepherd's purse, squirrel's shoe, whip-poor-will's shoe. The pink lady's-slipper is usually called simply the lady's-slipper when referring to the provincial flower of Prince Edward Island, but other species of *Cypripedium* are also called lady's-slipper. The words "slipper" and "mocassin" are based on the shape of the largest petal, which forms a pouch resembling shoeware.

French Names

Le sabot-de-la-vierge, sabot-de-Vénus, cypripède acaule, cypripède rose, soulier-de-Notre-Dame.

HISTORY

Canada

The "lady's-slipper" was chosen as the floral emblem of Prince Edward Island in 1947, but a particular species was not mentioned. Of the three species of *Cypripedium* found in the province, the showy lady's-slipper (*C. reginae*) was generally accepted as the floral emblem. However, in the early 1960s not enough plants of this locally rare species could be found on the island to prepare a display for the Fathers of Confederation Building in Charlottetown. Naturally there was concern that the showy lady's-slipper was too rare in the province to be an emblem. In 1965 the much better known and widespread pink lady's-slipper, *C. acaule*, was recognized as the new emblem in an amendment to the Prince Edward Island Floral Emblem Act.

The pink lady's-slipper is the logo of Native Orchid Conservation Inc. (founded in Manitoba in 1998; http://www.nativeorchid.org/aboutnoci.htm).

Foreign

Orchids are official flowers of Belize, Brazil, Cayman Islands, Columbia, Costa Rica, Ecuador, Guatemala, Honduras, Indonesia, Panama, Seychelles, Singapore, and Venezuela. *Cypripedium acaule* was adopted as the official state wildflower of New Hampshire in 1991. The showy lady's-slipper (*C. reginae*) became the state flower of Minnesota in 1902.

Painting of pink lady's-slipper (*Cypripedium acaule*) in its natural setting, from the Walter Coucill Canadian Centennial official flowers of Canada series (see Coucill 1966 cited in the first chapter of this book). Reproduced with the permission of the copyright holders, the Coucill family.

APPEARANCE

Cypripedium acaule generally grows in small colonies, although it has been observed to form populations of several thousand. The short, perennial, rhizome (underground stem) produces two (rarely three) dark green, strongly veined basal leaves (9–30 cm long × 2.5–15 cm wide, or 3.5–12 inches × 1–6 inches), and a flowering axis ("scape") with a single flower. A single green bract arises from the floral stalk and arches over the flower. The overall height of the plant is 10–60 cm (4–24 inches). The pink or white flowers are usually 30–65 mm (1.2–2.5 inches) long, and often have a pleasant fragrance. The size of the flower and the plant can vary greatly. In fact, a flower at one locality may be larger than a whole plant at another locality. A detailed description of the rather complicated floral structure is provided below in the discussion of pollination. After fertilization, the flower develops into a green capsule which turns brown, opening and liberating numerous tiny seeds (sometimes over 50,000). The plant also spreads vegetatively, the rhizome forming new rosettes very close to the old flowering plant, this process continuing for half a century or more if the habitat is not altered.

CLASSIFICATION

Family: Orchidaceae (orchid family).

The orchid family may be the largest family of flowering plants, with perhaps 25,000 species.

The name "lady's-slipper" is used in a broad sense for the orchid genera in subfamily Cypripedioidea, including *Cypripedium, Mexipedium, Paphiopedilum, Phragmipedium,* and *Selenipedium*. The genus *Cypripedium* has about 50 species, found in North America, Central America, Europe, and Asia. China has the largest number of species. Of the twelve North American species, eight are native to Canada.

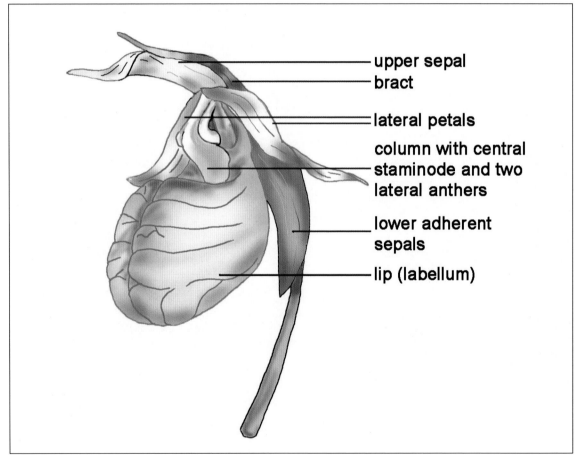

Parts of a flower of *Cypripedium acaule*. Drawn by B. Brookes.

upper sepal
bract
lateral petals
column with central staminode and two lateral anthers
lower adherent sepals
lip (labellum)

GEOGRAPHY

Cypripedium acaule is native to all provinces of Canada except British Columbia, as well as the Northwest Territories. In its northernmost range in Canada, pink lady's-slipper is distributed from the MacKenzie Valley in Northwest Territories through Lake Winnipeg and the Great Lakes area to the southern shore of James Bay and eastward to the Manicouagan Reservoir in Quebec, and to Newfoundland. In the eastern U.S., the plant extends from Minnesota south to Tennessee, Mississippi, Alabama, and Georgia.

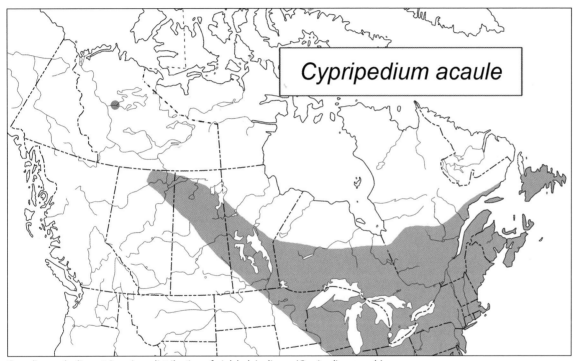

Canadian and adjacent American distribution of pink lady's-slipper (*Cypripedium acaule*).

Pink lady's-slipper (*Cypripedium acaule*), in Terra Nova National Park, Newfoundland and Labrador. Source: Wikipedia (photographer: D.G.E. Robertson; Creative Commons Attribution-Share Alike 3.0 license).

A BIODIVERSITY TREASURE

ECOLOGY

Cypripedium acaule appears to be adapted to growing in early forest succession, when gaps in the canopy allow moderate light to reach the forest floor. With increasing closure of the forest, growth of the orchid colony decreases. However, with canopy disturbances, increased light will re-invigorate the

A white-flowered pink lady's-slipper (*Cypripedium acaule*) in Norfolk Country, southwestern Ontario. Although rare in Ontario populations, this white form is frequent in some New Brunswick and Quebec populations. Photo by P.M. Catling.

plants for a period. Under natural circumstances, this orchid probably thrives in middle-aged and mature pineries (extensive pine groves) that developed on mineral soil following a fire. Individual plants may live for 100 years (the median age has been estimated to be 24 years), but flowering may be prevented by environmental conditions, and fruit formation is relatively uncommon in some populations.

Habitat
The pink lady's-slipper occurs in a variety of both wet and dry, shaded and semi-shaded sites in boreal and temperate regions. It is most common in shady coniferous woods, especially under pines, but also occurs in deciduous forests, swamps, sphagnum bogs, and barrens. The acidic substrate usually has considerable humus, but the species also is found in sand or gravel on rocky or mossy slopes. The roots generally are confined to the well-oxygenated humus layer, but occasionally extend into a lower mineral portion of the soil.

Inter-species Relationships
All orchid seeds are tiny and lack well-developed embryos. To germinate and grow in nature, the seeds must become associated with a fungus, often a *Rhizoctonia* species. The mycorrhizal fungus is thought to be necessary for the roots to obtain sufficient water and nutrients. To survive, the orchid seed must be penetrated by fungal filaments (hyphae). Although most of the literature describes the association as symbiotic, the extent to which the relationship is actually mutually beneficial is unclear, and it has been suggested that the orchid is actually a parasite on the fungus, at least for the first few years of growth. After an orchid seed germinates, it produces a small mass of below-ground tissue that relies for years on the fungal filaments to supply water, minerals, and carbohydrates.

Pollination and Dispersal
Orchid flowers are modified from those typical of most other plant families. There are three sepals and three petals, but one of the petals, called the labellum or lip, is highly modified. The male part of the plant usually consists of just one or two stamens, and these are fused to the female part of the plant, the pistil, to form a cylindrical structure called the gynostemium or column. The pollen in the stamen's anther sacs is picked up and transported as a sticky mass in many lady's-slipper orchids, but the pollen of *C. acaule* may be less sticky than that of other species. A sticky mass of pollen is often referred to as a pollinium or a pollinarium, but this term is probably best applied to the more complex structure by which pollen is transported in the majority of orchids.

In the case of pink lady's-slipper, one of the sepals is uppermost in the flower. The other two sepals are joined together behind the lip. The sepals and the two lateral petals are yellow-green to purplish-brown. The lip, at the bottom of the flower, is pink (less often white) with red or purplish veins. The pouch-like lip is specialized to act as a trap, temporarily imprisoning a visiting insect pollinator, and guiding its escape along a passageway that causes the insect to brush first against the stigmatic surface, depositing any pollen that it is carrying, and then passing against an anther, thereby picking up a new load of pollen as it exits by one of the openings at the base of the lip. The pollinator, usually a queen bee (of genera such as *Bombus* and *Psithyrus*), enters

ECOLOGY (CONT'D)

the lip through the large slit at the bottom, but the in-rolled edges and slippery inner surface make it difficult to escape from this entrance. Hairs on the inner surface lead to the two exits on either side of the column at the base of the flower. Once a flower is fertilized, the petals droop, discouraging additional bee visits. In the fall, slits open in the capsule and the tiny seeds are released and carried away by the wind.

Orchid flowers attract pollinators to transfer pollen by two principal methods: providing them with actual rewards such as nectar, or deceptively luring them to the flower. The pink lady's-slipper is thought to lure bees by using bright flower colour, nectar guides (petal markings that in most flowers actually guide pollinators to nectar), attractive odours, and the architecture of the opening.

In Canada, flowering occurs from the middle of May to early July. In the Great Lakes region, late hard spring frosts can ruin the flowers of most plants in a population, and such natural catastrophes appear to explain in part a generally very low production of seed capsules. A dearth of pollinators in much of the natural range of *C. acaule* also seems to be responsible for low seed set. Recent studies have suggested that a large population of bee pollinators, maintained by a local abundance of heath family shrubs, is a major factor in promoting seed production by the orchid. Aerial spraying of insecticides to control pests in New Brunswick forests has been shown to reduce bee populations with consequent reduction in seed set by *C. acaule*, and the species has been considered "high risk" with respect to insecticides. It has been found that the pink lady's-slipper can be artificially self-pollinated, but in nature only outcrossing occurs.

USES

The only modern substantial use of the pink lady's-slipper is as an ornamental, but in the past it was considered to be an important medicinal plant. The old name "nerve root" reflects wide use of the plant in nineteenth century North America as a sedative for nervous irritability, nervous headaches, hysteria, insomnia, menstrual irregularities accompanied by pre-menstrual syndrome, and mental depression. The old name "American valerian" is based on the similar use of *Valeriana officinalis* for nervous complaints. The roots have also been used to treat stomach ache, kidney and urinary tract disorders, and venereal disease. Today, there is only very limited medicinal use of *Cypripedium*, by herbalists (health practitioners who specialize on the use of crude plant materials).

TOXICITY

Contact with lady's-slipper can cause dermatitis in some individuals, which has been compared to poison ivy. The plant is covered with tiny glandular hairs, and the secretions can produce rashes. It has been suggested that this is more likely when the plants are wet. The causative agent is a quinone (defined as an aromatic benzene molecule containing a double ketone functional group) called cypripedin (a word more generally applied in the past to medicinal preparations of dried *Cypripedium* roots). Quinones from a variety of plant species, including several other *Cypripedium* species, are known to cause rashes.

Pink lady's-slipper (*Cypripedium acaule*), in La Ronge, Saskatchewan. Source: Wikipedia (photographer: Sasata; Creative Commons Attribution-Share Alike 3.0 license).

CULTIVATION

Growing orchids has become a popular activity, and several species are relatively easily cultivated in semi-shade, on a damp acidic soil rich in humus. Pink lady's-slipper seems like an appropriate subject for a woodland garden or shady border, but it is difficult to grow and is best left in the wild. The following comments are from our colleague Larry Sherk's out-of-print "Growing Canada's floral emblems" (Canada Dept. Agric. Publication 1288, 1967; cf. similar comments in French in Lamoureux and Nantel 1999, cited below):

"This is the hardest of the provincial flowers to grow and maintain in the garden over a long period. This plant, more than any of the other floral emblems, must be preserved in native stands. Buying plants from wildflower dealers is almost a complete waste of time and money. It contributes to the depletion of native stands because the dealers get their plants from the wild . . . .

To move plants endangered by construction, dig them either in early spring or in the fall. Take as large a block of earth as possible with them because the roots spread out near the surface for 2 feet [60 cm] or more. Plant them in a light acid mixture of pine needles and sand, in a spot that is shaded for at least the hottest part of the day, preferably under pine trees. These plants may grow and flower for a few years."

Lady's-slipper should not be picked or transplanted. It rarely survives a change of habitat. The extensive, fragile root system in particular is easily damaged. In nature, germination from seed to flowering can take 10–16 years. There has been extensive experimentation on growing the seeds in artificial culture without the use of the fungus necessary for reproduction in the wild, but it is not yet clear that a commercial method of doing this consistently has become available for the pink lady's-slipper (see Durkee 2000 for information on growing conditions). Unfortunately, some suppliers offering material claimed to have been commercially propagated have supplemented their stock with wild-collected plants. Amateurs can attempt to propagate the plant from seeds by surface-sowing them as soon as they are ripe, and maintaining them on continuously damp organic material, which should be taken from near an established plant to ensure that the required fungus is present. Division of pot-grown plants is also possible, separating part of the original rootball with the soil intact, although as noted above the plants respond poorly to having their roots disturbed. Division has been recommended either in early spring or towards the end of the growing season. As with other orchids, addition of fertilizers or fungicides can harm the fungus that the plants depend on to assist them in obtaining nutrients from the soil.

A white-flowered pink lady's-slipper (*Cypripedium acaule*). Photo by P.M. Catling.

CONSERVATION STATUS

Native orchids usually require specialized and often temporary habitats that are very vulnerable to human influence. Road building, draining of wetlands, and land clearing have reduced the living space of numerous orchids. Indiscriminate use of insecticides has eliminated many essential pollinators. Because they are so attractive, people have tried to transplant orchids, or simply to pick the flowers, reducing the chances of survival.

The pink lady's-slipper is fairly common in Canada, and therefore is not protected by federal legislation. In Nova Scotia, *C. acaule* is considered endangered (i.e., in danger of extinction throughout all or a significant portion of its range) and is a protected plant. In Alberta the species has been judged "May be at risk".

The pink lady's-slipper is not federally endangered in the U.S., but is at risk in some states. It is considered endangered in Illinois and Tennessee, and threatened in Georgia. The New Hampshire Plant Protection Act lists *C. acaule* as a plant of "Special Concern" (a species that is not rare in the state, but is vulnerable to over-collection because of its showy nature). Similarly in New York State, where all native orchids are protected, the pink lady's-slipper has the status "Exploitably Vulnerable". Although rare in some areas, *C. acaule* has become more abundant in parts of the northeast, especially in New England, due to the establishment of pine plantations and natural forest development on abandoned marginal farmlands.

Cypripedium orchids, along with many other orchid species, are listed in Appendix II of CITES (Convention on International Trade in Endangered Species), making it illegal to export any part of the plants without a permit. However, most countries will not accept trade in wild-collected slipper orchids, so essentially all legal international commerce in these plants is based on artificially propagated plants. *Cypripedium acaule* is not yet commonly propagated, so there is very little trade in this species.

Pink lady's-slipper (*Cypripedium acaule*), near Quebec City. Source: Wikipedia (photographer: Myric; Creative Commons Attribution-Share Alike 3.0 license).

MYTHS, LEGENDS, TALES, FOLKLORE AND INTERESTING FACTS

❦ In the nineteenth century, *C. acaule* was thought to possess narcotic properties, "especially when inhabiting dark swamps".

❦ Crab spiders (of the family Thomisidae) sometimes sit on the pouches of *Cypripedium* orchids in the distribution range of *C. acaule*, using the flowers as convenient locations to ambush small insect visitors. Crab spiders are commonly called "flower spiders" because of this hunting method. They are called crab spiders because their first two pairs of legs are held out to the side giving them a crab-like appearance, and they move sideways and backwards more easily than forwards, like crabs. These attractive spiders, variously coloured yellow, white, and pink, are harmless to humans.

❦ Prince Edward Island, the only province of Canada to have an orchid as a provincial symbol, is the only province that does not have an orchid society. (For a list of Canadian orchid societies, see http://www.chebucto.ns.ca/Recreation/orchidcongress/cocmemb.html.)

❦ Although the orchid family is huge, *Vanilla planifolia*, the source of vanilla, is the only species that has commercial significance as food. Plain old vanilla is the favourite ice cream flavour, accounting for 29% of all North American sales. Recently, flowers of orchids such as *Dendrobium phalaenopsis* have been used to garnish meals in expensive restaurants. Most of those used for this purpose are edible.

Pink lady's-slipper (*Cypripedium acaule*). Source: S. Katovich, United States Department of Agriculture, Forest Service.

SOURCES OF ADDITIONAL INFORMATION

Baird, B. 1983. Wild orchids: exquisite, irresistible, vulnerable. Canadian Geographic 103(1): 46–51.

Cribb, P., and Green, P. 1997. The genus *Cypripedium*. Kew Royal Botanic Gardens, U.K. 358 pp.

Davis, R.W. 1986. The pollinator biology of *Cypripedium acaule* (Orchidaceae). Rhodora 88: 445–450.

Durkee, S. 2000. *Cypripedium acaule* and *Cypripedium reginae*. Successful cultivation of two North American lady's-slipper orchids. Orchids 69: 864–869.

Lamoureux, G., and Nantel, P. 1999. Cultiver les plantes sauvages. Fleurbec, Saint-Henri-de-Lévis, QC, Canada. 80 pp.

O'Connell, L.M., and Johnston, M.O. 1998. Male and female pollination success in a deceptive orchid, a selection study. Ecology 79: 1246–1260.

Primack, R. 1996. Science and serendipity. The pink lady's slipper project. Arnoldia 56(1): 8–14.

Sheviak, C.J. 2002. *Cypripedium. in* Flora of North America. Vol. 26. *Edited by* Flora of North America Editorial Committee. Oxford University Press, Oxford, U.K. pp. 499–507.

St.-Arnaud, M., and Barabé, D. 1987. Une orchidée du Québec, le sabot de la vierge. Quatre-temps 11(4): 16–23.

White-flowered form of pink lady's-slipper (*Cypripedium acaule*). Source: Wikipedia (photographer: Orchi; Creative Commons Attribution 2.0- Generic license).

Pink lady's-slipper (*Cypripedium acaule*). Photo courtesy of Brian L. Simpson, Government of Prince Edward Island.

TREE: RED OAK

This red oak (*Quercus rubra*) was planted by His Royal Highness the Duke of Connaught, Governor General of Canada on October 18th, 1911. The 100-year old tree on the Central Experimental Farm in Ottawa frames the Saunders Building, which houses the largest research collection of dried plants and the largest botanical research library in Canada. Photo by P.M. Catling in 2007.

SYMBOLISM

As the provincial tree of Prince Edward Island, red oak has been said to represent growth, strength, and longevity. The tree appears on the flag, and also on the coat of arms which bears the Latin motto *Parva sub Ingenti* ("Little under the Great"), with a large oak tree (representing England) beside three small oak trees (representing the three provincial counties of Kings, Queens, and Prince).

The "Black Rod" traces to 1348, when the British monarchy used a kind of club to deny admission of unauthorized persons to Windsor Castle. By 1642, the British House of Commons had reversed this usage, using the club to symbolically deny entry to King Charles I. As in several other provinces, in Prince Edward Island the Sergeant-at-Arms or some other designated official now carries a Black Rod preliminary to several ceremonies and occasions. In Prince Edward Island, the Black Rod is made from the Island's red oak.

Two 1871 pennies, with the provinces oak motif, are the only coins ever minted for Prince Edward Island alone. They show Queen Victoria on the face, and the red oak on the reverse.

1871 bronze penny minted for Prince Edward Island. The province joined Canada in 1873. The large red oak symbolizes Great Britain and the three small oaks symbolize the three counties of Prince Edward Island.

NAMES

Latin Names

Quercus rubra L. (The old synonym *Q. borealis* is occasionally encountered in the literature.)

The genus name *Quercus* is the old Roman word for oak (less plausibly, some authorities derive the word from the Celtic *quer*, fine + *cuez*, a tree). *Rubra* in the scientific name is Latin for reddish, and much of the plant is indeed reddish. The buds are dark reddish-brown (and may have tufts of reddish hairs), the twigs are reddish-brown, the leaves (petioles and blades) are frequently red-tinged (especially in the autumn, when the leaves turn deep red, rust, or copper), and the wood often is reddish.

English Names

Red oak has also been called common red oak, American red oak (a name used in Europe), eastern red oak, gray oak, mountain red oak, and northern red oak (for additional information, see Classification).

French Names

Chêne rouge; also: le chêne rouge d'Amérique (name used in Europe), chêne boréal.

HISTORY

Canada

The red oak was adopted in 1987 as the provincial tree of Prince Edward Island.

Foreign

Oaks are among the most important of political symbols. The oak is the national tree of the Republic of Ireland. It is also an unofficial emblem of England, for example having appeared on money (e.g., pound coins). Latvia has two national trees, one of which is the English oak (*Q. robur*), and oak branches are shown on the national coat of arms. The coat of arms of Cuba shows a palm, along with an oak and laurel branch. In 2004 the United States Congress designated the oak (no particular species) as the National Tree of the U.S. The live oak (*Q. virginiana*) was adopted as the state tree of Georgia in 1937. Live oak branches occur on the state seal of Texas. Illinois adopted the oak as its state tree in 1908, and in 1973 specified that the state tree is the white oak (*Q. alba*). Maryland recognized the white oak as its state tree in 1941. The official Arms of the state of Connecticut bears clusters of white oak (*Q. alba*) leaves and acorns (the official state tree, "the charter oak", does not specify a species). The oak (*Quercus*, no particular species) was designated the state tree of Iowa in 1961 (many authors have erroneously listed bur oak, white oak, or northern red oak as the state tree of Iowa). The seal of West Virginia contains a wreath of bay laurel emblematic of valour and oak leaves emblematic of strength. The District of Columbia declared the scarlet oak (*Q. coccinea*) to be its official tree in 1960. The red oak was adopted as the state tree of New Jersey in 1950, although in 1951 the American dogwood (*Cornus florida*) became the "state memorial tree".

APPEARANCE

Red oak is considered to be the tallest and most rapidly growing of the North American oaks. It often reaches 20–30 m (66–98 feet) in height, and 60–90 cm (2–3 feet) in diameter. In the U.S., trees that are 49 m (160 feet) high and 3 m (10 feet) in diameter have been recorded. In closed forests, the red oak grows straight and tall, often columnar in outline, clear of large lower branches but with scraggly small branches persisting for years on the lower trunk before being shed. In the open, the tree becomes shorter, with a stouter trunk, and develops a broad, roundish-topped, more spreading crown. The trees often develop a taproot and a network of spreading lateral roots. The mature leaves are 12–20 cm (5–8 inches) long. The leaves tend to remain on the trees into late autumn and early winter. The bark is gray to grayish-brown, with shallow vertical furrows and low ridges, tending to become checkered with age. The ridges of younger bark may appear to have stripes down the trunk or branch (several other oaks have such bark).

The remaining base of trees that have been cut down frequently develop sprouts (also known as suckers), and a single stump can produce several new trunks (a phenomenon called "coppice growth"). Indeed, sprouting seems to be an important kind of reproductive insurance in red oak. After fires and other kinds of injury, basal sprouts are often developed.

Drooping yellowish male catkins (clusters of flowers) are produced in the leaf axils of the previous year's growth. The female catkins are produced on small flowering branches in the axils of the current year's growth. Acorns are developed singly or in groups of two to five. They are 12–25 mm (0.5–1 inch) long (rarely as long as 35 mm or 1.4 inch), with a shallow, saucer-shaped cup, and they contain a large, white, bitter kernel.

Silhouette of a red oak (*Quercus rubra*) tree. Source: J.L. Farrar 1995. Trees in Canada. Canadian Forest Service and Fitzhenry and Whiteside, Markham, ON, Canada. Reproduced with permission.

Red oak (*Quercus rubra*). Source: S. Katovich, United States Department of Agriculture, Forest Service.

A BIODIVERSITY TREASURE

CLASSIFICATION

Family: Fagaceae (beech family).

There are about 400 species of *Quercus*, which are native to all continents except Australia. Most are indigenous to the temperate regions of the Northern Hemisphere, and to high altitudes in the tropics. Acorns, the scaly-cupped fruits (commonly called "nuts") of oak trees, have provided nourishment for people since prehistory. Ninety species are native to North America north of Mexico, and twelve of these are in Canada (three foreign species are commonly planted). The majority of Canada's native oaks are mostly in eastern Canada. Bur oak (*Q. macrocarpa*) ranges into the Prairie Provinces and Garry oak (*Q. garryana*) is found in British Columbia.

There are two groups of oaks in North America, the "white oaks" and the "red or black oaks". The white oaks have leaves with rounded lobes. The seed is relatively sweet. The red oaks have leaves mostly with pointed and bristle-tipped lobes. The red oak group includes the live oaks of the U.S. and Mexico, also known as the evergreen oaks. Most species of the red oak group have acorns that are edible but are extremely bitter, except for the live oaks, which tend to bear relatively sweet acorns. Red oak species can be difficult to identify. Red oak hybridizes with many other oak species, making identification still more problematical.

The acorns of red oak have saucer-shaped or cup-shaped acorn cups that cover one-quarter to one-third of the nut. The acorn cups of scarlet oak and northern pin oak are more likely to be inversely conical and to cover one-third to one-half of the nut. *Quercus rubra* trees with large nuts that are only one-fourth covered by flat, saucer-shaped cups are sometimes treated as var. *rubra*, while those with smaller nuts one-third covered by cup- or bowl-shaped cups have been recognized as var. *borealis* (Michx. f.) Farw., sometimes called gray oak or northern red oak. Many Canadian plants are referable to the latter variety. The two kinds have been found to differ chemically. *Quercus rubra* var. *rubra* is sometimes called southern red oak, but this name is usually applied to *Q. falcata* (also known as Spanish oak).

KEY TO THE RED OAK GROUP IN CANADA

1a. Leaf stalk 10–25 mm long; leaves densely hairy below . . . . . . *Q. ilicifolia* (bear oak; southern Ont.)
1b. Leaf stalk 20–70 mm long; leaves smooth or with tufts of hair where major veins diverge or with scattered hair 2

2a. Terminal buds pubescent throughout. . . . . *Q. velutina* (black oak; southern Ont.)
2b. Terminal buds smooth or pubescent only in the upper half 3

3a. Terminal buds hairy on all of upper half 4
3b. Terminal buds essentially smooth. 6

4a. Leaf blade dull green or glossy green; leaf sinuses extending to less than ⅓ distance to midrib: lobes of leaves developed in full sun not expanded outwardly . . . . *Q. rubra*
4b. Leaf blade glossy green; leaf sinuses extending to more than ½ distance to midrib: lobes of leaves developed in full sun expanded outwardly 5

5a. Acorn scales with a broad glossy base and strongly concave margins; acorn with one or more concentric rings of pits at the apex . . . . . *Q. coccinea* (scarlet oak; only planted)
5b. Acorn scales hairy and with straight or slightly concave margins; acorn lacking rings of pits at the apex . . . . *Q. ellipsoidalis* (northern pin oak; southern Ont.)

6a. Twigs reddish-brown; acorn cup thin, 3–6 mm high . . . . *Q. palustris* (pin oak; southern Ont.)
6b. Twigs gray to light brown; acorn cup thick, 7–12 mm high . . . . . . *Q. shumardii* (Shumard oak; southern Ont.)

Bark of trees of red oak (*Quercus rubra*) of different ages. Photos by P.M. Catling.

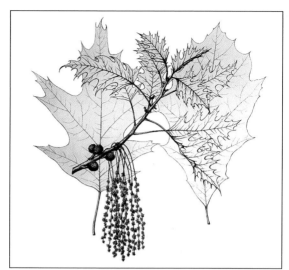

Flowering branch of red oak (*Quercus rubra*), with hanging catkins of male flowers and short spikes of young female flowers. Source: Sargent, C.S. 1895. The silva of North America. Houghton, Mifflin and Company, Boston, MA. Vol. 8, plate 409.

Red oak leaf and branch with acorns. Source: Sargent, C.S. 1895. The silva of North America. Houghton, Mifflin and Company, Boston, MA. Vol. 8, plate 410.

Red oak (*Quercus rubra*). Source: Wikipedia (released into the public domain).

GEOGRAPHY

Red oak is indigenous to eastern North America. In Canada, it is native to Prince Edward Island, Nova Scotia, Quebec, and Ontario. It has become naturalized in Revelstoke, British Columbia. In the U.S., the species has been collected from 40 states, and local populations are found as far south as Louisiana and Mississippi. Red oak is common in the following eastern Canadian forest regions: Deciduous Forest, Great Lakes-St. Lawrence Forest, Acadian Forest.

Dr. Peter Ball has advised us that red oak does not occur in northwestern Ontario, despite numerous reports of its presence. It has been known since the 1970s that northern pin oak (*Q. ellipsoidalis*) occurs in the region, and it is now believed that this is the only species present, having previously been misidentified as red oak. *Quercus ellipsoidalis* can be distinguished by sun-grown leaves, which are deeply divided, but shade-grown leaves are less divided and are easily confused with the leaves of red oak. It appears that the northwestern-most occurrence of

Q. rubra is on the islands off the east coast of Lake Superior north of Sault-Ste.-Marie. As well as being absent from northwestern Ontario, red oak may also be absent from the northernmost tier of counties in Minnesota.

During the last major North American glaciation, 10,000 years ago, many hardwood species were pushed far to the south. Red oak, however, occurred in the cool meadows and spruce forests close to the edge of the glacier.

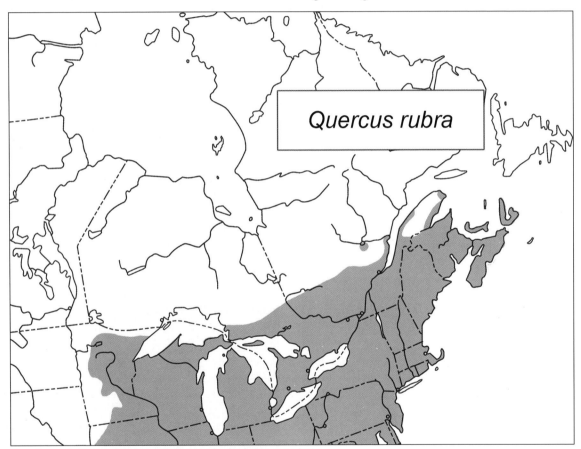

Canadian and adjacent American distribution of red oak (*Quercus rubra*).

The provincial flag of Prince Edward Island. The golden lion represents England, as does the largest oak tree.

ECOLOGY

Red oak is a dominant species in some locations, and often the trees are more or less even-aged. The seedlings are unable to reproduce in the shade of a climax red oak forest, and the species is often replaced successively by more shade-tolerant species such as sugar maple and American basswood. "Northern red oak is neither an aggressive colonizer that is characteristic of early successional species nor an enduring, shade-tolerant, slow-grower that is typical of late successional species. Its regeneration requires an edge environment: one that is more mesic than exposed, open sites, but less competitive than the deep shade of a forest understory" (Crow 1988). In historical times, red oak forests were promoted by relatively frequent disturbances, such as fire and windstorms. During European settlement, timber harvest and man-made fires favoured the growth of red oak, which reproduces quickly both from acorns and stump sprouts. The result was that in recent centuries stands of red oak were greater than they are today. Many researchers believe that because recurrent fires are a key to oak dominance, the suppression of fire in eastern North America has led to the decline of oak and the increase in maple.

Habitat

Red oak grows on a variety of dry to moderately moist sites, often on sloping land. It occurs on a range of soil textures, including gravelly soils, sand, loam, and clay. The best growth is on deep, fertile, slightly acidic, well-drained soils with a high water table. Red oak is intermediate in shade tolerance.

Inter-species Relationships

White-tailed deer browse on the leaves and, less commonly, so do elk, hares, cottontail rabbits, and moose. The acorns are consumed by a variety of small mammals including mice, chipmunks, and squirrels. Larger mammals that eat the acorns include fox, raccoon, red-tailed deer, and black bear. Numerous birds, especially bluejays, feed on the acorns. The extinct passenger pigeon depended heavily on acorns. They are a particularly important food for wild turkeys. A single wild turkey can consume over 200 at a meal. Gypsy moths and many other insects feed on red oak, but only occasionally cause serious harm. Red oak acorns have twenty times the concentration of tannic acid compared to white oak (Q. alba), and this is thought to provide protection against some insects. One of the most conspicuous results of insects on red oak is the development of large circular leaf galls, often called "oak apples". Typically, 80 to 100% of the crop is eaten by animals and, in poor acorn years, virtually every acorn is consumed. However, in good acorn years thousands of acorns per hectare can survive.

Good crops of acorns occur once every 2 to 5 years. Following years of heavy nut production, black bear reproduction often increases. On the other hand, it has been reported that in years of light nut production, the bears cause increased damage to crops, livestock, and beehives.

In the eastern U.S., years in which acorns are abundant appear to reduce the harvest of white-tailed deer in forested areas. Why? The deer gorge on acorns in the autumn and, when acorns are relatively scarce, the animals flock to the limited number of trees with good production. Knowledgeable hunters stake out such trees, making it easier to kill their prey. However, in years of acorn abundance it is harder to predict where the deer will congregate.

In addition to providing food, red oak furnishes cover and/or habitat for a wide variety of birds and mammals. Birds in particular employ the trees as perching and nesting sites, and also use the twigs and leaves as nesting material.

A condition known as "oak decline" affects red oaks in particular. It is apparently due to a combination of conditions (such as air pollution, drought, frost, defoliation, and pathogens) which cause progressive dieback from the top down and outside in. It has damaged many trees in the central Appalachian region.

Pollination and Dispersal

Red oak reproduction occurs mostly by acorns, and these are distributed by animals. The nuts can remain viable for 2 or 3 years, but most successful germination occurs in the spring following the season of production. Buried nuts are much more successful than nuts that remain on the surface of the soil; one reason for this is that exposed nuts are very vulnerable to rodents. "Scatter-hoarder" animals, notably the gray squirrel, are very important for seed dispersal. Gray squirrels are known to bury as much as 20% of the crop, and to fail to retrieve many of the acorns, leaving them to germinate. Gray squirrels have been observed to bury many seeds just a few metres from the tree; mice and chipmunks to move acorns 10–30 m (33–100 feet) away; and blue jays to transport the seeds from several hundred metres to 5 km (i.e., up to about 3 miles).

USES

Except for the softwood (coniferous) species, oaks furnish more timber annually than any other group of trees in North America. Red oak is an important source of hardwood lumber, used for furniture, cabinets, panelling, flooring, and caskets. Red oak is cheaper than white oak, and so is preferred for flooring and for cheaper grades of cabinets and furniture. In the past, when hardwood was available in greater supply, red oak was also used for railroad ties, fenceposts, and firewood. In the U.S., the species has been used to rehabilitate coal mine spoils. Red oak is a popular ornamental shade tree in eastern North America, as well as in Europe and Australia.

North American Indians removed the bitter tannins from acorns by using several techniques, and employed the nuts in a variety of food preparations. The dependence on acorns was so great that in some places a person would eat a ton of acorn flour yearly. Acorns were so important that some Indian calendars were based on the acorn harvest date. Such calendars indicated how far away or how much time has passed from the acorn harvest season. Native people also used red oak bark as a source of medicines, especially for digestive disorders, respiratory diseases, and skin infections. The Wintu Indians of California used to mix acorn flour with water and let it mould. The mould was used as a medicine much like penicillin. The bark was also once used as a source of yellowish, brownish, and reddish dyes, and for extracting tannins for hide preparation.

In early times, oak trees were very widespread, and acorns were an extensively consumed food throughout the world. Today, acorns are gathered occasionally for personal use, and are very rarely encountered in trade for food purposes. Acorns do not suit the taste of many people, but the sweeter nuts of some of the species have been compared to chestnuts. Although acorns are rarely found in commerce, and are an uncommon food for humans, they are still often eaten by people in southern Europe, and are very widely used as mast (i.e., nuts accumulated on forest floors) to feed hogs. (There are reports that cattle have been poisoned by eating acorns.) Although not cultivated for nuts, acorns constitute an annual crop that exceeds all other nuts put together.

The bitter chemicals in acorns, called tannins, are water soluble and can be leached away to produce a sweeter, nut-flavoured product. An old European method of leaching the bitter tannins out of the acorns was to place them in a cloth bag in a stream. Still another traditional method was to bury the acorns in boggy ground overwinter. The following provides a home method for preparing acorns. As noted above, relatively sweet acorns can be collected from the white oak group, while species of the red oak group should be avoided. Place acorns in a pot of water, and discard any that float. Boil them for about 15 minutes. Shell the acorns, crunch them up and boil them again. When the water turns brown, pour it off and boil again, repeating until the water does not turn brown. This works best if the nuts are crushed into quite small pieces, and to avoid losing pieces, they can be boiled in cheese cloth. If the water is clear but still tastes bitter, boil them until they are not bitter. Dry the material in an oven. The nuts can be eaten this way and can also be used as a replacement for nuts in recipes. The flour can be used in baked foods, but not alone in breads, since it lacks gluten.

"Acorn coffee" was once widely consumed in Germany, and to a lesser extent in England during World War I. Ripe acorns were cut into pieces, dried in an oven, roasted, and ground, a little butter was added to the powder, and it was used in the same way as regular coffee. Acorns of the white oak were used as an inferior coffee substitute during the American Civil War, when blockades and wartime conditions in general made coffee scarce.

Oak leaves are very rich in tannins. Tannins were originally used in tanning leather, because they coagulate and toughen proteins, especially those in skin. Tannins can be used in pickling to assist in firming vegetables and, in Poland, oak leaves have commonly been used for this purpose.

Red oak (*Quercus rubra*) flooring. Source: Thinkstock.

CULTIVATION

The red oak is an excellent, large shade tree that can withstand the pollution of cities. It also is suited to the cold temperatures of Canada, and is grown as far north as Edmonton. It does best in full sun and moist, slightly acidic, well-drained, rich deep soil. Establishing plants from acorns is not as easy as it might seem (acorns may not be viable for various reasons, and they need to be stored properly), but the tree is relatively easy to transplant, and so homeowners can simply purchase a small, potted plant from a nursery. The main drawback is that the tree grows too large for most city lots. Extensive information on how to collect, store, and evaluate acorns, establish the plant from these, and how to cultivate nursery stock is found in Dey and Buchanan (1995).

Red oak branch with acorns. Photo by P.M. Catling.

CONSERVATION STATUS

Red oak was one of the dominant trees of the original mixed-wood forest (part of the Acadian Forest) of Prince Edward Island. The Acadian Forest dominated the Maritime region until the eighteenth century, and by the end of the nineteenth century 80% of Prince Edward Island's land was cleared for settlements. As a result of conversion of the land for agriculture (especially potatoes), forest harvesting, road building, and urbanization, only fragments of the original ecosystem remain in the province.

Forty-five percent of Prince Edward Island is still forested, but much of this is white spruce, which has done well following clearcutting. Unlike the rest of Canada, where government and industry manage and/or own the forests, in Prince Edward Island almost 90% of the forested area is in the form of thousands of small, privately owned woodlots. Rather than cutting selectively, which would promote a return to the original forest, many landowners prefer to use their property to establish relatively profitable (at least in the short term) conifer plantations. This so-called "cut-and-run" management policy is increasingly being viewed as incompatible with society's growing concern for the welfare of the planet. Given the present situation, it might seem hopeless that a meaningful resurrection of the Acadian Forest could be achieved, but this is the aim of a coalition of Prince Edward Island environmentalists (note the following text box).

Red oak. (*Quercus rubra*). Source: International Wood Collectors Society. 2000. Canada's arboreal emblems. An overview of Canada's official trees and their wood. Reproduced with permission of C. Holder (author) and J. Monty (president) of the Canada Tree Foundation.

RESTORING THE BIODIVERSITY OF PRINCE EDWARD ISLAND

"We have a real opportunity to restore the native Acadian forest. True, this will take time, but it will also be an effort that brings great reward. We can continue the large-scale degradation that has taken place since Europeans first set foot on this Island. Or we can create healthy, diverse forest systems that provide a huge array of products, and also serve many other valuable roles—cleaning air, purifying water, protecting streams, storing carbon, housing wildlife and providing places for recreation."

—Gary Schneider, in *"Restoring biodiversity"* (http://www.elements.nb.ca/Theme/invasive_species/gary/schneider.htm)

A BIODIVERSITY TREASURE

MYTHS, LEGENDS, TALES, FOLKLORE AND INTERESTING FACTS

🍁 People today will find it difficult to fathom, but oak worship was widespread in the Middle Ages in Europe, sometimes by devout Christians. Orthodox Christians in Russia worshipped a holy oak until the 1870s, fixing candles to its trunk and branches and praying to it. The famous heroine of France, Joan of Arc (1412–1431), was accused of worshipping a bewitched oak.

🍁 Perpetual oak fires in homage to oaks were well known. In Rome, the Vestal Virgins used oak for their perpetual fire. A perpetual fire of oak wood was kept burning at Novgorod (north of Moscow, Russia), and the death penalty was imposed for allowing the fire to go out.

🍁 According to an old practice, If lovers put two acorns, representing themselves, in a bowl of water and they float towards each other then they will marry, but if they drift apart, so will they.

🍁 In Roman times the oak symbolized bravery, and a crown of oak leaves often rewarded military or civic achievements. In the U.S. military, the Oak Leaf Cluster is awarded as an additional honour to those who have already been decorated for exceptional service.

🍁 England ruled the seas in part because of its large oak forests that were used to build the finest warships. About 3,500 oaks or 364 ha (900 acres) of oak forest were needed to supply the timber required for a large battleship.

🍁 Large red oak trees can produce over 4,000 acorns in one season.

🍁 Poison oak is not an "oak" (nor is poison ivy an "ivy').

Red oak (*Quercus rubra*). Source: Loudon, J.C. 1844. The trees and shrubs of Britain. Longman, Brown, Green, and Longmans, London, U.K. Vol. 8.

OAK HUMOUR
How do you get an elephant to the top of an oak tree? Stand him on top of an acorn and wait 50 years.

How do you get an elephant down from an oak tree? Tell him to sit on a leaf and wait until autumn.

Red oak wood grain is so open that smoke can be blown through it from end-grain to end-grain on a flatsawn board (i.e., with growth rings approximately parallel to the wide face of the board; a quartersawn board has the annual growth rings approximately perpendicular to the surface of the board's wide face). Alternatively, the porosity of red oak can be demonstrated by dipping one end of a twig in soapy water and blowing on the other end; bubbles will be produced. White oak, by contrast, has relatively closed vessels so that the wood is waterproof, and can be used for whiskey barrels and outdoor furniture. Figure drawn by B. Brookes.

SOURCES OF ADDITIONAL INFORMATION

Crow, T.R. 1988. Reproductive mode and mechanisms for self-replacement of northern red oak (*Quercus rubra*)—a review. Forest Sci. 34: 19–40.

Dey, D., and Buchanan, M. 1995. Red oak (*Quercus rubra* L.) acorn collection, nursery culture and direct seeding: a literature review. Forest Research Information Paper No. 122, Ontario Forest Research Institute, Ontario Ministry of Natural Resources, Sault Ste. Marie, ON. 46 pp.

Johnson, P.S., Shifley, S.R., and Rogers, R. 2002. The ecology and silviculture of oaks. CABI, Wallingford, Oxon, U.K. 503 pp.

Miller, H.A., and Lamb, S.H. 1985. Oaks of North America. Naturegraph Publishers, Happy Camp, CA. 327 pp.

Nixon, K.C., Manos, P.S., Jensen, R.J., and Muller, C.H. 1997. *Quercus. In* Flora of North America. Vol. 3. *Edited by* Flora of North America Editorial Committee. Oxford University Press, Oxford, U.K. pp. 447–506.

Short, H.L. 1976. Composition and squirrel use of acorns of black and white oak groups. J. Wildl. Manage. 40: 479–483.

Trelease, W. 1924. The American oaks. National Academy of Sciences Memoirs, vol. XX. Govt. Print. Off., Washington, D.C. 255 pp. (Reprinted 1969, J. Cramer; New York, NY.)

Red oak (*Quercus rubra*) leaves and acorns. Source: Wikipedia (photographer: Lynk media; Creative Commons Attribution-Share Alike 3.0 Unported license).

The provincial Coat of Arms. The blue jay (provincial bird) at the top holds a leaf and acorn of red oak. The native foxes reflect the old industry of fur farming. The fox at the left wears a necklace of potato blossoms, while the fox at the right has a necklace made of fishing net, again symbolic of Prince Edward Island natural resource industries. Botanical symbols at the bottom include roses for England, lilies for France, thistles for Scotland, shamrocks for Ireland, and lady's-slipper for the Island.

A BIODIVERSITY TREASURE

Grove of red oak (*Quercus rubra*) trees in early fall foliage. Source: Thinkstock.

QUEBEC

Provincial flag of Quebec.

A QUEBEC LANDSCAPE: a forested hillside in the autumn in southern Quebec.

FLORAL EMBLEM: BLUE FLAG

Blue flag (*Iris versicolor*) in Forillon National Park, Quebec. Source: Wikipedia (photographer: D. Langlois; Creative Commons Attribution-Share Alike 3.0 Unported license).

SYMBOLISM

Blue flag, the subject of this chapter is an iris. Irises have represented important figures and sentiments for millennia. Dating back 4,000 years in Crete, the iris was the symbol of royalty and priests. To the early Egyptians, the iris represented power and majesty. The flower was depicted on the brow of the Sphinx and on regal sceptres. In ancient Greece, irises were planted on the tombs of women. By Islamic tradition, white-flowered irises were planted on the graves of soldiers. In Christianity, it has been claimed that many Biblical "lilies" were actually irises. Irises have represented the birth of Christ in several well-known paintings, including Dürer's *Madonna with the Iris*, and da Vinci's *Madonna of the Rocks*. The three-parted flower has been interpreted as reflecting the three virtues of faith, wisdom, and courage.

The flag of Quebec, showing four images of the fleur-de-lis and a white cross. Image courtesy of the Government of Quebec.

The fleur-de-lis symbol of heraldry is probably the iris, but its identity has been the subject of considerable controversy. The symbol has been said to be based on a spearhead (indeed, as the famous French author Voltaire pointed out, the shape is strikingly like the obsolete halberd or halbert), but it has also been claimed that the fleur-de-lis was modelled on crowns, bees, and even toads. In France, "fleur-de-lis" has been applied to the European yellow iris (*I. pseudacorus*), a species which occurs along the Lys River, suggesting the fleur-de-lis is based on "flower of the Lys [River]". French Royalty adopted the fleur-de-lis as a symbol (Charles the Bald about 840 used it on his sceptre; Louis VII chose it in 1147 as the national emblem of France), but it had previously been used in other European nations and perhaps even in ancient Egypt, so the symbol is not of French origin. Nevertheless, French explorers, missionaries, and pioneers in North America employed flags bearing the fleur-de-lis, which now adorns the flag of Quebec and other official artefacts of the province. In recent times, the fleur-de-lis has been adopted as the almost universal symbol of scouting, and as the logo of the New Orleans Saints professional football team.

Because many have interpreted the fleur-de-lis symbol as based on an iris flower (the resemblance is striking), and the fleur-de-lis is emblematic of Quebec, and indeed reflects the relationship of Quebec to France, it is natural that an iris was chosen as the floral emblem of the province. Quite aside from the relationship of the blue flag and the fleur-de-lis, the blue flag is a very beautiful flowering plant that is native to Quebec and widespread in the most populated and developed areas, and so is

an excellent floral emblem choice for the province. The different colours of the flower have been said to signify a multicultural province. It has been pointed out that *I. versicolor* flowers on St. Jean Baptiste Day, June 24, Quebec's national holiday.

The fleur-de-lis is the symbol of world scouting that was adopted about 1909 by the founder of scouting, Lord Baden-Powell. It has been worn proudly by over 200 million scouts since that time. Scouting is for boys and girls of all ages and (in Canada) includes Beavers, Cubs, Scouts, Venturers, and Rovers, and teaches sensitivity and cooperation that has benefited communities throughout the world. The three tips of the fleur-de-lis represent the three main parts of the scout promise: duty to God, obedience to law and service to others. The two five-point stars are for truth and knowledge and the total of ten points is a reminder of the ten points of the scout law. The circular rope and reef knot represents the bond of brotherhood.

NAMES

Latin Names
Iris versicolor L.

The genus name *Iris* is based on *iris*, Latin and Greek names meaning "a sweet smelling plant" and "rainbow". Sometimes the name is explained as a reference to the many attractive colours of the flowers of the species being reminiscent of the colours of a rainbow. The epithet *versicolor* in the scientific name is Latin for "variously coloured", likely a reference to the colour varying in different parts of the flower.

English Names
The blue flag has also been called harlequin blue flag, blue iris, great blue flag, larger blue flag, northern blue flag, and poison flag. Still additional names sometimes attributed to the species are American blue flag, dagger flower, dragon flower, flag lily, fleur-de-lis, flower-de-luce, liver lily, purple flag, snake lily, water flag, water iris, wild blue flag, and wild iris. As well as being the scientific name, iris is also very widely used as a common name and refers to all *Iris* species, and sometimes also species in related genera.

French Names
Iris versicolore, iris sauvage. The name clajeux is occasionally used, but is also a name applied to other species, including *I. pseudacorus*, introduced into Canada.

HISTORY

Canada
The white lily (*Lilium candidum*) was designated as the floral emblem of Quebec on January 23, 1963. This species was chosen by interpreting the fleur-de-lis emblem (discussed above) as a lily (*lis* is French for lily). However, botanists and others found this interpretation to be without merit, and the choice of the lily as highly inappropriate. Indeed, it was pointed out that not only is the white lily not indigenous to Quebec, it is apparently not even indigenous to France. The blue flag was selected as the new floral emblem of Quebec, so recognized by the Flag and Emblems of Quebec Act assented to on November 5, 1999. For a detailed history of events leading to the replacement of the white lily with the blue flag as the floral symbol of Quebec, see Lamoureux, (2002) and Catling and Mitrow (2004).

Foreign
Iris species are fairly widely afforded official symbolic status. *Iris giganticaerulea* (giant blue iris or giant blue flag), a native of the southeastern U.S., was declared to be the official state wildflower of Louisiana in 1990. *Iris lacustris* (dwarf lake iris), a tiny plant endemic to the northern shores of Lake Michigan and Lake Huron, was designated the state wildflower of Michigan in 1998. It occurs in the Bruce Peninsula and Manitoulin Island in Ontario, and has been designated a threatened species in the U.S. and Canada. Iris (no particular species) was recognized as the "state cultivated flower" of Tennessee in 1933. *Iris nigricans* (black iris) is the national flower of Jordan. *Iris croatica* is the national flower of Croatia. The "iris" is often claimed to be the national flower of France. Several cities have designated the iris as their official flower, including Kansas City, Brussels, and Athens.

Blue flag (*Iris versicolor*), by Lavonia R. Stockelbach (1874–1966). A collection of her paintings of Canadian provincial and territorial flowers is associated with the herbarium of Agriculture and Agri-Food Canada in Ottawa.

A BIODIVERSITY TREASURE

Painting of the former official flower of Quebec, the white garden lily (*Lilium candidum*), from the Walter Coucill Canadian Centennial official flowers of Canada series (see Coucill 1966 cited in the first chapter of this book). Reproduced with the permission of the copyright holders, the Coucill family.

OFFICIAL PLANT EMBLEMS OF CANADA

APPEARANCE

Blue flag arises from a stout, creeping, branching, cylindrical rhizome 1–2.5 cm (0.4–1 inch) in diameter, dark brown externally, with long slender roots and leaves borne on the currently growing terminal ends of the rhizomes. The rhizomes produce an annual joint. The leaves are basal, sword-like (long, narrow, rigid and lanceolate), folded on the midribs, (10)60–90 cm ((4)–24–36 inches) long, 1–3 cm (0.4–1.2 inches) wide, projecting upwards from the rhizomes in two-ranked flat fans. Large showy flowers, usually violet-blue or rarely white, are borne on vertical, branching flower stalks which appear in the spring, the inflorescence usually with only two to four flowers. The flower stalks are 20–80 cm (8–32 inches) long, typically over-topping the leaves. Superficially, the flowers appear to have nine petals, but actually these are sets of three large sepals, small petals, and petal-like style lobes. The flowers are divided into three sections, each with a sepal (called a "fall" by iris enthusiasts), petal ("standard"), stamen, and style branch (also commonly called a "style arm"). Each of the three sections functions as a separate flower. The showy sepals are light to deep blue or blue-purple with yellow and whitish markings at their base. Rarely, white or reddish-purple flowers are encountered. The sepals and style branches tend to be similar in colour to the petals, but see the information presented below on colour of cultivated varieties. The sepals hang down, while the much smaller petals are erect. The petal-like style branches split at their upper ends into two decorative horns called crests, and attached to the bottom of each style branch is a stigma flap ("stigmatic lip"). A stamen is pressed against the bottom of each style branch, its long anther terminating close to the stigma flap. A diagram of this rather complicated floral anatomy is given in the discussion of pollination presented below. Small, dark-brown seeds are produced in three-celled capsules 1.5–6 cm (0.6–2.4 inches) long, with two rows of densely packed brown seeds in each cell. The fruits dry out and shatter in the fall, scattering the seeds, but the fruits often persist on the plants over the winter.

The flag of Montreal, one of Canada's most important and diverse cities, contains four floral emblems, and a bold red heraldic cross. The cross is said to represent either the Christian motives and principles which governed the founders of the city, or St. George's Cross, commemorating a visit to Montreal by King George VI. The four floral emblems represent the four main European ethnic groups that initially settled the city. Clockwise from top left: the fleur-de-lys of the Royal House of Bourbon, representing the French; a Lancastrian rose, representing the English; a shamrock, representing the Irish; a thistle, representing the Scottish.

Blue flag (*Iris versicolor*) in Forillon National Park, Quebec. Source: Wikipedia (photographer: D. Langlois; Creative Commons Attribution-Share ALike 30 Unported license).

CLASSIFICATION

Family: Iridaceae (iris family).

The genus *Iris* has close to 300 species of perennial herbs, which occur primarily in the Northern Hemisphere, with the greatest diversity in Eurasia.

In North America 34 species have been recognized north of Mexico. Some infra-specific groups have been recognized in *I. versicolor*, none of these having received much recognition by botanists. They include forma *murrayana* (with somewhat yellowish flowers), and forma *albocaerulea* (with white and blue flowers). More than 25,000 cultivars of *Iris* have been named.

Iris versicolor is known to have evolved as a hybrid between *I. virginica* and *I. hookeri* (*I. setosa* var. *canadensis*). The research that revealed the hybrid origin of blue flag was carried out by a rather famous botanist, Edgar Anderson, at the Missouri Botanical Garden. *Iris versicolor* inherited the sets of chromosomes of both its parental species, and has a total of 108, the most of any *Iris* species. The parental species do not grow together now, but did in the past, when ancient glaciers advancing southward forced the northerly *I. hookeri* into the range of *I. virginica*. [In another major scientific contribution, Anderson collected measurements of various floral features of *I. versicolor*, *I. hookeri*, and *I. virginica*. The well known statistician R.A. Fisher used the data (called "Anderson's Iris Data" and "Fisher's Iris Data") to invent a mathematical model (linear discriminant analysis) that is now commonly used to aid in species identification.] *Iris versicolor* hybridizes with both *I. virginica* and *I. hookeri*. The hybrid of *Iris versicolor* and *I. hookerii* is called *I. ×sancti-cyri*. The hybrid of *I. versicolor* and *I. virginica* is *I. ×robusta*.

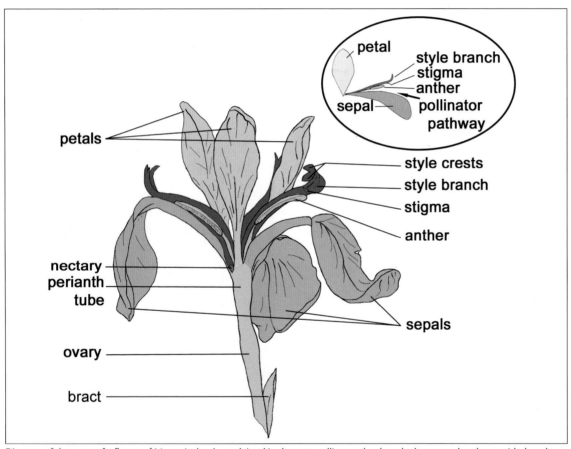

Diagram of the parts of a flower of *Iris versicolor*. As explained in the text, pollinators land on the large sepal and are guided, to the basal nectary, down a tunnel formed by the base of the sepal and the overhead style branch. During the inward trip, the pollinator deposits previously collected pollen on the upper (receptive) part of the stigma flap, and then picks up pollen from the anther; during the outward trip it brushes against the lower part of the stigma flap, but this is non-receptive to prevent self-fertilization. Prepared by B. Brookes.

GEOGRAPHY

Iris versicolor is native in Canada from Manitoba to Newfoundland, and extends south in the U.S. to Minnesota, Illinois, Ohio, Maryland, and Virginia.

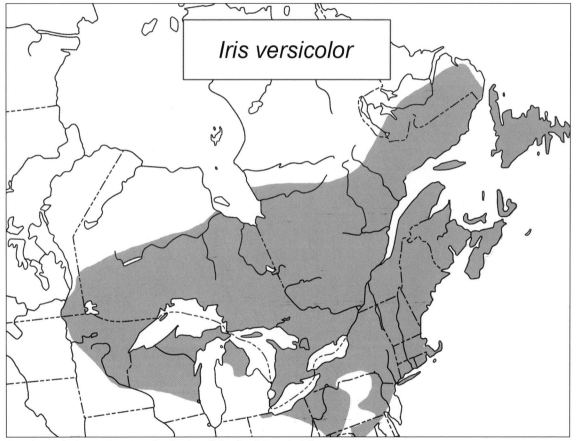

Iris versicolor

Canadian and adjacent American distribution of blue flag (*Iris versicolor*).

ECOLOGY

Habitat

The blue flag is a "subaquatic" or "emergent aquatic" plant that occupies shallow water or wet substrates, including bog mats, flood plains, wet pastures and meadows, forested wetlands, marshes, swamps, ditches, streambanks, and shorelines. The plants grow naturally in full sun to part shade.

Inter-species Relationships

Iris versicolor provides shoreline habitat for an array of wildlife, particularly furnishing cover for marsh birds, fish, and amphibians. The seeds are eaten by waterfowl and marsh birds, and the rhizomes (poisonous to humans) are consumed by moose and aquatic rodents, especially muskrats.

Pollination and Dispersal

Iris versicolor spreads vegetatively by rhizomes, often producing large clones. The species also produces seeds. A cavity in the seeds makes them buoyant, so they can be distributed by floating on water.

The large, nectar-producing flowers attract various pollinators as well as nectar robbers. Like the flowers of many insect-pollinated plant species, the stigma of *Iris* flowers receives pollen from visiting pollinators (especially bees) and the anthers provide a fresh load of pollen to the visitors to fertilize other flowers. However, the *Iris* flower is peculiar in the architectural way it separates these two events. The large petal-like sepals of the iris flower function as a landing platform for flying insects, and markings (guides) direct the visitors to the nectary at the base of the flower. The petal-like style branch (above) and the petal-like sepal (below) provide a channel towards the basal nectary. However, this channel is partially

blocked by the stigma, in the form of a flap, which is cleverly arranged so that the receptive side faces the incoming pollinator. As the pollinator pushes against the stigma flap, the receptive surface removes pollen that was acquired by the insect from previous floral visits. The insect next contacts an anther, and acquires a new load of pollen grains, before reaching the nectary. Finally, while backing out of the flower, the insect comes in contact only with the non-receptive face of the stigma flap. Thus the insect is prevented from depositing its newly collected batch of pollen on the stigma of the same flower. Despite this elaborate way of promoting outcrossing, self-pollination is very common in *I. versicolor*.

Blue flag (*Iris versicolor*) flower. Photograph courtesy of the Government of Quebec.

USES

Iris species are extensively used as ornamentals. *Iris versicolor* is not one of the principal garden species, but is often employed in water gardens (so are several other species adapted to standing water). Cultivars include 'Kermesina' (with red-purple flowers, probably the most popular variety), 'Candy Striper' (white flowers with bright reddish veins), 'Mysterious Monique' (with deep violet flowers), 'Rosea' (with pink flowers), and 'Bridesmaid' (flowers creamy yellow and lilac). *Iris versicolor* has been hybridized with other species to produce ornamental varieties. 'Gerald Darby' (a hybrid of *I. versicolor* and *I. virginica*) is particularly popular. It may be noted that cultivars of *I. versicolor* can only be maintained by vegetative propagation; some unscrupulous dealers have sold seedlings as the true cultivars, although they do not match the expected quality.

"Orrisroot powder", prepared by drying and pulverizing the rhizomes of certain *Iris* species (especially the closely related *I. florentina*, *I. pallida*, and *I. germanica*), has been used in spices, perfumes (to produce a violet odour), and medicine since the eras of the classical Greeks and Romans. Much of orrisroot today is produced in Italy. The juice of steeped *Iris* rhizomes has been employed to impart a flowery bouquet to Chianti wine.

North American Indians used *I. versicolor* "root" for a variety of medicinal purposes, especially topically to treat wounds, sores, and burns, and internally as a purgative, and to treat rheumatism, as well as disorders of the kidney and liver. The Potawatomi employed the leaves to weave baskets, mats, rugs, and bedding. Iridin (irisin) is a bitter extract of *I. versicolor* that has been used in herbal medicine for its diuretic (urine-stimulating), laxative, and blood-cleansing properties. Blue flag has been planted to stabilize and protect shorelines from erosion.

Blue flag (*Iris versicolor*) in Forillon National Park, Quebec. Source: Wikipedia (photographer: D. Langlois; Creative Commons Attribution-Share Alike 3.0 Unported license).

TOXICITY

Iris species are well known for their toxicity. Small amounts of the rhizomes or large amounts of the leaves, even if dried, are quite purgative, and can also cause depression and respiratory problems. The juice of the plant can cause dermatitis in sensitive individuals. Livestock avoid eating iris foliage. Cases of death of humans have been recorded, and ornamental rhizomes that are stored for planting are a potential risk to dogs. Irisin (mentioned above) may be responsible for some of the poisonous effects, but other compounds are suspected of being more toxic.

Flowers of blue flag (*Iris versicolor*). Source: Canadian Heritage. 2002. Symbols of Canada (revised). Canadian Heritage, Ottawa, ON. Reproduced with permission of Canadian Heritage, Public works, and Government Services Canada.

A BIODIVERSITY TREASURE

CULTIVATION

Iris species are among the most commonly grown ornamental plants, and there are numerous books dedicated to horticultural aspects. A number of species are grown in damp soil or standing water, and are often displayed in water gardens. Blue flag is one of these, although other *Iris* species are more often cultivated. Seeds used to grow *I. versicolor* are best stratified (stored at about 5 °C in wet paper towelling or moist peat moss for 3 months) to promote good germination. Seeds can be sown outdoors, spring planting preferred to fall. Young seedlings are best grown for a year in pots, then transplanted to their permanent positions. To reproduce by division, clumps of rhizomes should be replanted directly into their new positions, preferably in early autumn (mid-spring is also possible). Alternatively, smaller clumps can be potted and grown until well-rooted before final transplantation. This species may be grown in 4–10 cm (2–4 inches) of shallow, standing water in containers or artificial ponds, or in moist shoreline soils, or in constantly moist humus-rich soils of a garden border. *Iris versicolor* generally does not tolerate strong fluctuations in water level, and indeed can survive better than several more popular aquatic irises in soil that is merely damp. The plants should not be placed near aggressive, tall emergent aquatics like cattails, which will easily over-top them. After frost, the leaves may be trimmed back to about 2.5 cm (1 inch) above the crown.

CONSERVATION STATUS

Iris versicolor is a widespread species, not considered in need of conservation protection. The species is rare in Manitoba. It quickly colonizes newly available moist soils in New Brunswick, Prince Edward Island, and Nova Scotia, and has been listed as a noxious introduction in Nevada. Depending on location, it may be advisable to construct barriers to prevent the spread of *I. versicolor* where it is cultivated as an ornamental. The European *I. pseudacorus*, often grown in gardens, has escaped and is regarded as invasive in some areas of the U.S. It is displacing *I. versicolor* in some regions.

European yellow iris (*Iris pseudacorus*), often interpreted as the basis of the fleur-de-lis. As noted in the text, this species is commonly cultivated in North America, and in some regions is displacing *I. versicolor*. Source of illustration: Thomé, O.W. 1903. Prof. Dr. Thomé's Flora von Deutschland, Österreich und der Schweiz. Band 1, Fig. 139. H.V. Verlag, Berlin-Lichterfelde, Germany.

The Quebec blue flag coin issued in 2006. This is part of the provincial and territorial symbols gold coin series (0.99999% gold), initiated in 1998 (see the first chapter of this book). This coin has a face value of $350 but, reflective of its value to collectors, the purchase price is about $1,300. Only 2006 coins were made, matching the year of mintage. Coin image© courtesy of the Royal Canadian Mint.

MYTHS, LEGENDS, TALES, FOLKLORE AND INTERESTING FACTS

❧ In ancient Greece, Iris was the Greek goddess of the rainbow, daughter of the ocean spirit Electra, and a messenger of the gods. Always depicted with rainbow wings, she is said to have used the rainbow as a pathway through the sky, and wherever her feet touched earth there appeared iris flowers in a rainbow of colours.

❧ The oldest-known illustrations of irises are stylized flowers that appeared nearly 4,000 years ago on a wall fresco of the Priest-King in the palace of Minos at Knossos, Greece.

❧ Shah Jihan had the world-famous Taj Mahal erected in India after the death of his favourite wife in 1631. Some of the rooms are decorated with stone inlay based on an iris motif.

❧ The Ojibwa carried a piece of blue flag as a charm against snakes. The Arizona Indians are believed to have chewed blue flag before holding rattlesnakes in their mouths during snake dances, the odour said to be protective against bites.

❧ A solution of the flowers of blue flag produces a blue dye that has been employed like litmus paper to test for pH.

❧ The leaves of *I. florentina* yield iris green, a natural colouring once popular with artists. Curiously, irises have also been popular subjects for artists, particularly Vincent Van Gogh.

One of Vincent van Gogh's several paintings entitled *Irises*, currently owned by the Getty Museum in Los Angeles. In 1987 this painting sold for $53,900,000 (equivalent to $100,000,000 today).

SOURCES OF ADDITIONAL INFORMATION

Anderson, E. 1928. The problem of species in the northern blue flags, *Iris versicolor* L. and *Iris virginica* L. Annals Missouri Botanical Garden 15: 241–332.

Catling, P. M., and Mitrow, G. 2004. The white lilies—what are they? Can. Bot.Assoc.Bull. 37(1): 15–16.

Henderson, N.C. 2002. *Iris. In* Flora of North America North of Mexico. *Edited by* Flora of North America Editorial Committee. Oxford University press, Oxford, U.K. Vol. 26. pp. 371–395.

Köhlein, F. 1987. Iris. (Translated from German.) Timber Press, Portland, OR. [An excellent, non-technical guide to gardening with irises.]

Kron, P., Stewart, S.C., and Back, A. 1993. Self-compatibility, autonomous self-pollination, and insect mediated pollination in the clonal species *Iris versicolor*. Can. J. Bot. 71: 1503–1509.

Lamoureux, G. 2002. Flore printanière. Fleurbec, Saint-Henri-de-Lévis, Quebec. 576 pp. [Includes discussion of *I. versicolor* and its adoption as the floral emblem of Quebec; see pages 248, 364–371.]

Lim, K.Y., Matyasek, R., Kovarik, A., and Leitch, A. 2007. Parental origin and genome evolution in the allopolyploid *Iris versicolor*. Ann. Bot. 100: 219–224.

Shear, W. 1998. The gardener's iris book. Taunton Press, Newtown, CT. 170 pp. [Written in a popular style, a quite competent presentation.]

Warburton, B., and Hamblen, M. (Editors). 1978. The world of irises. Publishers Press, Salt Lake City, UT. 494 pp. [Available only from the American Iris Society; often called "the iris bible".]

Blue flag (*Iris versicolor*) in Forillon National Park, Quebec. Source: Wikipedia (photographer: D. Langlois; Creative Commons Attribution-Share Alike 3.0 Unported license).

TREE: YELLOW BIRCH

A maple (*Acer saccharum*)—yellow birch (*Betula alleghaniensis*) forest. Photo courtesy of the Government of Quebec.

SYMBOLISM

The forests of southern Quebec, which are highly productive and cover a large portion of the main areas of habitation, contain some of the largest concentrations of yellow birch in the world. It has been estimated that about 50% of the commercial stock of the species is in Quebec. Moreover, the tree has been of considerable use historically in the province, making its choice as the provincial arboreal emblem particularly appropriate.

Silhouette of yellow birch (*Betula alleghaniensis*). Source: J.L. Farrar 1995. Trees in Canada. Canadian Forest Service and Fitzhenry and Whiteside, Markham, ON, Canada. Reproduced with permission.

NAMES

Latin Names

Betula alleghaniensis Britton (*B. lutea* Michx. f.)

The genus name *Betula* is based on *betulla*, the Latin name for birch. *Alleghaniensis* in the scientific name is Latin for "of the Allegheny Mountains" that border the Appalachian plateau from Pennsylvania to Virginia. [The spelling of the epithet *alleghaniensis* in contrast to the spelling in "Allegheny Mountains" reflects past differences in usage in the literature.]

English Names

Yellow birch has also been called black, cherry, curly, gold, gray, hard, Quebec, red, silver, swamp, sweet, and tall birch, and Newfoundland oak. All of these alternative names are undesirable, and most of them have been applied to other species. The "yellow" in the name yellow birch refers to the golden yellow colour of the bark of mature trees. (*Lutea* in the old name *B. lutea*, Latin for yellow, is also a reference to bark colour. The name gold birch is similarly explained.)

French Names

Bouleau jaune. Other French names include bouleau des Alléghanys, bouleau frisé, bouleau merisier, merisier (a name used in France for the "wild cherry," and also used in Quebec for the pin cherry, *Prunus pensylvanica*), merisier blanc, merisier jaune, and merisier ondé.

HISTORY

Canada

Yellow birch was adopted in November 1993 as the provincial tree of Quebec. A related species, the white or paper birch (*B. papyrifera*), was adopted as the official tree of Saskatchewan in 1988.

Foreign

Some other birch species have been recognized as symbols in other countries. The white birch was designated the New Hampshire state tree in 1947. The silver birch (*B. pendula*) is the national tree of Finland. The "birch" is the national tree of Russia.

Bark of yellow birch (*Betula alleghaniensis*). Photo courtesy of the Government of Quebec.

APPEARANCE

The yellow birch is the tallest of the native birch species in Canada, growing to heights of 15–25 m (49–82 feet) and developing trunks 60–100 cm (24–39 inches) in diameter (trees 30 m (98 feet) high and 1.4 m (54 inches) wide have been recorded). In the forest the trunk is long and straight, supporting a relatively narrow crown. In the open, the branch system is wide, but usually with a well-developed central axis. Birches are known for their characteristic bark that usually separates readily into thin, papery sheets and has conspicuous, horizontal lenticels. (Lenticels are areas of the bark with numerous intercellular spaces that allow gas exchange through the cork cells of the bark which otherwise prevent the passage of water and gases.) The bark of yellow birch is thin (on small trunks), shiny, produces thin papery shreds but does not peel easily, and is initially reddish, gradually turning yellowish or bronze. On mature trunks the bark is dark and broken into large, ragged-edged plates. The leaves are alternate, 6-12 cm (2.4–4.7 inches) long and 4–9 cm (1.6–3.5 inches) broad, oval, and taper gradually from the middle to a slender, sharp point at the tip and to a narrow, rounded or slightly heart-shaped base. The margin is finely double-toothed. The root system is wide-spreading and may also be quite deep on well-drained loam and sandy loam soils (shallow roots are developed on shallow or poorly drained soils). When seeds germinate on rotting logs or decaying stumps, the roots may grow for some length down to the soil, and a curious "octopus-rooted habit", sometimes termed prop-rooted, may develop, the trunk supported by large roots the upper portions of which are above-ground.

Birch flowers occur in many-flowered catkins (cones), with male and female catkins on the same trees. The male catkins are pendulous while the female catkins are erect. The male catkins develop during the summer but remain fairly small, and the following spring they expand and shed their pollen before or during leaf expansion. In yellow birch the male catkins are about 2 cm (0.8 inch) long during the winter, but expand to about 8 cm (3.1 inches) in length at pollination time in the spring. The female catkins develop in the fall, remain on the branches over the winter, and the next season they reveal stigmas in the spring and later produce fruits (often called seeds) that are single-seeded with two wings, each in the axil of a three-lobed scale. In yellow birch the female catkins grow to 2.5–4 cm (1–1.6 inches) in length when the seeds are mature. The seeds ripen in September, the nutlets shedding in subsequent months, leaving behind the catkin axis and its scales that may remain on the tree over the following winter. Vegetative reproduction from stumps also occurs to some extent.

CLASSIFICATION

Family: Betulaceae (birch family).

There are about 35 species of *Betula*, distributed in north temperate regions of the world. About 18 species are native to North America north of Mexico, most of these occurring in Canada.

Betula alleghaniensis var. *macrolepis* (Fern.) Brayshaw, once called witch-hazel in Newfoundland, is said to have relatively long cone bracts (8 mm (0.3 inch) or more long). *Betula alleghaniensis* var. *fallax* (Fassett) Brayshaw is said to have dark brown bark that typically does not exfoliate into shreds or curly flakes at the surface. The unusual bark of var. *fallax* has led to confusion with cherry birch, *B. lenta*, and is the basis for reports of the latter north of its very restricted Canadian range.

Yellow birch has been hybridized with a dozen other species of *Betula*. A natural hybrid of *B. alleghaniensis* and *B. pumila* (bog birch), named purpus birch (*B. ×purpusii*), occurs occasionally in Canada. Natural hybrids of yellow birch and paper birch have rarely been reported but are suspected to occur with some frequency. Some researchers have considered *B. papyrifera* var. *cordifolia* to be this hybrid. Studies have shown that these hybrids are best recognized by their intermediate leaf characters. *Betula alleghaniensis* may also hybridize with *B. lenta*, but the hybrids are difficult to recognize. *Betula lenta* differs from both *B. alleghaniensis*

and such hybrids by increased numbers of hairs on bracts and fruiting catkins. Murray's Birch (*Betula murrayana*) is believed to have originated from a hybrid of purpus birch and yellow birch. It is intermediate in most characters and best distinguished from *B. alleghaniensis* by its acute instead of acuminate leaf tips, and leaves with 7–10 instead of 12–18 pairs of veins.

Yellow birch (*Betula alleghaniensis*). 1, Branch with mature male catkins. 2, Branch with immature male catkins during the winter. 3, Scale of a male flower. 4, Branch with mature female catkins. 5, Single-seeded fruit with two wings. 6, Scale of a female fruit. Source: Sargent, C.S. 1896. The silva of North America. Houghton, Mifflin and Company, Boston, MA. Vol. 9, plate 449.

Male catkins of yellow birch (*Betula alleghaniensis*). Source: BugwoodImages/ForestryImages (photographer: B. Cook; Creative Commons Attribution 3.0 license).

GEOGRAPHY

Yellow birch ranges from southeastern Manitoba through the Atlantic Provinces to southern Newfoundland, and southwards over the northeastern U.S., as far south as South Carolina, Tennessee, and the Appalachian Mountains of northern Georgia. The main concentrations of the species occur in Quebec, Ontario, New Brunswick, Maine, upper Michigan, and New York.

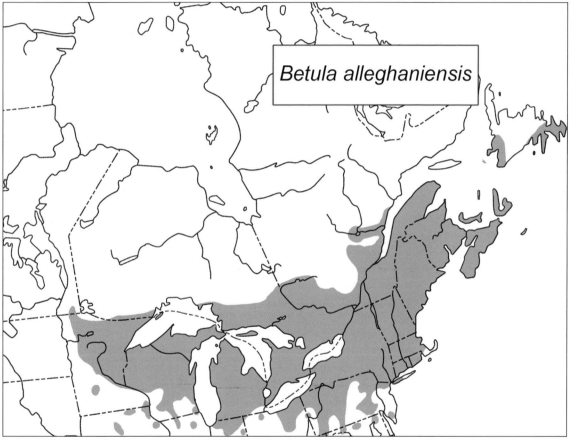

Betula alleghaniensis

Canadian and adjacent American distribution of yellow birch (*Betula alleghaniensis*).

Yellow birch (*Betula alleghaniensis*) forest in Quebec.
Source: Thinkstock.

A BIODIVERSITY TREASURE

ECOLOGY

This species is a member of Canada's southern hardwood forests in the Deciduous, Great Lakes–St. Lawrence, and Acadian forest regions, and is also found in the southeastern part of the Boreal Forest. Yellow birch occasionally occurs in nearly pure stands or as a dominant tree, but is usually a co-dominant or minor species. Its most common and important associates are spruce, balsam, hemlock, beech, and maple. It is more resistance to ice damage than other birches.

Yellow birch is one of the slowest growing trees in northern hardwood forests, typically increasing in trunk diameter less than 2.5 cm (1 inch) in ten years. Average longevity is about 150 years, and the trees can live to 400 years of age. However, several factors limit the life of yellow birch. The bark is flammable and the tree is highly vulnerable to fire. Yellow birch does not do well in hot dry sites, and it is suspected that "birch dieback", a condition that widely affected the species in Canada from the 1930s to the 1950s, is the result of hot spells.

Habitat

Yellow birch grows in cool areas well supplied with precipitation. The species occurs on a variety of soils, but achieves its best development on rich, moist, well-drained soils. The tree is tolerant of a range of soil pH. It is often found along stream banks, swampy woods, and forested slopes. *Betula alleghaniensis* cannot reproduce under a closed canopy, but is moderately shade tolerant (the most tolerant of eastern Canadian birches), although not as much so as the sugar maple and beech. It is able to occupy stands dominated by sugar maple. The seeds develop best in places free of leaf litter, and seeds may remain alive in the soil for several years. It has been shown that the roots of sugar maple seedlings produce a chemical that inhibits the growth of yellow birch seedlings.

Inter-species Relationships

As a large and frequent species, yellow birch plays an important role in the biodiversity of northeastern forests. Moose, snowshoe hare and (especially) white-tailed deer browse on the twigs. The seeds are consumed by a variety of birds, squirrels, mice, and voles. Ruffed grouse feed so frequently on catkins and buds that in northern Maine and Canada the bird is often called the "birch partridge". Yellow-bellied sapsuckers feed on the sap by drilling rows in the bark, and commonly feed on the same birch trees for years (occasionally the many individual wounds combine to girdle the tree, and mortality of the trees is sometimes a problem for logging companies). Red squirrels have been observed feeding on the sap of young plants. Beaver and porcupine consume the bark and wood (actually the cambium or "inner bark" is the desired part). Like sapsuckers, porcupine can cause significant losses and may tend to return to the same trees.

Birches, like most trees, are fed on by an almost endless variety of insects, but usually only one or a few cause serious damage. The bronze birch borer (*Agrilus anxius*) is considered to be the most serious pest of yellow birch by the logging industry. Adults of this beetle deposit eggs in bark crevices of upper branches, the larvae bore tunnels under the bark causing dying of the tree top, and over 2 or 3 years the insects kill the rest of the tree. Numerous other insects feed on yellow birch. These in turn provide food for other insects, birds and mammals. Different insects are adapted to different parts of the tree. The larvae of a tiny fly, the birch seed midge (*Oligotrophus betheli*) live in the developing seeds. Other insects feed only on the leaves or only on the flowers.

Bronze birch borer (*Agrilus anxius*). Left, adult (photo courtesy of Barry Lyons, Natural Resources Canada). Centre, gallery bored by larvae (photo by Thérèse Arcand, Ressources naturelles Canada, Service canadien des forêts, Centre de foresterie des Laurentides). Right, larva (photo courtesy of Canadian Forest Service, reproduced by permission).

Pollination and Dispersal

Birches are wind-pollinated. The light seeds are also spread by wind, usually within a few hundred metres of the parent trees. Most seeds are distributed no farther than two to four times the height of the tree. Because the fruits ("seeds") are sometimes held into winter and gradually dispersed from the cones, they are sometimes blown over glazed snow, occasionally as far as 400 m (1,300 feet). As with most trees, there are "mast years" marked by very large seed production with intervening relatively poor years. It has been estimated that out of every 10 years, yellow birch averages one heavy seed year, 3.5 medium years, 4.5 light or very light years, and 1 year of seed failure.

USES

Yellow birch is an important timber hardwood of eastern Canada, and indeed most wood sold as "birch" in North America is from this tree. The wood is very hard (comparable to white oak), strong, heavy, fine-grained, and takes stain well. Yellow birch wood is slightly harder and stronger than paper birch, and is considered superior to if for manufacture of furniture. It is employed for fine furniture, cabinets, panelling, interior trim, doors, plywood, veneer, parquet flooring, tool handles and woodenware. Lower quality logs have been used for railroad ties, pulpwood, and boxes. Birch is a preferred wood in the manufacture of toothpicks. The wood of yellow birch is very resistant to decay, and in the eighteenth century it was used in preference to oak for constructing the underwater parts of ships.

The tree has several very minor culinary uses. As with other birches, the sap can be tapped to yield a sugar or syrup but, compared to sugar maple, the amount produced is much less and it is more expensive. Between 80 and 100 litres of birch sap are required to make just 1 litre of syrup (30–40 litres are needed for maple syrup), which sells for about $80 wholesale. Birch syrup is a very minor commodity in Europe and Alaska. There are only a handful of producers of birch syrup in Canada, and paper birch is the main source. Birch syrup is darker and slightly more bitter than maple syrup, and is sometimes encountered as a glaze or flavouring used on very fancy meals in high-end restaurants. "Birch beer" is usually a carbonated soft drink made with birch twigs or bark from various *Betula* species, but may also be alcoholic, prepared by fermenting the sap or adding honey or sugar to promote fermentation. Very recently the Manitoba Liquor Control Commission allowed birch wine to be sold. Birch leaves and twigs have been employed to make tea.

Yellow birch is quite aromatic, the bark, twigs, buds, and leaves smelling and tasting of wintergreen when broken or bruised. The tree was once used as a commercial source of oil of wintergreen, which is added to medicines to mask their objectionable flavour. Oil of wintergreen formerly was also obtained from wintergreen (*Gaultheria procumbens*) and cherry birch (*B. lenta*). Today, this volatile oil is usually produced synthetically.

Yellow birch is one of the hardwood species that is most commonly employed to prepare wood alcohol, acetate of lime, charcoal, and essential oils. "Birch tar" ("Russian oil" when obtained from Russian species), extracted from the bark, was once used as a glue, lubricant, and medicine.

The oily bark of yellow birch is often used as kindling by campers and hunters in the north woods, because it can be used to start cooking or warming fires even when wet.

Collecting and preparing Canadian birch syrup. Photos courtesy of Dave Challen and Beth Kuiper, Boreal Birch Syrup Company (Thunder Bay).

CULTIVATION

The literature cited below can be used to find information on forestry management of yellow birch, and the following remarks are oriented to

Yellow birch (*Betula alleghaniensis*). Photo courtesy of the Government of Quebec.

growing the tree as an ornamental. Birch seeds do not require stratification if sown outdoors in the fall. To condition the seeds for spring planting, stratification can be accomplished by soaking the seeds in tap water for 24 hours, draining off excess water and storing the seeds in a plastic bag a few degrees above freezing for a month. Alternatively, nursery-grown saplings can simply be purchased. Seedlings may require protection from mice, and saplings from deer and rabbits. Birch trees are not easily excavated and transplanted, but well-grown younger trees that are balled or container-grown can be planted, preferably in early spring. Although somewhat tolerant of adverse conditions, yellow birch is best provided with moderately deep, well-drained loam soil, and a sunny or at least only partly-shaded location, preferably with some protection from wind. Because yellow birch is long-lived and potentially will grow into a moderately large tree, care should be exercised that this will not cause problems in the future. The species is tolerant of roadside salt and was judged to be moderately resistant to the Ice Storm of 1998. White-barked birches (especially paper birch) are usually preferred for home planting (because of the attractive white bark, the tendency to develop a clump of trunks, and a somewhat hardier nature), although the yellow birch provides extremely attractive yellow foliage in the fall, and is somewhat less prone to the bronze birch borer than are white-barked birches.

CONSERVATION STATUS

Yellow birch is not threatened over the major portion of its range.

Wood of yellow birch (*Betula alleghaniensis*). Source: Thinkstock.

MYTHS, LEGENDS, TALES, FOLKLORE AND INTERESTING FACTS

❦ Witches are said to have preferred birch twigs to make the ends of their broom sticks.

❦ Cradles were once made of birch wood in the belief that this would protect babies.

❦ In Finland, Scandinavia, Estonia, Latvia, and Russia, birch twigs with the foliage left on are traditionally employed to slap one's body in the sauna as a form of massage and to open the pores and increase blood circulation.

❦ At the end of their life cycle, yellow birch trees frequently decay extensively under the bark (which is extremely resistant to decay), and the rotten, spongy wood is often referred to as "punkwood". Aboriginal Peoples in eastern Canada dried punkwood and carried it with them as tinder for starting fires by friction.

❦ It takes about 100,000 seeds of yellow birch to weigh 1 kg (there are about 45,000 seeds in a pound). In bumper seed years a yellow birch forest may shed about 90 million seeds per hectare (36 million/acre).

❦ Yellow birch wood is very heavy, so much so that freshly fallen birch logs tend to sink. Loggers determined to float yellow birch logs downriver to a sawmill once resorted to lashing birch logs to other logs (particularly pine) that would float. Another technique was to dry the logs out for a period until their specific gravity was less than that of water. This was accomplished either by not removing the branches for several weeks, so that the leaves would suck water out, or scoring the trunks longitudinally to encourage desiccation.

Birch twigs bound in a bundle (called a birch) were once widely employed as a whip to "birch" (punish) people. Sapling branches from birch trees were a favourite disciplinary tool of stern schoolmasters in early colonial North America.

SOURCES OF ADDITIONAL INFORMATION

Barnes, B.V., Dancik, B.P., and Sharik, T.L. 1974. Natural hybridization of yellow birch and paper birch. Forest Sci. 20: 215–221.

Dancik, B.P., and Barnes, B.V. 1972. Natural variation and hybridization of yellow birch and bog birch in southeastern Michigan. Silvae Genetica 21: 1–9.

Dancik, B.P., and Barnes, B.V. 1974. Leaf diversity in yellow birch (*Betula alleghaniensis*). Can. J. Bot. 52: 2407–2414.

Dansereau, P., and Pageau, G. 1966. Phytogeographia laurentiana. IV. Distribution géographique et écologique du *Betula alleghaniensis*. Mémoires du Jardin Botanique de Montréal 58: 1–56.

Furlow, J.J. 1997. *Betula*. *In* Flora of North America North of Mexico. *Edited by* Flora of North America Editorial Committee. Oxford University press, Oxford, U.K. Vol. 3. pp. 516–530.

Gilbert, A.M. 1965. Yellow birch. *In* Silvics of forest trees of the United States. *Compiled by* H.A. Fowells. Department of Agriculture Handbook 271, Washington, DC. pp. 104–109.

Higginbotham, J.W., Curtis, M., and Parks, C.R. 1989. Morphological variation in southern Appalachian *Betula alleghaniensis* and *B. lenta* (Betulaceae). Rhodora 91: 172–187.

Larson, E.H. (Editor). 1969. The birch symposium. Northeastern Forest Experiment Station, Forest Service, U.S. Dept. Agriculture, Upper Darby, PA. 183 pp.

Robitaille, L., and Roberge, M. 1981. La sylviculture du bouleau jaune au Québec. Revue Forestière Française (France) 33: 105–112.

Tubbs, C.H. 1969. The influence of light, moisture, and seedbed on yellow birch regeneration. USDA Forest Service Research Paper NC-27. 12 pp.

Base of an old yellow birch (*Betula alleghaniensis*) tree, showing exposed, stilted roots ("octopus-rooted habit") indicative of the plant having grown as a seedling upon a log which has since disintegrated. Source: Wikipedia (photographer: Nicholas; Creative Commons Attribution 2.0 Generic license).

SASKATCHEWAN

Provincial flag of Saskatchewan.

A SASKATCHEWAN LANDSCAPE: an open prairie with the big sky so characteristic of the southern prairies.

FLORAL EMBLEM: WESTERN RED LILY

Flower of western red lily (*Lilium philadelphicum*), photographed by P.M. Catling.

SYMBOLISM

Lilium philadelphicum is perhaps the most attractive of the plants that thrive in the rugged environment of the prairies of northwestern North America. It symbolizes both the beauty of the natural landscape and the resourcefulness of its people. Accordingly it is an excellent floral emblem for the province of Saskatchewan.

Lilies in religion and art generally symbolize purity and spirituality, and as the flower of the Resurrection and of the Virgin in Christianity, white lilies are widely displayed at Easter. However, as explained in the discussion of iris in the chapter on Quebec emblems, many references to "lilies" in the Bible probably refer to the iris, or perhaps other wildflowers.

The Coat of Arms of Saskatchewan. The scroll at the bottom is decorated with western prairie lily flowers. The deer carries a pendant with a lily flower, and the beaver holds another flower in its paw. The inscription *Multis E Gentibus Vires* means "From Many Peoples Strength".

NAMES

Latin Names
Lilium philadelphicum L.

As noted below, legislation in Saskatchewan specifically recognized *L. philadelphicum* var. *andinum* (Nutt.) Ker Gawl. as the official flower of the province. This is one of two varieties (the other is var. *philadelphicum*) recognized as distinct by some authorities but not by others.

The genus name *Lilium* is based on the Greek *lirion*, white lily (assumed to be the Madonna lily, *L. candidum*). The epithet *philadelphicum* in the scientific name is Latin for Philadelphia. The botanist John Bartram sent a collection of the species from Philadelphia to Carolus Linnaeus, the Swedish taxonomist, who named it in 1762 after the Philadelphia area. The epithet *andinum* was coined by botanist Thomas Nuttall, based on a collection he made in North Dakota in 1811. Nuttall thought he was near the Rocky Mountains, which he called the "Andes" (a name now reserved for the Andes Mountains of South America) and he applied the descriptive word *andinum*, meaning "of the Andes".

English Names
Western red lily. Also: Philadelphia lily, prairie lily, red lily, wood lily. The name wood lily is sometimes restricted to *L. philadelphicum* var. *philadelphicum*. While "wood lily" is used chiefly for *L. philadelphicum* it is applied also to some species of *Trillium* and *Clintonia*; wintergreen (*Pyrola minor*); lily of the valley (*Convallaria majalis*); an Australian orchid, *Dendrobium speciosum*; and other plants. The names western red lily and western red wood lily are sometimes restricted to *L. philadelphicum* var. *andinum*. As discussed below, the evidence that

western plants deserve to be recognized separately is quite inconclusive. Therefore, the "western" in the name "western red lily" is perhaps debatable, but it is retained here since this common name is used in the legislation recognizing the species as the floral emblem of Saskatchewan. The name "tiger lily" is sometimes applied to the species, although it usually refers to the widely planted *L. lancifolium* Thunb., a native of China, Korea, and Japan.

The name "lily" is used chiefly for *Lilium* species, but is applied to plants of other families, especially in the amaryllis family (Amaryllidaceae, which is often included in the Liliaceae). Other examples are water lilies (of the Nymphaeceae) and calla lily (*Zantedeschia aethiopica* of the Araceae).

French Names
Lis de Philadelphie. Also: lis des prairies, lis rouge orangé (lis and lys are often interchanged). Lis des bois could refer to the species as a whole, just to *L. philadelphicum* L. var. *philadelphicum*, or to other species such as *Trillium grandiflorum* (Michx.) Salisb.

The provincial flag of Saskatchewan, bearing the official floral emblem, the western red lily.

HISTORY

Canada

In 1935, the Regina Natural History Society began a search for an appropriate floral emblem for Saskatchewan. Being common in the province at the time, having attractive red flowers, and not used as a symbol elsewhere, the western red lily was a natural choice. Saskatchewan's *Floral Emblem Act* of 1941 designated variety *andinum* of *L. philadelphicum*, referred to as the "prairie lily", as the official floral emblem of the province. The subsequent Floral Emblem Act of 1981 also referred specifically to *L. philadelphicum* L. var. *andinum*, but called it "the western red lily". Another lily, the white lily (*L. candidum*), was the floral emblem of Quebec from 1963 to 1999 (see the chapter on Quebec emblems).

Foreign

No particular species of *Lilium* appears to have current official designation as the emblem of a political region, except in Saskatchewan. *Lilium bosniacum* has been claimed to be the national flower of Bosnia and Hertzegovina, but this seems to be based primarily on (a) a tradition of it being a national emblem among the Bosniacs, and (b) the interpretation that the fleur-de-lis symbol that has been used officially is based on this lily species. Several so-called "lilies" are emblems of regions, but are not species of *Lilium* (e.g., the flame lily, *Gloriosa rothschildiana*, is the national flower of Zimbabwe).

APPEARANCE

The plants are perennials, developing a bulb 1.5–2.9 cm (0.6–1.1 inches) wide, with loosely arranged, jointed scales. The bulb is typically located 3–10 cm (1–2 inches) below the surface of the soil. Thin branched roots spread laterally from it, and somewhat thicker "contractile roots" arise from the base, serving to pull the bulb downward as the plant matures (a widespread strategy in herbaceous perennials, preventing the plants from popping out of the soil as they grow). Flowering occurs from late spring to summer. Flowering stems may rise up to 1.2 m (53 inches), and bear narrow leaves that are sometimes single but often arranged in whorls. The flowers commonly are solitary, but are also often in umbels of two or three or occasionally up to six. Young plants normally produce just one flower. The flowers are most often red-orange, fading to a yellowish throat with dark speckles. The tepals (petals and sepals that are very similar) are 4.5–8.2 cm (1.8–3.2 inches) long. Deep red, orange, pink, and rarely pure yellow flowers also occur. The fruits are cylindrical capsules, 2.2–7.7 cm (0.9–3 inches) long, the largest with up to 200 or so dark brown seeds that mature in the fall.

Western red lily (*Lilium philadelphicum*). Source: D. Powell, United States Department of Agriculture Forestry Service.

CLASSIFICATION

Family: lily family (Liliaceae).

The genus *Lilium* consists of about 100 species of the temperate northern Hemisphere, extending south to mountains of the Asian tropics. There are 22 species in North America north of Mexico. *Lilium philadelphicum* is the only species of the genus native to Canada with erect flowers (i.e., the only one with flowers that normally face upward instead of nodding), perianth segments (petals or sepals) that are highly clawed (i.e., with a well-developed stalk), and floral spots confined to well-defined nectar guides (streaks that guide pollinators to nectaries).

Lilium philadelphicum is a highly variable species. Features claimed to distinguish varieties *andinum* and *philadelphicum* are given in the following table. As detailed in Skinner (2002), cited below, plants in various areas of North America frequently cannot be identified by the characters alleged to discriminate the two varieties, and "the status of var. *andinum* is unsettled".

Alleged Differences between the Varieties of *Lilium philadelphicum*

Character	Variety *andinum*	Variety *philadelphicum*
Location	Primarily western	Primarily eastern
Ecology	Low grassy vegetation	Open woods and thickets
Capsule length	4–8 cm (1.6–3.1 inches)	2.5–3.5 cm (1–1.4 inches)
Mean plant height	48 cm (19 inches)	81 cm (32 inches)
Number of whorls of leaves with three or more leaves in a whorl on the stem (average in parenthesis)	0–5 (1.3)	2–5 (3.8)
Mean leaf length	5.1 cm (2 inches)	6.9 cm (2.7 inches)
Mean leaf width	0.6 cm (0.24 inch)	1.3 cm (0.5 inch)
Leaves usually scattered on stem?	Yes	No
Stem usually topped by a whorl of leaves?	Yes	No

Western red lily (*Lilium philadelphicum*). Source: D. Powell, United States Department of Agriculture Forestry Service.

GEOGRAPHY

Lilium philadelphicum is the widest-ranging of the North American species of *Lilium*. It extends from eastern British Columbia across southern Canada into the northern United States from Montana to the east coast.

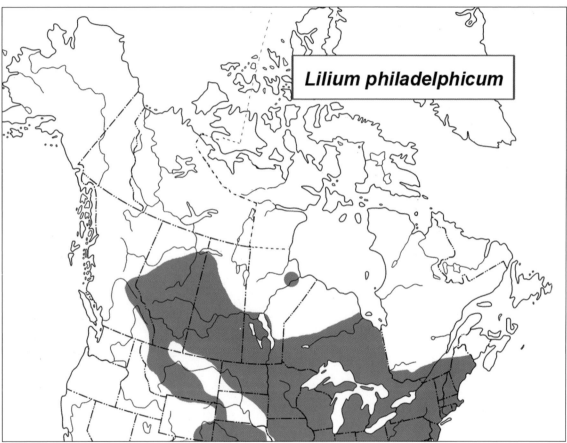

Canadian and adjacent United States distribution of *Lilium philadelphicum*.

Lilium philadelphicum. Source: Elwes, H.J. 1880. A monograph of the genus *Lilium*. Taylor and Francis, London.

ECOLOGY

The number of flowering plants in an area varies from year to year and is decreased by unusually dry conditions. Herbivores eat most of the plants in some years. Moderate grazing reduces competition (because *L. philadelphicum* is relatively resistant to grazing) and contributes to successive flowering. Some lightly grazed pastures and rangelands have consistently good displays of lilies. Sometimes the creation of new roadside ditches disturbs the soil in such a way that lilies flourish for a short period.

Habitat

Numerous habitats are occupied. The species is particularly common in open prairie grasslands, but also occurs in moist meadows, semi-wooded areas, and the understory of semi-open boreal forests.

Inter-species Relationships

White-tailed deer and some small mammals (such as mice, voles, gophers, squirrels, and hares) consume the plants, occasionally down to ground level, and sometimes also eat the bulbs. Deer are particularly fond of the flowers, whereas some other large herbivores, such as cattle and bison, tend to consume the whole plants. A wide variety of insects (including true bugs, ants, and some bees) "steal" nectar from the flowers (i.e., "rob" the nectar but rarely if every transfer pollen), but only some species of butterflies are good pollinators, as noted below.

Pollination and Dispersal

Lilium philadelphicum is pollinated principally by butterflies, particularly swallowtail butterflies (*Papilio* species), the pollen transfer taking place by sticking to the wings of the insects. The pollen-containing sacs (thecae) of the anthers have been observed to close in the rain, apparently an adaptation to protect the pollen from being washed away during rainy periods (when butterflies do not visit the flowers). The flowers lack fragrance, and rely on their size and colour to attract pollinators. Hummingbirds occasionally visit the flowers for nectar, but are not thought to act as pollinators (lily flowers in general have been hypothesized to have evolved characteristics that attract both Lepidoptera and hummingbirds). Nectar is produced by glands at the bases of three alternating members of the six tepals (these have been interpreted as the "sepals", the remaining three tepals as "petals").

Occasionally small mammals such as voles, that harvest the bulbs, disperse some of the scales that make up the bulbs. The individual scales of mature bulbs are capable of producing new plants, so the animals sometimes establish the plants in new locations by this method. However, most dispersal is by seeds, which are produced in large numbers.

WHY "PRAIRIE PHOENIX"?

Bonnie J. Lawrence and Anna L. Leighton were thinking of ecology when they developed the title for their wonderful book[1] about Saskatchewan's floral emblem. The sudden appearance of hundreds of spectacular vivid red lilies after a fire inspired the name "prairie phoenix". The mythical phoenix is a bird that is reborn from its own ashes. Fires, once a frequent natural event on the prairies, often resulted in explosive appearances of lilies (and other flora and fauna). Despite temperatures of up to 400 °C (752 °F) at the surface during the fires, the lily bulbs are protected since they are 3 to 5 cm (about 1–2 inches) below the ground surface where there is very limited temperature change. Fires often occurred in the spring and fall when there was ample fuel, but because the lily grows mainly in summer, the above-ground parts were infrequently burned. Bulbs can remain dormant but they are ready and waiting to grow as soon as fire nourishes the soil and reduces competition from grasses. Lawrence and Leighton suggested that the benefit of a fire may last 5 years, after which the population begins to decline—only to be reborn with the next fire.

[1]Reviewed in Blue Jay 63(3): 159. 2005.

USES

Historically, Native North Americans used *L. philadelphicum* for medicine and food, albeit to a limited extent. Dakota Indians employed pulverized or chewed flowers of western red lily as an antidote for spider bites, Algonquins chewed the "root" for stomach disorders, Chippewa employed a poultice of the bulbs to treat wounds, Iroquois used the plant to ease removal of the placenta after childbirth, and the Malecite used the roots as a cough medicine and to treat fevers. The Cree, Woodland, and Blackfoot Indians snacked on the bulbs. Today, the principal use of *L. philadelphicum* is as an ornamental.

TOXICITY

The lily family (Liliaceae) includes the edible onion, garlic, and asparagus, but also poisonous plants. Bulbs of *Lilium* are generally thought to be edible, although all species are not palatable and some are quite bitter. *Lilium philadelphicum* is generally not considered toxic to humans or other animals, and as noted above it is consumed by a variety of animals. The internet has some warnings about toxicity of "red lily" and *L. lancifolium* to pets, and there have been reports about nephrotoxicosis (kidney poisoning) in cats resulting from consumption of lilies, but specific, authoritative information for *L. philadelphicum* is lacking.

CULTIVATION

Detailed advice on cultivating *L. philadelphicum* is found in Lawrence and Leighton (2005), cited below. The species can be grown from seeds or bulb scales, but it may require 4 years for the plants to produce flowers (plants grow somewhat faster from bulb scales, but still may require 4 years to produce flowers). While some recently collected seeds may germinate, cold stratification (e.g., 6 to 8 weeks in a refrigerator) is recommended to improve germination. Germination is also enhanced by repeated washing (presumably removing water-soluble germination inhibitors). Bulbs may be purchased from some suppliers, or transplanted from fellow gardeners (preferably not from wild plants). The bulbs can be moved without soil in early fall after the leaves have died down, but it is better to take them in a sod of earth. Bulbs can be planted either in the spring or fall. Although the lilies grow in a wide variety of soil conditions, a humus-rich, well-drained, friable soil 22 cm (9 inches) deep is recommended. A mixture of sandy soil and peat moss is ideal. Large bulbs (2 cm or 0.8 inch or more in diameter) should be planted 5–7.5 cm (2–3 inches) below the soil surface; smaller bulbs may be planted more shallowly. Bulbs should be spaced 30–50 cm (12–18 inches) apart, in a fairly open location, although some shade from the hot afternoon sun is preferable. Protection from weeds and regular watering will increase growth and survival.

MACOUN'S FLOWER GARDEN

Exploring the Canadian prairies in July 1879, the famous Canadian field biologist, John Macoun, described the "Flower Garden of the Northwest" near Long Lake: "Sometimes, lilies (*Lilium philadelphicum*) are so abundant that they cover an acre of ground, bright red." His party celebrated the 12th of July by decorating their horses with these lilies and marching from camp to the beat of an old tin pan. (Page 141 in Autobiography of John Macoun, Canadian explorer and naturalist, 1831–1920, second edition. Ottawa Field-Naturalists' Club, 1979.) The general region of Macoun's "Flower Garden of the Northwest", north of Last Mountain Lake, became Canada's first migratory bird sanctuary in 1887, 8 years after Macoun's visit. Fire has been used in the management of the last Mountain Lake National Wildlife Area since the early 1980s, and this may explain why lilies are still abundant there today.

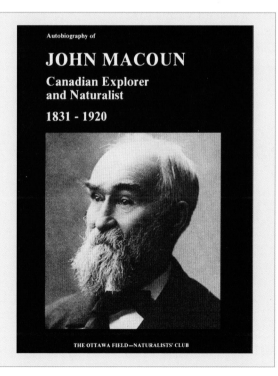

Autobiography of
JOHN MACOUN
Canadian Explorer and Naturalist
1831 - 1920

THE OTTAWA FIELD–NATURALISTS' CLUB

CONSERVATION STATUS

"Tom, Tom, the farmer's son
Found some lilies but picked not one—
He picked not because he knew
It was better to leave them where they grew."
—*From Morrison (1948)*

The western red lily was once widespread in Saskatchewan. Agricultural expansion and urbanization have been the main factors responsible for considerable decrease of the species in the province, but picking the very attractive red flowers, once a popular activity, also contributed to the decline. Diminishing numbers of the lilies have also been attributed in part to fire suppression. The western red lily is now protected by Saskatchewan's *Floral Emblem Act* of 1981, which makes it an offence to transplant, pick, uproot, or in any way damage the plant, but has exceptions for necessary work and for property owners on their own land. *The Provincial Emblems and Honours Act* provides for fines ranging from $50 to $500. *Lilium philadelphicum* is rare in the lower Midwestern prairies of the United States, and in the southern Appalachians. It is listed as Endangered in Maryland, New Mexico, Tennessee, and North Carolina, and Threatened in Kentucky and Ohio. In the northeastern United States, the species has declined rapidly with the disappearance of prairies and increase of white-tailed deer. The article cited below by Olson provides suggestions for methods of conserving lily species that require protection. A new threat to lilies in North America is the lily leaf beetle (see text box).

A MODERN MESSAGE HALF A CENTURY OLD
"Man has destroyed the balance of nature. By conserving the lily, you can help to tilt the balance back again."

The illustration below is slightly redrawn from Morrison's 1948 book entitled "The prairie lily. Saskatchewan's floral emblem". This book, written in elementary language, is a remarkable early attempt to educate very young school children of the importance of preserving nature.

WILL INVASIVE ALIEN BEETLE THREATEN THE WESTERN RED LILY?

The lily leaf beetle (*Lilioceris lilii*) has devastated cultivated lilies in eastern Canada and was recently found on the wild Canada lily (*L. canadense*) in New Brunswick. This beetle apparently feeds on all species of *Lilium*. It became established in North America in Montreal in 1943. Based on its rapid recent spread in the east, its catholic tastes, and the fact that it reached Portage La Prairie, Manitoba in 1999, the future large scale destruction of the western red lily seems inevitable. The insect is 6–8 mm (about 0.25 inch) long, red above except for the head which is black, and often produces distinct chirping sounds when picked up. Biological control of the beetle is being vigorously pursued in the United States, and should be considered for implementation in Canada.

For more information see Majka, C.G. and LeSage, L. 2008. Introduced leaf beetles of the maritime provinces, 5: The lily leaf beetle, *Lilioceris lilii* (Scopoli) (Coleoptera: Chrysomelidae). Proc. Entomol. Soc. Wash. 110: 186–195.

Lily leaf beetles (*Lilioceris lilii*). Source: Dr. H. Goulet.

CONSERVATION STATUS (CONT`D)

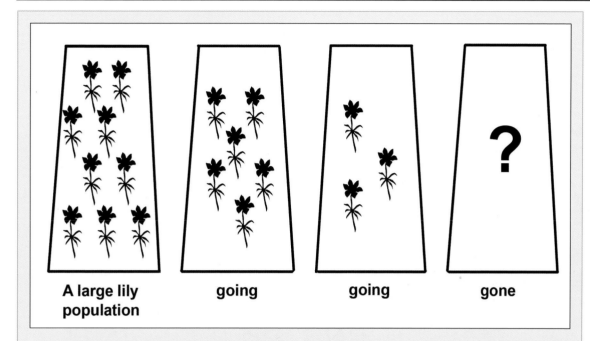

A large lily population   going   going   gone

SAVING LILIES—A FOUR POINT PRESCRIPTION

(1) Protect and create natural habitat wherever possible.

(2) Allow and promote disturbance events such as fire, grazing, rodent tunneling, haying, and brush removal.

(3) Stop planting invasive exotics, such as crested wheatgrass and smooth brome (for "improving" pasture and creating cover along road allowances). Wherever possible, replace invasive vegetation with native species.

(4) Remember that "to conserve the wild places where lilies grow is to preserve a vital part of ourselves—our cultural and spiritual well-being".

—*Adapted from Lawrence and Leighton (2005).*

Western red lily (*Lilium philadelphicum*) by Lavonia R. Stockelbach (1874–1966). A collection of her paintings of Canadian provincial and territorial official flowers is associated with the herbarium of Agriculture and Agri-Food Canada in Ottawa.

Painting of the official flower of Saskatchewan, western red lily (*Lilium philadelphicum*), from the Walter Coucill Canadian Centennial official flowers of Canada series (see Coucill 1966 cited in the first chapter of this book). Reproduced with the permission of the copyright holders, the Coucill family.

OFFICIAL PLANT EMBLEMS OF CANADA

MYTHS, LEGENDS, TALES, FOLKLORE AND INTERESTING FACTS

❦ According to Chippewa lore, a poultice of western red lily applied to the wounds of someone bitten by a dog would cause that animal's fangs to fall out.

❦ Iroquois tradition held that if the stems of two harvested western red lilies were allowed to dry out in the sun near each other, and they twisted together, one's wife was unfaithful.

❦ Still another belief among the Iroquois was that a boiled tea of the roots of western red lily should be used internally as an emetic and externally as a wash to cleanse a wife if her husband was unfaithful.

❦ In the Victorian era, "floriography" or the language of flowers was the basis of sending messages by careful choice of the composition and colour of the flowers included. A white lily conveyed the sentiment that the receiver was pure and sweet; a yellow lily could mean gratitude or jubilation; an orange lily, however, indicated hatred.

❦ The rose is the leading flower for the names of people ("Rose", "Rosie", "Rosalyn", etc.). The lily is the second most popular basis for floral names ("Lily", "Lil", Lilliane", etc.).

SOURCES OF ADDITIONAL INFORMATION

Barrows, E.M. 1979. Flower biology and arthropod associates of *Lilium philadelphicum*. Michigan Botanist 18: 109–115.

Edwards, J., and Jordan, J.R. 1992. Reversible anther opening in *Lilium philadelphicum* (Liliaceae): a possible means of enhancing male fitness. Am. J. Bot. 79: 144–148.

Lawrence, B. 1996. *Lilium philadelphicum* in Saskatchewan. The lily yearbook of the North American Lily Society 48/49: 115–117.

Lawrence, B.J., and Leighton, A.L. 2005. Prairie phoenix. *Lilium philadelphicum*. The red lily in Saskatchewan. Nature Saskatchewan, Regina, SK. 139 pp.

May, J.L. 2007. Forcing cycles speed growth in western red lily. Native Plants Journal 8(1): 11, 12, 14, 16.

Morrison, D. 1948. The prairie lily. Saskatchewan's floral emblem. School Aids and Text Book Publishing Company, Regina, SK. 40 pp.

Olson, J. 1991. Native lily conservation in Wisconsin. The lily yearbook of the North American Lily Society 44: 74–78.

Skinner, M.W. 2002. *Lilium*. *In* Flora of North America North of Mexico. *Edited by* Flora of North America Editorial Committee. Oxford University press, Oxford, U.K. Vol. 26. pp. 172–197.

Western red lily (*Lilium philadelphicum*). Source: D. Powell, United States Department of Agriculture Forestry Service.

Western red lily (*Lilium philadelphicum*). Source: D. Powell, United States Department of Agriculture Forestry Service.

TREE: WHITE BIRCH

A stand of white birch (*Betula papyrifera*). Courtesy of J. O'Brien, United States Department of Agriculture Forest Service.

SYMBOLISM

White birch is common in the northern three-quarters of Saskatchewan, and is a significant component of the province's forest resources. It is also an exceptionally attractive, easily recognized tree. Accordingly, the species is a good choice as the province's arboreal emblem. In several native North American cultures, birch symbolizes the feminine, or Mother Nature and, in the Old World, birch species have been associated historically with renewal rites of spring.

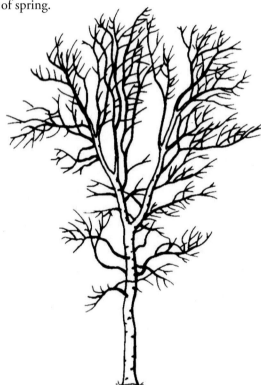

Silhouette of white birch (*Betula papyrifera*). Source: Farrar, J.L. 1995. Trees in Canada. Canadian Forest Service and Fitzhenry and Whiteside, Markham, ON, Canada. Reproduced with permission.

NAMES

Latin Names
Betula papyrifera Marsh.

The genus name *Betula* is based on *betulla*, the Latin name for birch (some authorities ascribe *Betula* to the Celtic *betu*, meaning tree and shining, a reference to the white bark of some species). *Papyrifera* is from the Greek word *papurus*, meaning papyrus or paper, referring to the paper-thin bark that has actually been used as paper, + the Greek *fero*, or Latin *ferre*, to bear, carry, or bring, i.e., "paper bearing".

English Names
White birch. Also: American white birch, canoe birch, paper birch, silver birch. The names white and silver birch are based on the bark colour; the names canoe birch and paper birch reflect the historical use of the bark by Native Americans for canoes and writing parchment, respectively. The name "white birch" is sometimes used for white-barked *Betula* species other than *B. papyrifera* (especially Eurasian species), but is adopted here as it is the name used in legislation recognizing the species as the arboreal emblem of Saskatchewan. Paper birch is a more widely used name for *B. papyrifera*.

French Names
Bouleau blanc. Also bouleau à papier, bouleau à canot.

HISTORY

Canada
The white birch was designated the provincial tree of Saskatchewan in 1988. Another birch species, yellow birch (*B. alleghaniensis*), was adopted in 1993 as the provincial tree of Quebec.

Foreign
The white birch was recognized as the New Hampshire state tree in 1947. The silver birch (*B. pendula*) is the national tree of Finland. The "birch" is the national tree of Russia.

Young birch tree hugger. Source: Thinkstock.

APPEARANCE

Betula papyrifera grows occasionally as a shrub but is usually a deciduous tree up to 35 m (115 feet) in height and 80 cm (32 inches) in diameter at breast height.

Most trees in Canada are 15–25 m (49–82 feet) and 30–40 cm (12–16 inches) in diameter at maturity. There may be a single or several stems (trunks), and often the presence of several trunks is the result of damage to a young plant by browsing animals. The tree is shallow-rooted, most of the roots found in the top 60 cm (2 feet) of soil. The bark of young trunks and branches is dark reddish brown, and smooth, and in mature trunks it is creamy to chalky white or pale (infrequently dark brown) with small black marks and scars, and elongated horizontal lenticels (natural openings in the bark that allow for gaseous exchange). The chalky white covering on the bark can rub off onto clothing. The inner bark is often reddish-orange, turning black with age. The outer bark is easily peeled off in sheets; however, doing so results in the reddish-orange bark dying and turning an ugly black; the papery white outer bark never grows back, although a new bark develops if removal of bark is not so extensive that it kills the tree. The flowers appear in male and female catkins. The male catkins are 4–10 cm or 1.5–4 inches long at maturity in the spring, shorter during the previous late fall when they develop, and during the winter. They hang down, singly or up to five in a cluster, from the ends of branches. The female catkins, up to 5 cm or 2 inches long, are upright and somewhat back from the ends of branches where the male catkins are located. The fruiting cones hang down, and are cylindrical, brownish, and 2.5–5 cm (1–2 inches) long. The tiny, papery "seeds" (fruits or nutlets) are two-winged. White birch is considered to be a short-lived species; few trees live longer than 140 years (some for up to 200 years), and most survive for no longer than 70 years.

White birch (*Betula papyrifera*) in fall, photographed in Ottawa in 2001. Photo© courtesy of Daniel Tigner, Canadian Forest Tree Essences, www.essences.ca.

A BIODIVERSITY TREASURE

CLASSIFICATION

Family: Betulaceae (birch family).

There are about 35 species of *Betula*, distributed in north temperate regions of the world. About 18 species are native to North America north of Mexico, most of these occurring in Canada. *Betula papyrifera* is a very variable species, some authorities recognizing as many as six varieties. As well, hybridization with several other species of *Betula* occurs, complicating identification. White birch crosses with most of the other birches that it comes in contact with across Canada, even with species as different as yellow birch (*B. alleghaniensis*) or bog birch (*B. pumila*). There are four other birches that occur naturally in Saskatchewan and white birch hybridizes with three of them; with water birch (*B. occidentalis*) to produce *B. ×utahensis*, with resin birch (*B. neoalaskana*) to produce *B. ×winteri*, and with bog birch (*B. pumila*) to produce *B. ×sandbergii*. Hybrids with *B. glandulosa* which also occurs in Saskatchewan remain to be documented. Canadian taxonomists J.R. Dugle, W.H. Brittain, and W.F. Grant have contributed much to an understanding of the evolution and classification of birches. Grant received the Lawson Medal from the Canadian Botanical Association in 1989 (CBA Bulletin 22(4): 37), largely for his work on birch. For a series of important papers by Brittain and Grant, see Furlow (1997).

White birch (*Betula papyrifera*). A, a branch bearing three, hanging, flowering male catkins at the end and two upright, flowering female catkins farther back. B, branches bearing young male catkins at the tips and fruiting catkins farther back. C, branch in winter with young male catkins. D, branch in early spring, with unfolding leaves and a female catkin. E, scale from a fruiting catkin. F, two-winged "seed" (nutlet). Source: Sargent, C.S. 1896. The silva of North America. Houghton, Mifflin and Company, Boston, MA. Vol. 9, plate 451.

GEOGRAPHY

Betula papyrifera occurs across northern North America, from Newfoundland to northwestern Alaska, from the treeline in the north southward to the northern United States, from Washington state to New York, with scattered populations in Iowa, Nebraska, the Dakotas, and on a few high mountains in North Carolina. The tree occurs in all provinces and territories of Canada, except Nunavut.

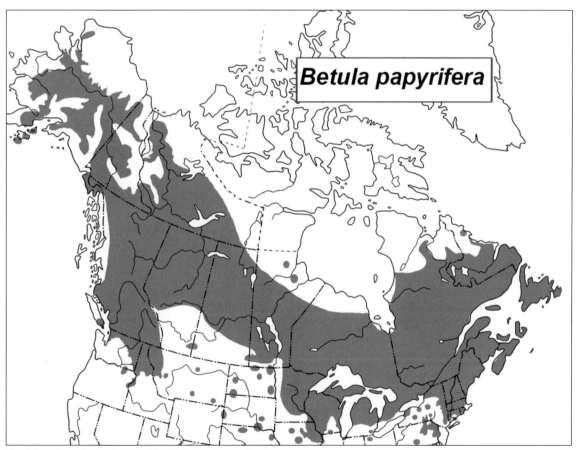

Betula papyrifera

North American distribution of white birch (*Betula papyrifera*).

White birch (*Betula papyrifera*) in the Saguenay Region of Quebec. Source: Wikimedia (photographer: D. Ménard; Creative Commons Attribution-Share Alike 2.0 license).

A BIODIVERSITY TREASURE

ECOLOGY

White birch is adapted to colonizing areas cleared by fire, often regenerating by stump sprouts, and often appearing following logging and abandonment of cleared land. The thin, inflammable bark makes the tree susceptible to fire. The species frequently grows in pure stands or in associations with conifers.

Birch trees are susceptible to dieback, a condition in which there is a general deterioration and eventual death of the trees. Symptoms may include sparse, stunted foliage near the top of the tree, followed by progressive dieing off of branches from the top of the tree downwards. The foliage that remains on the tree may be stunted and chlorotic (yellow). White birch die-back in eastern Canada and the adjacent U.S. has been interpreted as due in part to global warming, fungus disease, or a physiological response to heat and drought.

Habitat

White birch occurs in moist, more or less open, upland forests, often on rocky slopes, and sometimes in swampy woods. It is common on the margins of forests, in clearings in closed forests, on rock cliffs, in ravines, and along shores. The tree occupies a wide range of soil types, including peat, but does best on deep, well-drained, fertile soils. It is intolerant of shade, and prefers cool, moist sites.

Inter-species Relationships

White birch is an important browse plant for moose and white-tailed deer. Snowshoe hares consume the seedlings and saplings, and porcupines feed on the inner bark of trees. Hare and beaver also eat the young plants. Birds and small mammals eat the buds, catkins, and seeds. Voles and shrews also eat the seeds. Yellow-bellied sapsuckers peck holes in the bark to feed on the sap, and subsequently hummingbirds and red squirrels feed on the resulting sapwells. In addition to furnishing food for animals, white birch also provides cover for deer and moose, and many cavity-nesting birds. The bronze birch borer (described in the chapter on Quebec emblems) is the most well known insect found on white birch.

Pollination and Dispersal

Flowering occurs in late spring, and pollination is by wind. The fruiting cones shed winged seeds that are mostly wind-distributed in the fall. The seeds are quite small, about 3.4 million in a kilogram (1.5 million in a pound). In good seed years, some trees can produce more than 10 million seeds. Most seeds fall from 30–61 m (100–200 feet) from the parent tree, but seeds may travel considerable distances by being blown across crusted snow. Most successful seeds germinate the following spring, but a small proportion of the seeds may remain viable for several years on the forest floor.

Peeling bark of white birch (*Betula papyrifera*). Photo taken on June 6, 1999 in the Ottawa National Forest in Michigan's Upper Peninsula, courtesy of Joseph G. O'Brien, USDA Forest Service, and Bugwood.org.

Native American village scene showing birch bark canoes. Source: Thinkstock.

USES

Historically, North American Indians used white birch for a wide range of medicinal and construction purposes. The bark is waterproof because of a high oil content. It was especially used for many items, including canoes, baskets, containers for food and liquids, shelters, bathtubs, clothing, kindling, torches, drums, moosecallers, paper, playing cards, and even as a cast for broken limbs. Canoes were made by stretching stripped bark over frames of white cedar, sewing the pieces of bark together with tamarack roots, and caulking the seams with pine or balsam fir resin. The bark has been used to make "sunglasses" to prevent damage from snow glare; this was simply a strip of bark about 5 cm (2 inches) wide in which lenticels were used as eye apertures. Indians used the strong, flexible wood to construct such items as spears, bows, arrows, snowshoes, and sleds. Occasionally Indians ate fresh cambium (the growing portion of the trunk, between the wood and the bark).

Today, white birch wood is mostly valuable as lumber, plywood, veneer, fuel, and pulpwood. It is employed for furniture and cabinets, flooring, and for specialty wood products including clothespins, spools, pool cues, golf tees, broom handles, and toys. The odourless and tasteless qualities of the wood, as well as its uniform texture and white appearance, make it useful for ice cream sticks, toothpicks, and tongue depressors. Although burned as firewood, giving off considerable heat even when green, birch tends to coat chimneys with a layer of creosote, posing a fire danger.

White birch syrup, produced in the manner of maple syrup, is a cottage industry in North America,

especially in Canada and Alaska. Birch trees are occasionally used to produce alcoholic or non-alcoholic birch beer in Europe and North America (for more information, see the discussion of culinary uses of yellow birch, *B. alleghaniensis*, in the chapter on Quebec emblems). Occasionally the species is used as a source of medicinal extracts.

Cree hunter calling a moose on a birch-bark trumpet. Source: http://publicdomainclip-art.blogspot.com/2007/10/native-american-heritage-month-calling.html.

White birch is a popular ornamental or landscape tree, because of its graceful form (often forming clumps) and attractive bark. It is also used for revegetation and soil stabilization, including severely disturbed sites such as mine spoils.

TOXICITY

Birch sawdust can cause dermatitis in sensitive individuals, but generally birches are not considered toxic, either to humans or animals, and as noted above, birch syrup is considered a gourmet item.

Birch syrup. Photo courtesy of Kahiltna Birchworks, http://www.alaskabirchsyrup.com/.

CULTIVATION

White birch is a significant forestry species, and there is considerable information on its management. Although there are several white-barked birch species native to Europe, *B. papyrifera* has been a popular ornamental there since about 1750. Wild plants are occasionally transplanted from nature, but homeowners can conveniently plant containerized stock, and ornamental cultivars are available. Roots spread at least twice the height of the tree, so ample space should be allowed. The soil should be well draining (sand, silt, or loam), but nevertheless considerable moisture may be required (during the spring, a large tree can consume enough water in one day to fill about ten bathtubs). An open site providing full sun is best, and some protection from wind is beneficial. Birches tend to be well-formed, not requiring much pruning. Because cut branches exude considerable sap, as with maples, pruning should not be done in early spring when sap is flowing, or in late summer or fall, when cuts may be slow to heal. It has been recommended that *B. papyrifera* not be planted where it will grow above cars, because honeydew from aphids on the tree can coat vehicles with a sticky slime that attracts dirt.

WHY IS MY BIRCH TURNING BROWN?

Browning of the leaves of white-barked birches, including *B. papyrifera*, is usually due to the birch leafminer (*Fenusa pusilla*), a sawfly wasp introduced from Europe. The greenish-white larvae (up to 6 mm or 0.24 inch in length) feed on tissue between the upper and lower leaf surfaces and this causes portions of the leaf to die and turn brown. Although a number of birch trees are resistant to the insect, most of these do not have white bark and are not popular as ornamentals. Attempts to produce resistant cultivars through hybridization have not yet been successful. Trees can withstand a heavy infestation but become weakened if the attacks continue. Some birches sold as white birch are short-lived hybrids of the European *B. pendula* that die after a few decades regardless of leafminer infestations. *Betula papyrifera* can be distinguished from these plants by its short pointed instead of long pointed leaves.

Birch leaf almost totally mined by several larvae of birch leafminer (*Fenusa pusilla*). Source: Thérèse Arcand, Natural Resources Canada, Canadian Forest Service, Laurentian Forestry Centre.

CONSERVATION STATUS

Throughout most of its range, white birch is abundant, and not at risk. However, in some places along its southern range limit it is threatened. For example, it is Vulnerable in Indiana, Imperiled in Illinois, Virginia, West Virginia, and Wyoming, and Critically Imperiled in Colorado and Tennessee.

YES! PEELING OFF THE ATTRACTIVE WHITE BARK CAN KILL BIRCH TREES.

Damage caused by peeling the bark from the trunk of a white birch (*Betula papyrifera*). Source: Thinkstock.

MYTHS, LEGENDS, TALES, FOLKLORE AND INTERESTING FACTS

✤ White birch was a sacred tree for the Ojibwa Indians, who placed bark on the coffins when burying their dead. While gathering material from the trees, offerings of tobacco were made to the Great Spirit, Winabojo, and to Grandmother Earth.

✤ Ojibwas claimed that the birch was never struck by lightning and offered a safe place during thunderstorms. Curiously reminiscent, European farmers sometimes planted birch trees around their houses in the belief that this would protect them against lightning. (Since birches are generally not the tallest trees in a region, perhaps they are less likely to be struck by lightning and this gave rise to the impression that they are immune.)

✤ The Ukrainian word for the month of March is *berezen*, meaning "time when the birch trees flower".

✤ Native Americans produced a beautiful art form called birch bark biting, by which marks were made to create intricate designs. Birch bark bitings, a tradition dating back centuries, were usually made by First Nations women as a social activity at gatherings.

✤ White birch has an entirely positive image, making it a good choice as a symbol, in contrast to the negative reputation of some other trees. White poplar (*Populus alba*), for example, spreads very aggressively from root suckers and is regarded as a serious weed. (For a discussion of "bad trees" see http://forestry.about.com/b/2007/05/23/pick-a-tree-you-simply-cant-stand.htm.)

✤ Bark from white birch was used by North American Indians to prepare scrolls, inscribed with figures, maps, and in some cases ancient language systems. Some of these scrolls, deposited in museums, are at least 400 years of age. Birch bark scrolls (based on other species of *Betula*) are also known from the Old World. The British Museum has some birch scrolls from Afghanistan that are 2,000 years old, inscribed with Buddhist hymns, medical treatments, and historical details.

White birch (*Betula papyrifera*) in winter, photographed in Val-des-Monts, Quebec, in 2001. Photo© courtesy of Daniel Tigner, Canadian Forest Tree Essences, www.essences.ca.

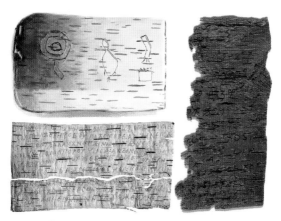

Portions of ancient birch bark scrolls: top left: Ojibwe hieroglyphics (considered sacred, these symbols are known only to some elders, and their meanings are usually kept secret); bottom left: 800 year old Russian scroll; right 2,000 year old Afghanistan scroll. Source: Wikipedia.

SOURCES OF ADDITIONAL INFORMATION

Assing, K., Nielsen, C.H., and Poulsen, L.K. 2006. Immunological characteristics of subjects with asymptomatic skin sensitization to birch and grass pollen. Clinical & Experimental Allergy 36: 283–292.

Barnes, B.V., Dancik, B.P., and Sharik, T.L. 1974. Natural hybridization of yellow birch and paper birch. Forest Sci. 20: 215–221.

Clennett, C., and Sanderson, H. 2002. *Betula papyrifera*. Curtis's Botanical Magazine 19: 40–48.

Dugle, J.R. 1966. A taxonomic study of western Canadian species in the genus *Betula*. Can. J. Bot. 44: 929–1007.

Furlow, J.J. 1997. *Betula. In* Flora of North America North of Mexico. *Edited by* Flora of North America Editorial Committee. Oxford University press, Oxford, U.K. Vol. 3. pp. 516–530.

Haack, R.A. 1996. Will global warming alter paper birch susceptibility to bronze birch borer attack? *In* Dynamics of forest herbivory: quest for pattern and principle. *Edited by* W.J. Mattson, P. Niemelä, and M. Rousi. U.S. Dept. Agriculture Forest Service General Technical Report NC 183. pp. 234–247.

Hutnik, R.J., and Cunningham, F.E. 1961. Silvical characteristics of paper birch. U.S. Dept. Agriculture, Forest Service, Northeastern Forest Experiment Station, Upper Danby, PA, Station Paper No. 141. 24 pp.

Hyvarinen, M.J. 1968. Paper birch, its characteristics, properties, and uses: a review of recent literature. North Central Forest Experiment Station, Forest Service, U.S. Dept. Agriculture Forest Service General Technical Report NC 22, Saint Paul, Minn. 12 pp.

Oldenmeyer, J.L. 1982. Estimating production of paper birch and utilization by browsers. Can. J. Forest Res. 12: 52–57.

Peterson, E.B. 1997. Paper birch managers' handbook for British Columbia. British Columbia. Ministry of Forests, Victoria, B.C., and Forestry Canada. 133 pp.

Safford, L.O. 1983. Silvicultural guide for paper birch in the Northeast (revised). United States Department of Agriculture, Forest Service, Northeastern Forest Exp. Station, Broomall, PA, Research Paper NE 535. 29 pp.

Wilder, N., Lousier, J.D., and Hawkins, C. (*Editors.*) 2002. Proceedings of the Paper Birch Workshop and Conference, September 19-22, 2001, Prince George, BC, Canada. University of Northern British Columbia, Prince George, B.C. 166 pp.

White birch (*Betula papyrifera*) trees by a lake. Source: Wikipedia (photographer: W.-C. Poon; Creative Commons Attribution-Share Alike 2.5 Generic license).

GRASS: NEEDLE-AND-THREAD GRASS

Hesperostipa comata, growing in a field near Lyons, Colorado. Source: Wikipedia (photographer: C.M. Sauer: Creative Commons Attribution-Share Alike Unported license).

SYMBOLISM

Needle-and-thread grass has become symbolic of the movement to protect declining natural prairie grasslands. As the dominant grass of the province's mixed grassland eco-region, and also common in the moist mixed grassland and aspen parkland eco-regions, it is an excellent representative of the natural prairie ecosystems of Saskatchewan. Moreover, since the plant is a protein-rich grass that provides important forage for grazing cattle, the species well represents the sustainable agricultural industry of the province.

Needle-and-thread grass (*Hesperostipa comata*). Source: Looman, J., and Best, K.F. 1979. Budd's flora of the Canadian prairie provinces. Agriculture Canada Research Branch Publication 1662.

NAMES

Latin Names

Hesperostipa comata (Trin. & Rupr.) Barkworth subsp. *comata* (= *Stipa comata*, a name used in the older literature). The genus name *Hesperostipa* is from the Greek *hesperos*, "west" (for the western North American distribution), + the name of the Eurasian grass genus *Stipa*. The name *Stipa* is based on the Latin *stipa*, meaning "oakum", i.e., a combination of fibres and tar used to caulk joints; the name was applied to the plants because the grass inflorescences were reminiscent of a loose bunch of fibres; as well, a species of *Stipa*, *S. tenacissima*, was employed as a source of fibres used for cordage, a component of oakum. *Comata* in the scientific name is a Latin word meaning "head of hair", and is also based on the appearance of the mass of hair-like awns of the inflorescence.

English Names

Needle-and-thread grass. Also: speargrass, common speargrass, western speargrass, needle and thread, needleandthread, sewing needlegrass, western needlegrass. Subspecies *intermedia* has been called intermediate needle and thread. The name needle-and-thread grass is based on the sharp, needle-like "seeds" (fruits, technically caryopses) attached to a long thread-like, thin awn that when dried often becomes curly, all of this resembling a threaded needle.

French Names

Stipe chevelue. Also: stipe comateuse.

HISTORY

Canada

Needle-and-thread grass was chosen as the provincial emblem by a coalition of environmental, wildlife, and agricultural organizations, acting through the "Prairie Conservation Action Plan", in order to maintain the native prairie ecosystem of Saskatchewan. It was designated the official grass of Saskatchewan in 2001. The conservation-oriented groups backed *H. comata* because of its value to both prairie ecosystems and to ranching. Rough fescue (*Festuca scabrella*), another prominent native prairie grass, became the official grass emblem of Alberta in 2003.

Foreign

Hesperostipa species have not received any form of honourary recognition, except for *H. comata* as the official grass of Saskatchewan. Seventeen U.S. states have official grasses (http://en.wikipedia.org/wiki/List_of_U.S._state_grasses). Given the fact that grasses provide more food for humans and livestock than any other family of plants, grass species are remarkably absent as official emblems of political regions of most of the world.

APPEARANCE

Needle-and-thread grass is a "bunchgrass", the small clumps generally from 2.5–10 cm (1–4 inches) in diameter at the base, and widely spaced. The plant is a perennial herb, growing from its base in early spring or when moisture becomes available. The leaves have narrow blades (generally 3–8 mm or 0.1–0.4 inch) that are usually inrolled, are 5–40 cm (2–16 inches) long, and taper to a sharp point. The fruiting stems are generally 30–90 cm (1–3 feet) tall. The plant reproduces by seed and also by tillers (rooting branches produced from the base). The flowering head is nodding, loosely spreading, and 10–50 cm (4–20 inches) long. The seeds have a sharp attachment point.

"Awns" in botany are either hair-like or bristle-like appendages on a larger structure, or in the case of the Asteraceae (daisy family), the individual elements of the set of bracts (scales, bristles, or hairs) at the base of the florets. Awns are characteristic of many grass species, where they extend from the lemmas of the florets (lemmas are the outer, and paleas are the inner, of the pair of bracts typically subtending a grass floret). Awns may be several centimetres long or short, straight or curved, single or multiple per floret.

At maturity, the "seeds" (strictly these are fruits) are enclosed in the floral bracts (lemma and palea), and the awn is attached to the tip of the lemma. For simplicity, the entire dispersal unit (i.e., lemma, palea, seed) is commonly referred to as an "awned seed".

Needle-and-thread grass (*Hesperostipa comata* subsp. *comata*), courtesy of S. Hagwood, United States Bureau of Land Management.

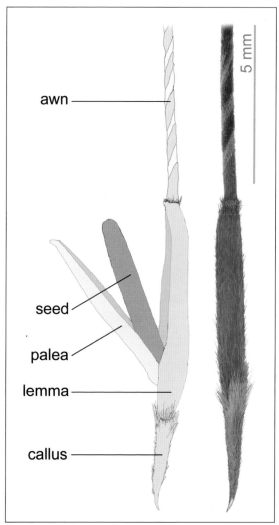

Parts of a mature floret of *Hesperostipa comata*. Drawings by P.M. Catling based on a specimen in the vascular plant collection of Agriculture Canada, collected by W.G. Dore on the high arid banks of the Qu'Appelle Valley in Saskatchewan on July 5, 1951. Dore made major contributions to the understanding of Canada's grass flora.

CLASSIFICATION

Family: Poaceae (Gramineae; grass family).

Hesperostipa is a genus of four North American species, all of which occur in Canada (a collection from Mexico has been represented as a fifth species, but is of uncertain status). *Hesperostipa comata* differs from the other species in having scabrous (rough to the touch) instead of pilose (hairy) awns and lemmas that are evenly white-pubescent instead of unevenly brown-pubescent. *Hesperostipa comata* subsp. *comata* has awns that are 4–12 cm (1.6–4.7 inches) long and are sinuous to curled at maturity. *Hesperostipa comata* subsp. *intermedia* (Scribn. & Tweedy) Barkworth has terminal awn segments that are 3–8 cm (1.2–3.1 inches) long, and are straight. Some authors recognize the two subspecies as varieties.

Needle-and-thread grass (*Hesperostipa comata* subsp. *comata*), courtesy of S. Hagwood, United States Bureau of Land Management.

GEOGRAPHY

Needle-and-thread grass grows throughout western Canada and western and Midwestern United States, from the Yukon to California, extending east to Ontario, Indiana, and Texas, and south into Mexico. Occasional populations occur as far east as Rhode Island and New York. The species is often the most common grass of the dry prairies of western Canada. It is rare in Ontario, Rhode Island, and Oklahoma.

Hesperostipa comata subsp. *comata* is widespread and frequently abundant in western and central North America. *Hesperostipa comata* subsp. *intermedia* is found from the Rocky Mountains of southern Canada through the Sierra Nevada to New Mexico. The two subspecies overlap geographically, but infrequently grow together.

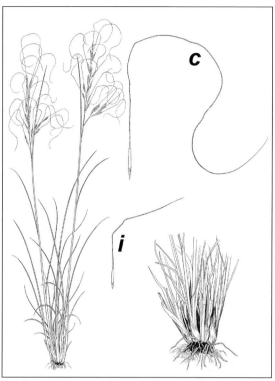

Needle-and-thread grass (*Hesperostipa comata*). Source: Unpublished drawings housed in the botanical illustration collection of the AAFC Vascular Plant Herbarium (DAO) in Ottawa. Prepared by Anne Hanes under the direction of M.E. Barkworth. c = subspecies *comata*, i = subspecies *intermedia*.

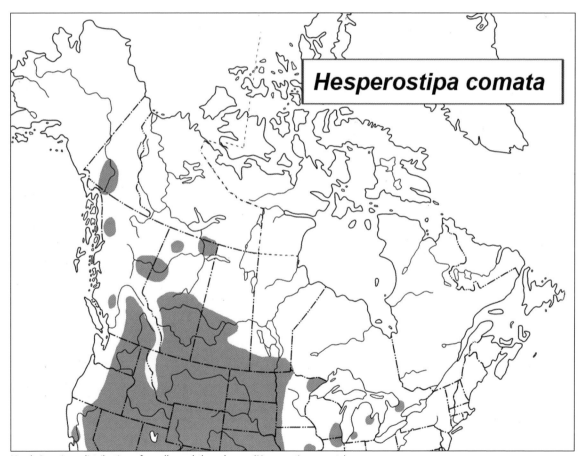

North American distribution of needle-and-thread grass (*Hesperostipa comata*).

ECOLOGY

Hesperostipa comata is adapted to well-drained, sandy and rocky soils. The fibrous root system may reach as deep as 1.5 m (5 feet), making the plant somewhat drought-resistant. However, much of the root system is quite shallow, and during hot weather the plants may become dormant, resuming growth when sufficient moisture becomes available. The species helps to protect drier soils from erosion from wind, heavy rains, and spring snow melt. The plants withstand grazing well, and indeed often increase in frequency under moderate grazing.

The prairies where needle-and-thread grass occurs once experienced periodic natural fires, and indeed it appears that North American Indians also frequently burned native prairies. The plant sprouts from its base following a fire, if the heat was not sufficiently severe to kill the underground parts.

Needle-and-thread is one of the grasses that have "rhizosheaths" formed by sand grains adhering to the roots. Rhizosheaths are especially common in grass species found in sandy soils where drought is frequent. Sticky mucilage secreted from the roots results in them becoming encased in a layer of sand. These structures are important because it has been found that nitrogen-fixing bacteria are associated with them, and enrich the soil around the roots, benefiting the plants. Also, water uptake and retention by the plants are sometimes improved, and it has been hypothesized that rhizosheaths are protective against pests and low temperatures. Rhizosheaths are thought to improve the success of species under stressful conditions, such as drought and soil infertility.

Habitat

Hesperostipa comata subsp. *comata* occurs in cool deserts, grasslands, and sagebrush associations, at elevations of 200–2,500 m (650–8,200 feet). It is often found in disturbed areas. *Hesperostipa comata* subsp. *intermedia* occurs in pinyon-juniper woodlands at elevations of 2,175–3,075 m (7,100–10,000 feet).

Inter-species Relationships

Hesperostipa comata is eaten by wildlife, including mule deer, rabbits, and black-tailed prairie dogs. Mostly it is the foliage that is attractive, but seeds and roots may also be eaten. To some extent, animals avoid grazing mature plants, because of the damaging awned seeds. The plants provide cover for sage grouse, other birds, and small mammals.

Pollination and Dispersal

Grasses are usually wind-pollinated, but wind is of limited pollination significance in needle-and-thread grass since it produces mostly cleistogamous seeds (i.e., developing from self-pollination in closed flowers). The seeds are dispersed soon after they mature. The long awns and hairs on the lemmas and awns facilitate attachment to fur, and the 50 million bison that formerly roamed the North American plains may have been significant dispersal agents. As with some other grasses, the seeds have hygroscopic awns that bend with changes in humidity. In response to humidity, the sharp awn twists through several turns. The long awn braces against surrounding objects, and this transmits the twisting force to the seed, screwing the seed into the soil. Upon drying, the awn twists, and upon becoming moist as humidity increases, the awn untwists. Because backwardly-directed hairs on the lemma (which covers the seed) fix the position

of the seeds in the soil, and act like barbs, ensuring that the seeds move in only one direction, the seeds are propelled into the soil. (Commonly, this is compared to a screw, but in this case the screw twists downward regardless of the direction of rotation, and cannot be removed by any rotation.) The tip of the seed is slightly bent to facilitate digging into the soil (it digs a hole large enough for the body of the seed to more easily enter the soil).

"Seed" (fruit) and attached awn of needle-and-thread grass (*Hesperostipa comata*). Source: Wikipedia (photographer: S. Sauer; Creative Commons Attribution-Share Alike 3.0 Unported license).

USES

Needle-and-thread grass is most important as a key component of native prairies, and therefore for sustainable ranching. *Hesperostipa comata* is protein-rich (up to 20% in the early spring) and has some value for livestock. The plant is useful as forage during the spring before seeds develop, and again during the fall after the seeds have dropped. As noted below, when seeds are present the plants can be injurious. Accordingly, this grass is rarely planted for forage. It is, however, planted for prairie reclamation. The species has often been used in native prairie reclamation projects, to stabilize eroded or degraded sites, and to assist in rehabilitation of mining sites. The fibrous root system binds soil, reducing water and wind erosion.

TOXICITY

This species is not known to be poisonous, but mechanical injury to animals is common. The corkscrew action of the awned seeds coupled with the backwardly-projecting hairs not only serve to drill into soil, but also the skin of animals, including livestock, dogs, and people, sometimes damaging eyes, mouths, and ears. The barb-like hairs on the fruit prevent the seed from reversing its direction, and the seed continues to embed itself with every slight movement. Sheep have been known to shed their fleece because of excessive irritation of the skin by the awns. Livestock often exhibit avoidance of needle-and-thread grass while it is in its dangerous fruiting stage, but more readily consume it before and after the fruiting stage.

CULTIVATION

Needle-and-thread grass is a suitable subject for cultivation as an ornamental, especially in native plant gardens, and seeds are available from some garden sources. Seeds are sometimes dormant, requiring a period of cold, but generally plants can be established without pre-treatment. When the seeds are planted in containers, the awn end should be uppermost, with the pointed end down. This grass is preferably grown in well-drained soils, in full sunlight. Massed plantings make for an especially elegant appearance. Generally seeds are limited in availability, both for prairie rehabilitation and horticultural purposes. Seed sources can be found by searching the internet.

CONSERVATION STATUS

Hesperostipa comata is a widespread grass, not in need of special conservation measures over most of its range, but it may be threatened on the periphery of its range (such as in Ontario), where genetically unique plants are likely present. The prairie habitat in which it is typically found has been catastrophically diminished in North America since the arrival of European settlers. In Saskatchewan, more than three-quarters of the native prairie has been eliminated.

Fruiting branch of needle-and-thread grass (*Hesperostipa comata*). Source: Wikipedia (photographer: S. Sauer; Creative Commons Attribution-Share Alike 3.0 Unported license).

A BIODIVERSITY TREASURE

MYTHS, LEGENDS, TALES, FOLKLORE AND INTERESTING FACTS

🍁 In past times, Blackfoot Indians used the maturing of seed heads of needle-and-thread grass as a guide to the best time in the fall to hunt buffalo (i.e., bison) cows.

🍁 During a budgetary crisis in Colorado in 2003, it was suggested that the state adopt AstroTurf as the state's official grass, to encourage saving money by replacing lawns that require expensive maintenance (The Colorado Springs Gazette, October 21, 2003). Using native drought-tolerant vegetation, such as needle-and-thread, should have been considered as an option.

🍁 The children of Native American tribes used the seeds of needle-and-thread grass as toy darts.

🍁 As Lewis and Clark travelled through Montana in 1806, Lewis noted in his journal that the seeds of needle-and-thread penetrated his shoes and leather pants and caused his dog great suffering. This is one of the earliest references to the remarkable characteristics of the seeds.

SOURCES OF ADDITIONAL INFORMATION

Barkworth, M.E. 2007. *Hesperostipa* (M.K. Elias) Barkworth. *In* Flora of North America, Vol. 24, Magnoliophyta: Commelinidae (in part): Poaceae, part 1. *Edited by* M.E. Barkworth et al. Oxford University Press, New York, NY. pp. 157–161.

Moen, H. 1998. Managing your native prairie parcels. Your guide to caring for native prairies in Saskatchewan. Saskatchewan Wetland Conservation Corporation. Regina, SK. 50 pp. http://www.swa.ca/Publications/Documents/ManagingNativePrairieParcels.pdf.

Reece, P.E., Bode, R.P., and Waller, S.S. 1988. Vigor of needle and thread and blue grama after short duration grazing. J. Range. Manage. 41: 287–291.

Saskatchewan Agriculture and Food. 2004. Managing Saskatchewan rangeland. 99 pp. http://www.vido.org/beefinfonet/management/images/ManagingSKRangeland.pdf

Trottier, G.C. 2002. A landowner's guide. Conservation of Canadian prairie grasslands. Environment Canada, Edmonton, AB. http://www.mb.ec.gc.ca/nature/whp/prgrass/df03s00.en.html.

Wasowski, S. 2002. Gardening with prairie plants. How to create beautiful native landscapes. University of Minnesota Press, Minneapolis, MN. 286 pp.

Wullstein, L.H., Bruening, M.L., and Bollen, W.B. 1979. Nitrogen fixation associated with sand grain root sheaths (rhizosheaths) of certain xeric grasses. Physiologia Plantarum 46: 1–4.

Needle-and-thread grass (*Hesperostipa comata* subsp. *comata*), courtesy of S. Hagwood, United States Bureau of Land Management.

YUKON

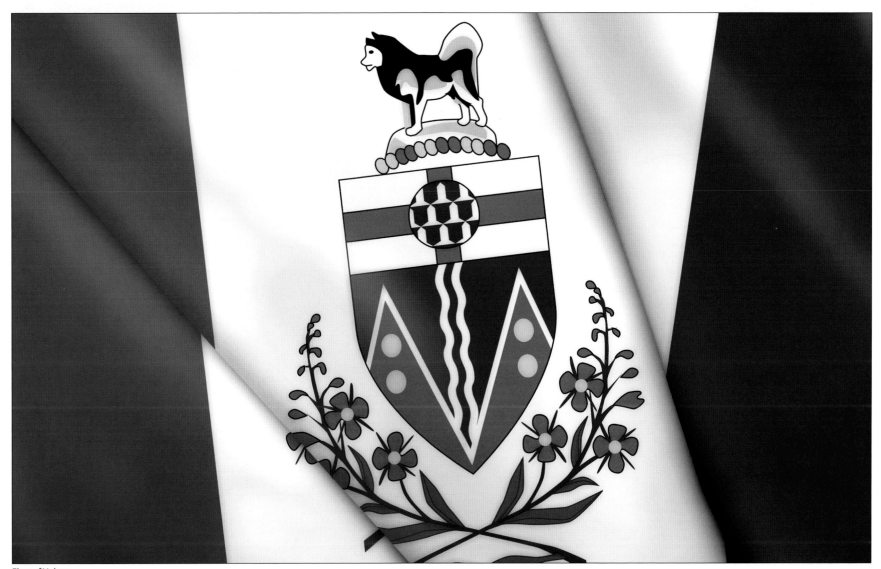

Flag of Yukon.

A YUKON LANDSCAPE: an autumn view of alpine shrub tundra.

FLORAL EMBLEM: FIREWEED

Fireweed (*Chamerion angustifolium*), at an elevation of 1,550 m (5,100 feet) in the West Julian Alps, Italy, photographed August 3, 2004. Photo courtesy of Amadej Trnkoczy.

"YUKON" OR "THE YUKON"?

"When the Yukon Act came into effect in 2003, in legal documents references to the government, its departments and officials became 'Yukon'. It is no longer Yukon Territory or The Yukon Territory.

HOWEVER, and this is direct from the communications officer of the Executive council Office: 'in speech, correspondence and in media coverage, it is a matter of style and preference.' 'Yukon' or 'the Yukon' are both acceptable."
—*Ryerson Review of Journalism, Dec. 23, 2008.*

"In body text, either 'Yukon' or 'the Yukon' is acceptable. However, Yukon-specific article, category and list titles should always use the form *Yukon* **without** the word *the*. For *the Northwest Territories*, however, the preferred form is the Northwest Territories in article text and in the titles of list articles, but geographic articles about the Northwest Territories (e.g., Ukulhaktok, Northwest Territories) do *not* use the word *the* in the title."
—*Wikipedia Manual of Style: http://en.wikipedia.org/wiki/Wikipedia:Manual_of_Style_(Canada-related_articles)*

YUKON IS BOTH TOUGH AND BEAUTIFUL . . . LIKE FIREWEED.

"This is the law of the Yukon, and ever she makes it plain:
Send not your foolish and feeble; send me your strong and your sane . . . "
—Robert Service in *The Law of the Yukon*

"Some say God was tired when He made it,
Some say it's a fine land to shun;
Maybe; but there's some as would trade it
For no land on earth—and I'm one."
—Robert Service in *The Spell of the Yukon*

SYMBOLISM

The hardiness and attractiveness of the ubiquitous fireweed make it a natural botanical representative of Yukon. Dazzling blankets of magenta or pink flowers along the sides of roads and mountains always impress visitors to the territory, and the displays are evident for many weeks during the summer and fall, from June to August. The ability of the plant to beautify areas that have been denuded by natural disasters and man-made disturbances reflect well on the people who have chosen to live with the challenges of Canada's north.

Fireweed (*Chamerion angustifolium*) on the Klondike Highway in British Columbia. Source: Wikipedia (photographer: Wknight94; Creative Commons Attribution-Share Alike 3.0 Unported license).

NAMES

Latin Names

Chamerion angustifolium (L.) Holub is a name that has been adopted recently. The species is known in most of the North American literature as *Epilobium angustifolium* and in much of the European literature as *Chamaenerion angustifolium*. The reason for the name change is discussed below.

Close-up photo of flowers of fireweed (*Chamerion angustifolium*), courtesy of G.D. Carr. The plants were growing near Cheney, Spokane Co., Washington State, on July 17, 2003.

The genus name *Chamerion* is based on the Greek *chamai*, dwarf + nerion, oleander; fireweed has narrow leaves like the ornamental oleander shrub. *Angustifolium* in the scientific name is from the Latin *angustus*, narrow + *folium*, leaf, indicating that the species has narrow leaves.

English Names

Fireweed. Also: common fireweed, perennial fireweed, narrow leaved fireweed, great willow herb, spiked willow-herb, rosebay willow herb, French willow, blooming Sally, wild asparagus, pink tops, purple rocket, wickup, wicopy.

The name "fireweed" usually refers to *Chamerion angustifolium* in North America, but in some parts of the world other species quickly colonize fire-ravaged areas, and are also known as fireweed. The name wild asparagus results from consumption of the young shoots which are sometimes eaten like asparagus. The "willow" in some variants of the name refers to the willow-like shape of the leaves; in Europe the plant has been called flowering willow, French willow, Persian willow, and rosebay willow. The name Sally is a corruption of *Salix* (the willow genus), still another reference to willow-like leaves. The name rosebay is a reference to the rosy flowers and the (allegedly) bay-like leaves (bay is the culinary plant *Laurus nobilis*).

French Names

Épilobe à feuilles étroites. Also: asperge, bouquet rouge, bouquets rouges, herbe à feu, lilas de montagne. In France: épilobe en épi, osier fleuri, laurier de Saint-Antoine.

Flowering and fruiting shoots and details of flower, fruit, and seed of fireweed (*Chamerion angustifolium*). Source: Hallier, E.H. 1885. Flora von Deutschland, edition 5 of D.F.L. von Schlechtendal et al. F.E. Köhler, Gera-Untermhaus, Germany. Vol. 22, plate 2256.

HISTORY

Canada

Fireweed was chosen as the floral emblem of the Yukon Territory by members of the Yukon Territorial Government on March 27, 1957, and the choice was made official by an ordinance on November 16, 1957. The prairie crocus had also been under consideration, but was rejected because it is the official flower of Manitoba (see the chapter on floral emblems of the province).

Foreign

It appears that no other political region of the world has employed fireweed or any of its close relatives as an official symbol.

APPEARANCE

Fireweed is a robust perennial herb, 1–3 m (3–10 feet) tall, with erect, reddish stems which are somewhat stout and slightly woody. The plant is topped by a long inflorescence of very attractive purple or pink (rarely white) flowers with petals 1–2 cm (0.4–0.8 inch) long. The alternate, lance–shaped leaves are 3–20 cm (1–8 inches) long, and characteristically reticulate-veiny on the lower surfaces. The flowers have four petals. The slender fruit is a linear capsule that splits from the apex. It is 5–8 cm (1–3 inches) long, and contains many brown seeds. The seeds are 1–1.3 mm (about 0.05 inch) long, and have a tuft of fine, white hairs at the apex.

CLASSIFICATION

Family: evening primrose family (Onagraceae).

Until the early 1990s, the genus *Epilobium* was generally considered to comprise about 170 species, including fireweed. Molecular analysis (see Baum et al. 1994) showed that eight species now placed in *Chamerion* are well separated from the remaining species, now left in *Epilobium*. All eight species of *Chamerion* are perennial herbs, restricted to the Northern Hemisphere, six of them native only to Eurasia. *Chamerion angustifolium* and the closely related *C. latifolium* (L.) Holub are circumboreal/circumarctic. The genus name *Chamaenerion*, which had also been employed, is not acceptable under the rules of nomenclature. For an authoritative review of the taxonomy of *Chamerion* and its relatives, see Wagner et al. (2007), cited below.

Chamerion angustifolium varies geographically in size and leaf shape, and in the past the classification of the species has been problematical. In North America, *C. angustifolium* subsp. *angustifolium* is characterized by small to medium-sized leaves lacking pubescence on the ribs of the lower side of the leaves, triporate (three-pored) pollen grains, and a chromosome number of $2n$ = 36. By contrast, subsp. *circumvagum* Mosquin has small to very large leaves with glabrous to densely pubescent leaf ribs, quadriporate (four-pored) pollen as well as triporate, and a chromosome number of $2n$ = 72. Subspecies *angustifolium* occurs in the arctic, boreal, and cordilleran regions of Canada, south to the approximate southern border of the boreal forest, while subspecies *circumvagum* occupies the area to the south and east. Plants with white petals and sepals are occasionally seen and may occur in groups. They have been recognized as f. *albiflorum* (Dumort.) Haussk. Another unusual color form is f. *spectabile* (Simmons) Fern., which has white petals with contrasting bright red sepals.

Chaemerion latifolium is often called broad-leaved fireweed (also river-beauty). Natural hybridization between it and *C. angustifolium* has been reported but is apparently rare. The former is the only species likely to be confused with *C. angustifolium* in North America and they can be separated as follows:

1a. Stems solitary or few, erect 0.1–3 m (mostly 1–2 m) long (tall); leaves membranous, reticulate-veiny beneath; petals 1–2 cm long; style pilose at base, longer than stamens; seeds 1–1.3 mm long. . . . . *C. angustifolium*

1b. Stems numerous, tufted, depressed or arched, less than 0.5 m long; leaves fleshy, not veiny; petals 1.8–3 cm; style glabrous at base, much shorter than stamens; seeds approx. 2 mm long . . . *C. latifolium*

GEOGRAPHY

Fireweed occurs in all Canadian provinces and territories. It is also extensively distributed in the U.S., except the southeastern states and Texas. The species is circumboreal, occurring widely in Eurasia.

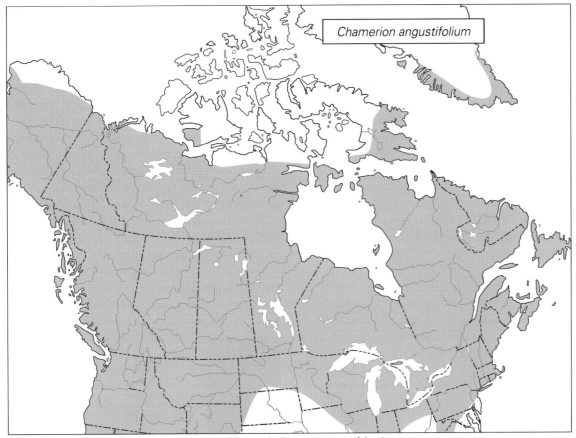

Chamerion angustifolium

Canadian and adjacent United States distribution of fireweed (*Chamerion angustifolium*).

Fireweed (*Chamerion angustifolium*). Source: Canadian Heritage. 2002 (revised edition). Symbols of Canada. Canadian Heritage, Ottawa, ON. Reproduced with permission.

A BIODIVERSITY TREASURE

ECOLOGY

Fireweed dominates many plant communities undergoing succession. It is common in streamside and upland habitats, and in logged and burned areas. This species is adapted to rapidly colonize newly disturbed habitats, especially where moist mineral soil is laid bare and considerable light is available.

Despite the "weed" in fireweed, this species is usually not a problem. Competition with conifer seedlings in revegetating burned land, and serving as the alternate host of conifer rusts have been noted as potential difficulties for forest managers. Fireweed has been observed as a weed of some vegetable crops in northern regions.

Habitat

Although fireweed can tolerate considerable shade, it grows well only in open locations. In North America it characteristically grows on gravelly, acidic soils, pH varying from as low as 3.5 to circumneutral, but the plant also tolerates somewhat basic soils. Favourite habitats include coniferous and mixed forests, aspen parklands, grasslands, and muskegs, disturbed regions such as cut-over or burned forests and swamps, avalanche zones, riverbars, embankments of highways, and railways, waste places, and old fields.

Inter-species Relationships

Numerous wild mammals (including moose, caribou, elk, deer, mountain goats, muskrats, and hares), and some wild birds graze on fireweed, which is moderately nutritious and palatable. Fireweed will also be consumed by domestic livestock, although it is considered only fair as forage. The seeds are eaten by small mammals such as chipmunks. Hummingbirds are attracted to the nectar. Butterflies and bees collect both the nectar and pollen. Hundreds of insect species feed on fireweed.

Pollination and Dispersal

Inbreeding depression (reduced fitness following self-fertilization, resulting in poor seed production) is sometimes extreme in fireweed, making cross-pollination very important. Individual flowers mature their pollen before the stigma is receptive, to prevent selfing. Bees, moths, and butterflies are important pollinators of fireweed. They characteristically move from the bottom towards the top of the flowering stem. The insects first deposit pollen on the older, lower flowers, which have receptive stigmas, but receive no pollen from them since their pollen was released earlier. Then, they acquire pollen from the younger, upper flowers, which have not yet opened their stigmas.

The two North American subspecies sometimes grow together, and population biologists have been interested in studying how they can coexist and remain distinct. Most hybrids are sterile. Hybridization between the two is difficult, partly because they differ in chromosome number, and partly because they differ in flowering time. Additionally, pollinators behave differently on the two subspecies.

The seeds have a tuft of long hairs at one end, which serves as a sail for wind distribution. The extremely numerous seeds produced can be carried by wind for hundreds of kilometers. A Swedish study revealed that up to half of the seed disperses over the landscape more than 100 m (328 feet) above the ground. Humidity expands the diameter of the seed hairs, decreasing loft, an adaptation which tends to deposit the seeds in humid areas and during wet periods, thus ensuring adequate moisture for germination. The seeds are non-dormant and short-lived, rarely remaining viable for more than 3 years, and generally germinating as soon as a suitable site is found. Although seeds account for the remarkable ability of fireweed to colonize new areas, once germination occurs, vegetative reproduction by rhizome spread becomes more important than sexual reproduction for propagating the plant at a given site. Fragmenting the rhizomes stimulates production of shoots, as with dandelions, contributing to the reputation of fireweed as a hard-to-eradicate weed. Most of the rhizomes and roots occur in the top 5 cm (2 inches) of mineral soils, and this underground portion can survive relatively intense fires. Indeed, the rhizomes sprout new shoots vigorously a few weeks following destruction of the old shoots. Young plants overwinter as rosettes. The aboveground shoots of older plants are killed by frost, but the plants overwinter as rhizomes.

The Yukon flag, showing fireweed at the base of the central, white vertical panel.

USES

Food. The most important agricultural significance of fireweed is as a honey plant, providing considerable nectar to bees. Near Seattle, Washington, fireweed is common and beekeepers in the area market "fireweed honey" as a specialty item. Indeed, in the past, beekeepers in coastal Washington and Oregon often set up their hives in areas that were being colonized by fireweed. Indigenous people in both the Old and New Worlds have used fireweed as food, for example the young shoots consumed as greens, the leaves used to make tea, the petals made into jelly, and the roots eaten as a vegetable. In Russia, fireweed leaves are still used as a tea called "Kaporie tea". The Russian name "Ivan's tea" also reflects the use of fireweed for tea in Russia. (The high tannin content suggests that consumption of fireweed tea should be limited. As is well-known, tannins in common tea are denatured by adding milk, a practice that is medically sensible.)

Fibre. An antiquated use of the plant was the incorporation of the down of the seeds into cotton and fur to make clothing. Native Americans in the Pacific Northwest employed the stem fibres to make twine and fishnets.

Reclamation. The species is widely used for revegetation and soil stabilization of northern and alpine disturbed sites, such as mined lands, roadways, and logged areas. It is also useful for providing plant cover where oil spills have occurred, as well as for strip-mined areas and mine spoil deposits.

Medicines and Cosmetics. Native Americans employed fireweed juice to soothe skin irritation and burns, a practice also found in European herbal medicine. In both European and North American folk medicine, fireweed has been used as tea to relieve stomach upset, respiratory complaints (including whooping cough and asthma), and constipation. These uses could be explained by the high tannin content (and therefore astringency) of fireweed, or by the presence of antiseptic, healing compounds. Commercial creams, lotions, after-sun balms, after-shave ointments, and baby care products that include fireweed extracts have been introduced to the marketplace in recent years.

BEHIND THE BEAUTY

Fireweed transforms a burned black and grey landscape into a rolling pinkish sea extending to the horizons. The visual impact and the strength of natural rejuvenation are compelling. But fireweed is also a key player in the dynamic rebirth of the boreal forest, which is forever locked in a cycle of destruction and regeneration. Fires are a natural process occurring in different places at different times. Fireweed is the first stage in a succession of habitat and vegetation changes that culminate in the restoration of the original forest. Mature boreal forests contain only a fraction of the biodiversity of the boreal forest ecosystem. Most biodiversity is distributed among the series of changing habitats that follow fires. Fireweed is the most important of many plants and animals that are uniquely adapted to early post-fire situations. Many of these are virtually absent from the mature forest. Without fire and the resulting gradient of habitats beginning with the fireweed community, biodiversity in the boreal forest would be greatly reduced.

Young girl with an excavated plant of fireweed (*Chamerion angustifolium*). Photo taken July 3, 2002 in Benewah County, Idaho, courtesy of Richard Old (XID Services, Inc.) and Bugwood.org.

CULTIVATION

Fireweed is occasionally grown as an ornamental, admired for its easy cultivation, spectacular floral display, and deep red fall foliage, although its weedy, aggressive tendencies sometimes make it undesirable. Nevertheless, fireweed is an excellent addition to wild-flower gardens in cold climates. The plants can grow in shade, but will develop best in sunny locations. They tolerate a variety of soils, but should not be drought-stressed, especially while being established.

Instructions on how to grow fireweed, from former Central Experimental Farm horticulturalist and co-worker Larry Sherk, are reproduced below from his popular but out-of-print (1967) guide (cited in the first chapter of this book) to growing Canada's floral emblems:

"This plant will become weedy and take over large areas if you grow it in rich garden soil. It is best to plant it in dry, well drained soil, preferably sterile and without any added nutrients. Choose a place where its vigorous suckers cannot encroach on other garden plants. The ripe seed pods should be cut off before they scatter the seeds, which self sow readily. Seeds germinate quickly when they are scattered on the soil and lightly raked in. Or you can sow the seed in sandy, sterile soil in seed pans and transplant the seedlings when the first true leaves appear. Plants may also be propagated by suckers, root cuttings, or division of older crowns, in either early spring or early fall."

PROSPECTING WITH PLANTS . . . AND PLANT PROSPECTING

Prospecting with plants (sometimes called geobotany) is the process of using the presence, appearance, or chemical content of plants to find mineral resources. Plants vary in their usefulness in this respect and different plants absorb different elements to different degrees. The white-flowered forms of fireweed have been associated with uranium deposits after being found in abundance around the "Glory Hole" mine at Port Radium on Great Bear Lake. It has been suggested that mutations from the radiation near uranium deposits result in a relatively high frequency of white-flowered variants, and that this phenomenon can be used to find uranium. High positive correlations between soil uranium content and that in leaves of fireweed have been reported.

Plant prospecting is finding plants for the development of new foods, prescription drugs, dietary supplements, fragrances, flavours, cosmetics, industrial materials, pesticides, and other valuable products. A first step is the selection of plants for testing. In many cases plants like fireweed, which already have a history of use and are aggressive and easy to grow, are ideal candidates. In fact, there has been appreciable success in Canada in developing and marketing fireweed as a source of cosmetics and medicinal extracts.

CONSERVATION STATUS

Fireweed is so widespread, and is often such an aggressive colonizer that it does not seem to be in any need of conservation. However, the pattern of genetic variability across its range is still not well documented. Areas of the Rockies in Alberta where both subspecies occur together are restricted and of interest from an evolutionary perspective.

A rare white form of fireweed (*Chamerion angustifolium*), at Churchill, Manitoba. Photo courtesy of Joy Viola and Bugwood.org.

MYTHS, LEGENDS, TALES, FOLKLORE AND INTERESTING FACTS

❋ The Cree and Woodland Indians employed the time of flowering of fireweed as a seasonal indicator that moose were in their fattening stage.

❋ According to an old Alaska saying, the first snow will fall 6 weeks after the last fireweed flower on a plant opens and the first fruit releases its seeds to the wind (fireweed blooms mature sequentially from the bottom to the top of the floral stalk, the first seeds scattering from the lowest fruits).

❋ Fireweed sprouted quickly from surviving rhizomes, following the burning of the forest following the volcanic eruption on Mount St. Helens, Washington in 1980. One year after the explosion, 81% of all seedlings present were from fireweed.

❋ One fruit of fireweed can contain as many as 500 seeds. A single plant can produce as many as 80,000 seeds in a year.

Stand of fireweed (*Chamerion angustifolium*) in the Quebec national park of l'Île-Bonaventure-et-du-Rocher-Percé. Photograph taken on August 5, 2011 by J. Cayouette.

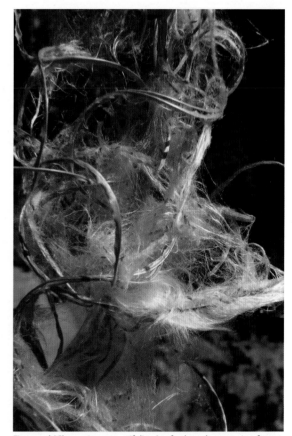

Fireweed (*Chamerion angustifolium*) tufted seeds scattering from the fruits. Source: Wikipedia (photographer: W. Siegmund; Creative Commons Attribution-Share Alike 3.0 Unported license).

A BIODIVERSITY TREASURE

Painting of the official flower of Yukon, fireweed (*Chamerion angustifolium*), from the Walter Coucill Canadian Centennial official flowers of Canada series (see Coucill 1966 cited in the first chapter of this book). Reproduced with the permission of the copyright holders, the Coucill family.

OFFICIAL PLANT EMBLEMS OF CANADA

SOURCES OF ADDITIONAL INFORMATION

Baum, D.A., Sytsma, K.J., and Hoch, P.C. 1994. The phylogeny of *Epilobium* (Onagraceae) based on nuclear ribosomal DNA sequences. Syst. Bot. 19: 363–388.

Brenchley, W.E., and Heintze, S.G. 1933. Colonization by *Epilobium angustifolium*. J. Ecol. 21: 101–120.

Broderick, D.H. 1990. The biology of Canadian weeds: 93. *Epilobium angustifolium* L. (Onagraceae). Can. J. Plant Sci. 70: 247–260.

Galen, C., and Plowright, R.C. 1985. The effects of nectar level and flower development on pollen carry-over in inflorescences of fireweed (*Epilobium angustifolium*) (Onagraceae). Can. J. Bot. 63: 488–491.

Henderson, G., Holland, P.G., and Werren, G.L. 1979. The natural history of a subarctic adventive: *Epilobium angustifolium* L. (Onagraceae) at Schefferville, Quebec. Nat. Can. 106: 425–437.

Husband, B.C., and Schemske, D.W. 1997. Effects of inbreeding depression in diploid and tetraploid populations of *Epilobium angustifolium*: implications for the genetic basis of inbreeding depression. Evolution 51: 737–746.

Husband, B.C., and Sabara, H.A. 2003. Reproductive isolation between autotetraploids and their diploid progenitors in fireweed, *Chamerion angustifolium* (Onagraceae). New Phytol. 161: 703–713.

Keating, R.C., Hoch, P.C., and Raven, P.H. 1982. Perennation in *Epilobium* (Onagraceae) and its relation to classification and ecology. Syst. Bot. 7: 379–404.

McColl, J. 2002. Willowherb (*Epilobium angustifolium* L.): biology, chemistry, bioactivity, and uses. Agro-Food Industry Hi-Tech. 13: 18–22.

Michaud, J.P. 1990. Observations on nectar secretion in fireweed, *Epilobium angustifolium* L. (Onagraceae). J. Apicult. Res. 29(3): 132–137.

Mitich, L.W. 1999. Fireweed, *Epilobium angustifolium*. Weed Technol. 13: 191–194.

Mosquin, T. 1966. A new taxonomy for *Epilobium angustifolium* L. Brittonia 18: 167–188.

Mosquin, T. 1967. Evidence for autopolyploidy in *Epilobium angustifolium* (Onagraceae). Evolution 21: 713–719.

Mosquin, T., and Small, E. 1971. An example of parallel evolution in *Epilobium* (Onagraceae). Evolution 25: 678–682.

Myerscough, P.J., and Whitehead, F.H. 1980. Biological flora of the British Isles. *Epilobium angustifolium* L. (*Chamaenerion angustifolium* (L.) Scop.). J. Ecol. 68: 1047–1074.

Shacklette, H.T. 1964. Flower variation of *Epilobium angustifolium* L. growing over uranium deposits. Can. Field-Nat. 78: 32–42.

Solbreck, C., and Andersson, D. 1987. Vertical distribution of fireweed, *Epilobium angustifolium*, seeds in the air. Can. J. Bot. 65: 2177–2178.

Wagner, W.L., Hoch, P.C., and Raven, P.H. 2007. Revised classification of the Onagraceae. Syst. Bot. Mongraphs 83: 1-239.

Flowering top of fireweed (*Chamerion angustifolium*), photographed in south-central Colorado. Photo courtesy of Dave Powell (USDA Forest Service) and Bugwood.org.

Fireweed (*Chamerion angustifolium*) in Alaska. Source: Thinkstock.

OFFICIAL PLANT EMBLEMS OF CANADA

TREE: SUBALPINE FIR

Subalpine fir (*Abies lasiocarpa*). Source: Wikipedia (photographer: W. Siegmund; Creative Commons Attribution-Share Alike 3.0 Unported license).

SYMBOLISM

The abilities of subalpine fir to withstand cold, heavy snows, and a short growing season coincide with and symbolize the capacities of citizens of the Yukon to withstand the challenges of their northern climate. The strikingly symmetrical spire-like form of the trees is exceptionally attractive, reflective of the natural beauty of the territory. The traditional use of subalpine fir for food, medicine, shelter, and implements by indigenous people was also recognized by Yukon in its choice of the tree as an emblem.

Tracing largely to the Old World, fir trees have long been respected, indeed often venerated. They have been associated with a winter solstice celebration since ancient pagan times in Europe, when the ritual of decorating a conifer represented tribute to the rebirth of the sun god. Gradually the custom was taken up by Christians, and at least since the sixteenth century in Europe small fir trees have been used to decorate houses at Christmas time. In Europe, the silver fir (*A. alba*) has long been the fir of choice for Christmas trees. In North America, the balsam fir, a close relative of the subalpine fir, has been the most desirable Christmas tree for many years. Subalpine fir is also used as a Christmas tree, but to a lesser extent. Fir trees have been a symbol of fertility in many cultures, for their ability to last through long winters, but the religious symbolism is now considered more important.

NAMES

Latin Names
Abies lasiocarpa (Hook.) Nutt.

The genus name *Abies* is based on the Latin *abed*, a word used by the classical Romans to refer to the silver fir of Europe (the word abies was also used in ancient Latin for the silver fir). Alternatively, the name is said to be based on the Latin *abire*, to rise up, referring to the great height of some of the species. *Lasiocarpa* in the scientific name is based on the Greek *lasios*, woolly, and *karpos*, fruit, a reference to the cone-scales which are covered with fine hairs.

English Names
Subalpine fir. Also: alpine fir; uncommonly: caribou fir, mountain fir, sweet fir, sweet-pine.

The word "fir" in modern English traces back to Old English and Old High German words meaning fir forest and a Goth word meaning mountain. Today "fir" is usually restricted to the genera *Abies* and *Pseudotsuga*. The names alpine fir and subalpine fir indicate the frequent high-altitude habitat of the species. The names balsam, balsam fir, western balsam, mountain balsam fir, western balsam fir, and white balsam reflect the similarity with *A. balsamea*, the true balsam fir (treated in the chapter on the emblems of New Brunswick), which grows in eastern North America. (A few taxonomists have considered *A. balsamea* and *A. lasiocarpa* to be sufficiently close to merit placement in the same species.) The "white" in the name "white balsam" (and in "white fir", although this is the usual name of *A. concolor*) reflects the often almost-white wood and the occasionally whitish bark. "Sweet" in the names "sweet fir and "sweet-pine" is based on the pleasant aroma. The name Rocky Mountain(s) subalpine fir (or Rocky Mountain alpine fir) is sometimes applied to the whole species, sometimes just to variety *bifolia*. The name Pacific subalpine fir (or Pacific alpine fir) is often restricted to variety *lasiocarpa*. The name corkbark fir is applied to variety *arizonica*. These varieties are discussed below. The name caribou fir reflects the attractiveness of the tree as browse for caribou and other large herbivores.

French Names
Sapin subalpin. Also: sapine concolore, sapin de l'Ouest, sapin des montagnes Rocheuses.

Silhouette of subalpine fir (*Abies lasiocarpa*). Source: Farrar, J.L. 1995. Trees in Canada. Canadian Forest Service and Fitzhenry and Whiteside, Markham, ON, Canada. Reproduced with permission.

HISTORY

Canada

Subalpine fir was chosen as the official tree of Yukon in 2001, the result of a contest held by the government that year. Most of the voters were students, of whom about one-third voted for the tree, the others for the other three choices: flatleaf willow, trembling aspen, and balsam poplar. One journalist reported "The willows are weeping, the aspens are trembling and the poplars are pleading, but no matter; the subalpine fir has been formally designated as the Yukon's official tree."

The closely related balsam fir, *A. balsamea* (L.) Mill., was adopted as the provincial tree of New Brunswick in 1987.

Foreign

North Carolina adopted the related Fraser fir (*A. fraseri* (Pursh) Poir.) as its "Official Christmas Tree" in 2005. The Frazer fir constitutes more than 90% of Christmas tree production in North Carolina and was chosen ten times over the period 1971–2007 as the White House Christmas Tree. No species of *Abies* is an "official state tree" of any of the U.S. states, although Douglas fir (*Pseudotsuga menziesii*) is the official state tree of Oregon. Spanish fir (*A. pinsapo* Boiss.) has been called the national tree of the Andalusian region of Spain, but this is an unofficial designation.

APPEARANCE

The trees develop a narrow, dense crown that is spire-like at the top in open-grown trees, narrowly conical with a very elongated, extremely narrow top in trees growing in forests. Subalpine firs are typically 15–30 m (49–90 feet) in height, rarely as tall as 45 m (148 feet), with a diameter at breast height up to 120 cm (4 feet), rarely 2 m (6.5 feet). The bark is grayish (sometimes reddish when young), covered with resin blisters, later becoming scaly (rough and fissured) and dark gray or whitish. The needles are mostly 1.5–2.5 cm (0.6–1 inch) long (sometimes as long as 4.5 cm or 1.8 inches), flattish, and grayish-green to bluish green. The needles are arranged spirally around the twigs, but twist at the leaf bases so that they are mostly above and at the sides of the twigs where they are exposed to the sun. Male and female flowers are produced on the same trees, in compact clusters called cones. The greenish or bluish male cones are 13–20 mm (0.5–0.8 inch) long and are borne in pendulous clusters on lower twigs of the tree, often abundantly. The seed cones are cylindrical or ovoid, borne upright on the twigs, singly or often in small clusters, in the upper part of the crown. The seed cones are usually less frequent than the male cones, and are 4–12 cm (1.6–4.7 inches) long and 2–4 cm (0.8–1.6 inches) wide. They are dull purple when young, purplish brown or brown at maturity, and often covered by resin. The cone scales disintegrate to release the ripe winged seeds in the fall. The bare axis of the cones may remain on the trees for years. The seeds are brown or purple, about 6 mm (0.25 inch) long, with a wing 10–18 mm (0.4–0.7 inch) in length. Subalpine fir has a shallow, wide-spreading root system, and because the anchorage is often poor, the tree is occasionally toppled by wind. Frequently the plants are stunted or develop into shrubs on exposed ridges at tree line.

The oldest known tree is from Yukon and had 501 annual growth rings (subalpine firs rarely grow longer than 200 years). The tallest was from the Alpine Lakes Wilderness area in Washington and was 52 m (170 feet) in height. The tree with the broadest trunk had a diameter at breast height of 204 cm (6.7 feet) and was from Olympic National Park, Washington State.

Subalpine fir (*Abies lasiocarpa*), growing on the southwest shore of Crystal Lake, Mount Rainier National Park, Washington State. Photo courtesy of Walter Siegmund.

CLASSIFICATION

Family: Pinaceae (pine family).

There are about 40 species of *Abies*, distributed in north temperate regions of the world, as well as in Mexico, Central America, and North Africa. Four species are native to Canada (five if *A. lasiocarpa* and *A. bifolia* are considered to be separate species). A key to the Canadian species of Abies is presented in the chapter on the emblems of New Brunswick.

Abies lasiocarpa is known to hybridize with some other species, particularly the rather similar *A. balsamea*, where the two species overlap in central Alberta.

Across the continental divide in the northern Rocky Mountains, the western subalpine fir trees differ somewhat from the eastern trees, and the two kinds have been recognized by some taxonomists as different species. However, most authorities recognize them as different subspecies or varieties. *Abies lasiocarpa* var. *lasiocarpa*, known as Pacific alpine fir, occurs west of the continental divide, on the Pacific slope from eastern Alaska and the Yukon to northwestern California. *Abies lasiocarpa* var. *bifolia* (A. Murray) Eckenwalder (= *A. bifolia* A. Murray), known as Rocky Mountain subalpine fir, occurs east of the continental divide, from Yukon to Utah and central Colorado. The two are distinguished in the following table.

A comparison of some key characters of the two varieties of *Abies lasiocarpa*

Character	Variety *lasiocarpa*	Variety *bifolia*
Fresh leaf scars (evident upon pulling off a few needles)	Red periderm (tissue observable in fresh leaf scar)	Yellow or tan periderm
Foliar buds	Basal scales are equilaterally triangular with crenate or dentate margins	Basal bud scales are long, narrow-triangular to spathulate with crenate to entire margins
Leaf dimensions	18–31 mm × 1.5–2 mm	11–25 × 1.25–1.5 mm
Leaf odour	Sharp (from ß-phellandrene)	Similar to camphor
Leaf colour, upper surface	Blue-green, very glaucous	Light green to blue-green, usually glaucous

In southern Colorado through Arizona and New Mexico, there are trees known as corkbark fir, which have a thick, corky bark and especially glaucous foliage (i.e., bluish needles). These are often classified as *A. lasiocarpa* var. *arizonica* (Merriam) J. Lemmon, but are also considered by many authorities to simply be part of *A. lasiocarpa* var. *bifolia*.

Populational geneticists have been intrigued by the genetic nature of subalpine fir; genetic variation is very high among some high elevation sites on different mountains, and also very high among different altitudinal growth forms on the same mountain.

Resin-blistered trunk of subalpine fir (*Abies lasiocarpa*) growing in south-central Colorado. Photo courtesy of Dave Powell (USDA Forest Service) and Bugwood.org.

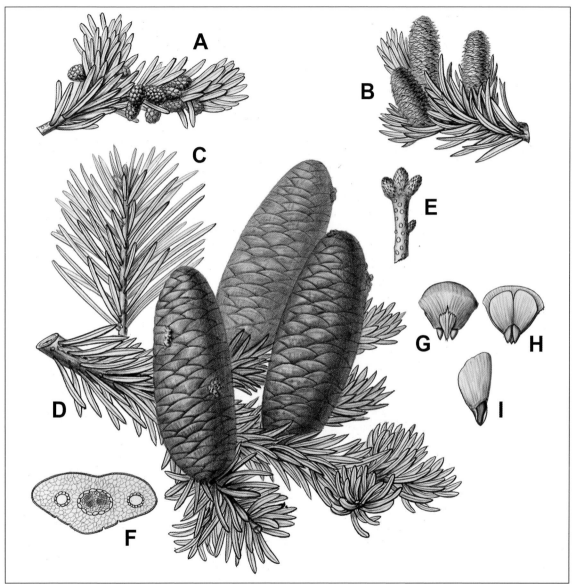

Subalpine fir (*Abies lasiocarpa*). A, branch with male cones; B, branch with young female cones; C, end of a lateral branch; D, fruiting branch; E, winter buds; F, cross section of a leaf; G, lower side of a mature cone scale with its bract; H, upper side of a mature cone scale with its winged seeds; I, winged seed. Source: Sargent, C.S. 1898. The silva of North America. Houghton, Mifflin and Company, Boston, MA. Vol. 12, plate 611.

Subalpine fir (*Abies lasiocarpa* var. *lasiocarpa*) among mountain hemlock (*Tsuga mertensiana*). Source: Wikipedia (photographer: W. Siegmund; Creative Commons Attribution-Share Alike 3.0 Unported license).

A BIODIVERSITY TREASURE

GEOGRAPHY

Subalpine fir (including both varieties) is the most widely distributed of the western North American species of *Abies*, and the second most widespread fir species in North America. It is found in the subalpine region, extending from southeastern Alaska east to central Yukon Territory, south through British Columbia and western Alberta to Colorado, southwestern New Mexico, northeastern Nevada, and southeastern Arizona. The species occurs in the Coast Mountains of British Columbia, the mountains of Alaska, Washington, Oregon, and California, frequently up to treeline. Scattered populations are distributed throughout the Rocky Mountains, more so in the north. Subalpine fir extends east as far as the eastern margins of the Rocky Mountains. Towards its southern limit, it is found in scattered montane sites in Arizona, northwestern California, and New Mexico. Subalpine fir grows (rarely) down to sea level in the north of its range, and up to 3,650 m (12,000 feet) in altitude in the southernmost part of its range. The approximate distributions of the two varieties are separated by a dashed line in the distribution map.

Some ecologists have speculated that the isolated occurrences of the species are where the trees survived glaciation in refugia (areas not covered with ice). However, in one region of isolated occurrences it was concluded that the trees are simply in areas with underlying limestone, which is presumably advantageous to the plants. Fossil pollen assemblages in lakebeds suggest that 200,000 years ago subalpine fir was more abundant in Yukon and grew as far north as Old Crow, which is 400 km (250 miles) north of the tree's present northern limit near Dawson. Interestingly lodgepole pine is a relative newcomer, having arrived in Yukon about 1,000 years ago.

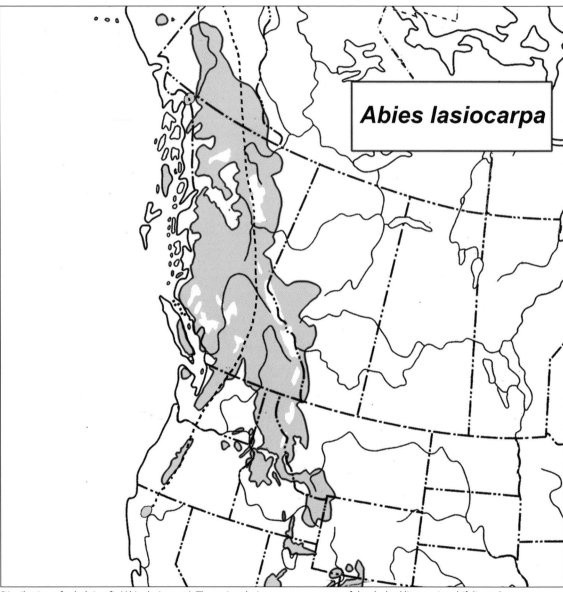

Distribution of subalpine fir (*Abies lasiocarpa*). The variety *lasiocarpa* occurs west of the dashed line, variety *bifolia* to the east.

ECOLOGY

Abies lasiocarpa grows in pure stands in some places, more often in associations with other conifers, and sometimes with cold-hardy deciduous trees including aspen (*Populus*) and birch (*Betula*) species. Subalpine fir is a pioneer on severe and disturbed sites, but often becomes less competitive when forests approach maturity. The trees are slow-growing, and once stands are established they sometimes persist for a century or more, but are often replaced by other species. *Abies lasiocarpa* is common at and near the tree line, occurring in subalpine forests in mountainous regions, and in the northwestern part of North America's boreal forest, where it has a competitive advantage. The very narrow, spire-like crown is adaptive to the heavy snowfall often encountered in the subalpine zone, the trees shedding snow easily as the relatively short branches bend downward.

Habitat

The trees occur on a variety of soils, often colonizing newly exposed ground. They do best on deep, moist, well-drained, loamy soils, but are capable of growing on very poor, thin soils, sometimes acting as the main pioneer species in such sites. Subalpine fir is tolerant of semi-shade. The species is adapted to a short growing season associated with cold winters, cool summers, frequent summer frosts, and heavy snowpack. Although they can tolerate some drought, the trees are naturally adapted to moist environments.

Inter-species Relationships

Subalpine fir is an important source of browse for wildlife, including grouse, deer, elk, and bighorn sheep. The seeds are consumed by squirrels, chipmunks, mice, and several birds. The cones are a favourite food of squirrels, which tear the cones open to obtain the seeds. The trees also provide cover for both small and large mammals, such as bear, porcupine, pine marten, fisher, lynx, hares, mice, voles, chipmunks, and shrews, as well as numerous birds. Many kinds of insects feed on subalpine fir, and some (including the western spruce budworm, western balsam bark beetle, and balsam woolly aphid) are considered to be quite damaging.

Pollination and Dispersal

Subalpine fir is wind-pollinated, the male flowers shedding pollen in late spring and early summer. Although the trees are capable of self-pollination, a substantial degree of cross-pollination occurs. The female flowers (and consequently the seed cones) are predominantly at the top of the trees, a strategy for increasing reception of pollen from distant trees. The seeds ripen in late summer and early fall, and are wind-dispersed, the seed wings acting as sails. In open areas, most seeds fall within 30 m (100 feet) on the windward (upwind) side, and within 80 m (260 feet) on the leeward (downwind) side. Most seeds are distributed by the wind, but some are dispersed by squirrels as a result of being carried to and stored in caches; seeds that escape being eaten often germinate in clumps to produce a group of trees. As with many tree species, masting occurs, i.e., seed production is very high in one year, followed by several years of limited production, a strategy to prevent seed consumers from building up large populations in lean years, and to generate so many seeds in good years that there are too few animals to eat them all. In subalpine fir, abundant seed years occur about every 3 to 5 years.

The lower branches sometimes droop and touch the ground, where layering may occur, i.e., the branches take root, producing new plants. This is much more frequent at high elevations, where snow load increases the likelihood of branches contacting the ground, and because the plants are smaller, indeed often dwarfed, the branches are nearer to the ground.

Subalpine fir (*Abies lasiocarpa*). Source: Thinkstock.

A BIODIVERSITY TREASURE

USES

Lumber & Pulp. Subalpine fir is mainly employed for construction lumber (often included in shipments of spruce) and pulp, occasionally for other uses such as boxes, veneer, finish carpentry, and poles. The often inaccessible high-mountain and northern habitats, and small size frequently developed in much of the range of the species, limits the tree's economic importance. The trunk seems to be susceptible to interior defects from middle age onwards, decreasing the value of the wood. Subalpine fir is one of four species harvested together, by British Columbia and Western Alberta lumber manufacturers as part of the SPF (spruce-pine-fir) group. The other species are white spruce (*Picea glauca*), Engelmann spruce (*Picea engelmannii*), and lodgepole pine (*Pinus contorta*). Of these species, subalpine fir is considered the most difficult to process and market because of its relatively low wood density, high moisture content, high presence of moisture pockets, and lower drying rate compared to the other species. In British Columbia, the four SPF species are processed together for dimension lumber, with the residuals used for pulp and paper.

Other. As noted elsewhere, the species is also used to a limited extent as a Christmas tree and as an ornamental. The resin (known commercially as Canada balsam and Strasbourg turpentine) from firs is employed as a cement for optical lenses and microscope slides, as a varnish, and for medicinal purposes. However, subalpine fir is a minor source of the resin.

Traditional. North American Indians chewed the resin of subalpine fir to clean their teeth, and also employed the resin as a topical antiseptic, and even for tea. The resin was also used to patch holes in canoes and preserve the strings of bows. Hair tonic was prepared by mixing powdered leaves with deer grease. All parts of the plant were used for a variety of medicinal purposes. Because the foliage has a pleasant aroma, it was employed to scent rooms, clothing, and even people. The wood, bark, and boughs were used for roofing.

TOXICITY

Working with subalpine fir lumber can cause dermatitis or eczema in some individuals, but the species is not considered to pose a significant health problem.

ARCTIC AND ALPINE TREE-LINES

Subalpine fir is geographically limited by tree-lines. The term tree-line has sometimes been used loosely. The area in which a tree can grow can be limited by various factors, including cold (or heat), wind, soil features, water availability, herbivores, disease, and competitors. However, "tree-lines" are best known when they are latitudinal (such as the taiga-tundra boundary of northern Canada), or altitudinal (such as occurs on the side of a tall mountain, where subalpine communities are replaced by low-growing alpine plants). An "inverted treeline" can occur where cold air drains into a mountain basin, producing a tree-line based on a lower instead of an upper altitudinal limit. Some ecologists dislike the phrase tree-line, since frequently the "line" isn't sharp, and many prefer the phrase "tree zone". In any event, European ecologists often use three terms to specify more exactly the areal limits of tree growth. These terms are:

"Timber-line" (*waldgrenze*): upper limit of tall, erect tree growth at forest densities.

"Transition zone" (*rampfzone*): the area between the timber-line and the tree-line.

"Tree-line" (*baumgrenze*): the area where trees are often deformed, dwarfed, or prostrate because of the severe environment.

In North America and Europe, a community of dwarfed and deformed (usually coniferous) trees such as occur at tree-lines is often referred to as *"Krummholz"* or *"Krumholtz"* from the German *krumm* meaning crooked, bent, or twisted and *Holz* meaning wood. The term "elfin-wood" is also sometimes applied but is also used to describe many kinds of tropical and subtropical dwarf woody vegetation.

See the chapter on Nunavut for additional information on the northern tree line of Canada.

CULTIVATION

Abies lasiocarpa is planted to some extent in North America for landscape rehabilitation, and as an ornamental park or roadside tree in areas where it grows naturally, but it is not grown much for agroforestry purposes. In Scandinavia, particularly in Norway, subalpine fir cultivation is expanding for production of Christmas trees.

Subalpine fir is adapted to high altitudes and cool, moist conditions, and so does not grow well in many areas outside its natural range. In low-elevation gardens, the trees often do not develop their characteristic spire-like form. Nevertheless subalpine fir is very picturesque and symmetrical, and is grown as an ornamental to some extent. Seedlings grow very slowly in their first year (one-year-old seedlings are often less than 2.5 cm (1 inch) in height), and container nursery stock is usually employed for ornamental purposes. Dwarf cultivars are popular, especially of variety *arizonica*, which as noted earlier has attractively-bluish needles. Dwarf cultivars. include: 'Argentea' ('Arizonica Glauca', noted for its silvery-blue foliage); 'Compacta' ('Glauca Compacta', with silvery-blue foliage and a conical shape); 'Mulligan's Dwarf', 'DuFlon', and 'Green Globe' (rounded and somewhat flat on top).

CONSERVATION STATUS

Subalpine fir is not thought to be in need of conservation measures, although curious forms have been described at the periphery of its range. These are not well understood at present, but some of them might merit conservation measures.

Subalpine fir (*Abies lasiocarpa*) growing in southwestern Colorado. Photo courtesy of Dave Powell (USDA Forest Service) and Bugwood.org.

A BIODIVERSITY TREASURE

MYTHS, LEGENDS, TALES, FOLKLORE AND INTERESTING FACTS

✤ The ancient Irish were Celts who had migrated to the Irish isles from Central Europe nearly 2,000 years before the coming of Christianity to Ireland. Their unique language, Gaelic, was written in a special alphabet called the "Celtic Tree Alphabet", comprised of letters that signified trees found in abundance in Ireland. In "Ogham script", the lettering of old Gaelic, "A" (Ailm) stood for the fir tree (sometimes interpreted as a pine), and was represented by a cross with equidistant arms within a circle. This is sometimes displayed in Irish tattoos.

The character indicates purity, as the fir tree was synonymous with purity and considered sacred. After the sixteenth century, Gaelic clans in Scotland frequently adopted tree symbols as clan badges, and the fir was often chosen.

✤ Beginning about the seventh century, fir trees were hung upside down from ceilings in Central Europe as a symbol of Christianity at Christmas time. This practice (still sometimes encountered) seems curious, even sacrilegious today, although it appears to originally have been simply a way of giving the tree a lofty prominence in the home.

✤ Colours are often very difficult to characterize. "Fir green" is defined (Webster's Third New International Dictionary) as "a dark grayish green that is yellower and stronger than average ivy, yellower and deeper than Persian green, and yellower, lighter, and stronger than hemlock green."

✤ According to an old wives' tale, consumed fresh plant parts or seeds that aren't sufficiently chewed might grow inside a person. In 2009, Russian surgeons, operating on a 28-year-old man suspected of having a tumour in one of his lungs, discovered instead a fir sprig about 5 cm (2 inches) long. Newspapers subsequently published X-ray radiographs of what appeared to be a small fir plant inside the man's chest, with the suggestion that it had grown inside his lung. Botanists asked by journalists to comment on the report noted the unsuitability of the interior of the human body for plant growth.

Subalpine fir (*Abies lasiocarpa*) forest around a lake. Source: Wikipedia (photographer: W. Siegmund; Creative Commons Attribution-Share Alike 3.0 Unported license).

A FIR POEM
I remember, I remember
The fir-trees dark and high;
I used to think their slender tops
Were close against the sky:
It was a childish ignorance,
But now 'tis little joy
To know I'm farther off from heaven
Than when I was a boy.
—*Thomas Hood (1799–1845; British poet)*

SOURCES OF ADDITIONAL INFORMATION

Alexander, R.R., Shearer, R.C. and Shepperd, W.D. 1984. Silvical characteristics of subalpine fir. USDA Forest Service General Technical Report 115. U.S. Dept. Agric., Rocky Mountain Forest and Range Experimental Station, Fort Collins, CO. 29 pp.

Alexander, R.R., Shearer, R.C., and Shepperd, W.D. 1990. *Abies lasiocarpa* (Hook.) Nutt., subalpine fir. *In* Silvics of North America. Volume 1, Conifers. Agric. Handbk. 654. *Coordinated by* R.M. Burns and B.A. Honkala USDA Forest Service Washington, DC. pp. 60–70.

Dietrichson, J. 1971. Genetic variation in subalpine fir (*Abies lasiocarpa* (Hook.) Nutt.). Meddelelser fra det Norske Skogforsoeksvesen 29(1): 1–19.

Eckenwalder, J.E. 2009. Conifers of the world: the complete reference. Timber Press, Portland, OR. 704 pp.

Edwards, G.W. 2008. Abies P. Mill. *In* The woody plant seed manual. *Edited by* F.T. Bonner and R.P. Karrfalt. USDA Forest Service, Agricultural Handbook 727, Washington, D.C. pp. 148–198.

Ettl, G.J., and Peterson, D.L. 2001. Genetic variation of subalpine fir (*Abies lasiocarpa* (Hook.) Nutt.) in the Olympic Mountains, WA, USA. Silvae Genetica 50: 145–153.

Hansen, O.B., and Leivsson, T.G. 1990. Germination and seedling growth in *A. lasiocarpa* (Hook.) Nutt. as affected by provenance, seed pretreatment, and temperature regime. Scandinav. J. Forest Res. 5: 337–345.

Henderson, J.A. 1982. Ecology of subalpine fir. *In* Proceedings (1981), symposium on the biology and management of true fir in the Pacific Northwest. *Edited by* C.D. Oliver and R.M. Kenady. University of Washington, Institute of Forest Resources, Seattle/Tacoma, WA. pp. 53–58.

Hunt, R.S. 1993. *Abies. In* Flora of North America, vol. 2. *Edited by* Flora of North America Editorial Committee. Oxford University Press, Oxford, U.K. pp. 354–362.

Hunt, R.S., and von Rudloff, E. 1979. Chemosystematic studies in the genus *Abies*. IV. Introgression in *Abies lasiocarpa* and *Abies bifolia*. Taxon 28: 297–305.

Hunt, R.S., and von Rudloff, E. 1983. Further clarification on the *Abies balsamea–A. bifolia–A. lasiocarpa* complex with reference to the Parker and others publication. Taxon 32: 444–447.

Leadem, C.L. 1989. Stratification and quality assessment of *Abies lasiocarpa* seeds. FRDA Rep. 095. Forestry Canada/British Columbia Development Agreement, Victoria, BC. 23 pp.

Liu, T.-S. 1971. A monograph of the genus *Abies*. Dept. of Forestry. Nat. Taiwan Univ. Taipei, Taiwan. 608 pp.

Parker, W.H., and Maze, J. 1984. Intraspecific variation in *Abies lasiocarpa* from British Columbia and Washington. Amer. J. Bot. 71: 1051–1059.

Parker, W.H., Maze, J., and Bradfield, G.E. 1981. Implications of morphological and anatomical variation in *Abies balsamea* and *Abies lasiocarpa* (Pinaceae) from western Canada. Amer. J. Bot. 68: 843–854.

Parker, W.H., Bradfield, G.E., Maze, J., and Lin, S.C. 1979. Analysis of variation in leaf and twig characters of *Abies lasiocarpa* and *Abies amabilis* from north-coastal British Columbia. Can. J. Bot. 57: 1354–1366.

Parker, W.H., Maze, J., Bennett, F.E., Cleveland, T.A., and McLachlan, D.G. 1984. Needle flavonoid variation in *Abies balsamea* and *A. lasiocarpa* from western Canada. Taxon 33: 1–12.

Peterson, D.W., Peterson, D.L., and Ettl, G.J. 2002. Growth responses of subalpine fir (*Abies lasiocarpa*) to climatic variability in the Pacific Northwest. Can. J. Forest Res. 32: 1503–1517.

Worley, I.A., and Jacques, D. 1973. Subalpine fir (*Abies lasiocarpa*) in coastal western North America. Northw. Sci. 47 265–273.

Subalpine fir (*Abies lasiocarpa*) growing in northeastern Oregon. Photo courtesy of Dave Powell (USDA Forest Service) and Bugwood.org.

CANADA'S MAPLES

Sugar maple trees in Quebec in the autumn. Source: Thinkstock.

Sugar maple trees in Ontario in the autumn. Source: Thinkstock.

NATIONAL EMBLEM: THE MAPLE LEAF

Sugar maple (*Acer Saccharum*). Photograph taken by Michael Weigand on October 20, 2011 at Stanley's Olde Maple Lane Farm, Edwards, Ontario.

CANADA'S OFFICIAL MAPLES

Although no particular species is honoured as the official emblem of Canada, as detailed below tradition and legislation make it clear that the native species are the basis of the emblem. The "maple leaf" and "the maple", both in a generic sense, constitute the most important Canadian icons. Various artistic renditions of the maple leaf are employed on the Canadian flag and other official symbols of Canada, and while these are not consistently identifiable as a particular native Canadian species, they tend to be closest to sugar maple and red maple. The five-lobed stylized leaf on the Canadian flag is closest to the sugar maple, which is the national tree of Canada. Canada does not have an "official flower" or "official floral emblem", although sometimes the maple is claimed to have this status.

SYMBOLISM

As the arboreal emblem of Canada, the sugar maple tree reflects the extraordinary forest resources of the nation, which have played important roles in the social and economic development of Canada. Many forestry companies display the maple tree as a symbol of Canada's efforts to promote sustainable forest management. However the maple leaf considerably surpasses the maple tree in symbolic importance. The maple leaf is not only Canada's national emblem, it has become the leading symbol of Canada, adorning the Canadian flag and innumerable other governmental artefacts and commercial products. The maple leaf is Canada's most recognizable and respected icon, both within the country and internationally. Maple leaf pins are proudly displayed by Canadians while travelling abroad, and they are a reminder of Canadian values, including respect for the wild, natural landscape and the protection of the natural environment.

Important Canadian heraldic symbols featuring the maple leaf. Top: The Arms of Canada represents the authority of government agencies and officials, including the Prime Minster, Cabinet, Speaker of the House of Commons, Parliament, and most courts, including the Supreme Court. It is present on all Canadian paper currency, and on the cover of Canadian passports. Bottom: The Royal Standard of Canada is the Queen's personal Canadian flag, deployed only when the monarch is in Canada or represents Canada at an official event. As the monarch personifies the Canadian state, her flag takes precedence over all other Canadian flags, including the national flag.

The national flag of Canada, adopted in 1965. This features an 11-pointed generalized maple leaf. February 15, the official anniversary, is celebrated as National Flag of Canada Day.

PROCLAMATION DESIGNATING THE MAPLE TREE AS NATIONAL ARBOREAL EMBLEM OF CANADA
(Officially proclaimed April 25, 1996; published in the Canada Gazette May 15, 1996)

Whereas the maple leaf is recognized nationally and internationally as representing Canada and Canadians, as a symbol of our natural heritage and national identity;

And Whereas the maple tree has played a meaningful role in the historical development of Canada, first as discovered and utilized by the First Nations, later contributing to the lifestyles and economy of the European settlers, and more recently for its commercial, environmental and aesthetic importance to all Canadians;

And Whereas the maple tree is an important and environmentally sustainable source of economic activity;

And Whereas the maple tree (genus *Acer*) has ten species native to Canada;

Now Know You that We, by and with the advice of Our Privy Council for Canada, do by this Our Proclamation designate the maple tree (genus *Acer*) as national arboreal emblem of Canada.

The taming of the Canadian lion. The Governor General's standard, a symbol of the Sovereignty of Canada, is composed of an imperially crowned gold lion on a wreath of the official colours of Canada, holding the maple leaf, emblematic of the country. Roméo LeBlanc (Governor General 1994–1999) had the official crest redrawn from the ferocious tongue-protruding version shown above left to the less offensive Disneyesque rendition shown above right. While sticking one's tongue out is in bad taste today, the protruding tongue is traditional in heraldry, and has been said to emphasize the readiness of the animal to be in the service of the bearer of the heraldic symbol. Along with the loss of his tongue and his scowl, the new lion was de-whiskered, declawed, neutered, and hair styled. The maple leaf was diminished in size and its lobes were made less threatening. The modifications were reversed by LeBlanc's successor.

MAPLE STAMPS AND COINS

The maple in four seasons", a stamp set issued in 1971. Stamp images supplied by and reproduced with the permission of ©Canada Post Corporation.

Canada Day maple tree stamp set issued in 1994. The stamps are arrayed in the following positions:

A. macrophyllum A. saccharum   A. saccharinum A. pensylvanicum
A. platanoides   A. negundo   A. nigrum   A. glabrum var. douglasii
A. spicatum   A. circinatum A. campestre   A. rubrum

Acer nigrum is considered here to be *A. saccharum* subsp. *nigrum*. *Acer platanoides* (Norway maple) and *A. campestre* (hedge maple) are native to Eurasia, but are grown in Canada as ornamentals. They are not native to Canada, and were inappropriately honoured by being included in this stamp set. Norway maple is a widely planted tree, but is less desirable because its deep shade limits the growth of lawn and garden plants, and its autumn colouration is inferior to many other maples. Moreover, it has escaped from cultivation and become invasive, crowding out some native Canadian maples and other plants. Stamp images supplied by and reproduced with the permission of ©Canada Post Corporation.

Some of the many Canadian maple image coins. The four coloured coins at left were issued from 2001 to 2004 to illustrate the four seasons. They were nominally $5.00 coins, but sold uncirculated for $34.95 each. The coin at upper right was part of a set of six bimetallic gold coins issued from 1979 to 2004 that sold as a set for $2,500.00. The coin at lower right is a one-ounce gold coin, nominally $50.00, issued from 1979 to 2005, with a purchase price ranging from less than $100.00 to almost $2,000.00 depending on year. Coin images supplied by and reproduced with the permission of ©The Canadian Mint.

Several of the many Canadian maple leaf stamps. Bottom left issued 1964, top left issued 1966; right: sugar maple stamp issued in 2003. Stamp images supplied by and reproduced with the permission of ©Canada Post Corporation.

NAMES

Names of the native Canadian maple (*Acer*) species.

Latin Names	English Names	French Names
A. saccharum Marsh.	Sugar maple (bird's-eye maple, Caddo maple (for the cultivar 'Caddo'), curly maple, hard maple, head maple, rock maple, sugartree, sweet maple)	Érable à sucre (érable du Canada, érable dur, érable franc, érable franche, érable moiré, érable ondé, érable piqué, érable sucrier)
A. saccharum subsp. *nigrum* (Michx. f.) Desmarais (*A. nigrum* Michx. f.)	Black maple (black sugar maple)	Érable noir
A. macrophyllum Pursh	Bigleaf maple (British Columbia maple, broadleaf maple, broadleaved maple, common maple, Oregon maple)	Érable à grandes feuilles (érable grandifolié, érable de l'Oregon)
A. rubrum L.	Red maple (curled maple, scarlet maple, soft maple, scarlet maple, swamp maple, water maple)	Érable rouge (érable tendre, plaine, plaine rouge, plane rouge)
A. saccharinum L.	Silver maple (river maple, soft maple, white maple)	Érable argenté (érable à fruits cotonneux, érable blanc, plaine blanche, plaine de France, plane blanche)
A. negundo L.	Manitoba maple (ashleaf maple, ash-leaved maple, box elder)	Érable négundo (érable à feuille(s) de frêne, (érable à feuilles composées, érable à Giguère, érable du Manitoba, érable négondo, frêne à fruits d'érable, plaine à Giguère, plane négundo)
A. spicatum Lam.	Mountain maple (dwarf maple, low-moose maple, whiterod, white maple, whitewood (in New Brunswick)	Érable à épis (bâtarde, érable bâtard, fouéreux, plaine, plaine bâtarde, plaine bleue, plâne bâtard)
A. pensylvanicum L.	Striped maple (goosefoot maple, moose maple, moosewood, moosewood maple, whistle wood)	Érable de Pennsylvanie (bois barré, bois d'orignal, bois noir, érable jaspé (France), érable strié, érable barré)
A. glabrum Torr. var. *douglasii* (Hook.) Dipp.	Douglas maple (dwarf maple, Rocky Mountain maple, western mountain maple)	Érable circiné, (érable glabre (France), érable nain)
A. circinatum Pursh	Vine maple	Érable circiné (érable à feuilles rondes)

NAMES (CONT'D)

Names of cultivated maples (*Acer species*) that have escaped to the wild in Canada.

Latin Names	English Names	French Names	Occurrence
A. campestre L.	Hedge Maple, field Maple	Érable champêtre	Rare: Ontario
A. ginnala Maxim. (*A. tataricum* L. subsp. *ginnala* (Maxim.) Wesm.)	Amur maple (ginnala maple)	Érable ginnala (érable de l'Amour, érable du fleuve Amour)	Rare: British Columbia, New Brunswick, Nova Scotia, Ontario
A. platanoides L.	Norway maple	Érable de Norvège (érable plane, érable platane, érable platanoïde)	Common: built-up areas across much of southern Canada
A. pseudoplatanus L.	Sycamore Maple (English maple, great maple, Scottish maple, sycamore)	Érable sycomore (faux platane, Sycomore)	Rare: British Columbia, New Brunswick, Nova Scotia, Ontario
A. negundo L.	Manitoba maple (also see previous table)	Érable négundo (also see previous table)	Common: likely introduced in parts of eastern and northern Canada from Western Canada

DERIVATION OF NAMES

The genus name *Acer* is derived from *acer*, the classical Latin word for maple. The Latin word means hard, referring to the wood. The name "maple" apparently originated in England, based on the Old English *mapul*, which may be related to *möpurr*, the Old Norse name for the maple. The names "flowering maple" and "parlour maple" refer to species of the genus *Abutilon*, quite unrelated to *Acer*.

HISTORY

Canada

Well before the arrival of European settlers, Canada's aboriginal peoples used maples for various purposes, particularly for production of maple syrup. The maple leaf began to serve as a Canadian symbol as early as 1700. In 1834 the Société Saint-Jean Baptiste reportedly adopted the maple leaf as its emblem (other accounts state that the maple leaf was simply given consideration as the possible emblem of Canada during the 1834 founding of the organization). In 1836, *Le Canadien*, a newspaper published in Lower Canada, characterized the maple leaf as a suitable emblem for Canada. In 1848 the Toronto literary annual *The Maple Leaf* called it the chosen emblem of Canada. The maple leaf was incorporated into the badge of the Queen's Own Rifles of Canada in 1860. That same year the maple leaf was used extensively in emblematic decorations for the visit of the Prince of Wales. In 1867, Toronto schoolmaster and poet Alexander Muir wrote "The Maple Leaf Forever" as Canada's confederation song, and it was regarded as Canada's national song for several decades. In 1868 both Ontario and Quebec included the maple leaf in their new coats of arms. Between 1876 and 1901, all Canadian coins displayed the maple leaf, which continues to appear on Canadian currency. During the First World War the badges of many Canadian regiments included the maple leaf. Since 1921, the Royal Arms of Canada have included three maple leaves. With the start of World War II, many Canadian troops displayed the maple leaf on regimental badges and Canadian military equipment. In 1965 the red and white maple leaf flag was inaugurated as the National Flag of Canada. In 1996, the maple leaf was formally recognized as Canada's national emblem.

Foreign

The sugar maple is the state tree of New York (declared in 1956), Vermont (in 1949), West Virginia (in 1949), and Wisconsin (in 1949). The red maple has been the state tree of Rhode Island since 1964. Maple was declared to be the "state flavour" of Vermont in 1993.

CLASSIFICATION

Family: Soapberry family (Sapindaceae; formerly placed in the maple family, Aceraceae).

The genus *Acer* has about 125 species, mostly deciduous trees and some shrubs, the majority native to the north temperate zone, particularly to eastern Asia, with about a dozen species indigenous to North America and some in Central America and North Africa. Nine species are native to Canada (ten if *A. nigrum* is considered to be separate from *A. saccharum*).

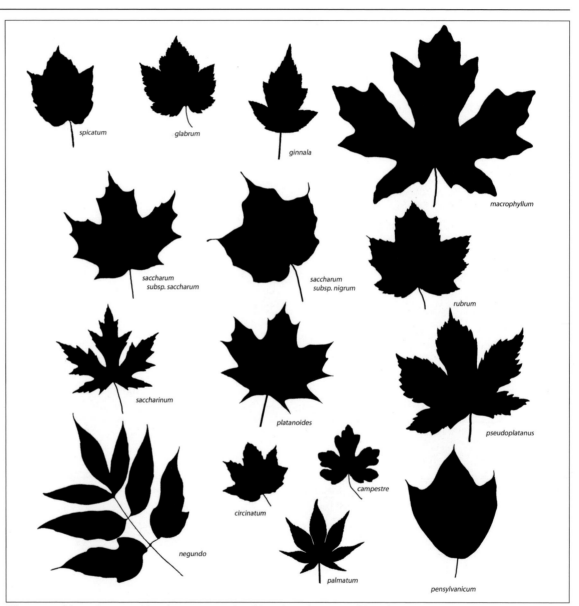

Silhouettes of the native, escaped, and most commonly cultivated maple species of Canada.

APPEARANCE

Maple leaves are arranged in opposite pairs on the stems, and are usually simple (i.e., not divided into leaflets) and palmately lobed, although sometimes they are compound (i.e., with several leaflets). Individual trees may bear unisexual flowers, or hermaphrodite flowers, or a mixture of both. Some species produce nectar and are insect pollinated, others are wind pollinated, and still others are both insect and wind pollinated. The distinctive fruit consists of two attached seeds, each encased by a protective fruit wall which expands into a wing on both sides of the pair of seeds. The pair may or may not separate; as the seed falls the wing rotates like the blade of a helicopter, maintaining the seed in the air and resulting in dispersal away from the parent tree, depending on the force of the wind.

Identification Key to the Native and Commonly Cultivated Foreign Maples of Canada

Note: Several maple species are widely grown as ornamental trees in lawns and parks, and along streets. The following key includes the most popular foreign species of *Acer* grown in Canada (indicated by * in the key). This key is based mostly on J.L. Farrar's *Trees in Canada*.

1. Leaves pinnately compound (with 3–9 stalked, coarsely toothed or lobed leaflets) . . . . Manitoba maple (*A. negundo*)
1. Leaves simple, lobed, or rarely with 3 leaflets lacking stalks 2

2. Leaves typically 7–9 lobed, outline of blade broadly oval to circular 3
2. Leaves typically 3–7 lobed, outline of blade square or rectangular 4

3. Leaf lobes triangular (about as long as wide), widest at their base; margins with short-pointed single or double teeth. Seed wings forming angle of about 180° . . . . Vine maple (*A. circinatum*)
3. Leaf lobes elongated (notably longer than wide), widest about their middle, leaf margins with long-pointed double teeth. Seed wings forming an angle of about 100° . . . . Japanese maple (*A. palmatum*)*

4. Central leaf lobe narrowing gradually from base to tip 5
4. Central leaf lobe with sides parallel or diverging above the base 7

5. Leaf blades longer than wide, margins coarsely and irregularly single-toothed; seeds wings forming and angle of less than 90° . . . . Mountain maple (*A. spicatum*)
5. Leaf blades as wide as or wider than their length, margins double-toothed 6

6. Leaves unlobed or shallowly 3-lobed; marginal teeth fine and regular. Bark conspicuously striped. Seed wings forming an angle of 90° . . . . Striped maple (*A. pensylvanicum*)
6. Leaves 3 or 5-lobed (lobing sometimes indistinct or 3 unstalked leaflets present); marginal teeth coarse and irregular. Bark not striped. Seed wings forming an angle of less than 45° . . . . . . Douglas maple (*A. glabrum* var. *douglasii*)

7. Leaves more than 15 cm (6 inches) wide, central and lateral lobes often overlapping. Seeds hairy . . . . Bigleaf maple (*A. macrophyllum*)

7. Leaves less than 15 cm (6 inches) wide, central and lateral lobes rarely overlapping. Seeds hairless 8

8. Leaves with numerous double teeth on the margin. Fruit maturing and falling before midsummer 9
8. Leaves with coarse, single teeth on the margin. Fruit maturing and falling in autumn. 10

9. Leaves deeply notched between central and lateral lobes, central lobe with sides diverging above the base. Seeds ribbed, often only one developed. Seed wings more than 4 cm (1.6 inch) long, forming an angle of 90° . . . . . Silver maple (*A. saccharinum*)
9. Leaves shallowly notched between the central and lateral lobes, central lobe with sides parallel to the midrib. Seeds swollen, both seeds developing. Seed wings less than 2.6 cm (1 inch) long, forming an angle of 60° . . . . Red maple (*A. rubrum*)

10. Central lobe not less than twice the length of the lateral lobes . . . . Amur maple (*A. ginnala*)*
10. Central lobe about equal in length to the lateral lobes 11

11. Leaves thick, wrinkled, lobes with numerous coarse teeth and white hair on each side of the main vein on the lower surface. Mature bark scaly, shedding. Seeds occasionally in groups of three . . . . . Sycamore maple (*A. pseudoplatanus*)*
11. Leaves thin, smooth, lobes with a few irregular, wavy teeth, hairless or entirely covered with hair on the lower surface. Mature bark ridged, not shedding. Seeds always in pairs 12

APPEARANCE (CONT'D)

12. Leaves 5–7 lobed, teeth and lobes bristle-tipped, leaf stalks exuding milky sap when cut. Flowers appearing with the leaves in the spring. Seeds flattened, seed wings 3.5–5 cm (1.4–2 inches) long, forming an angle of 180°.... Norway maple (*A. platanoides*)*

12. Leaves 3–5 lobed, teeth and lobes blunt-tipped, leaf stalks not exuding milky sap when cut. Flowers appearing before the leaves in the spring. Seeds plump, seed wing 3–3.6 cm (1.2–1.4 inches) long, almost parallel 13

13. Leaves typically 5–lobed, not appearing wilted and droopy, pale green and hairless below, central lobe square, separated from lateral lobes by wide, round notches, brilliant orange or scarlet in autumn ....Sugar maple (*A. saccharum*)

13. Leaves typically 3-lobed, appearing wilted and droopy, yellowing-green and covered with dense, velvety brown hair below, central lobe slightly tapered, separated from the lateral lobes by shallow, open notches, yellow in autumn..... Black maple (*A. saccharum* subp. *nigrum*)

The flowers of native maples, although short-lived, are extraordinarily beautiful. A selection is shown on this and the facing page. Left to right: male flowers of silver maple (*Acer saccharinum*); bisexual flowers of silver maple; bisexual flowers of red maple (*A. rubrum*); male flowers of Manitoba maple (*A. negundo*).

ECOLOGICAL RELATIONSHIPS

In some cases there is enough information to write an entire book about the interactions of a particular plant with other animals and plants. The maples are a good example. They are dominant in ecosystems and many organisms depend entirely on one or more maple species. Only a few of these interactions come regularly to the attention of the public.

One of these, the tar spot fungus, is featured later in this article. Another interaction that attracts attention is elongate warts which frequently occur on the upper surface of the leaf of silver and red maples. They are caused by tiny spider-like creatures called bladdergall mites, and they will not kill the trees. Abnormal growths on plants, such as these warts,

are referred to as galls and are usually a consequence of either bacteria or insects. A specific gall-causing insect (or arachnid, like mites) will produce a particular substance that will have a distinctive effect on plant growth resulting in a characteristic kind of gall.

The rosy maple moth (*Dryocampa rubicunda*) is the most attractive insect associated with maples. The larval caterpillars feed on red, silver and sugar maples. The spectacular adults are vibrant pink and yellow. Although many maples are wind-pollinated, some such as sugar maple, provide nectar and pollen for a host of bee species which serve as important pollinators of other plants. The use of maples by other animals is extensive and some uses are noted under particular species in the following pages.

Flowers of the two largest introduced cultivated maples. Left: Bisexual flowers of Norway maple (*A. platanoides*). Right: Bisexusal flowers of sycamore maple (*A. pseudoplatanus*).

A BIODIVERSITY TREASURE

SUGAR MAPLE (*ACER SACCHARUM*)

The sugar maple is probably the most important maple species in the world. It is one of the most common trees of eastern North America. There are several subspecies, best known of which is the widely distributed subsp. *saccharum*, which includes the majority of Canadian trees. The black maple (*A. saccharum* subsp. *nigrum*) is discussed later. When growing in a forest, the sugar maple develops a straight, branch-free trunk as high as 40 m (131 feet). Open-grown trees produce a rounded crown. The trunk may exceed 1.5 m (5 feet) in diameter at maturity. Sugar maples are widely planted as shade trees, valued for their spectacular yellow, gold, orange, and red autumn foliage.

Sugar maple is known of course for sugar maple products. Squirrels are fond of maple sap, and commonly lap it up from natural wounds on maple trees. The eastern grey squirrel (*Sciurus carolinensis*) is said to deliberately bite into maple trees to stimulate the flow of sap, upon which it can later feed. Legends relate how observing such squirrel behaviour led North American Native People to prepare maple syrup. Virtually all indigenous people within the range of sugar maple used the tree. Indeed it was often important to native people and colonists during the "hungry months" when food stocks were low, some mammals still hibernating, and fishing difficult due to melting ice. Spring runs of fish had not begun, nor had migratory birds returned, and the ground would be frozen for another several weeks so that tubers could not be dug. Native people collected sap in wooden (particularly birchbark) or pottery vessels in the early spring. Since metal buckets were not available prior to Columbus' discovery of the New World, present-day technology of lighting fires under containers of sap could not be used. The sap was concentrated by boiling, achieved by dropping hot rocks into the filled vessels that were available. Alternatively, the containers of sap were left until a layer of ice formed at the top; this (mostly sugar-free) ice was removed, and the process repeated until the sap was sufficiently concentrated. Maple syrup was the principal confection of the Eastern Woodlands Indians, who used the syrup to flavour and season vegetables, fruits, stews, cereals, and fish. A variety of beverages, including fermented drinks, were also prepared from sugar maple. By the seventeenth century, European colonists improved on the native techniques of collection, and boiled the sap to obtain sugar. Until cane sugar became

Children enjoying maple sugar excursion at Upper Canada Village, Ontario.

SUGAR MAPLE (*ACER SACCHARUM*) (CONT'D)

available, about 1860 in New England, maple syrup was an important component of the colonists' limited culinary fare. During the maple syrup season, New Englanders used to drink collected sap as a spring tonic. North American colonists often apologized for serving maple sugar instead of the scarce manufactured brown sugar of the time, which was actually more costly and rather inferior. Today, the mantle of inferiority has passed to sugared, maple-flavored imitations of real maple syrup.

Sugar maple syrup is now generally considered to be a luxury item, since cane and beet sugar, and corn syrup are produced very much more cheaply. The quantity of sugar maple syrup is only commercially important in primarily northern or alpine areas, where alternate spring freezing and thawing produces an exceptionally high sap yield. Sugar maple production is a uniquely North American industry, with over 10 million L (188,000 American gallons) often harvested annually. Canada accounts for three quarters of world production, with Quebec yielding three quarters of Canada's output. In the remainder of Canada the industry is located in eastern Ontario, Nova Scotia, and New Brunswick. In the United States, maple sugar syrup is produced commercially in 13 northern states from Maine to Minnesota. The leading states are Vermont, New York, Pennsylvania, Michigan, and Ohio. Sugar maple syrup production is a seasonal industry, conveniently occurring during a farm's slack season. Although a multimillion dollar industry, few producers rely on it as the chief source of income. Some operations have expanded to sugar bush attractions, with sleigh rides and breakfast pancakes with maple syrup. Harvesting syrup is labour-intensive, and in

A sugar maple forest. Photo courtesy of J. O'Brien, USDA Forest Service, and Bugwood.org.

Sugar maple autumn foliage. Left photo courtesy of J. O'Brien, USDA Forest Service, and Bugwood.org; right photo courtesy of Jean-Pol Grandmont.

A BIODIVERSITY TREASURE

SUGAR MAPLE (*ACER SACCHARUM*) (CONT'D)

North America approximately 60,000 part-time workers are employed each year. There are more than 10,000 maple syrup producers in Canada. Preparing maple syrup is generally a task for professionals, although the syrup has been made in home kitchens, boiling sap down on the kitchen stove. A frequent result is that the huge volume of water vapour produced has condensed on walls, sometimes peeling wallpaper away.

Sugar concentration averages less than 3% sucrose in the sap (some trees have as much as 8% sugar content), so that 30–40 units of sap often must be boiled down to produce one unit of syrup. Production varies considerably from year to year, and the factors responsible for this are largely unknown. The running of sap in the spring is poorly understood. In the previous growing season, sugars formed in the leaves by photosynthesis and moved down to the trunk and roots, where they were converted into starch and stored in living ray cells of the wood. When the trunk warms up sufficiently in the spring, the starch is first converted into glucose sugar, then into invert sugar (a mixture of glucose and fructose), and finally into sucrose. Ideal temperatures for the sap to run are 7 °C (45 °F) in the daytime and -4 °C (25 °F) at night. Warm days and freezing nights create a pumping action. Cold nights induce a negative pressure within the tree, with moisture being absorbed through the roots. Warm days provide positive pressure, forcing the sap out of the tree. However, the actual physiological mechanisms causing the development of positive and negative pressure in maple trees are poorly appreciated. Only a small percentage of the sap of the tree is removed each year, and trees can be used repeatedly for a century or more. An excessive number of holes in the trees or extra-large holes may damage trees by encouraging decay.

The early runs of sap produce light-coloured, aromatic "fancy" grades of syrup, slightly less concentrated in sugar. However, sugar concentration remains more or less constant during the season. As the season progresses, the syrup darkens, and eventually the maple taste becomes strong and almost unpleasant, so that the product is used mainly to flavour breakfast cereals and junk food. Although high in sugar content, maple syrup spoils at room temperature; once opened, containers should be stored in the refrigerator. Commercially, potassium sorbate and sodium citrate are widely used as preservatives. Maple sugar is prepared by concentrating the sucrose to the point that it will crystallize out of solution when the syrup cools; this occurs at -114 °C (-173 °F) at sea level. Maple cream is a malleable mixture of very fine crystals in a small amount of dispersed syrup, prepared by cooling the syrup very rapidly to about 21 °C (70 °F) by immersing a pan of syrup in a bath of iced water, and then beating it continuously until it become very stiff. The mass of material is then rewarmed in a double boiler, becoming smooth and semisoft.

As well as being a source of syrup, the sugar maple is one of the most valuable commercial hardwoods in Canada and the northern United States. Maple wood is in great demand for flooring, furniture, cabinetry, and interior decorative woodwork, veneer, small woodenware, and even walking sticks. It is the preferred wood for bowling pins, piano frames, shoe lasts, billiard cues, and many other products. Its strength makes it an outstanding choice for factory, dance-hall, and bowling-alley floors. One of the most widely recognized woods is "birdseye maple". The distinctive pattern results from a distortion of the grain in sugar maple wood, associated with conical indentations in the growth rings. Its causes are poorly understood, but the attractive pattern of "eyes" in the wood grain make the lumber from affected trees as much as 40 times as valuable as normal sugar maple lumber. Not surprisingly, birdseye maple has been widely copied on synthetic "wood" veneers.

Birdseye maple, a remarkably attractive and popular wood for furniture and ornamental wood products.

SUGAR MAPLE (*ACER SACCHARUM*) (CONT'D)

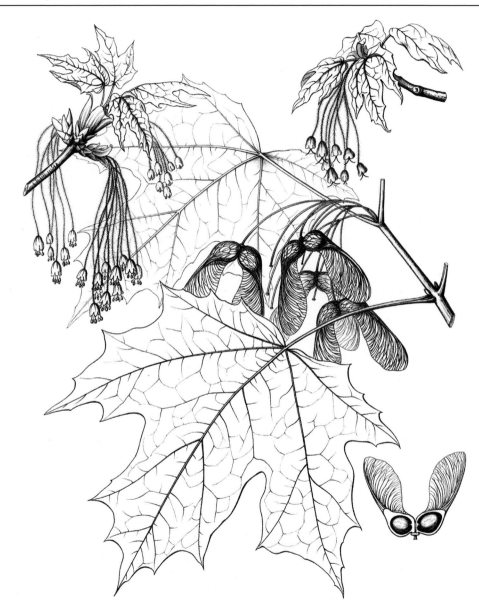

A BIODIVERSITY TREASURE

SUGAR MAPLE (*ACER SACCHARUM*) (CONT'D)

Currier & Ives 1872 lithographic print of the painting *Maple Sugaring*.

SUGAR MAPLE (*ACER SACCHARUM*) (CONT'D)

Currier & Ives 1856 lithographic print of the painting *American Forest Scene – Maple Sugaring*.

BIGLEAF MAPLE (*ACER MACROPHYLLUM*)

Bigleaf maple occurs in the forests of southwestern British Columbia. It is native to western North America, from southern Alaska to southern California, mostly near the Pacific Ocean. As the name implies, this species is easily recognized by its large leaves, the largest of any maple in the world. The leaves regularly reach 30 cm (1 foot) in width, and are sometimes as wide as 60 cm (2 feet). When the leaf stalks are broken, they exude a milky sap (the same occurs with the introduced Norway maple). The bark retains moisture, and in the warm, moist climate of the West Coast the trunk and larger branches are often covered with mosses, ferns, and other plants. In Canada the trees grow as high as 30 m (98 feet) with a diameter at breast height up to 1 m (about a yard). Bigleaf maple is considered to be the largest native maple species in Canada, and is the only native maple species that reaches notable tree size on the Pacific coast (compare Douglas maple and vine maple, described below). Bigleaf maple is also the only maple species that provides a significant lumber harvest on the West Coast of North America. The wood is used for much the same purposes as sugar maple, described above, but the supply is quite limited. Many aboriginal groups made paddles out of the wood and called the species "paddle tree". It produces very attractive yellow and orange foliage in the fall and is planted as an ornamental. Big-leaf maple was used as food to a minor extent by various tribes in Canada: the Lower Nlaka'pamux (Thompson) of British Columbia ate raw young shoots and boiled, sprouted seeds; the Sechelt also consumed the seeds of this species and the Saanich ate the inner bark. Today, wild food enthusiasts sometimes consume the flowers. The trees have been tapped for sugar syrup, but are less suitable for this purpose than sugar maple. Honeybees visiting the flowers produce a delicious honey.

Bigleaf maple (*Acer macrophyllum*), photographed November 29, 2003 in Quinault Rain Forest, Olympic National Park, Washington. Note the epiphytes growing on the branches, a phenomenon that is possible because of the mild, humid environment. Reproduced by courtesy of the photographer, W. Leonard.

BIGLEAF MAPLE (*ACER MACROPHYLLUM*) (CONT'D)

BLACK MAPLE (*ACER SACCHARUM* SUBSP. *NIGRUM*)

The black maple (*A. saccharum* subsp. *nigrum*) is so-named for its relatively black bark. This subspecies is quite similar to sugar maple (*A. saccharum* subsp. *saccharum*) discussed above, but usually has leaves with three rather than five lobes, and these often have a wilted appearance, the ends of the leaf lobes curving downwards. The distinctive hair on the underside of the leaf of black maple can be seen by folding the leaf with the lower surface outside and holding the edge of the fold up to the light. The two subspecies of *A. saccharum* hybridize, and trees of intermediate appearance are common. Black maple has a limited distribution in Canada, ranging from southern Ontario and Quebec to southern Minnesota, south to West Virginia and Arkansas, but it is abundant only in the eastern portion of its range. Black maple is used in the same ways as sugar maple, i.e., primarily for lumber and maple syrup, neither of which has been found to differ significantly between sugar maple and black maple. There are a few ornamental cultivars available, but far fewer than for *A. saccharum* subsp. *saccharum*. It has been speculated that global warming will cause black maple to increase (because it is better adapted to a warmer, drier climate) while sugar maple decreases in the northern part of its range. In Quebec, where it is uncommon, the black maple is afforded partial protection under a statute.

Black maple (*Acer saccharum* subsp. *nigrum*) in Tennessee on October 13, 2005. Photos courtesy of S.J. Baskauf (http://bioimages.vanderbilt.edu). Note the dark bark and the droopy appearance of the leaves.

BLACK MAPLE (*ACER SACCHARUM* SUBSP. *NIGRUM*) (CONT'D)

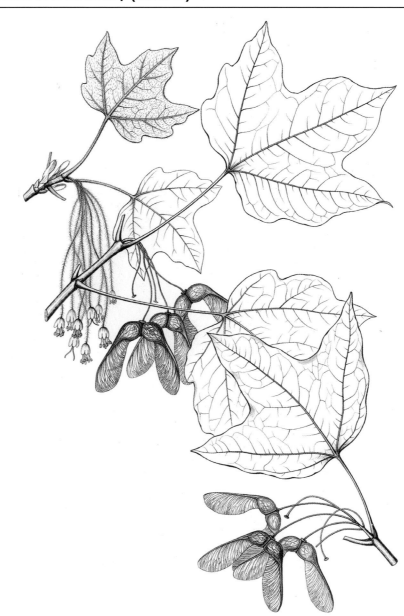

DOUGLAS MAPLE (*ACER GLABRUM* VAR. *DOUGLASII*)

Douglas maple commemorates David Douglas (1799–1834), a famous Scottish botanist who travelled through the interior of British Columbia, and introduced over 200 North American plants to Britain. The species is usually a large shrub but sometimes becomes a very small tree in its southern Canadian range, growing up to 10 m (33 feet) and 25 cm (10 inches) in diameter. Unlike some other Canadian maples, male and female flowers usually are on different trees. Variety *douglasii* of the species is the main variety in Canada. This western North American maple is found from southeastern Alaska to the southwestern United States. It occurs along streams and other moist sites in southwestern Alberta and in much of British Columbia (but is not native to northern British Columbia or the Queen Charlotte Islands). Unlike another British Columbia maple, the vine maple, it does not tolerate shade and usually grows in open habitats. The tough, pliable wood has no commercial importance, but was used by aboriginal people to make tools and ornamental items. The Blackfoot used the dry, crushed leaves to spice stored meat. The Saanich of southern Vancouver Island used the bark to make an antidote for poisoning. The species has attractive fall foliage (but not as brilliant as the vine maple discussed below); it is particularly suitable for dry areas, and is planted occasionally as an ornamental.

Douglas maple (*Acer glabrum* var. *douglasii*) growing in Crater Lake National Park, Oregon, September 9, 2006. Photo courtesy of K. Morse.

David Douglas. Portrait published in Curtis's Botanical Magazine in 1834.

DOUGLAS MAPLE (*ACER GLABRUM* VAR. *DOUGLASII*) (CONT'D)

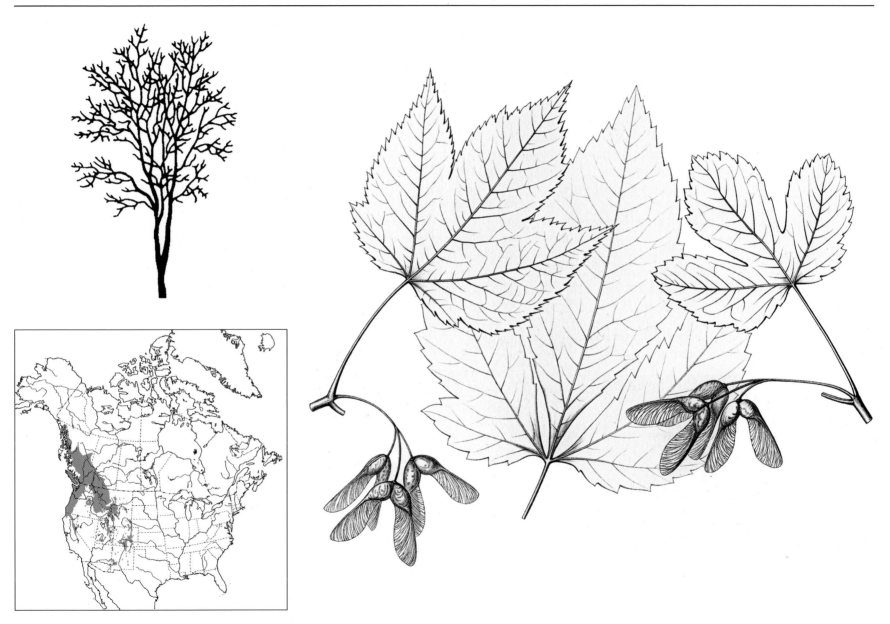

MANITOBA MAPLE (*ACER NEGUNDO*)

In Canada, Manitoba maple appears to have once been confined to Manitoba and adjacent provinces (hence the "Manitoba" in the name), but it has been spread quite widely to other provinces. Over much of Canada, this tree is an abundant colonizer of gardens and vacant lots. This fast-growing tree can become 20 m (66 feet) in height and 75 cm (30 inches) in diameter, sometimes larger. The trunk frequently branches irregularly, producing a rather asymmetrical appearance that discourages use of the tree as an ornamental. However, the species is hardier than most other hardwood trees in the Prairie Provinces, and accordingly has been widely planted there. Male and female flowers occur on different trees. Manitoba maple has weedy and invasive tendencies, and is difficult to eradicate because it sprouts readily from stumps. There are variegated-leaf cultivars, such as 'Flamingo', which are considered to be non-invasive. The alternative names "box elder" and "ashleaf maple" (the much more frequently encountered common names in the United States) reflect the fact that the leaves, uniquely for Canadian maples, are compound, with three or more leaflets (like elder and ash trees). Very young plants with three leaflets are often confused with poison ivy. The "box" in the name box elder reflects the occasional past use of the lumber for making boxes, although Manitoba maple is not a significant source of lumber. First Nations peoples and prairie settlers used the tree as a source of maple sugar, although it is a very poor producer.

Manitoba maple is quite unlike all other Canadian maples in many respects. One interesting difference is that the trees often retain many of their seeds over the winter. This may be advantageous in the native prairie range, in allowing wind dispersal over the snow crust of the open terrain. Birds that consume the seeds extensively, especially evening grosbeaks, and some mammals, may also assist in dispersal by carrying the seeds.

Three varieties and a number of forms of *A. negundo* have been recognized in Canada. The classification of these requires more study. They are listed below.

Variety *interius* (Britt.) Sarg. f. *interius*, Alberta and Northwest Territories to Ontario, grayish-velvety twigs and greenish seeds.

Variety *interius* (Britt.) Sarg. f. *loeveorum* Boivin, Manitoba, grayish-velvety twigs and deep red seeds.

Variety *violaceum* (Kirsch.) Jaeg. var. *violaceum*, Alberta to Nova Scotia, twigs glabrous and purple beneath a white bloom, seeds yellowish.

Squirrel eating seeds of Manitoba maple (*Acer negundo*). Photographed October 27, 2009 in Calgary, Alberta. Photo courtesy of Aires Mario da Cruz.

Variety *violaceum* (Kirsch.) Jaeg. var. *dorei* Boivin, Manitoba to Quebec, twigs glabrous and purple beneath a white bloom, seeds deep red.

Variety. *negundo* f. *negundo*, across much of Canada, at least as an escape, twigs glabrous and green, seeds greenish.

Variety *negundo* f. *sanguinium* Martin, Manitoba and Ontario, at least as an escape, twigs glabrous and green, seeds deep red.

Manitoba maple (*Acer negundo*). Public domain photo from Wikimedia Commons (from Herman, D.E. et al. 1996. North Dakota tree handbook.).

MANITOBA MAPLE (*ACER NEGUNDO*) (CONT'D)

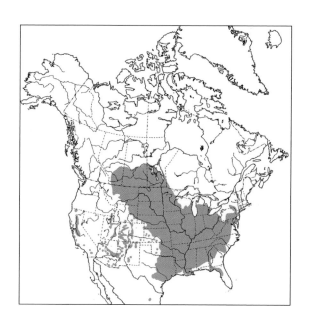

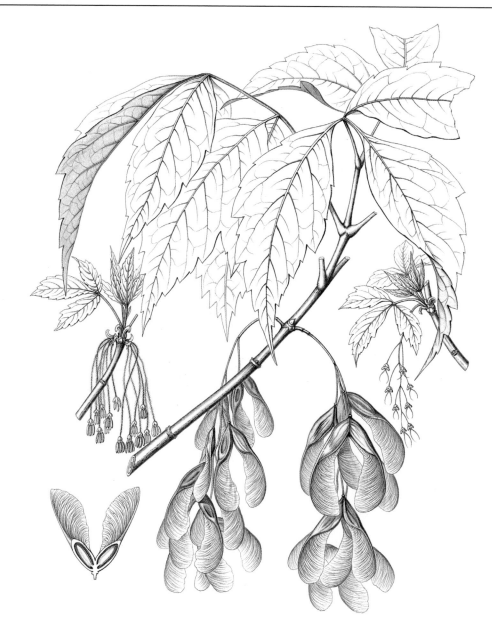

MOUNTAIN MAPLE (*ACER SPICATUM*)

Mountain maple is a large shrub or very small tree rarely taller than 5 m (16 feet) in height and 15 cm (6 inches) in diameter. The species is the smallest and the most adapted to northern conditions of the Canadian maples. It grows in the shade of the forests of eastern Canada and in the northeastern United States. The "mountain" in the name has been questioned. Mountain maple does grow in the southern Appalachian Mountains in the southern part of its range, but the name is somewhat inappropriate and can lead to confusion with other maples called mountain maple (particularly *A. glabrum*, called Douglas maple in this presentation). Mountain maple has no value as lumber, but the species is sometimes planted as an ornamental. It produces brilliant yellow, orange, and especially red foliage in the autumn, and forms with strikingly reddish fruits have been selected. Extracts have been used to flavour tobacco, non-alcoholic beverages, ice cream, candy, and baked goods. The species provides food for deer and birds, and is important in prevention erosion on banks and steep slopes.

Mountain maple (*Acer spicatum*) growing in the Dominion arboretum in Ottawa. Photographed May 7, 2010 by E. Small.

Foliage of Mountain maple (*Acer spicatum*). Photo courtesy of Jean-Pol Grandmont.

MOUNTAIN MAPLE (*ACER SPICATUM*) (CONT'D)

RED MAPLE (*ACER RUBRUM*)

Red maple is one of the most common and widespread trees in the forests of eastern North America, occurring in Canada from Ontario to Newfoundland. The species grows in an extensive range of habitats, including drylands and swamps. It is frequent in the acid substrates of bogs and granite rocklands whereas sugar maple and black maple are more common in alkaline soils over limestone. In Canada, trees grow up to 25 m (82 feet) in height, and 60 cm (2 feet) in diameter. True to its name, the leaves usually turn a striking scarlet in the autumn, and the twigs, buds, flowers, immature fruits, and leaf-stalks are also often bright red. The species hybridizes extensively with silver maple, described below, and many trees are difficult to distinguish. The wood is used for various purposes, but red maple is considered to be a minor source of lumber. There are numerous cultivars of red maple, and it is often grown as a shade and park tree because it is exceptionally tolerant of urban conditions. Red maple is sometimes tapped for maple sugar. The Iroquois of the Lake Ontario region pounded the dried bark of red maple into flour for bread. Although the leaves of maples are consumed by many animals, and sometimes are fed to livestock, the foliage of red maple (even when dead) is extremely toxic to horses, consumption of 1.4 kg (3 pounds) leading to death. The toxin is probably gallic acid, which also occurs in other maples, but in lesser amounts. Obviously horse pastures should not include red maple trees.

In the floodplains along major rivers in parts of the Northeast, particularly the Ottawa Valley, red and silver maples often occur near to each other and plants of intermediate appearance are not uncommon. These intermediates are presumed to be hybrids and may be referred to *Acer ×freemanii* A.E. Murray (*A. rubrum* × *A. saccharinum*), commonly known as Freeman's maple. At least some of these hybrids produce viable seed. For additional information, see "united maple" under "Myths, Legends, Tales, Folklore, and Interesting Facts".

Red maple (*Acer rubrum*) growing near water. Photo courtesy of C. Evans (River to River CWMA), and Bugwood.org.

Red maple (*Acer rubrum*) foliage in autumn. Photo courtesy of R. Gillis, Dow Gardens (Michigan) and Bugwood.org.

Red maple (*Acer rubrum*) cultivar 'Northwood'. Photo courtesy of R. Gillis, Dow Gardens (Michigan) and Bugwood.org.

RED MAPLE (*ACER RUBRUM*) (CONT'D)

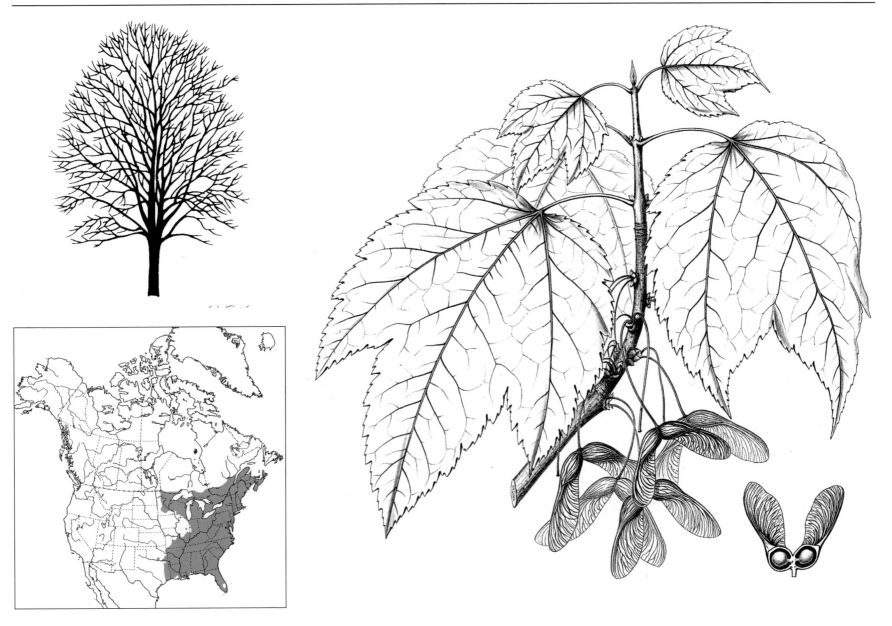

A BIODIVERSITY TREASURE

SILVER MAPLE (*ACER SACCHARINUM*)

Silver maple resembles red maple, described above, and hybridizes with it extensively, so that many trees are difficult to distinguish. (For information on a hybrid, see section on red maple.) The leaves of silver maple normally have much deeper lobes than the leaves of red maple, and have a silvery-white appearance on their underside (hence the "silver" in the name). Like red maple, silver maple is also an eastern Canadian tree, but has a more restricted distribution, and is frequently found growing beside streams and in wet soil. In Canada it grows to 35 m (115 feet) in height and 1 m (40 inches) in diameter. Silver maple is the first native maple to flower in the spring. The relatively soft wood is used to a small extent for various purposes, but the supply is limited. Silver maple is exceptionally impressive in form, relatively tolerant of air pollution and urban conditions, and quite fast growing. Accordingly, it is widely planted as a shade and street tree, although its foliage is not particularly colourful in the autumn (mostly pale yellow, but rarely orange or red). Many cultivated varieties have exceptionally deeply lobed leaves. Unfortunately because the roots are adapted to wet soil, when planted near sewer pipes the roots often clog them. The roots can also crack sidewalks and foundations, and the extensive roots near the soil surface make it difficult to mow grass or plant shrubs near the tree. The Iroquois pounded the bark to make flour for bread, but native peoples used the tree mostly as a source of sugar and syrup. The seeds are the largest of the native North American maples, and are a food source for wildlife, particularly squirrels (wild food enthusiasts sometimes roast and consume the seeds). Squirrels also heavily consume the youngest buds in the spring.

Silver maple (*Acer saccharinum*) growing on the Central Experimental Farm, Ottawa.

Foliage of silver maple (*Acer saccharinum*). Photo courtesy of Thomas Voekler.

SILVER MAPLE (*ACER SACCHARINUM*) (CONT'D)

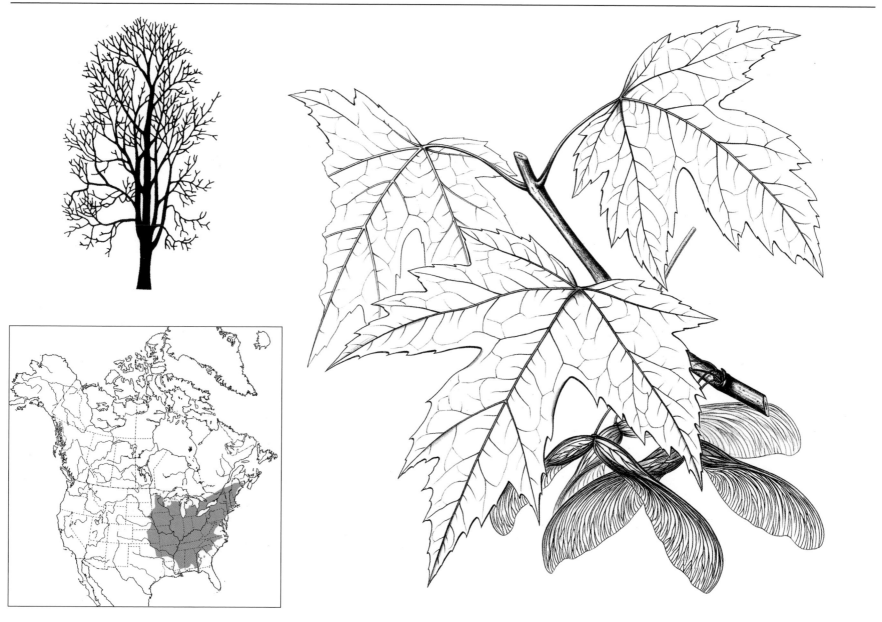

STRIPED MAPLE (*ACER PENSYLVANICUM*)

Striped maple is a large shrub or very small tree, in Canada rarely taller than 10 m (33 feet) and more than 25 cm (10 inches) in diameter. The species is distinctive in having striped bark. The long, vertical, greenish-white stripes are particularly conspicuous when young, but with age become grayish. Sex expression is curious in striped maple, some trees always producing only male flowers, others only female flowers, still others both kinds of flowers, and some trees producing male flowers in some years and female flowers in other years. Striped maple has been called "goosefoot maple" because of the shape of the leaf. The species is a native of southeastern Canada and northeastern United States. It occurs in the shade of eastern Canadian forests from Ontario to the Maritimes, often in association with mountain maple. Striped maple is occasionally planted as an ornamental, valued for its striking bark and tolerance to shade. The leaves turn pale yellow in the autumn. The wood is soft and does not have commercial value. The expression "(tiger) striped maple" refers to wood with stripes like those of a tiger, used for very high quality ornamental applications; it is not obtained from striped maple. The Micmacs of the Maritimes made tea from the bark. An anti-tumour substance has been isolated from the plant. The alternative names "moosewood" and "moose maple" reflect the fact that the leaves and young shoots are a favourite food of moose, but a wide variety of wildlife also consume the plant. Buck deer are fond of rubbing the velvet off their antlers against striped maple prior to the late-autumn breeding season, and consequently the resulting scars on the branches and trunks are called "buck rubs". The spelling *pensylvanicum* (with one "n") was the correct spelling when the name was coined, and must be retained according to the rules of botanical nomenclature.

Foliage of striped maple (*Acer pensylvanicum*). Photo courtesy of Jean-Pol Grandmont.

Striped maple (*Acer pensylvanicum*) growing at the edge of a forest at Zena, New York, with pine and hickory in the background. Source: Wikipedia (public domain photo).

Bark of young tree (left) and mature tree (right) of striped maple (*Acer pensylvanicum*) growing in Great Smoky Mountains National Park, Tennessee. Photos courtesy of C. Evans (River to River CWMA), and Bugwood.org.

STRIPED MAPLE (*ACER PENSYLVANICUM*) (CONT'D)

VINE MAPLE (*ACER CIRCINATUM*)

Vine maple is a large, contorted, gnarled, crooked, multi-stemmed shrub or very small tree up to 10 m (33 feet) in height and 15 cm (6 inches) in diameter. Branches sometimes touch the ground and take root. The species occurs along stream banks and in the shade of forests, from southwestern British Columbia to northern California, within 300 km (186 miles) of the Pacific Ocean. Dense thickets are sometimes formed. *Circinatum* in the scientific name means coiled, referring to the branches, which tend to coil around other trees, like a vine; also, the branches often become depressed by snow, extending horizontally as far as the height of the plant (another characteristic leading to the name "vine maple"). Early wilderness travellers called the plant "Devil's wood" because they often stumbled over the low-spreading branches.

The wood has very little commercial value, but is occasionally used for tool handles and fuel. First Nations people also carved household objects such as bowls, spoons, and platters, as well as a variety of tools from the wood. Aboriginal people on the West Coast boiled the bark of the roots to make a tea for colds, and used teas prepared with burned wood to combat dysentery and polio; they ritually collected the bark and wood early in the morning from the sunrise side of the tree. Karok Indian women of California made a love potion out of the branches. There are several ornamental cultivars of vine maple, which is often grown in its native area. The species is browsed to some extent by wildlife.

A range of leaf colouration in vine maple (*Acer circinatum*). Leaves collected by D. Otis, photo courtesy of D. Mosquin.

Vine maple (*Acer circinatum*), photograph October 1, 1959 in Oregon. Photo courtesy of G. Dallas and M. Hanna, and the California Academy of Sciences.

VINE MAPLE (*ACER CIRCINATUM*) (CONT'D)

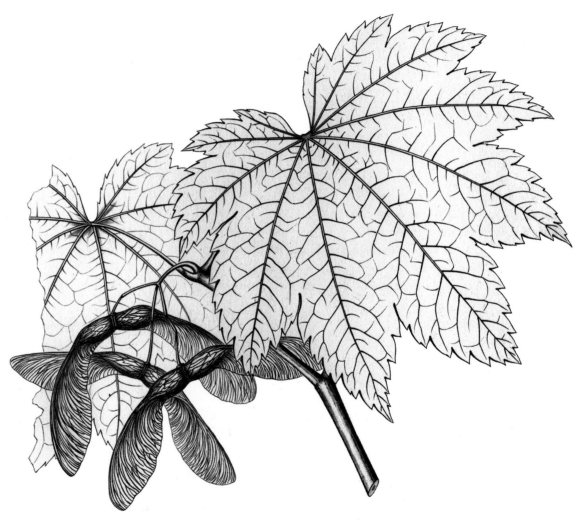

Vine maple (*Acer circinatum*), growing in an exposed site within E.C. Manning Provincial Park, British Columbia. Plants in sunny areas tend to develop much more intense autumn colouration, as shown here. Photo courtesy of D. Mosquin.

OFFICIAL PLANT EMBLEMS OF CANADA

CONSERVATION STATUS

About a third of the world's maples are considered to be in danger of extinction, most of these native to China (see *Gibbs and Chen* cited below). However, North American maple species are not considered to be endangered, although there is concern that populations at the range limits, which almost certainly are genetically distinct, are in danger of elimination. Decline of certain forest tree species in parts of their distribution range has been documented in various regions of the world for hundreds of years, but especially during the last century. Maple dieback or decline in recent years has caused great concern in the sugar maple industry. Among the possible causes are 1) insect defoliation, 2) fungus attack, 3) deep soil freezing at times of low snow cover, 4) atmospheric deposition of acid rain and heavy metals and 5) ozone.

Collecting sugar maple sap. Source: Thinkstock.

TAR SPOT DISEASE OF MAPLES IN THE OTTAWA DISTRICT

Maples are host to considerable biodiversity including numerous insects and fungi. Much of this goes unnoticed, but the maple tar spot fungus which discolours leaves with tar-like spots draws a lot of attention. Is the tree going to die? What are the spots? During a year when it is prevalent, they make the newspaper and people want to know what to do. People want to burn theirs leaves and apply fungicides. These spots are actually nothing to worry about and they do not mean that the tree is going to die. Often for a few years after a big tar spot year, there is not enough to be noticed and it is again forgotten for a while.

Corlett, M.P. and Catling, P.M. 2009. What is it?—1. Tar spot disease of maples in the Ottawa District. Trail and Landscape 43(4): 145–150.

1 cm

Maple tar spots fungus on a leaf of Norway maple from Ottawa. Photo by P.M. Catling.

A BIODIVERSITY TREASURE

MYTHS, LEGENDS, TALES, FOLKLORE AND INTERESTING FACTS

✤ On journeys, the Iroquois carried maple syrup in empty quail and duck eggs, the first "no-deposit-no-return" biodegradable containers.

✤ Indigenous peoples of northeastern North America sometimes used maple products as currency.

✤ In pioneering days of the United States, apples and such root crops as carrots and potatoes were stored separately between layers of maple leaves to help in their preservation.

✤ In the Alsace region of France, it was believed that storks place a piece of maple in their nests to frighten away bats, fearing that the touch of the bats would make the eggs infertile.

✤ The most prolific composer of ragtime music was Scott Joplin (1868–1917). He published approximately 50 rags, but probably composed about 600. The most famous of Joplin's rags was *Maple Leaf Rag*, which sold hundreds of thousands of copies in the first ten years it was published.

✤ All maples are "hardwoods", a term used to designate most deciduous trees, as opposed to the "softwoods", the contrasting term referring in general to coniferous, evergreen trees, which generally have softer wood than the hardwoods. Most North American species of *Acer*, including sugar maple, are "hard maples", so-called because of the very hard texture of the wood. Some maples, like silver maple and red maple, are "soft maples", with softer, although still quite hard, wood. Maple wood can be identified as hard or soft by applying a solution of ferric salt to the sapwood; blue stain indicates a soft maple and green stain identifies the tree as a hard maple. In Maine, it was once thought that too much fertilizer and rich earth could change a hard maple into a soft maple.

✤ Maple sap that flows in the spring appears to come from all directions (not just from the roots): from above, below, and sideways within the tree, apparently to prepare critical areas of the plant for growth. The lateral flow provides sugar to the growing part of the tree trunk (cambium), near the bark, for active growth in the spring.

✤ Maple keys (the winged seeds, technically called samaras) have an exquisite aerodynamic design. With a moderate wind blowing, these can travel as much as 160 m (525 feet) away from the tree. The key design features that seem to provide better flight performance are the thickened leading edge of the wing part and the roughened surface, characteristics similar to bird wings. The samaras are often compared to helicopters but, in flight, they cut into the air at very sharp angles that would cause stalling in a helicopter.

✤ Some large red maple trees can produce a million seeds in one season.

✤ "Big Yo", the world's largest yo-yo, displayed in the National Yo-yo Museum in Chico, California, weighs 116 kg (256 pounds) and is partly made of maple.

✤ The Canadian botanist W.G. Dore (1912–1996) pointed out that two North American maples, silver maple and red maple, widely hybridize and intermingle in Canada to produce "a tree of mixed parentage, a vigorous and vital breed, newly sprung from the particular milieu which pertains to Canada!" Dr. Dore proposed the name "united maple" for the hybrid tree, and recommended that it be identified as Canada's emblematic maple.

✤ The Toronto Maple Leaf hockey team of the National Hockey League has a problem with the plural of leaf. The usual spelling when referring to the team collectively is "Toronto Maple Leafs," although occasionally those who are offended by this ungrammatical spelling call them the "Toronto Maple Leaves". As pointed out on one website, "Maple Leafs? Did Elmer Fudd name this team? I guess they have chifes on their baked potatoes, and cut them with knifes."

✤ According to an ancient Oriental gardening rule, maples should always be planted on the western side of a house. Whether or not this is rationale, it does mean that in the fall the late afternoon sun streaming through the crown will show up the colourful foliage in its most attractive light.

SOURCES OF ADDITIONAL INFORMATION

Alward A., Corriher, C.A., Barton, M.H., Sellon, D.C., Blikslager, A.T., and Jones, S.L. 2006. Red maple (*Acer rubrum*) leaf toxicosis in horses: a retrospective study of 32 cases. J. Vet. Intern. Med. 20: 1197–1201.

Dansereau, P., and Desmarais, Y. 1947. Introgression in sugar maples—II. Am. Midl. Nat. 37: 146–161.

Deschênes, J.-M. 1970. The history of the genus *Acer*, a review. Naturaliste Can. 97: 51–59.

Dore, W.G. 1967. A mingling of maples. Trail & Landscape (Ottawa Field-Naturalist Club) 1: 64–67.

Gelderen, D.M. van, de Jong, P.C., Oterdoom, H.J., and van Hoey Smith, J.R.P. 1994. Maples of the world. Timber Press, Inc., Portland, OR. 512 pp.

Gelderon, C.J. van, and Gelderon, D.M. van. 1999. Maples for gardens: a color encyclopedia. Timber Press, Portland, OR. 294 pp.

Gibbs, D., and Chen, Y. 2009. The red list of maples. Botanic Gardens Conservation International, Richmond, U.K. 40 pp.

Gunter, L.E., Tuskan, G.A., Gunderson, C.A., and Norby, R.J. 2000. Genetic variation and spatial structure in sugar maple (*Acer saccharum* Marsh.) and implications for predicted global scale environmental change. Glob. Chang. Biol. 6: 335–344.

Harris, J. 2000. The gardener's guide to growing maples. David & Charles, Newton Abbot, Devon, U.K. 160 pp.

Hibbs, D.E., and Fischer, B.C. 1979. Sexual and vegetative reproduction of striped maple (*Acer pensylvanicum* L.). Bull. Torrey Bot. Club 106: 222–227.

Hibbs, D.E., Wilson, B.F., and Fischer, B.C. 1980. Habitat requirements and growth of striped maple (*Acer pensylvanicum* L.). Ecology 61: 490–496.

Horsley, S.B., and Long, R.P. (*Editors*). 1999. Sugar maple ecology and health: proceedings of an international symposium, June 2–4, 1998, Warren, Pennsylvania. USDA Forest Service, Northeastern Research Station, Radnor, PA. 120 pp.

Horsley, S.B., Long, R.P., Bailey, S.W., Hallett, R.A., and Wargo, P.M. 2002. Health of eastern North American sugar maple forests and factors affecting decline. Northern J. Appl. For. 19: 34–44.

Foliage of Japanese maple (*Acer palmatum*), cultivar 'Osakazuki'. This colourful shrubby tree native to eastern Asia is widely grown as an ornamental in Canada . Photo courtesy of Jean-Pol Grandmont.

SOURCES OF ADDITIONAL INFORMATION (CONT'D)

Kriebel, H.B. 1957. Patterns of genetic variation in sugar maple. Ohio Agric. Expt. Stat. Res. Bull. 791. 56 pp.

Kriebel, H.B. 1989. Genetic improvement of sugar maple for high sap sugar content. I. Clone selection and seed orchard development. Can. J. For. Res. 19: 917–923.

Kriebel, H.B. 1990. Genetic improvement of sugar maple for high sap sugar content. II. Relative effectiveness of maternal and biparental selection. Can. J. For. Res. 20: 837–844.

Larsson, H.C., and Jaciw, P. 1967. Sap and syrup of five maple species. Ontario Department of Lands and Forests, Research Report 69. Maple, ON. 62 pp.

Le Hardÿ de Beaulieu, A., and Mechelynck, A.L. 2003. An illustrated guide to maples. Timber Press, Portland, OR. 464 pp.

Maeglin, R.R., and Ohmann, L.F. 1973. Boxelder (*Acer negundo*): A review and commentary. Bull. Torrey Bot. Club 100: 357–363.

Millers, I., Lachance, D., Burkman, W.G., and Allen, D.C. 1991. North American sugar maple decline project: organization and field methods. U.S. Dep. Agric. For. Serv. Gen. Tech. Rep. NE-154. 26 pp.

Munson, P.J. 1989. Still more on the antiquity of maple sugar and syrup in aboriginal eastern North America. J. Ethnobiol. 9: 159–170.

Nearing, H., and Nearing, S. 1950. The maple sugar book. The John Day Company, New York, NY. 271 pp.

Northeastern Forest Experiment Station 1982. Sugar maple research: sap production, processing, and marketing of maple syrup. U.S. Dep. Agric. For. Serv. NE For. Exp. Stn. Gen. Tech. Rep. NE-72. 109 pp.

Pendergast, J.F. 1982. The origin of maple sugar. National Museums of Canada, National Museum of Natural Sciences, Ottawa, ON. 79 pp.

Schaberg, P.G., Van Den Berg, A.K., Murakami, P.F., Shane, J.B., and Donnelly, J.R. 2003. Factors influencing red expression in autumn foliage of sugar maple trees. Tree Physiol. 23: 325–333.

Skepner, A.P., and Krane, D.E. 1997. cpDNA of *Acer saccharum* and *Acer nigrum* are very similar. Ohio J. Sci. 97: 90–94.

Skepner, A.P., and Krane, D.E. 1998. RAPD reveals genetic similarity of *Acer saccharum* and *Acer nigrum*. Nature 80: 422–428.

Sullivan, J.R. 1983. Comparative reproductive biology of *Acer pensylvanicum* and *A. spicatum* (Aceraceae). Am. J. Bot. 70: 916–924.

ACKNOWLEDGMENTS

The maps in this chapter are based on: Little, E.L., Jr. 1971. Atlas of United States Trees. U.S. Department of Agriculture, Forest Service, Washington, D.C. Vol. 1, 1971 (plates 95–99, 101), Vol. 3. 1976 (plates 8, 9), Vol. 4, 1977 (plates, 3, 4). The black and white illustrations of maple species are based on: Sargent, C.S. 1891. The silva of North America. Houghton, Mifflin and Company, Boston, MA. Vol. 2 (plates 83, 85, 87–91, 3, 94, 96). The tree silhouettes are reproduced with permission from: Farrar, J.L. 1995. Trees in Canada. Canadian Forest Service and Fitzhenry and Whiteside, Markham, ON, Canada.

The world's largest coin. Five copies of this coin featuring a sprig of three maple leaves were produced in 2007 by the Canadian Mint. The coin measures 53 cm (almost 21 inches) in diameter, 3 cm (1.2 inches) in width, weighs 100 kg (220 pounds), and is 99.999% pure gold. It is listed in the Guinness Book of World Records as the world's largest coin. Although it carries a face value of $1 million Canadian, with the current high price of gold the bullion in the coin is worth considerably more. In 2010, one of the coins was sold at auction for more than $4 million. Coin image supplied by and reproduced with the permission of ©The Canadian Mint.

APPENDIX: THOUSANDS OF OTHER CANADIAN PLANTS: A GUIDE TO INFORMATION

Northern Canadian plant biodiversity. Source: Thinkstock.

In addition to the official plant emblems of Canada, its provinces, and its territories, several native Canadian species are recognized locally in official legislation, such as salmonberry (*Rubus spectabilis* Pursh) shown here. Salmonberry is a shrub native to British Columbia, with berries that are valued by First Nations people and wild food enthusiasts. The Badge and Insignia of the village of Port Alice, British Columbia, featuring a bald eagle in a circle of salmonberry flowers, is shown in the centre. The figure at left is from: Lindley, J. 1831. Edwards's Botanical Register, Vol. 17, Plate 1424, James Ridgway, London, U.K.; the figure at right is from Loddiges, C. and Sons. 1830. The botanical cabinet, Vol. 17, Plate 1602, Longman, Rees, Orme, Brown, & Greene, London, U.K.

INTRODUCTION

In concentrating on the official botanical symbols of Canada, this book has highlighted only about 1% of the more than 4,000 native flowering plants occurring in the nation. Many of the other plants are important for agriculture, forestry, medicine, recreation, and other purposes. Indeed virtually all plants are useful in one way or another. To utilize, protect, and enjoy Canada's plants, it is necessary to identify them, and to have sources of information about them. This appendix provides a guide to resources serving to identify and give basic information about the plants of Canada. References listed below include many with identification keys, descriptions, and illustrations. Frequently we have added comments [in square brackets] for publications that we have personally found useful as professional botanists for identifying plants. However, we have included not only the basic manuals that are utilized by professional biologists, but also many of the more user-friendly guides to common plants that are copiously illustrated with excellent photographs, making identification a pleasant pastime for the average person. We have often excluded works of narrow coverage where a more comprehensive or recent guide is available. Some of the references are based mostly on regions bordering Canada, but are nevertheless quite useful for identifying plants in adjacent parts of Canada. Geographically-based texts are not the only kinds of identification aids that are available. Others include special bibliographies, guides to vascular plant herbaria (museums with collections of preserved reference specimens) and their staff (specialists in classification and identification), manuals on to how to collect and preserve reference samples, and information organized in subject categories such as cultivated plants, woody plants, poisonous plants, edible plants, aquatic plants, and weeds. Also included in the following are special information sources that will assist with identifications, determining correct names, and finding related information. It is our hope that this book will stimulate many readers to become more familiar with the plants in their local areas, as well as in places they may visit in Canada, and some of the following guides should be very useful for these purposes.

Garden lupin (*Lupinus polyphyllus*) growing in Newfoundland. This native of western North America has become widely established elsewhere.

As well as searching under the geographical regions listed below, also examine the lists of special categories of plants for additional information. For example Brayshaw's work on the trees and shrubs of British Columbia is listed under "Trees and Shrubs" rather than under British Columbia.

LOCATION OF INFORMATION SOURCES

A lesson in plant identification. Frontispiece of: Pallas, P.S. 1784. Flora Rossica, vol. 1. Imperiali J.J. Weitbrecht, Petropoli (St. Petersburg), Russia. Coloured by B. Brookes.

GUIDES TO LARGE AREAS OF CANADA

Aiken, S.G., Dallwitz, M.J., Consaul, L.L. et al. 2007. Flora of the Canadian Arctic Archipelago: descriptions, illustrations, identification, and information retrieval. [CD-ROM] NRC Research Press, National Research Council of Canada, Ottawa, ON. [An important reference about northern Canadian plants.]

Boivin, B. 1966–1968. Énumération des plantes du Canada. Provancheria (Mémoires de l'Herbier Louis-Marie, Université Laval, Quebec) n° 6. Irregularly paginated. [An authoritative compilation of Canadian plant species, with an indication of their distribution and references to related classification literature. Also published in Naturaliste Canadian vols. 93 and 94.]

Boivin, B. 1967–1981. Flora of the Prairie Provinces. Provancheria (Mémoires de l'Herbier Louis-Marie, Faculté d'Agriculture, Université Laval). 5 vols. [Lacking illustrations (except for part 5) and distribution maps, nevertheless the most complete flora for the Prairie Provinces.] Part 1 (1967). Pteroids, ferns, conifers and woody dicopsids. Provancheria 2: 1–202. (Reprinted from Phytologia 15: 121–159, 329–446; 16: 1–47). Part 2 (1968–1969). Digitatae, Dimerae, Liberae. Provancheria 3: 1–185. (Reprinted from Phytologia 16, 17, 18). Part 3 (1972). Connatae. Provancheria 4: 1–224. (Reprinted from Phytologia 22, 23). Part 4 (1979). Monopsida. Provancheria 5: 1–189. (Reprinted from Phytologia 42, 43). Part 5 (1981). Gramineae. Provancheria 12: 1–107.

Boivin, B. 1992. Les Cypéracées de l'est du Canada. Provancheria 25: 1–230. [A guide to the sedge family of Canada, with all species illustrated.]

Budd, A.C., Looman, J., Best, K.F., and Waddington, J. 1987. Budd's flora of the Canadian Prairie Provinces. (Latest revision.) Research Branch Publication 1662. Agriculture Canada, Ottawa, ON. 863 pp. [Includes many illustrations but not distribution maps.]

Campbell, C.S., Hyland, F., and Campbell, M.L.F. 1975. Winter keys to woody plants of Maine. University of Maine Press, Orono, ME. 52 pp. + plates. [Useful for identifying leafless plants in winter of northeastern Canada.]

Fernald, M.L. 1950. Gray's manual of botany. 8th edition. Van Nostrand Reinhold, New York, NY. 1632 pp. [One of the most useful floras ever produced and still very valuable despite its age. Page 6 notes that this guide covers "the area south of the Straits of Belle Isle and from Anticosti Island westward along the 49th parallel of latitude in Quebec to the northwestern corner of Minnesota." This includes the southern tip of NF-LAB; all of NF-NFLD, NS, PE, and NB; southern, central, and northwestern ON; and southern QC; useful for southern MB, but not intended to cover this region. The 1970 printing includes corrections.]

Feilberg, J., Fredskild, B., and Holt, S. 1984. Flowers of Greenland. Ahrent Flensborgs Florag, Copenhagen, Denmark. [In English and Danish; a beautifully illustrated small guide that is useful for plants of arctic Canada.]

Flora of North America Editorial Committee. Flora of North America north of Mexico. Oxford University Press, New York, NY. [Sixteen of the 30 volumes planned to cover the entire flora of North America are currently available as outlined below. There is variation in the quality of the treatments in this work, but many are written by world authorities and include the most current taxonomic decisions. Most of the information is available online: http://www.efloras.org/flora_page.aspx?flora_id=1. To find the volume in which a family appears, see http://www.fna.org/FNA/families.shtml .]
1993. Vol. 1. Introduction. 372 pp.
1993. Vol. 2, Pteridophytes and Gymnosperms. 475 pp.
1997. Vol. 3, Magnoliophyta: Magnoliidae and Hamamelidae. 590 pp.
2000. Vol. 22, Magnoliophyta: Alismatidae, Arecidae, Commelinidae (in part), and Zingiberidae. 352 pp.
2002. Vol. 26, Magnoliophyta: Liliidae and Orchidales. 723 pp.
2002. Vol. 23, Magnoliophyta: Commelinidae (in part): Cyperaceae. 608 pp.
2003. Vol. 25, Magnoliophyta: Commelinidae (in part): Poaceae, part 2. 783 pp. [This volume covers over half of the grass family in North America north of Mexico. It and volume 24 (cited below) differ from the other *Flora of North America* volumes in that they were originally intended for publication under a separate title within a single volume—a successor to Hitchcock's classic *Manual of Grasses of the United States*. With identification a key focus, the two grass

GUIDES TO LARGE AREAS OF CANADA (CONT'D)

volumes have many more illustrations than other FNA volumes: almost every species is illustrated. Also included are species known only from cultivation, and species that are considered serious threats to North American agriculture but which are not yet established. Compare Barkworth et al. (2007) listed below in "Grasses", which provides essentially the same information.]

2003. Vol. 4, Magnoliophyta: Caryophyllidae, part 1. 559 pp.

2005. Vol. 5, Magnoliophyta: Caryophyllidae, part 2. 656 pp.

2006. Vol. 19, Magnoliophyta: Asteridae (in part): Asteraceae, part 1. 579 pp.

2006. Vol. 20. Magnoliophyta: Asteridae (in part): Asteraceae, part 2. 666 pp.

2006. Vol. 21. Magnoliophyta: Asteridae (in part): Asteraceae, part 3. 616 pp.

2007. Vol. 24. Magnoliophyta: Commelinidae (in part): Poaceae (part 1). 911 pp.

2007. Vol. 27. Bryophyta: Mosses, part 1. 713 pp.

2009. Vol. 8. Magnoliophyta: Paeoniaceae to Ericaceae. 585 pp.

2010. Vol. 7. Magnoliophyta: Salicaceae to Brassicaceae. 797 pp.

Gleason, H.A. 1968. The new Britton and Brown illustrated flora of the Northeastern United States and adjacent Canada. Hafner, New York, NY. 3 vols. [This very useful, illustrated manual is superseded by the combination of Gleason and Cronquist (1991) + Holmgren (1998).]

Gleason, H.A. and Cronquist, A. 1991 (7th printing, 2004). Manual of vascular plants of Northeastern United States and adjacent Canada. 2nd edition. The New York Botanical Garden, Bronx, NY. 993 pp. [Covers NS, PE, NB, southern QC, southern and central ON; useful for northwestern ON and southern MN, but not intended to cover this region. Page numbers in this non-illustrated manual correspond to the illustrations on the matching page numbers in Holmgren 1998, listed below. The 7th printing, 2004, includes corrections and other changes, outlined in Foreword on p. v).]

Hitchcock, C.L. and Cronquist, A. 1973. Flora of the Pacific Northwest. University of Washington Press, Seattle, WA. 730 pp. [An authoritative flora with illustrated keys. Includes "an indefinite fringe of British Columbia."]

GUIDES TO LARGE AREAS OF CANADA (CONT'D)

Hitchcock, C.L., Cronquist, A., Ownbey, M., and Thompson, J.W. (Editors). 1955–1969. Vascular plants of the Pacific Northwest. University of Washington Press, Seattle, WA. [A classic and popular flora that includes "an indefinite southern fringe of British Columbia." Has excellent descriptions, illustrations and keys. Hitchcock and Cronquist (1973), listed above, is a condensed version.]
1955. Part 5, Compositae. 343 pp.
1959. Part 4, Ericaceae through Campanulaceae. 510 pp.
1961. Part 3, Saxifragaceae to Ericaceae. 614 pp.
1964. Part 2, Salicaceae to Saxifragaceae. 597 pp.
1969. Part 1, vascular cryptogams, gymnosperms and monocotyledons. 914 pp.

Holmgren, N.H. 1998. Illustrated companion to Gleason and Cronquist's Manual. The New York Botanical Garden, Bronx, NY. 937 pp. [This is the illustrated companion to the most current floristic guide to northeastern North America (see Gleason and Cronquist 1991 listed above).]

Johnson, D., Kershaw, L., MacKinnon, A., and Pojar, J. 1995. Plants of the western boreal forest & aspen parkland. Lone Pine Publishing, Edmonton, AB. 392 pp. [This guide includes many colour photographs, as well as illustrated keys, and covers a large area of western Canada.]

Kartesz, J. T. and Meacham, C.A. 1999. Synthesis of the North American Flora, version 1.0. North Carolina Botanical Garden, Chapel Hill, North Carolina. [A CD-ROM with interactive software. This is a comprehensive, authoritative source of names of vascular plants and their synonyms combined with information on geography, common names, biological attributes, and uses.]

McGregor, R.L. and Barkley, T.M. (Editors.) 1977. Atlas of the Flora of the Great Plains. Iowa State University Press, Ames, IO. 600 pp. [Presents distribution maps for species treated in the following flora. Useful for determining which plants occur at the Canadian border.]

McGregor, R.L., Barkley, T.M., Brooks, R.E., and Schofield, E.K. (Editors.) 1986. Flora of the Great Plains. University Press of Kansas, Lawrence, KS. 1392 pp. [The plains region extends into the southern portions of AB, SK, and MB. Although most of the Great Plains are in the U.S., a large proportion of the species also occurs in Canada.]

McKenny, M. and Peterson, R.T. 1998. A field guide to wildflowers: Northeastern and North-Central North America (Peterson Field Guides). Houghton Mifflin Harcourt, Boston, MA. 448 pp.

Polunin, N. 1940. Botany of the Canadian eastern arctic. Bull. 92. Nat. Mus. Can., Ottawa, ON. 408 pp. [A classic and comprehensive work.]

Polunin, N. 1959. Circumpolar arctic flora. Oxford Univ. Press, Oxford, U.K. 514 pp. [Although dated, this is still a very valuable reference. Includes many illustrations, but no distribution maps.]

Scoggan, H.J. 1978–1979. The flora of Canada. National Museum of Natural Sciences, Ottawa, ON. 4 vols. [A valuable compilation of information on the Canadian flora, includes identification keys and information on distribution, but lacks detailed descriptions and illustrations.]
Part 1 (1978): General survey. Publications in Botany 7(1): 1–89.
Part 2 (1978): Pteridophyta, Gymnospermae, Monocotyledoneae. Publications in Botany 7(2): 93–544.
Part 3 (1978): Dicotyledoneae (Saururaceae to Violaceae). Publications in Botany 7(3): 547–1115.
Part 4 (1979): Dicotyledoneae (Loasaceae to Compositae). Publications in Botany 7(4): 1117–1711.

Swink, F. 1990. The key to the vascular flora of the northeastern United States and southeastern Canada. Plantsmen's Publications, Flossmore, IL. 514 pp. [A useful identification aid.]

Also note "Database of Canadian Vascular Plants (VASCAN)" http://data.canadensys.net/vascan/search/; this provides general information on names and distribution.

GUIDES TO PROVINCES AND TERRITORIES

Alberta

Faust, R. and Faust, P. 1999 Wildflowers of the Inland Northwest: Idaho, Montana, Washington, Oregon, British Columbia, & Alberta. Museum of North Idaho, Coeur d'Alene, ID. 141 pp.

Hallworth, B. and Chinnappa, C.C. 1997. Plants of Kananaskis Country, in the Rocky Mountains of Alberta. University of Alberta Press, Edmonton, AB. 366 pp. [An excellent guide with line drawings, keys, colour photographs, and descriptions. Although local, it applies to much of the Rocky Mountain area.]

Jennings, N.L. 2006. Uncommon beauty: wildflowers and flowering shrubs of southern Alberta and southeastern British Columbia. Rocky Mountain Books, Victoria, BC. 246 pp.

Kershaw, L. 2003. Alberta wayside wildflowers. Lone Pine, Edmonton, AB. 160 pp.

Kuijt, J. 1982. A flora of Waterton Lakes National Park. The University of Alberta Press, Edmonton, AB. 684 pp. [A well illustrated and useful guide, covering a large portion of the Rocky Mountains.]

Moss, E.H. and Packer, J.G. 1983. Flora of Alberta. 2nd edition. University of Toronto Press, Toronto, ON. 687 pp. [Has distribution maps, no illustrations.]

Royer, F. and Dickinson, R. 2007. Plants of Alberta. Trees, shrubs, wildflowers, ferns, aquatic plants & grasses. Lone Pine, Edmonton, AB. 527 pp.

Wilkinson, K. 1999. Wildflowers of Alberta: a guide to common wildflowers and other herbaceous plants. Lone Pine, Edmonton, AB. 364 pp.

British Columbia

Note: There are numerous excellent guides to specific groups of plants of British Columbia that were produced by the Royal British Columbia Museum, but these are superseded by Douglas et al., cited below, for identification purposes. However, in many cases they contain additional information, and deserve to be on the bookshelf of any serious student of the B.C. flora.

Angove, K. and Bancroft, B. 1983. A guide to some common plants of the southern interior of British Columbia. Ministry of Forests, Province of B.C., Victoria, BC. 225 pp.

Burbridge, J. 1989. Wildflowers of the southern interior of British Columbia and adjacent parts of Washington, Idaho, and Montana. University of British Columbia Press, Vancouver, BC. 398 pp.

Calder, J.A. and Taylor, R.L. 1968. Flora of the Queen Charlotte Islands. Part 1, Systematics of the Vascular Plants. Monograph No 4 Part 1. Canada Department of Agriculture, Ottawa, ON. 659 pp. [Includes a few illustrations and many distribution maps.]

Clark, L.J. 1973. Wildflowers of British Columbia. Gray's Pub., Canada. 591 pp.

Clark, L.J. 1998. Wild flowers of the Pacific Northwest. 3rd edition. Harbour, Madeira Park, BC. 604 pp.

Coupé, R., Parish, R., Lloyd, D., and Antos, J. 1996. Plants of southern interior British Columbia and the inland northwest. Lone Pine, Vancouver, BC. 463 pp.

Craighead, J.J., Craighead, F.C., Jr., and Davis, R.J. 1991. A field guide to Rocky Mountain wildflowers: northern Arizona and New Mexico to British Columbia. Houghton Mifflin, Boston, MA. 275 pp.

Douglas, G.W., et al. (Editors). 1999–2002. Illustrated Flora of British Columbia. [Note the two series below. This flora includes many illustrations in each volume and distribution maps in volume 8. Provides up-to-date and definitive coverage of the flora of British Columbia. Related to this is E-Flora BC, Electronic atlas of the plants of British Columbia, http://www.geog.ubc.ca/biodiversity/eflora/efloraintroductionpage.html, which presents much of the information in this flora (note cautions regarding validity of map data)]

Douglas, G.W., Straley, G.B., Meidinger, D., and Pojar, J. (Editors). 1999–2002. Illustrated Flora of British Columbia, Victoria, BC. Ministry of Environment, Lands and Parks, and Ministry of Forests, British Columbia. Vols. 1–2. Volume 1 (1998): Gymnosperms and Dicotyledons (Aceraceae through Asteraceae). 436 pp.
Volume 2 (1998): Dicotyledons (Balsaminaceae through Cuscutaceae). 401 pp.
[This series was continued below, without Straley as an editor.]

GUIDES TO PROVINCES AND TERRITORIES (CONT'D)

Douglas, G.W., Meidinger, D., and Pojar, J. (Editors). 1999–2002. Illustrated Flora of British Columbia. Ministry of Environment, Lands and Parks, and Ministry of Forests, British Columbia, Victoria, BC. Vols. 3–8.
Volume 3 (1999): Dicotyledons (Diapensiaceae through Onagraceae). 423 pp.
Volume 4 (1999): Dicotyledons (Orobanchaceae through Rubiaceae). 427 pp.
Volume 5 (2000): Dicotyledons (Salicaceae through Zygophyllaceae) and Pteridophytes. 389 pp.
Volume 6 (2001): Monocotyledons (Acoraceae through Najadaceae). 361 pp.
Volume 7 (2001): Monocotyledons (Orchidaceae through Zosteraceae). 379 pp.
Volume 8 (2002). General summary, maps and keys. 457 pp.

Eastham, J.W. 1947. The flora of southern British Columbia. British Columbia Provincial Museum. Victoria, Special Publication No. 1. 119 pp.

Fagan, D. 2006. Pacific Northwest wildflowers: a guide to common wildflowers of Washington, Oregon, Northern California, Western Idaho, Southeast Alaska, and British Columbia. Falcon Pub., Helena, MO. 229 pp.

Haber, E. and Soper, J.H. 1980. Vascular plants of Glacier National Park, British Columbia, Canada. National Museum of Natural Sciences, National Museums of Canada, Ottawa, ON. 34 pp.

Horn, E.L. 1994. Coastal wildflowers of British Columbia and the Pacific Northwest. Whitecap Books, Vancouver, BC. 179 pp.

Jennings, N.L. 2008. Central beauty: wildflowers and flowering shrubs of the southern interior of British Columbia. Rocky Mountain Books, Vancouver, BC. 303 pp.

Jennings, N.L. 2008. Coastal beauty: wildflowers and flowering shrubs of coastal British Columbia and Vancouver Island. Rocky Mountain Books, Vancouver, BC. 287 pp.

Klinkenberg, B. (Editor) 2010. E-Flora BC: Electronic Atlas of the Plants of British Columbia [eflora.bc.ca]. Lab for Advanced Spatial Analysis, Department of Geography, University of British Columbia, Vancouver. http://www.geog.ubc.ca/biodiversity/eflora/orchidsbc.html

Kershaw, L., MacKinnon, A., and Pojar, J. 1998. Plants of the Rocky Mountains. Lone Pine, Edmonton, AB. 384 pp.

Kozloff, E.N. 2005. Plants of western Oregon, Washington & British Columbia. Timber Press, Portland, OR. 512 pp.

Larrison, E.J. 1974. Washington wildflowers, including 1134 species of wildflowers most commonly found in the state of Washington and adjacent areas of Oregon, Idaho, and British Columbia. Audubon Society, Seattle, WA. 376 pp.

Lyons, C.P., and Merilees, B. 1996. Trees, shrubs, and flowers to know in British Columbia and Washington. Revised edition. Lone Pine, Vancouver, BC. 376 pp. [Based on Lyon's 1965 book.]

MacKinnon, A. and Pojar, J. 2004. Plants of coastal British Columbia. Revised edition. Lone Pine, Edmonton, AB. 528 pp.

MacKinnon, A., Pojar, J., and Coupé, R. 1999. Plants of Northern British Columbia. Revised edition. Lone Pine, Edmonton, AB. 352 pp. [A very useful, user-friendly text for the northern part of the province. It includes keys and illustrations (many in colour).]

Pojar, J. and MacKinnon, A. 2005. Plants of the Pacific Northwest coast: Washington, Oregon, British Columbia and Alaska. Revised edition. Lone Pine Edmonton, AB, 528 pp.

Royal British Columbia Museum Handbooks. These older BC guides are out of print but some are still available for sale at http://www.royalbcmuseum.bc.ca/Shop/out-of-print.aspx. Following is a list of botanical subjects with official handbook number in parentheses.
Edible plants, guide to common (20)
Ferns and fern allies (12)
Figwort family (33)
Food plants of B.C. Indians, Part 1: Coastal Peoples (34)
Grasses (9)
Heather family (19)
Lily family (25)

GUIDES TO PROVINCES AND TERRITORIES (CONT'D)

Orchids (16)
Pea family (32)
Plants in B.C. Indian technology (38)
Rose family (30)
Trees and shrubs, guide to (31)

Sept, J.D. 2006. Common wildflowers of British Columba. 2nd edition. Calypso Publ, Sechelt, BC. 95 pp.

Soper, J.H. and Szczawinski, A.F. 1976. Mount Revelstoke National Park wild flowers. National Museums of Canada (Ottawa) Natural History series No. 3. 96 pp.

Turner, M. and Gustafson, P. 2006. Wildflowers of the Pacific Northwest. Timber Press, Portland, OR. 512 pp.

Manitoba

Anonymous. 1968. Manitoba wildflowers. Dept. of Mines and Natural Resources, MB. 24 pp.

Cody, W.J. 1988. Plants of Riding Mountain National Park, Manitoba. Publication 1818. Research Branch, Agriculture Canada, Ottawa, ON. 319 pp. [Has keys and descriptions of 669 species, and hundreds of illustrations.]

Holland, G. 1996. Wild plants of Birds Hill Provincial Park, Manitoba, Canada. Manitoba Naturalists Society, Winnipeg, MB. 107 pp.

Johnson, K.L. 1987. Wildflowers of Churchill and the Hudson Bay region. Manitoba Museum of Man and Nature, Winnipeg, MB. 400 pp.

Kershaw, L. 2003. Manitoba wayside wildflowers. Lone Pine, Edmonton, AB. 160 pp.

Macdonald, H. 1982. Native Manitoba plants in bog, bush and prairie. Revised edition. Manitoba Agriculture, Winnipeg, MB. 108 pp.

Scoggan, H.J. 1957. Flora of Manitoba. National Museum of Canada Bulletin 140, Biological Series 47. Department of Northern Affairs and National Resources, Ottawa, ON. 619 pp. [An excellent, although dated, compilation of the vascular flora of the province, but lacks illustrations and distribution maps. Additions to this work have been published in the Canadian Field-Naturalist, and are on file in the Manitoba Museum of Man and Nature.]

Scott, P.A. 1996. Flora of Churchill, Manitoba. 8th edition. Dept. of Biological Sciences, University of Alberta, Edmonton, AB. 76 pp.

New Brunswick

Harries, H., MacKinnon, C.M., and Ellingwood, C. 1991. The flora of Cape Jourimain National Wildlife Area, New Brunswick. Canadian Wildlife Service, Atlantic Region, Sackville NB. 131 pp.

Hinds, H.R., Young, C.M., and Clayden, S.R. 2000. Flora of New Brunswick. 2nd edition. University of New Brunswick, Fredericton, NB. 699 pp. [Maps and illustrations are provided for most species. Additions and corrections are available at http://www.unb.ca/fredericton/science/biology/.].

Also see Haines and Vining (1998) under Quebec.

Newfoundland and Labrador

Alexander, A. 2000. Flora of peatland ecosystems in Newfoundland and Labrador and the French islands of St. Pierre and Miquelon. A. Robertson, St. John's NL. 209 pp.

Bouchard, A., Hay, S., and Rouleau, E. 1978. The vascular flora of St. Barbe South District, Newfoundland; an interpretation based on biophysiographic areas. Rhodora 80: 228–308. [This describes the flora of a large part of Newfoundland.]

Collins, M.A.J. 1994. Plants and wildflowers of Newfoundland. Jesperson Press, St. Johns, NL. 148 pp.

Damman, A.W.H. 1965. Key to the Carex species of Newfoundland by vegetative characteristics. Publication No. 1017. Canadian Department of Forestry, Ottawa, ON. 39 pp. [A useful guide to the identification of a large and difficult group of Newfoundland plants.]

Hay, S.A., Bouchard, A., and Brouillet, L. 1990. Additions to the flora of the Island of Newfoundland. Rhodora 92: 277–293.

Meades, S.J., Hay, S.G., and Brouillet, L. 2000. Annotated list of the plants of Newfoundland and Labrador. http://www.digitalnaturalhistory.com/meades.htm (from the Provincial Museum of Newfoundland and Labrador). ["This checklist documents over 1300 taxa of plants known to occur in the Province of Newfoundland and Labrador, Canada. It includes scientific

GUIDES TO PROVINCES AND TERRITORIES (CONT'D)

names, English and French common names, key synonyms, range and specific habitat preferences, and notes on scarcity, notable range extensions, questionable reports and taxonomic problems. The checklist is available for download as a set of WordPerfect, or MSWord files."]

Robertson, A.W. 1984. *Carex* of Newfoundland. Ministry of Supply and Services, Ottawa, ON. 252 pp. [Distributed by Canadian Forestry Services, St. John's Newfoundland. A guide to the sedges of Newfoundland.]

Rouleau, E. and Lamoureux, G. 1992. Atlas of the vascular plants of the island of Newfoundland and of the islands of Saint-Pierre-et-Miquelon./ Atlas des plantes vasculaires de l'île de Terre-Neuve et des îles de Saint-Pierre-et-Miquelon. Groupe Fleurbec, Saint Henri-de-Lévis, QC. 777 pp. [Presents a checklist and over a thousand excellent, detailed distribution maps.]

Rousseau, C. 1974. [This is listed below for Quebec, and gives information on many plant distributions for Labrador.]

Scott, P.J. 2000. Boreal flora: vascular flora of Newfoundland. Dept. of Biology Memorial University of Newfoundland, St. John, NL. 278 pp.

Northwest Territories and Nunavut

Aiken, S.G., Dallwitz, M.J. Consaul, L.L. et al. 1999–onwards. Flora of the Canadian Arctic Archipelago: descriptions, illustrations, identification, and information retrieval. Version:

April 29, 2003. http://www.mun.ca/biology/delta/arcticf/. [Provides illustrated, interactive, identification to the more than 300 taxa known to occur on the Canadian Arctic Islands. A useful source of information, including descriptions, illustrations, and distribution maps. Compare the more recent Aiken et al. listed in Guides to Large Areas of Canada, which is not available online.]

Catling, P.M., Cody, W.J., and Mitrow, G. 2005. A compilation of additions to the flora of the continental portions of Northwest Territories and Nunavut. Botanical Electronic News 353: 3–2. http://www.ou.edu/cas/botany-micro/ben/ben353.html [Includes all additions to Porsild and Cody (1980), below, reported up to 2004.]

Catling, P.M., Mitrow, G., and Bennett, B.A. 2008. A compilation of additions to the flora of the continental portions of Northwest Territories and Nunavut—n° 2. Botanical Electronic News (E-journal), 400(2). http://www.ou.edu/cas/botany-micro/ben/ben400.html.

Edlund, S. 1986, 1987. Common arctic wildflowers of the Northwest Territories. Geological Survey of Canada, Ottawa, ON. 32 pp.

Mallory, C. and Aiken, S. 2004. Common plants of Nunavut. Nunuvut Department of Education, Nunavut Wildlife Management Board, and Canadian Museum of Nature. Ottawa, ON. 400 pp. (200 in English, 200 in Inuktituk). [A popular guide with colour illustrations.]

Milburn, A. and Milburn, D. 2002. What's blooming: a guide to 100+ wild plants of Northwest Territories. What's Blooming, Yellowknife, NWT. 127 pp.

Milburn, A. and Pamplin, T. 2002. Wild and wacky plants of the NWT. Resources, Wildlife and Economic Development, Northwest Territories, Yellowknife, NWT. 73 pp. [Written for a juvenile audience.]

Porsild, A.E. and Cody, W.J. 1980. Vascular plants of Continental Northwest Territories, Canada. National Museums of Natural Sciences, National Museums of Canada, Ottawa, ON. 667 pp. [This flora includes the previous Districts of Mackenzie, Franklin, and Keewatin, portions of which are now included in Nunavut. Nunavut was created in 1999 from a large portion of the "Northwest Territories", including Keewatin, northeastern Mackenzie, and a portion of Franklin. Additions to this flora have been published mostly in the Canadian Field-Naturalist.]

Porsild, A.E. 1964. Illustrated flora of the Canadian Arctic Archipelago. National Museum of Canada Bulletin 146. 218 pp. [Covers Canadian Arctic Islands. Includes illustrations and distribution maps.]

Nova Scotia

LaRue, D. 2002. Pocket guide to roadside plants: a view from Nova Scotia highways. Transportation and Public Works, Halifax, NS. 78 pp.

LaRue, D. 2004. Common wild flowers & plants of Nova Scotia. Nimbus, Halifax, NS. 164 pp.

GUIDES TO PROVINCES AND TERRITORIES (CONT'D)

Roland, A.E. and Smith, E.C. 1969. The flora of Nova Scotia. The Nova Scotia Museum, Halifax, NS. 746 pp. [An updated version is indicated below, but this original manual remains very useful, and contains some information not included in the update.]

Roland, A.E. and Zinck, M. 1998. Roland's flora of Nova Scotia. Nimbus Publishing and Nova Scotia Museum, Halifax, NS. 2 vols. [Includes many illustrations and distribution maps.]

Nunavut
See "Northwest Territories and Nunavut". Also see Johnson (1987), listed for Manitoba.

Ontario
Baldwin, K.A. and Sims, R.A. 1990 and continued. Field guide to the common forest plants in northwestern Ontario. Forestry Canada, Sault Ste. Marie, ON. (Loose-leaf).

Baldwin, W.K.W. 1958. Plants of the Clay Belt of northern Ontario and Quebec. Bulletin n° 156. National Museum of Canada, Ottawa, ON. 324 pp. [Contains much information on the vegetation and status of plants in the Clay Belt region.]

Carmichael, I., MacKenzie, A., and Vance, A. 2006. Photo field guide to some wildflowers of Southern Ontario. St. Thomas Field Naturalist Club Inc., St. Thomas, ON. 150 pp.

Chambers, B., Legasy, K., and Bentley, C.V. 1996. Forest plants of central Ontario. Lone Pine, Edmonton, AB. 448 pp.

Contributions to a flora of New York state. [New York State Museum bulletins published by the State Education Department, Albany, NY. These comprehensive treatments have keys, extensive descriptions and useful illustrations, and can be used to identify plants from much of southern Ontario. Contribution 3, dealing with mosses, is not listed below.]
1. Mitchell, R.S. and Dean, J.K. 1978. Polygonaceae (buckwheat family) of New York State. Contr. to a Flora of New York State I. New York State Mus. Bull. 431. 80 pp.
2. Mitchell, R.S. and Beal, E.O. 1979. Magnoliaceae through Ceratophyllaceae of New York State. Contr. to a Flora of New York State II. New York State Mus. Bull. 435. 62 pp.
4. Mitchell, R.S. and Dean, J.K. 1982. Ranunculaceae (crowfoot family) of New York State. Contr. to a Flora of New York State IV. New York State Mus. Bull. 446. 100 pp.
5. Mitchell, R.S. 1983. Berberidaceae through Fumariaceae of New York State. Contr. to a Flora of New York State V. New York State Mus. Bull. 451. 66 pp.
6. Mitchell, R.S. 1988. Platanaceae through Myricaceae of New York State. Contr. to a Flora of New York State VI. New York State Mus. Bull. 464. 98 pp.

7. Clemants, S.E. 1990. Juncaceae (rush family) of New York State. Contr. to a Flora of New York State. VII. New York State Mus. Bull. 475. 68 pp.
8. Furlow, J.J. and Mitchell, R.S. 1990. Betulaceae through Cactaceae of New York State. Contr. to a Flora of New York State VIII. New York State Mus. Bull. 476. 94 pp.
9. Cope, E.A. 1992. Pinophyta (Gymnospermae) of New York State. Contr. to a Flora of New York State IX. New York State Mus. Bull. 483. 80 pp.
10. Clemants, S.E. 1992. Chenopodiaceae and Amaranthaceae of New York State. Contr. to a Flora of New York State X. New York State Mus. Bull. 475. 100 pp.
11. Mitchell, R.S. 1993. Portulacaceae through Caryophyllaceae of New York State. Contr. to a Flora of New York State XI. New York State Museum Bull. 486. 124 pp.

Crowe, J.M. 2004. First book of Ontario wildflowers. Le Courbeau Press, Owen Sound, ON. 106 pp.

Dickinson, T., Metsger, D., Ball, J., and Dickinson, R. 2004. The ROM field guide to wildflowers of Ontario. Royal Ontario Museum and McClelland and Stewart, Toronto, ON. 416 pp. [A valuable reference with colour photos, that treats 550 species (reviewed in CBA/ABC Bull. 38(3): 40 (2005).]

Dore, G.D. and McNeill, J. 1980. Grasses of Ontario. Agriculture Canada Research Branch Monograph 26, Ottawa, ON. 566 pp. [Includes illustrations and distribution maps.]

GUIDES TO PROVINCES AND TERRITORIES (CONT'D)

Hodgins, J.L. 978. A guide to the literature on the herbaceous vascular flora of Ontario. Botany Press, Toronto, ON. 73 pp.

Kershaw, L.J. 2002. Ontario wildflowers: 101 wayside flowers. Lone Pine, Edmonton, AB. 144 pp.

Legasy, K., LaBelle-Beadman, S., and Chambers, B. 1995. Forest plants of northeastern Ontario. Lone Pine, Edmonton, AB. 352 pp.

McKay, S.M. and Catling, P.M. 1979. Trees, shrubs & flowers to know in Ontario. J.M. Dent & Sons (Canada) Ltd., Don Mills, ON. 208 pp. [A useful and well-illustrated guide to common species.]

Meades, S.J., Schnare, D., Lawrence, K., and Faulkner, C. 2004 (and onwards). Northern Ontario Plant Database Website. Version 1, January 2004. Algoma University College and Great Lakes Forestry Centre, Sault Ste. Marie, ON. www.northernontarioflora.ca/ [Lists records in northern Ontario herbaria and provides links to descriptions and illustrations.]

Morton, J.K. and Venn, J.M. 2000. The flora of Manitoulin Island and the adjacent islands of Lake Huron, Georgian Bay and the North Channel. 3rd edition. University of Waterloo, Waterloo, ON. 375 pp. [Although this annotated checklist features Manitoulin Island, it can be used effectively as an identification aid for much of the northern Lake Huron region of Ontario.]

Newmaster, S.G. and Subramanyam, R. 2005. Flora Ontario - integrated botanical information system (FOIBIS), phase 1, 2005. http://www.uoguelph.ca/foibis/ [Latin, English, and French names as well as classification information are provided for 4,780 species including vascular plants, bryophytes and lichens.]

Newmaster, S.G., Lehela, A., Uhlig, P.W.C., McMurray, S., and Oldham, M.J. 1998. Ontario plant list. Forest Research Information Paper 123. Ontario Forest Research Institute, Sault Ste. Marie, ON. Irregularly paginated. [An authoritative, current list of plant names for Ontario, including synonyms and an indication of conservation status.]

Rabeler, R.K. 2007. Gleason's plants of Michigan: a field guide. University of Michigan Press, Ann Arbor, MI. 398 pp. [A current revision of a classic work that includes most of the flora of southern and central Ontario, and many plants likely to be found in the province.]

Reznicek, A.A., Voss, E.G. and Walters, B.S. 2001. Michigan Flora Online. University of Michigan. Web. 1-31-2012. http://michiganflora.net/home.aspx.

Riley, J.L. 2003. Flora of the Hudson Bay Lowland and its postglacial origins. NRC Research Press, Ottawa, ON. 236 pp. [A valuable list of species of an extensive northern region of the province. Includes distribution maps and considerable information.]

Soper, J.H., Garton, C.E., and Given, D.R. 1989. Flora of the north shore of Lake Superior: vascular plants of the Ontario portion of the Lake Superior drainage basin. National Museums of Natural Sciences, National Museum of Canada, Ottawa, ON. 61 pp.

Voss, E.G. 1972–1996. Michigan flora. Cranbrook Institute of Science, Bloomfield Hills, MI. 3 vols. [This outstanding guide to the plants of Michigan applies very well to much of southern and central Ontario. Includes some illustrations and distribution maps for Michigan.]
Part 1 (1972), Gymnosperms and monocots. Cranbrook Institute of Science Bulletin 55. 488 pp. [Printings with corrections in 1990 and 1992.]
Part 2 (1985), Dicots (Saururaceae-Cornaceae). Cranbrook Institute of Science Bulletin 59. 727 pp. [Second printing 1998, with corrections and additions on pages 725–727.]
Part 3 (1996), Dicots (Pyrolaceae-Compositae). Cranbrook Institute of Science Bulletin 61. 622 pp.

Walshe, S. 1980. Plants of Quetico and the Ontario shield. University of Toronto Press, Toronto, ON. 152 pp.

Prince Edward Island

Clough, K.S. 1992. Wildflowers of Prince Edward Island. Ragweed, Charlottetown, PEI. 150 pp.

Erskine, D.S., Catling, P.M., and MacLaren, R.B. 1985. The plants of Prince Edward Island, with new records, nomenclatural changes, and corrections and deletions. Research Branch Publication 1798. Agriculture Canada, Ottawa, ON. 272 pp. + maps. [Has distribution maps but not illustrations of species.]

Primrose, M. and Munro, M. 2006. Wildflowers of Nova Scotia, New Brunswick, & Prince Edward Island. 2nd edition. Formac, Halifax, NS. 159 pp.

GUIDES TO PROVINCES AND TERRITORIES (CONT'D)

Quebec

Beauséjour, S. 2008. Les Orchidées indigènes du Québec/Labrador. Les Éditions Native, Joliette, QC. 176 pp. [A superbly illustrated guide to the native orchids of Quebec and Labrador.]

Blondeau, M. and Roy, C. (Collaboration: A. Cuerrier and Avataq Cultural Institute). 2011. Atlas des plantes des villages du Nunavik/Atlas of plants of the Nunavik villages. Éditions MultiMondes, Sainte-Foy, QC. 737 pp. [A useful guide for the far northern regions of Quebec. Has excellent maps and photographs in colour. In French, English, and Inuktitut.]

Campbell, C.S. and Eastman, L.M. 1980. Flora of Oxford County, Main. Life Sciences and Agriculture Experiment Station, University of Main at Orono, Technical Bulletin 99. 244 pp. [Useful for identifying plants in adjacent areas of Quebec.]

Fleurbec (group: G. Lamoureux et al.). 1978. Plantes sauvages des villes et des champs, vol. 1. Fleurbec, Montreal, QC. 273 pp. [Colour photographs. Includes about 85 species.]

Fleurbec (group: G. Lamoureux et al.). 1983. Plantes sauvages des villes et des champs, vol. 2. Fleurbec, Saint-Augustin, QC. 208 pp. [Colour photographs, distribution maps. Includes about 90 species.]

Fleurbec (group: G. Lamoureux et al.). 1985. Plantes sauvages du bord de la mer. Fleurbec, Saint-Augustin, QC. 286 pp. [A guide to 55 species, colour photographs and distribution maps.]

Fleurbec (group: G. Lamoureux et al.). 1987. Plantes sauvages des lacs, rivières et tourbières. Fleurbec, Saint-Augustin, QC. 399 pp. [Colour photographs and distribution maps. Treats about 60 species.]

Fleurbec (group: G. Lamoureux et al.). 1993. Fougères, prêles et lycopodes. Fleurbec, Saint-Henri-de-Lévis, QC. 511 pp. [Colour photographs and distribution maps.]

Haines, A. and Vining, T.F. 1998. Flora of Maine: a manual for identification of native and naturalized vascular plants of Maine. V.F. Thomas Co., Bar Harbor, ME. 847 pp. [Can be used for parts of Quebec adjacent to Maine.]

Hammerly, T.E. 2000. Appalachian wildflowers: an ecological guide to flowering plants from Quebec to Georgia. University of Georgia Press, Athens, GA. 327 pp.

Lacoursière, E., and Therrien, J. 1998. Fleurs sauvages du Québec. Les Éditions de l'Homme, QC. 265 pp. + index.

Lamoureux, G. 2002. Flore printanière (une mise à jour de Plantes sauvages printanières, 1975). Fleurbec, Saint-Henri-de-Lévis, QC. 576 pp. [A guide to 123 spring-flowering wild plants of eastern North America, with colour photographs and distribution maps, as well as extensive ecological information.]

Louis-Marie, P. 1967. Flore-manuel de la province de Québec, Canada. 4th edition. Centre de Psychologie et Pédagogie, Montreal, QC. 317 pp. [An old but very popular and useful text. The 4th edition of 1967 is a re-impression in pocket book format of the 2nd edition (1953), with three pages added at the end. The 3rd edition (1959) presents drawings in colour.]

Marie-Victorin, Frère. 1997. Flore Laurentienne. 3rd edition. Updated and annotated by L. Brouillet, S.G. Hay, I. Goulet. M. Blondeau, J. Cayouette, and J. Labrecque. Presses de l'Université de Montréal, Montréal, QC (and also republished in 2002 by Gaëtan Morin, Boucherville, QC). 1093 pp. [The most complete flora of Quebec available at this time. Like the 1995 edition, this work has been referred to as the "third edition", although the 1997 and 2002 printings (which are identical) have many corrections and additions. Includes illustrations and many photographs in colour.]

Marie-Victorin, Frère, and Rolland-Germain, Frère. 1969. Flore de l'Anticosti-Minganie. Les Presses de l'Université de Montréal, Montréal, QC. 527 pp. [Provides useful coverage for the Gulf of St. Lawrence area.]

Rouleau, R. 1990. Petite flore forestière du Québec. 2nd edition. Ministère de l'energie et des ressources, QC. 250 pp.

Rousseau, C. 1968. Histoire, habitat et distribution de 220 plantes introduites au Québec. Nat. can. 95: 49–171. [A valuable source of information on introduced plants.]

Rousseau, C. 1974. Géographie floristique du Québec/Labrador. Distribution des principales

GUIDES TO PROVINCES AND TERRITORIES (cont'd)

espèces vasculaires. Les Presses de l'Université Laval, QC. 799 pp. [Not an identification guide, but presents ecological and distributional information for over 1,000 species, as well as distribution maps.]

Scoggan, H.J. 1950. The flora of Bic and the Gaspé Peninsula. National Museum of Canada Bulletin 115, Biological Series 47. Canada Department of Resources and Development, Development Services Branch, Ottawa, ON. 399 pp. [A classic flora, still very useful.]

Saskatchewan

Note: Although there are few comprehensive works dedicated to Saskatchewan alone, and no complete flora designed for identification, the guides listed for the adjacent provinces of Alberta and Manitoba are useful, and so are the general guides for the prairie region and boreal forest listed above.

Carmichael, L.T. 1976. Saskatchewan wildflowers: western area. Dept. of Natural Resources, Regina, SK. 108 pp. [Written for preschoolers.]

Kershaw, L.J. 2003. Saskatchewan wayside wildflowers. Lone Pine, Edmonton, AB. 160 pp.

Hudson, J.H. 1977. *Carex* in Saskatchewan. Bison Publishing House, Saskatoon, SK. 193 pp. [A guide to 100 species, with keys, descriptions, illustrations, and distribution maps.]

Harms, V.L. 2003. Checklist of the vascular plants of Saskatchewan and provincially and nationally rare native plants of Saskatchewan.

University of Saskatchewan Press, Saskatoon, SK. 328 pp. [A complete and authoritative annotated checklist.]

Johnson, D., Kershaw, L., MacKinnon, A., and Pojar, J. 1995. Plants of the Western Boreal Forest and Aspen Parkland. Lone Pine, Edmonton, AB. 392 pp. [Aspen parkland includes transitional zones between prairie and boreal forest, from northeastern British Columbia through central and northwestern Alberta, central Saskatchewan to central and southern Manitoba.]

Yukon

Anderson, J.P. 1959. Flora of Alaska and adjacent parts of Canada. Iowa State University Press, Ames, IA. 543 pp.

Bennett, B.A., Catling, P.M., Cody, W.J., and Argus, G.W. 2010. New records of vascular plants in the Yukon Territory VIII. Canadian Field-Naturalist. 124: 1–27. [This includes references to the other update lists in the series.]

Cody, W.J. 2000. Flora of the Yukon Territory. 2nd edition. NRC Research Press, Ottawa, ON. 669 pp. [The definitive identification guide to this region. Updates giving additions and range extensions have been published in the Canadian Field-Naturalist.]

Eaton, J.S. 1989. Discovering wild plants: Alaska, western Canada, the Northwest. Alaska Northwest Books, Anchorage, AK. 354 pp.

Hultén, E. 1968. Flora of Alaska and neighboring territories. Stanford University Press, Stanford, CA. 1008. [Includes illustrations and circumpolar distribution maps.]

Pratt, V.E. 1991. Wildflowers along the Alaska Highway. Alaskakrafts, Anchorage, AK. 230 pp.

Schofield, J.J. 1989. Discovering wild plants— Alaska, western Canada, the Northwest. Alaska Northwest Books, Bothell, WA. 354 pp.

Trelawny, J.G.S. 2003. Wild flowers of the Yukon, Alaska & northwestern Canada. 2nd edition. Harbour Pub., Madeira Park, BC. 224 pp.

Welsh, S.L. 1974. Anderson's flora of Alaska and adjacent parts of Canada. Brigham Young University Press, Provo, UT. 724 pp. [Includes a limited number of species illustrations but no distribution maps.]

White, H.A. and Williams, M. 1974. The Alaska-Yukon wild flowers guide. Alaska Geographic Society, Anchorage, AK. 112 pp.

SPECIAL GROUPS

Cultivated plants

Bailey, L.H. 1949. Manual of cultivated plants. MacMillan Publishing Co. New York, NY. 1116 pp. [Out of date, but this classic and extensive work is still very useful.]

Bailey, L.H., Bailey, E.Z., and staff of the Liberty Hyde Bailey Hortorium. 1976. Hortus Third. A concise dictionary of plants cultivated in the United States and Canada. Macmillan, New York, NY. 1290 pp. [A very large encyclopedia providing information on ornamental plants. This does not have keys and there are very few illustrations, but is useful when trying to find information about a cultivated plant when at least the genus is known.]

Facciola, S. 1998. Cornucopia II. A source book of edible plants. Kampong Publications, Vista, CA. 713 pp. [Does not have keys, but extremely useful for finding information on available cultivars when the species name is known.]

Huxley, A., Griffiths, M., and Levy, M. (Editors). 1992. The new Royal Horticultural Society dictionary of gardening. MacMillan, London, U.K. 4 vols. [An extremely large encyclopedia giving information on ornamental plants of the world. This does not have keys and there are very few illustrations, but has a wealth of information, particularly concerning cultivars.]

Lamoureux, L. and Nantel, P. 1999. Cultiver des plantes sauvages . . . sans leur nuire. Fleurbec, Saint-Henri-de-Lévis. QC. 81 pp. [Provides information on wild plants of Quebec that have potential to be cultivated.]

Rehder, A. 1951. Manual of cultivated trees and shrubs hardy in North America. 2nd edition. Macmillan, New York, NY. 996 pp. [An extensive classic work, treating over 2,500 species.]

Woody plants (trees & shrubs)

Brayshaw, T.C. 1996. Catkin-bearing plants of British Columbia. 2nd edition. Royal British Columbia Museum, Victoria, BC. 213 pp.

Brayshaw, T.C. 1996. Trees and shrubs of British Columbia. Royal B.C. Museum (Victoria, BC) and UBC Press (Vancouver, BC), 374 pp.

Brough, S. 1998. Wild trees of British Columbia. Pacific Educational Press, Vancouver, BC. 240 pp.

Burns, R.M. and Honkala, B.H. (Technical coordinators) 1990. Silvics of North America. Volume 1, Conifers. U.S. Department of Agriculture, Forest Service, Agriculture Handbook 654, 675 pp.; Silvics of North America Volume 2, Hardwoods. U.S. Department of Agriculture, Forest Service, Agriculture Handbook 654, 877 pp. [Considerable information on trees of interest to professionals.]

Core, E.L. and Amnons, N.P. 1958. Woody plants in winter; a manual of common trees and shrubs in winter in the Northeastern United States and southeastern Canada. Boxwood Press, Pittsburg, PA. 218 pp.

Cunningham, G.C. 1958. Forest flora of Canada. Dept. of Northern Affairs and National Resources, Forestry Branch, Ottawa, ON. 144 pp.

Farrar, J.L. 1995. Trees in Canada. Fitzhenry & Whiteside Ltd., Markham, ON, and Canadian Forest Service, Natural Resources, Ottawa, ON. 502 pp. [Includes useful line drawings, colour photographs, and distribution maps. This is the best basic guide to the trees of Canada.]

Graves, A.H. 1992. Illustrated guide to trees and shrubs: a handbook of the woody plants of the northeastern United States and adjacent Canada. Revised edition. Dover Publications, New York, NY. 271 pp.

Hilts, S. 1997. A pocket guide to Ontario trees & some woodland plants. Centre for Land and Water Stewardship, University of Guelph, Guelph, ON. 63 pp.

Hosie, R.C. 1979. Native trees of Canada. 8th edition. Fitzhenry & Whiteside, Don Mills, ON. 380 pp.

Kershaw, L. 2001. Trees of Ontario, including tall shrubs. Lone Pine, Edmonton, AB. 240 pp.

Lauriault, J. 1989. Identification guide to the trees of Canada. Fitzhenry & Whiteside, Markham, ON. 479 pp. [A basic, well-researched guide to Canadian trees, with information often not available in other publications.]

Little, E.L. 1971. Atlas of United States trees, vol. 1, Conifers and important hardwoods. U.S.D.A. Forest Service Misc. Publication 1146.

SPECIAL GROUPS (CONT'D)

Little, E.L. 1975. Atlas of United States trees, vol. 2, Alaska trees and common shrubs. U.S.D.A. Forest Service Misc. Publication 1146.

Little, E.L. 1976. Atlas of United States trees, vol. 3, Minor Western Hardwoods. U.S.D.A. Forest Service Misc. Publication 1314.

Little, E.L. 1979. Forest trees of the United States and Canada and how to identify them. Dover, New York, NY. 70 pp.

Parish, R. and Thomson, S.M. 1994. Tree book: learning to recognize trees of British Columbia. Ministry of Forests, Canadian forest Service, Victoria, BC. 183 pp. [Available online: http://www.for.gov.bc.ca/hfd/library/documents/treebook/]

Parrot, L. and Dignard, N. 2009, Arbres, arbustes et arbrisseaux du Québec: comment les identifier en toutes saisons. 9th edition. Publication du Québec. 103 pp.

Petrides, G.A. 1972. A field guide to trees and shrubs. 2nd edition. Houghton Mifflin, Boston, MA. 428 pp. [Applies to southeastern and south-central Canada and adjacent United States.]

Rowe, J.S. 1972. Forest regions of Canada. Canadian Forestry Service, 172 pp. [A classic reference describing the forest regions of Canada.]

Smith, W. R. 2008. Trees and shrubs of Minnesota. Minnesota Department of Natural Resources and University of Minnesota Press. Minneapolis, MN. 703 pp.

Soper, J.H. and Heimberger, M.L. 1982 (& 1985). Shrubs of Ontario. Revised edition. Royal Ontario Museum, Toronto, ON. 495. pp. [Includes illustrations and distribution maps for all species.]

Stephens, H.A. 1973. Woody plants of the North Central Plains. The University Press of Kansas, Lawrence, KS. 530 pp.

Wilkinson, K. 2010. Trees and shrubs of Alberta. Lone Pine, Edmonton, AB. 192 pp.

Poisonous plants

Poisonous plant guides have limited usefulness for identification unless it is already suspected that a certain genus is responsible for poisoning, or (in the case of guides organized by symptoms) there is knowledge of the specific effects that have resulted from suspected poisoning. This brief list is included because even limited identification value may be important in cases of poisoning of humans, pets, or livestock.

Anderson, J.R. 137. Trees and shrubs: food, medicinal, and poisonous plants of British Columbia. C.F. Banfield (Printer), Victoria, BC. 165 pp.

Burrows, G.E. and Tyrl, R.J. 2001. Toxic plants of North America. Iowa State Press (Blackwell Publishing Company), Ames, IA. 1342 pp. [The most extensive source of information on North American toxic plants, includes both wild and commonly cultivated plants, has many illustrations and distribution maps. Organized by plant family and genus. The keys deal only with a few species and are of very limited use. Review: Small, E. 2005. Agriculture, Ecosystem & Environment 110: 327–238.]

Frohne, D. and Pfänder, H.J. 1983. A colour atlas of poisonous plants. Wolfe Publishing Ltd., Stuttgart, Germany. 291 pp. [Includes descriptions, photographs and reference to microscopic characters]

Hardin, J.W. 1969. Human poisoning from native and cultivated plants. Duke University Press, Durham, NC. 167 pp. [A concise guide to over 300 plants with descriptions and illustrations.]

Johnston, A., Smoliak, S., and Wroe, R.A. 1975. Poisonous and injurious plants of Alberta. Alberta Agriculture, Edmonton, AB. 60 pp.

Kingsbury, J.M. 1964. Poisonous plants of the United States and Canada. Prentice-Hall, Englewood Cliffs, NJ. 626 pp. [Dated, but still useful. Organized by plant family and genus.]

Knight, A.P. and Walter, R.G. 2001. A guide to plant poisoning of animals in North America. Teton NewMedia, Jackson, WY. 367 pp. [Available as a book, CD, and online by subscription. Organized on the basis of symptoms (plants affecting digestive system, nervous system, kidneys, musculoskeletal system, etc.), rather than on taxonomic relationships of the plants. Colour photographs.]

Lampe, K.F. and McCann, M.A. 1985. A.M.A. handbook of poisonous and injurious plants. American Medical Association, Chicago, IL. 432 pp.

SPECIAL GROUPS (CONT'D)

Lewis, W.H. and Elvin-Lewis, M.P.F. 2003. Medical botany: plants affecting man's health. Second edition. John Wiley & Sons, Hoboken, NJ. 812 pp. [An extremely useful source of information on poisonous plants and the symptoms of poisoning.]

McLean, A. and Nicholson, H.H. 1958. Stock poisoning plants of the British Columbia ranges. Canada Dept. of Agriculture, Ottawa, ON. 31 pp.

Montgomery, F.H. 1965. Plants poisonous to livestock in Ontario. Ontario Dept. of Agriculture, Toronto, ON. 44 pp.

Mulligan, G.A. 1990. Poison-ivy, western poison oak and poison sumac (revised edition). Agriculture Canada Publ. 1699E. 13 pp.

Mulligan, G.A. and Munro, D.B. 1990. Poisonous plants of Canada. Agriculture Canada Publ. 1842E. 96 pp. [A useful source of information for those interested in plants that poison humans and livestock.]

Munro, D.B. Canadian poisonous plant information system. http://www.cbif.gc.ca/pls/pp/poison?p_x=pxtitle.html [Provides information on native Canadian and some cultivated plants that are toxic to livestock, pets and humans. Based on literature up to 1993.]

Edible plants

Anonymous. 1980s. Native cookery and edible wild plants of Newfoundland and Labrador. Dept. of Rural, Agricultural and Northern Development, St. John's NF. 96 pp.

Angier, B. and Foster, D. 2008. Field guide to edible wild plants. 2nd edition. Stackpole Books, Harrisburg, PA. 285 pp.

Choyce, L. and Shaler, K. 1976. Edible wild plants of Nova Scotia. Eastern Shore Pub. Collective, West Chezzetcook, NS. 47 pp.

Fleurbec (group: G. Lamoureux et al.). 1981. Plantes sauvages comestibles. Fleurbec, Saint-Cuthbert, QC. 167 pp. [Colour photographs. Includes 28 species.]

Fleurbec (group: G. Lamoureux et al.). 2005. Plantes sauvages au menu: cuisine raisonnée. 2nd edition. Fleurbec, Saint-Henri-de-Lévis, QC. 192 pp. [A guide to edible wild plants.]

Gibbons, E. 1966. Stalking the wild asparagus. David McKay Company Inc., New York , NY. 303 pp.

Kirk, D.R. 1970. Wild edible plants of the Western United States, including also most of southwestern Canada and northwestern Mexico. Naturegraph, Healdsburg, CA. 307 pp.

MacLeod, H., Brousseau, D., and MacDonald, B. 1976 & 1988. Edible wild plants of Nova Scotia. Nimbus, Halifax, NS. 135 pp.

Peterson, L. and Peterson, R.T. 1999. A field guide to edible wild plants: Eastern and central North America (Peterson Field Guides). Houghton Mifflin Harcourt, Boston, MA. 352 pp.

Porsild, A.E. 1937. Edible roots and berries of Northern Canada. Dept. of Mines and Resources, National Museum of Canada, Ottawa, ON. 17 pp.

Saunders, C.f. 1976. Edible and useful wild plants of the United States and Canada. Dover, New York, NY. 276 pp. [A reprint of a 1934 publication.]

Scott, P.J. 2010. Edible plants of Newfoundland and Labrador. Boulder Publications, Portugal Cove-St. Philips, NL. 180 pp.

Szczawinski, A.F. and Hardy, G.A. 1962. Guide to common edible plants of British Columbia. A. Sutton (Printer), Victoria, BC. 90 pp.

Szczawinski, A.F. and Turner, N.J. 1978. Edible garden weeds of Canada. National Museum of Natural Sciences, National Museums of Canada, Ottawa, ON. 184 pp.

Szczawinski, A.F. and Turner, N.J. 1980. Wild green vegetables of Canada. National Museum of Natural Sciences, National Museums of Canada, Ottawa, ON. 179 pp.

Turner, N.J. 1995. Food plants of the Coastal First Peoples. Royal British Columbia Provincial Museum, Victoria, BC. 164 pp.

Turner, N.J. 1997. Food plants of Interior First Peoples. Royal British Columbia Provincial Museum, Victoria, BC. 215 pp.

SPECIAL GROUPS (CONT'D)

Turner, N.J. and Szczawinski, A.F. 1978. Wild coffee and tea substitutes of Canada. National Museum of Natural Sciences, National Museums of Canada, Ottawa, ON. 111 pp.

Turner, N.J. and Szczawinski, A.F. 1979. Edible wild fruits and nuts of Canada. National Museum of Natural Sciences, National Museums of Canada, Ottawa, ON. 212 pp.

Tozer, F. 2006. The uses of wild plants: using and growing the wild plants of the United States and Canada. Green Man Pub., Santa Cruz, CA. 263 pp.

Walker, M. 1984. Harvesting the northern wild: a guide to traditional and contemporary uses of edible forest plants of the Northwest Territories. Outcrop, Yellowknife, NWT. 224 pp.

Walker, M. 2008. Wild plants of Eastern Canada: identifying, harvesting and using. Nimbus Publishing, Halifax, NS. 203 pp.

Weeds

The biology of Canadian weeds. A series of reviews on weeds of Canada, published in the Canadian Journal of Plant Science, starting in 1973, and continuing to the present (for information, see http://www.aic.ca/journals/weeds.cfm). The earlier papers have been republished as 5 volumes:

Mulligan, G.A. (Editor). 1979. The biology of Canadian weeds: contributions 1–32. Publication 1693. Agriculture Canada, Ottawa, ON. 512 pp.

Mulligan, G.A. (Editor). 1984. The biology of Canadian weeds: contributions 33–61. Publication 1765. Agriculture Canada, Ottawa, ON. 415 pp.

Cavers, P.B. (Editor). 1995. The biology of Canadian weeds: contributions 62–83. Agricultural Institute of Canada, Ottawa, ON. 338 pp.

Cavers, P.B. (Editor). 2000. The biology of Canadian weeds: contributions 84–102. Agricultural Institute of Canada, Ottawa, ON. 335 pp.

Cavers, P.B. (Editor). 2005. The biology of Canadian weeds: contributions 103–129. Agricultural Institute of Canada, Ottawa, ON. 516 pp.

The Biology of Invasive Alien Plants in Canada. This is a similar series to the above, started in 2003, and also published in the Canadian Journal of Plant Science.

Alex, J.F. 1992. Ontario weeds: descriptions, illustrations and keys to their identification. Ontario Ministry of Agriculture and Food, Toronto. 304 pp. [A very useful text for identifying common weedy plants.]

Bouchard, C., Néron, R, and Guay, L. 1999. Identification guide to the weeds of Quebec. Conseil des production végétales du Québec, Inc., QC. 253 pp.

Darbyshire, S.J., Favreau, M., and Murray, M. 2000. Common and scientific names of weeds in Canada / Noms populaires et scientifiques des plantes nuisibles du Canada. Research Branch Publication 1387/B. Agriculture and Agri-Food Canada, Ottawa, ON. 132 pp. [A valuable list giving accurate scientific and one selected common English name and one French name for 1130 taxa of weedy plants.]

Frankton, C. and Mulligan, G.A. 1987. Weeds of Canada (revised). NC Press Ltd., Toronto, and Agriculture Canada, Ottawa, ON. 217 pp. [A guide to 230 weedy species of Canada, mostly illustrated.]

Royer, F. and Dickinson, R. 1999. Weeds of the northern U.S. and Canada: a guide for identification. Lone Pine, Renton, WA. 434 pp.

Prairie, pasture, and rangeland plants

Abouguendia, Z.M. 1993. Identification of common range plants of southern Saskatchewan: field guide. Saskatchewan Agriculture and Food, Regina, SK. 53 pp.

Aiken, S.G. and Darbyshire, S.J. 1983. Grass genera of Western Canadian cattle rangelands. Monograph No. 29. Research Branch, Agriculture Canada, Ottawa, ON. 173 pp. [One of several useful tools for identifying Canadian grasses.]

Anonymous. 1994. Field guide: identification of common range plants of northern Saskatchewan. Saskatchewan Agriculture and Food, Regina, SK. 48 pp.

SPECIAL GROUPS (CONT'D)

Best, K.F. and Campbell, J.B. 1971. Prairie grasses identified and described by vegetative characters. Publication 1413, Canada Department of Agriculture, Ottawa, ON. 239 pp. [This guide includes a vegetative key, and describes and illustrates 104 grass species characteristic of rangelands of the Prairie Provinces. For each, details of the top of the leaf sheath are shown.]

Johnson, H. 1984. Prairie plants of southeast Alberta. 2nd edition. The Printer (Medicine Hat) Ltd., Medicine Hat, AB. 125 pp.

Looman, J. 1983. 111 range and forage plants of the Canadian prairies. Agriculture Canada, Ottawa, ON. 255 pp.

Aquatic plants

Brayshaw, T.C. 2000. Pondweeds, bur-reeds and their relatives of British Columbia: Aquatic families of monocotyledons. 2nd. edition. Royal British Columbia Museum, Victoria, BC. 250 pp.

Burland, R.G. 1989. An identification guide to Alberta aquatic plants. Pesticide Management Branch, Alberta Environment, Edmonton, AB. 78 pp.

Caldwell, J.R. 1960, 1962. Guide to Saskatchewan marsh plants. Ducks Unlimited (Canada), Winnipeg, MB. 77 pp.

Carmichael, L.T. 1967. Common marsh plants of Saskatchewan. Dept. of Natural Resoruces, Saskatchewan, Regina, SK. 40 pp.

Colberg, T. and Abouguendia, Z.J. 2000. Field guide: identification of common riparian plants of Saskatchewan. Grazing and Pasture Technology Program, Regina, SK. 40 pp.

Crow, G.E. and Hellquist, C.B. 2000. Aquatic and wetland plants of northeastern North America: a revised and enlarged edition of Norman C. Fassett's A manual of aquatic plants. University of Wisconsin Press, Madison, WI. 2 vols. [A useful and current text with keys and numerous line drawings.]

Hotchkiss, N. 1972. Common marsh, underwater, and floating-leaved plants of the United States and Canada. Dover, New York, NY. 124 pp. [A reprint of a 1970 publication.]

Newmaster, S.G., Harris, A.G., Kershaw, L.J., Foster, R.F., and Racey, G.D. 1997. Wetland plants of Ontario. Lone Pine, Edmonton, AB. 240 pp. [A guide to over 450 species of wetland plants, with numerous line drawings.]

Tiner, R.W. 2009. Field guide to tidal wetland plants of the northeastern United States and neighboring Canada: vegetation of beaches, tidal flats, rocky shores, marshes, swamps, and coastal ponds. University of Massachusetts Press, Amherst, MA. 459 pp.

Warrington, P.D. 1980. Aquatic plants of British Columbia. Ministry of Environment, Inventory and Engineering Branch, Province of British Columbia. 601 pp.

Warrington, P.D. 1994. Identification keys to the aquatic plants of British Columbia. Water Quality Branch, Victoria, BC. 139 pp.

Medicinal plants

Angier, B. 1978. Field guide to medicinal wild plants. Stackpole Books, Harrisburg, PA. 320 pp.

Brigham, T., Schröder, M., Cocksedge, W. et al. 2004. Good practices for plant identification for the herbal industry. Saskatchewan Herb and Spice Association, SK. 54 pp. [A practical guide prepared for the purpose of providing reliable identifications of plants collected for the Canadian herbal and medicinal industries. Available online at several websites.]

Elliott, D. 1995. Wild roots: a forager's guide to the edible and medicinal roots, tubers, corms, and rhizomes of North America. Healing Arts Press, Rochester, VT. 128 pp.

Fortin, D., Lacoursière, E., and Leduc, P. 1992. L'herbier médicinal: album d'ethnobotanique québécoise. Québec Science Éditeur, Sillery, QC. 118 pp.

Foster, S. and Duke, J.A. 1999. A field guide to medicinal plants and herbs: of Eastern and Central North America (Peterson Field Guides). Houghton Mifflin Harcourt, Boston, MA. 432 pp.

Gaudet, J.F. 1979. Medicinal and poisonous plants on Prince Edward Island. Forestry Branch, Dept. of Agriculture and Forestry, Charlottetown, PEI. 116 pp.

SPECIAL GROUPS (CONT'D)

Gibbons, E. 1989. Stalking the healthful herbs. A.C. Hood, Putney, VT. 301 pp. [Reprint. Originally published in 1966 by D. McKay, New York, NY.]

Hudson, I.B. 1950. Medicinal and food plants of British Columbia. Victoria, BC. 70 pp.

Kershaw, L.J. 2000. Edible and medicinal plants of the Rockies. Lone Pine, Edmonton, AB. 272 pp.

Lanthier, A. 1977. Les plantes médicinales canadiennes. Editions Paulines, Montréal, QC. 92 pp.

MacKinnon, A., Kershaw, L., Arnason, J.T., Owen, P., Karst, A., and Hamersley-Chambers, F. 2009. Edible & medicinal plants of Canada. Lone Pine, Edmonton, AB. 448 pp.

Moerman, D.E. 1986. Medicinal plants of native America. Univ. Mich. Mus. Anthropol. Tech. Rep. 19. 2 vols.

Naegele, T.A. 1996. Edible and medicinal plants of the Great Lakes Region. Revised edition. Wilderness Adventure Books, Davisburg,, MI. 200 pp.

Small, E. and Catling, P.M. 1999. Canadian medicinal crops. NRC Press, Ottawa. 240 pp. NRC Press, Ottawa. x + 240 pp.

Willard, T. 1992. Edible and medicinal plants of the Rocky Mountains and neighbouring territories. Wild Rose College of Natural Healing, Ltd., Calgary, AB. 277 pp.

Carnivorous plants

Barthlott, W. and Ashdown, M. 2007. The curious world of carnivorous plants: a comprehensive guide to their biology and cultivation. Timber Press, Portland, OR. 224 pp.

Schnell, D.E. 2002. Carnivorous plants of the United States and Canada. 2nd edition. Timber Press, Portland, OR. 468 pp.

Slack, A., and Gate, J. 1980. Carnivorous plants. MIT Press, Cambridge, MA. 240 pp.

Grasses

Barkworth, M.E., Anderton, L.K., Capels, K.M., Long, S., and Piep, M.B. (Editors). 2007. Manual of grasses for North America. Intermountain Herbarium and Utah State University Press, Logan, UT. 629 pp. [The definitive guide to identifying grasses of North America.]

Darbyshire, S.J. 2005. A key to the common grasses of southeastern Canada by vegetative characteristics. Can. Bot. Assoc. Bull. 38: 58–63. [A very useful tool for identifying grasses.]

Hitchcock, A.S. 1971. Manual of the grasses of the United States. 2nd edition. Dover, New York. 2 vols. (1051 pp.). [A much-used guide for identifying grasses, but supplanted by Barkworth et al., cited above. Abundantly illustrated.]

Orchids

Ames, D., Acheson, P.B., Heshka, L., Joyce, B., Neufeld, J., Reeves, R., Reimer, E., and Ward, I. 2005. Orchids of Manitoba, a field guide. Native Orchid Conservation Inc., Winnipeg, MB. 158 pp. (also see http://www.nativeorchid.org/contactnoci.htm)

Anonymous. 2010. The orchids of British Columbia. In: E-Flora BC: Electronic Atlas of the Plants of British Columbia [eflora.bc.ca]. Edited by B. Kinkenberg. Lab for Advanced Spatial Analysis, Department of Geography, University of British Columbia, Vancouver. http://www.geog.ubc.ca/biodiversity/eflora/orchidsbc.html

Beauséjour, S. 2008. Les orchidées indigènes du Québec/Labrador [Native Orchids of Quebec/Labrador]. Les éditions Native, Joliette, QC. 176 pp.

Bingham, M.T. 1939. Orchids of Michigan. Cranbrook Institute of Science, Bloomfield Hills, MI. 87 pp.

Boland, T. 1994. Orchids in Newfoundland. American Orchid Society Bulletin 63: 396–405.

Brackley, F. E. 1985. The orchids of New Hampshire. Rhodora 87: 1–117.

Brown, P.M. 1993. A field and study guide to the orchids of New England and New York. Orchis Press, Jamaica Plain, MA. 245 pp.

SPECIAL GROUPS (CONT'D)

Brown, P.M. 2003. The wild orchids of North America, north of Mexico. University Press of Florida, Gainesville, FL. 236 pp.

Brown, P.M. 2006. Wild orchids of the Canadian Maritimes and northern Great Lakes region. University Press of Florida, Gainesville, FL. 313 pp.

Brown, P.M. 2006. Wild orchids of the prairies and Great Plains region of North America. University Press of Florida, Gainesville, FL. 342 pp.

Brown, P.M. 2006. Wild orchids of the Pacific Northwest and Canadian Rockies. University Press of Florida, Gainesville, FL. 287 pp.

Brown, P.M. 2009. Wild orchids of the White Mountains of New Hampshire and Maine. North American Native Orchid Journal 15: 203–265. http://xtheastern United States. Comstock Publishing, Ithaca, NY. 236 pp.

Bruce-Gray Plant Committee (Owen Sound Field-Naturalists). 1997. The orchids of Bruce and Grey. Owen Sound Field-Naturalists, Owen Sound, ON. 105 pp.

Cameron, J.E.W. 1976. The orchids of Maine. University of Maine at Orono Press, Orono, ME. 80 pp.

Case, F.W. 1987. Orchids of the western Great Lakes region, rev. ed. Cranbrook Institute of Science Bulletin 48. Bloomfield Hills, MI. 251 pp.

Chapman, W.K. 1997. Orchids of the Northeast: a field guide. Syracuse University Press, Syracuse, NY. 200 pp.

Cormack, R.G.H. 1948. The orchids of the Cypress Hills. Canadian Field-Naturalist 62(5): 155–156.

Correll, D.S. 1950. Native orchids of North America north of Mexico. Chronica Botanica, Waltham, MA. 399 pp.

Cotterill, P. 2010. Orchids of Lakeland [Lakeland Provincial Recreation Area near Lac La Biche, Alberta], a field guide to Lakeland Provincial Park, Provincial Recreation Area and surrounding region. Alberta Environmental Protection, AB. 52 pp. www.anpc.ab.ca/assets/Orchid.pdf

Donly, J.F. 1963. The orchids of Nova Scotia. University College of Cape Breton Press, NS. 96 pp.

Fisher, R.M. 1980. Guide to the orchids of the Cypress Hills, including the most common orchids of Alberta and Saskatchewan. Published privately, Olds, AB. 44 pp.

Hapeman, J. R. 1996. Orchids of Wisconsin [Website]. http://www.botany.wisc.edu/Orchids/Orchids_of_Wisconsin.html

Johnson, L.P. 1996. Orchids of the Sibley Peninsula. North American Native Orchid Journal 2: 239–252.

Johnsson, R.G. 1963. The orchids of Isle Royale National Park. Wolf's Eye Press, Houghton, MI. 28 pp.

Keenan, P.E. 1983. A complete guide to Maine's orchids. DeLorme Press, Freeport, ME. 48 pp.

Keenan, P.E. 1999. Wild orchids across North America. Timber Press. Portland, OR. 321 pp.

Luer, C.A. 1975. The native orchids of the United States and Canada, excluding Florida. New York Botanical Garden, New York, NY. 361 pp.

Morris, F. and Eames, E. 1929. Our wild orchids. Charles Scribner's sons, New York, NY. 464 pp.

Mundin, C. 2001. Native orchids of Nova Scotia: a field guide. University College of Cape Breton Press, Sydney, NS. 96 pp.

Niles, G.G. 1904. Bog trotting for orchids. G.P. Putnam's Sons, New York, NY. 310 pp.

Nylander, O.O. 1935. Our northern orchids [Orchids of Northern Maine]. Aroostook Star [Star-Herald Pub. Co.], Presque Isle, ME. 32 pp.

Petrie, W. 1981. Guide to the orchids of North America. Hancock House, Blaine, WA. 128 pp.

Reddoch, J. M. and A. H. Reddoch. 1997. The orchids of the Ottawa District: Floristics, phyto-geography, population studies and historical review. Canadian Field-Naturalist 111: 1–185.

SPECIAL GROUPS (CONT'D)

Scott, P.J. 1981. Orchids in Newfoundland. Canadian Orchid Journal 1(2): 22–26.

Scott, P.J. 1985. The orchids of Newfoundland and Labrador. Osprey16(2): 183–198.

Scott, P.J. 1985. The orchids of Labrador and Newfoundland peatlands. Peat News 7(2): 7–12.

Sheviak, C.J. 1974. An introduction to the ecology of the Illinois Orchidaceae. Illinois State Museum, Springfield, IL. 89 pp.

Szczawinski, A.F. 1959. The orchids of British Columbia. British Columbia Provincial Museum Handbook No. 16. 124 pp.

Voitk, A. and Voitk, M. 2006. Orchids on the rock: the wild orchids of Newfoundland. Gros Morne Cooperating Association, Rocky Harbour, NL. 96 pp.

Whiting, R.E. and Catling, P.M. 1986. Orchids of Ontario. CanaColl Foundation, Biodiversity, Agricultue and Agri-Food Canada, Ottawa, ON. 169 pp.

Williams, L.O. 1937. The Orchidaceae of the Rocky Mountains. American Midland Naturalist 18: 830–841.

Williams, J.G., Williams, A.E., and Arlott, N. 1983. A field guide to the orchids of North America. Universe Books, New York, NY. 143 pp.

Ferns

Bruce-Gray Plant Committee (Owen Sound Field-Naturalists). 1997. The ferns of Grey and Bruce. Owen Sound Field-Naturalists, Owen Sound, ON. 117 pp.

Cody, W.J. 1978. Ferns of the Ottawa District. Revised edition. Canada Dept. of Agriculture Research Branch Publication 974. 112 pp.

Cody, W.J. and Britton, D.M. 1989. Ferns and fern allies of Canada. Publication 1829/E. Agriculture Canada Research Branch, Ottawa, ON. 430 pp. [Includes illustrations and distribution maps.]

Farrar, D.R. 2006 Moonwort (*Botrychium*) Systematics. http://www.public.iastate.edu/~herbarium/botrychium.html

Fleurbec (group: G. Lamoureux et al.). 1993. Fougères, prêles et lycopodes. Fleurbec, Saint-Henri-de-Lévis, QC. 511 pp. [Colour photographs and distribution maps.]

Lellinger, D.B. 1985. A field manual of the ferns and fern-allies of the United States and Canada. Smithsonian Institution Press, Washington, D.C. 389 pp.

Taylor, T.M.C. 1956. The ferns and fern allies of British Columbia. British Columbia Provincial Museum Handbook No. 12. Victoria, BC. 154 pp.

Taylor, T.M.C. 1970. Pacific Northwest Ferns and their allies. University of Toronto Press, Toronto, ON. 247 pp.

Tryon, A.F. and Moran, R.C. 1997. The ferns and allied plants of New England. Center for Biological Conservation, Massachusetts Audubon Society, Lincoln, MA. 325 pp.

Williston, P. 2001. The Botrychiaceae of Alberta. Alberta Natural Heritage Information Centre, Edmonton, AB. 61 pp.

Rare and endangered plants

Argus, G.W. and Pryer, K.M. 1990. Rare vascular plants in Canada: our natural heritage. Botany Division, Canadian Museum of Nature, Ottawa, ON. 191 pp. + maps.

Argus, G. W. and White, D.J. 1977. The rare vascular plants of Ontario. National Museum of Natural Sciences, Ottawa, ON. (Syllogeus Series nº 14.) 63 pp.

Argus, G.W., Pryer, K.M., White, D.J., and Keddy, C.J. (Editors). 1982–1987. Atlas of the rare vascular plants of Ontario. National Museum of Natural Sciences, Ottawa, ON. 4 vols.

Argus, G.W., Meidinger, D.V., and Penny, J.L. 2002. Rare native vascular plants of British Columbia. 2nd edition. British Columbia Conservation Data Centre, Victoria, BC. 358 pp.

SPECIAL GROUPS (CONT'D)

Bouchard, A., Barabé, D., Bergeron, Y., Dumais, M., and Hay, S. 1983. The rare vascular plants of Quebec. National Museum of Natural Sciences, Ottawa, ON. (Syllogeus Series nº 48.) 75 pp.

Centre de Données sur le Patrimoine Naturel de Québec. 2008. Les plantes vasculaires menacées ou vulnérables du Québec. 3ᵉ édition. Gouvernement du Québec, ministère du Développement durable, de l'Environnement et des Parcs, Direction du patrimoine écologique et des parcs, Québec. 180 pp.

Cody, W.J. 1979. Vascular plants of restricted range in the continental Northwest Territories. National Museum of Natural Sciences, Ottawa, ON. (Syllogeus Series No. 23.) 57 pp.

Comité Flore québecoise de FloraQuebeca. 2009. Plantes rare du Québec méridional. Guide d'identification produit en collaboration avec le Centre de données sur le patrimoine naturel du Québec (CDPNQ). Les Publications du Québec, Québec. 406 pp.

Day, R. and Catling, P.M. 1991. The rare vascular plants of Prince Edward Island. National Museum of Natural Sciences, Ottawa, ON. (Syllogeus Series nº 67.) 65 pp.

Dignard, N., Couillard, L., Labrecque, J., Petitclerc, P., and Tardif, B. 2008. Guide de reconnaissance des habitats forestiers, des plantes menacées ou vulnérables. Capitale-Nationale, Centre-du-Québec, Chaudière-Appalaches et Mauricie. Ministère des Ressources naturelles et de la Faune et ministère du Développement durable, de l'Environnement et des parcs. 234 pp.

Dignard, N., Petitclerc, P., Labrecque, J., and Couillard, L. 2009. Guide de reconnaissance des habitats forestiers, des plantes menacées ou vulnérables. Côte-Nord et Saguenay-Lac-Saint-Jean. Ministère des Ressources naturelles et de la Faune et ministère du Développement durable, de l'Environnement et des parcs. 144 pp.

Douglas, G.W., Argus, G.W., Dickson, H.L., and Brunton, D.F. 1981. The rare vascular plants of the Yukon. National Museum of Natural Sciences, Ottawa, ON. (Syllogeus Series No. 28.) 61 pp.

Douglas, G.W., Straley, G.B., and Meidinger, D.V. 1998. Rare native vascular plants of British Columbia. B.C. Ministry of Environment, Lands and Parks, Victoria, BC. 423 pp. [Text, illustration, and map are provide for each species.]

Hinds, H. 1983. The rare vascular plants of New Brunswick. National Museum of Natural Sciences, Ottawa, ON. (Syllogeus Series nº 50.) 38 pp.

Kershaw, L., Gould, J., Johnson, D., and Lancaster, J. 2001. Rare vascular plants of Alberta. Univ. Alberta Press, Edmonton, AB and Nat. Resour. Can., Can. For. Serv., North For. Cent., Edmonton, AB. 484 pp. [Describes and provides excellent colour photographs of about 485 species of rare native vascular plants of Alberta.]

Maher, R.V., Argus, G.W., Harms, V.L., and Hudson, J.H. 1979. The rare vascular plants of Saskatchewan. National Museum of Natural Sciences, Ottawa, ON. (Syllogeus Series nº 20.) 55 pp.

Maher, R.V., White, D.J., Argus, G.W., and Keddy, P.A. 1978. The rare vascular plants of Nova Scotia. National Museum of Natural Sciences, Ottawa, ON. (Syllogeus Series 18.) 37 pp.

McJannet, C.L., Argus, G.W., and Cody, W.J. 1995. Rare vascular plants in the Northwest Territories. National Museum of Natural Sciences, Ottawa, ON. (Syllogeus Series 73.) 104 pp.

McJannet, C., Argus, G.W., Edlund, S., and Cayouette, J. 1993. Rare vascular plants in the Canadian Arctic. National Museum of Natural Sciences, Ottawa, ON. (Syllogeus Series 72.) 79 pp.

Oldham, M.J. and Brinker, S.R. 2009. Rare vascular plants of Ontario, Fourth edition. Natural Heritage Information Centre, Ontario Ministry of Natural Resources. Peterborough, ON. 188 pp. [Available online: http://publicdocs.mnr.gov.on.ca/View.asp?Document_ID=15769&Attachment_ID=3330 1]

Packer, J.G. and Bradley, C.E. 1984. A checklist of the rare vascular plants in Alberta with maps. Natural History Occasional Paper 5. Provincial Museum of Alberta, Edmonton, AB. 112 pp.

SPECIAL GROUPS (CONT'D)

Pelletier, D. 1987. The rare plants of the Mingan Archipelago. Environment Canada, Ottawa, ON. 95 pp.

Petitclerc, P., Dignard, N., Couillard, L., Lavoie, G., and Labrecque, J. 2007. Guide de reconnaissance des habitats forestiers, des plantes menacées ou vulnérables. Bas-Saint-Laurent et Gaspésie. Ministère des Ressources naturelles et de la Faune, Direction de l'environnement forestier. 113 pp.

Straley, G.B., Taylor, R.L., and Douglas, G.W. 1985. The rare vascular plants of British Columbia. National Museum of Natural Sciences, Ottawa, ON. (Syllogeus Series Nº. 59.) 165 pp.

Talbot, S.S., Yurtsev, B.A., Murray, D.F., Argus, G.W., Bay, C., and Elvebakk, A. 1999. Atlas of rare endemic vascular plants of the Arctic. Conservation of Arctic Flora and Fauna Technical Report nº 3. U.S. Fish and Wildlife Service, Anchorage, AK. 73 pp.

Wallis, C., Fairbarns, M., Loewen, V., and Bradley, C.E. 1987. The rare vascular flora of Alberta. Alberta Forestry, Lands and Wildlife, Edmonton, AB. 4 vols.

White, D.J. and Johnson, K.L. 1980. The rare vascular plants of Manitoba. National Museum of Natural Sciences, Ottawa, ON. (Syllogeus Series nº 27.) 52 pp.

Canadian plants in art

Figzgibbon, A., and Traill, C.P. 1868. Canadian wild flowers. John Lovell, Montreal, QC. 86 pp. + plates.

Montreal Star, The. 1894. Wildflowers of Canada. The Monteal Star, Montreal, QC. Unpaginated. 288 plates.

Small, E., Catling, P.M., Cayouette, J., and Brookes, B. 2009. Audubon: beyond birds, plant portraits and conservation heritage of John James Audubon. National Research Council Press, Ottawa, ON. 266 pp.

Walcott, M.V. 1925. North American wildflowers. Smithsonian Institution, Washington, D.C. 5 vols.

ADDITIONAL SOURCES OF INFORMATION

Special bibliographies

Several bibliographies are available to help locate studies of plants of given regions. In some cases complete lists of references concerning the flora of a region exist only as a few copies of old unpublished documents on the shelves of provincial museums or provincial or regional conservation data centres (CDCs) (e.g., see the following (also see Pringle (1995) in "Experts"):

Catling, P.M., Brookes, B.S., Skorupinski, Y.M., and Malette, S.M. 1986. Bibliography of vascular plant floristics for New Brunswick, Newfoundland (insular) and Nova Scotia. Technical Bulletin 1986–3E. Agriculture Canada Research Branch, Ottawa, ON. 28 pp. [A comprehensive list of floristic references for the Maritimes.]

Douglas, G.W., Češka, A., and G.G. Ruyle, G.G. 1983. A floristic bibliography for British Columbia. Province of British Columbia Ministry of Forests, Land Management Report Number 15. 143 pp. [References are listed by plant family and author.]

With increasing frequency, plants are being imported or introduced to Canada that are not part of the established flora, and is it important to know what tools are available for identification of such foreign material. Frodin (2001) provides a list of the major references:

Frodin, D.G. 2001. Guide to the standard floras of the world. 2nd edition. Cambridge University Press, Cambridge, UK. 1124 pp. [A monumental guide to world floras.]

Plant museums (vascular plant herbaria)

Vascular plant herbaria in Canada contain authoritatively identified reference specimens that can be used for comparison in identification. Moreover, the staff includes experts on plants of the local region or on particular groups of plants. Some of the herbaria have websites that provide information on services available [see for example the Agriculture and Agrifood Canada vascular plant collection website http://www4.agr.gc.ca/AAFC-AAC/display-afficher.do?id=1251393521021&lang=eng]. Information on herbaria is available from various sources, ranging from regional to world coverage, and some principal guides are listed below. (Also see the appendix in Pringle (1995), listed in "Experts".)

Boivin, B. 1980. Survey of Canadian herbaria. Provancheria (Mémoire de l'Herbier Louis-Marie) 10. 187 pp. [A comprehensive review of Canadian herbaria, with much useful historical information.]

Brunton, D.F. 1986. An Inventory of Private Herbaria in Ontario. Plant Press 4: 51–55.

Rothfels, C. 2003. Synopsis of Ontario herbaria. Field Botanists of Ontario Newsletter 16(1): 7–19. [An example of a recent regional compilation, including some information that is not available elsewhere.]

Thiers, B. [continuously updated; previously Holmgren, P.K. and N.H. Holmgren]. Index Herbariorum: A global directory of public herbaria and associated staff. New York Botanical Garden's Virtual Herbarium. http://sweetgum.nybg.org/ih/ [The herbaria of the world are listed. This can be used to locate Canadian herbaria: in "Search by Institution" simply type in "Canada" for country, and details for more than 100 Canadian herbaria will be presented.]

Experts

Index Herbariorum mentioned above lists staff and their specialties (in "search by Person" type in "Canada" for country, and details of about 200 Canadians associated with herbaria will be presented). Local experts capable of assisting with plant identification may also be found in universities, museums, conservation data centres, natural resource departments, and the Canadian Botanical Association.

The website of the American Society of Plant Taxonomists (with about 1,300 members) lists experts by taxonomic groups (e.g., genera). See http://www.aspt.net/. (However, many experts are not members of the society, and will not be listed.)

Good sources of Canadian plant biodiversity specialists are the following:

Pringle, J.S. 1995. The history of the exploration of the vascular flora of Canada. Canadian Field-Naturalist 109: 291–356.

Small, E., Cayouette, J., Brookes, B., and Wojtas, W. 1995. Canadian biodiversity: a guide to botanical specialists and literature / Biodiversité canadienne: répertoire des botanistes actuels et de leurs publications. Agriculture and Agri-Food Canada, Research Branch, Central Experimental Farm, Ottawa. [Electronic publication in English and French. Provides full literature citations of thousands of publications dealing with Canadian plants.]

ADDITIONAL SOURCES OF INFORMATION (CONT'D)

Collecting reference specimens

Brayshaw, T.C. 1996. Plant collecting for the amateur. Royal British Columbia Museum, Victoria, B.C. 44 pp.

Bowles, J.M. Guide to plant collection & identification http://www.queensu.ca/biology/facilities/herbarium/collecting.html [An online version of a booklet prepared by Dr. Bowles, containing much useful information.]

Forman, L., and Bridson, D. (Editors). 1989. The herbarium handbook. Royal Botanic Gardens, Kew, U.K. 214 pp.

MacFarlane, R.B. 1985. Collecting and preserving plants. Dover, New York, NY. 184 pp.

Savile, D.B.O. 1962. Collection and care of botanical specimens. Research Branch Publication 1113. Canada Department of Agriculture, Ottawa, ON. 124 pp. [A comprehensive and excellent source of information on making plant collections.]

Plant descriptive terms

Featherly, H.I. 1965. Taxonomic terminology of the higher plants. Hafner, New York, NY. 166 pp.

Harris, J.G. and Harris, M.W. 2001. Plant identification terminology: an illustrated glossary. Spring Lake Pub., Spring Lake, UT. 206 pp.

Hickey, M., and King, C. 2000. The Cambridge illustrated glossary of botanical terms. Cambridge University Press, Cambridge, U.K. 208 pp.

Jackson, B.D. 1971. A glossary of botanic terms with their derivation and accent. Gerald Duckworth & Co., London, U.K. 481 pp.

Little, R.J., and Jones, C.E. 1980. A dictionary of botany. Van Nostrand Reinhold, New York, NY. 400 pp.

Plant families and plant taxonomy (classification)

Baumgardt, J.P. 1982. How to identify flowering plant families: a practical guide for horticulturists and plant lovers. Timber Press, Portland, OR. 269 pp.

Cullen, J., and Davis, P.H. 1997. The identification of flowering plant families: including a key to those native and cultivated in north temperate regions. 4th edition. Cambridge University Press, Cambridge, U.K. 215 pp.

Elpel, T.J. 2000. Botany in a day: Thomas J. Elpel's herbal field guide to plant families. 4th ed. HOPS Press, Pony, MT. 196 pp.

Glimn-Lacy, J., and Kaufman, P.B. 2006. Botany illustrated: introduction to plants, major groups, flowering plant families. 2nd edition. Springer, New York, NY. 146 pp.

Heywood, V.H. 2006. Flowering plant families of the world. Revised edition. Firefly Books, Buffalo, NY. 424 pp.

Jacques, H.E. 1948. Plant families: how to know them: picture keys for determining the families of nearly all of the members of the entire plant kingdom. 2nd edition. W.G. Brown, Dubuque, IA. 177 pp.

Lawrence, G.H.M. 1955. An introduction to plant taxonomy. Macmillan, New York, NY. 179 pp.

Leadlay, E., and Jury, S.L. (Editors). 2006. Taxonomy and plant conservation: the cornerstone of the conservation and the sustainable use of plants. Cambridge University Press, Cambridge, U.K. 343 pp.

Simpson, M.G. 2006. Plant systematics. Elsevier Academic Press, Boston, MA. 590 pp.

Smith, J.P., Jr. 1977. Vascular plant families. Mad River Press, Eureka, CA. 320 pp. [A manual on the families of vascular plants native to North America. Harris and Harris cited above will be useful to understand the complex terminology.]

Stuessy, T.F. 2009. Plant taxonomy: the systematic evaluation of comparative data. 2nd edition. Columbia University Press, NY. 539 pp.

Zomlefer, W.B. 1994. Guide to flowering plant families. University of North Carolina Press, Chapel Hill, NC. 430 pp.

ADDITIONAL SOURCES OF INFORMATION (CONT'D)

Online information sources for plant names
It is sometimes desirable to ensure that the most current classification and nomenclature have been employed. There are numerous monographs of specific genera, families, etc. that are more up to date than some of the references listed above. These can be found through standard database literature searches (e.g., AGRIS, AGRICOLA, BIOSIS, etc.).

The International Plant Names Index (IPNI), online at http://www.ipni.org/index.html, is a database of the names and associated basic bibliographical details of all seed plants, ferns and fern allies. Its goal is to eliminate the need for repeated reference to primary sources for basic bibliographic information about plant names. The data are freely available and are gradually being standardized and checked. This is an excellent source for confirming bibliographic details of names, but is by no means infallible.

The Integrated Taxonomic Information System (ITIS), available online at http://www.itis.usda.gov, is another important developing source of basic information on plant names.

The Plants database (of the United States Department of Agriculture) http://plants.usda.gov/index.html has illustrations, U.S. distribution maps, and considerable information on thousands of North American species.

Flora of North America Newsletter http://hua.huh.harvard.edu/FNA/newsletter.shtml presents current information on the Flora of North America project (see "Guides to large areas of Canada"), and the status of upcoming FNA volumes, as well as new publications and resources concerned with plant identification and classification.